THE FIFTEENTH CENTURY
VOLUME XX

The Fifteenth Century
ISSN 1479-9871

General Editor
Dr Linda Clark

Assistant Editor
Dr Hannes Kleineke

Editorial Advisory Committee
Professor Matthew Davies, *Birkbeck, University of London*
Dr Catherine Nall, *Royal Holloway, University of London*
Dr Stephen Mileson, *Oxfordshire Victoria County History*
Professor A.J. Pollard, *University of Teesside*
Professor Carole Rawcliffe, *University of East Anglia*
Dr Benjamin Thompson, *Somerville College, Oxford*
Professor John Watts, *Corpus Christi College, Oxford*

THE FIFTEENTH CENTURY
XX

ESSAYS PRESENTED TO ROWENA E. ARCHER

Edited by
LINDA CLARK and JAMES ROSS

THE BOYDELL PRESS

© Contributors 2024

All Rights Reserved. Except as permitted under current legislation
no part of this work may be photocopied, stored in a retrieval system,
published, performed in public, adapted, broadcast,
transmitted, recorded or reproduced in any form or by any means,
without the prior permission of the copyright owner

First published 2024
The Boydell Press, Woodbridge

ISBN 978-1-83765-199-3

The Boydell Press is an imprint of Boydell & Brewer Ltd
PO Box 9, Woodbridge, Suffolk IP12 3DF, UK
and of Boydell & Brewer Inc.
668 Mt Hope Avenue, Rochester, NY 14620-2731
website: www.boydellandbrewer.com

A catalogue record for this title is available
from the British Library

The publisher has no responsibility for the continued existence or accuracy of
URLs for external or third-party internet websites referred to in this book, and
does not guarantee that any content on such websites is, or will remain, accurate or
appropriate

CONTENTS

List of Illustrations	ix
Abbreviations	x
Preface	xi

A Rich Old Lady Getting Poorer: Maud, Countess of Oxford, and the De Vere Estates, 1371–1413   1
JAMES ROSS

The Adoption of the English Language by Henry V   20
SAMUEL LANE

The Origins and Development of the Body Corporate in Late Medieval England   37
EDWARD POWELL

'The Principal Place of Honour about the Person of the Queen.' Margaret of Anjou and Alice Chaucer, Duchess of Suffolk: the Making of a Friendship   46
DIANA DUNN

'Broken by Age and Reduced by Poverty': Care for the Elderly in Late Medieval Almshouses   67
CAROLE RAWCLIFFE

Butlerage and Prisage: a Cinderella Tax? The Bristol Evidence   92
MARGARET CONDON

From the Welsh Marches to the Royal Household: the Leominster Riots of 1487 and Uncertain Allegiances at the Heart of Henry VII's Regime   116
S.J. PAYLING and SEAN CUNNINGHAM

Burials and Memorialisation at the Command of Henry VII   131
RALPH A. GRIFFITHS

Justice, Good Ladyship and the Queen's Council in Late Medieval England, 1450–1550   149
LAURA FLANNIGAN

The 'Last Yorkist' Revealed? Richard de la Pole, Charles, duc de Bourbon, and a Contentious Panel Portrait of the 1520s 168
ANTHONY GROSS

Imperial Echoes: English Gascony and British India. A Preliminary Survey 195
MALCOLM VALE

Contributors 206
Dr Rowena E. Archer 208
Index 218
Tabula Gratulatoria 232

ILLUSTRATIONS

Frontispiece: Rowena E. Archer

Margaret Condon, Butlerage and Prisage

1   Grotesque from TNA, E351/454, m. 33   112

Anthony Gross, The 'Last Yorkist' Revealed?

1   Anon., *Richard de la Pole*, ante 1525, private collection   169
2   Anon., *Charles de Bourbon*, Colección del Museo de Bellas Artes de
    València   171
3   Lucas Vosterman, *Charles III de Bourbon*, 1622–8, British Museum,
    London © The Trustees of the British Museum   172
4   Thomas de Leu, *Charles, duc de Bourbon*, c. 1600, Royal Collection
    Trust, London © His Majesty King Charles III   172
5   Aix en Provence, Bibliothèque Méjanes MS 442 (Rés. Ms 20), f. 17   177
6   Anon., *Portrait d'homme tourné de profil à gauche, portant un chaperon
    à résille*, BNF   178
7   École Française, *Monsieur de Bourbon,* c. 1590, Musée Condé, Chantilly 179
8   Anon., *Ritratto di Carlo di Borbone*, ante 1568, Uffizi Gallery, Florence 180
9   BL, Add. MS 17385, ff. 25v–26   182
10 Anon., medal depicting Renée de Bourbon and Antoine de Lorraine,
    1520–9, British Museum, London © The Trustees of the British Museum   183

The editors, contributors and publisher are grateful to all the institutions and persons listed for permission to reproduce the materials in which they hold copyright. Every effort has been made to trace the copyright holders; apologies are offered for any omission, and the publisher will be pleased to add any necessary acknowledgement in subsequent editions.

ABBREVIATIONS

BJRL	*Bulletin of the John Rylands Library*
BL	British Library, London
BNF	Bibliothèque Nationale de France, Paris
Bodl.	Bodleian Library, Oxford
Cal. Inq. Misc.	*Calendar of Inquisitions Miscellaneous*
CCR	*Calendar of Close Rolls*
CFR	*Calendar of Fine Rolls*
CIPM	*Calendar of Inquisitions Post Mortem*
CP	G.E. Cokayne, *The Complete Peerage of England, Scotland, Ireland, Great Britain and the United Kingdom*, ed. V. Gibbs *et al.* (12 vols, 1910–59)
CPR	*Calendar of Patent Rolls*
EETS	Early English Text Society
EHR	*English Historical Review*
Foedera	Thomas Rymer, *Foedera, Conventiones, Literae et Cujuscunque Generis Acta Publica* (20 vols, 1704–32)
HMC	Historical Manuscripts Commission
HR	*Historical Research*
Letters and Papers	*Letters and Papers, Foreign and Domestic, of the Reign of Henry VIII* (21 vols, 1862–1932)
Oxford DNB	*Oxford Dictionary of National Biography from the Earliest Times to the Year 2000*, ed. H.C.G. Matthew and Brian Harrison (61 vols, Oxford, 2004)
PPC	*Proceedings and Ordinances of the Privy Council of England*, ed. N.H. Nicolas (7 vols, 1834–7)
PROME	*Parliament Rolls of Medieval England, 1275–1504*, ed. Chris Given-Wilson *et al.* (16 vols, Woodbridge, 2005)
RO	Record Office
Rot. Parl.	*Rotuli Parliamentorum* (6 vols, 1767–77)
RS	Rolls Series
Statutes	*Statutes of the Realm* (11 vols, 1810–28)
STC	*A Short-Title Catalogue of Books Printed in England, Scotland and Ireland and of English Books Printed Abroad, 1475–1640*, ed. A.W. Pollard and G.R. Redgrave, 2nd edn, revised by W.A. Jackson *et al.* (3 vols, 1976–91)
TNA	The National Archives, Kew
TRHS	*Transactions of the Royal Historical Society*
VCH	*Victoria County History*

Unless stated otherwise, the place of publication of books cited is London.

PREFACE

The present volume, a *festschrift* for Dr Rowena E. Archer, draws inspiration from her own research interests, writing and teaching, so that the essays collected here – offered by her colleagues, friends and pupils – reflect on themes which help to expand our wider understanding of complex relationships in medieval Britain and Europe, particularly during the fifteenth century, which has always been a focal point of her endeavours. Her personal interest in Alice, duchess of Suffolk, ensured that prominent among these themes are the influence exerted by wealthy ladies possessed of widespread estates: how they, by participating in the foundation of almshouses might provide care for the elderly, how queens consort played a part in the implementation of justice through their councils, and how certain queens involuntarily became political pawns. A strong sense of ancestry among the English nobility led to Henry VII's sensitive attitude towards the burial and memorialisation of his relatives (even those executed on his orders). Yet also examined here are the damaging effects of rivalries in the localities which spread their contagion to the royal household, and we are reminded that Yorkist claimants to the crown persisted well into the sixteenth century. In her role as a supervisor of doctoral theses, Rowena warmly encouraged studies concerned with Anglo-French relations, and these are well represented in the contributions printed here, notably those regarding Gascony or Henry V's use of the English language while in France. Nor are her appreciation of fine wines and connection with Bristol overlooked, for they both find reflection in an essay about how such imports were taxed.

Linda Clark and James Ross

A RICH OLD LADY GETTING POORER: MAUD, COUNTESS OF OXFORD, AND THE DE VERE ESTATES, 1371–1413[1]

James Ross

The importance of landed estates to noblemen and noblewomen has been one of the primary themes of Rowena Archer's work. From her doctoral thesis on the Mowbray dukes of Norfolk, with its meticulous handling of the financial records of the family, through her seminal article on rich old ladies, which demonstrated the impact of dowagers on noble estates, to her study of noblewomen's land management in theory and in practice, she has underscored the importance of understanding the dynamics of noble landownership and estate management.[2] She has also outlined the way late medieval noblewomen were 'in general, competent, workmanlike, and active', and 'frequently manipulative, influential, sometimes political, often formidable… eschewing neither ruthlessness nor aggression if circumstances so demanded'.[3] Maud, countess of Oxford, is in one respect an example of one of Rowena's rich old ladies, a dowager who outlived her husband for more than forty years, and occupied half of the de Vere family estates. Yet she was atypical for a number of reasons, notably in her dispersal of many landed estates to the detriment of her marital family and in consequence suffering significant financial difficulties. Maud also had many – but not all – of the personal qualities Rowena outlined. Rowena has always had a keen eye for an exception to a generalisation and I hope, therefore, that this case study of a complex and not entirely successful late medieval noblewoman is fitting in a volume published in honour of her career.[4]

[1] I am grateful to Dr Simon Payling for reading a draft of this essay and making a number of valuable suggestions. All manuscript references are to the National Archives (TNA) unless otherwise stated.
[2] R.E. Archer, 'The Mowbrays, Earls of Nottingham and Dukes of Norfolk to 1432' (D.Phil. thesis, Oxford University, 1984); *eadem*, 'Rich Old Ladies: the Problems of Late Medieval Dowagers', in *Property and Politics. Essays in Late Medieval English History*, ed. A.J. Pollard (Gloucester, 1984), 15–35; *eadem*, 'The Estates and Finances of Margaret of Brotherton, c.1320–1399', *HR*, lx (1987), 264–80; *eadem*, '"How Ladies … Who Live on their Manors Ought to Manage their Households and Estates": Women as Landholders and Administrators in the Later Middle Ages', in *Woman is a Worthy Wight: Women in English Society, c.1200–1500*, ed. P.J.P. Goldberg (Stroud, 1992), 149–81.
[3] R.E. Archer, 'Piety in Question: Noblewomen and Religion in the Later Middle Ages', in *Women and Religion in Medieval England*, ed. Diana Wood (Oxford, 2003), 119.
[4] Rowena supervised my thesis on the de Veres, when I first came across Maud, and indeed suggested her as a topic for my first paper at the Fifteenth Century conference in 2001, which subsequently became my first publication in 2003. My debt to her supervision and support is immense. The 2003 article focused primarily on Maud's rebellion of 1403, although I touched briefly on her landed estates

I

Maud was the daughter of Sir Ralph Ufford (d. 1346), chief justice of Ireland, and Matilda of Lancaster (d. 1377), great-grand-daughter of Henry III. She was probably born in late 1345 or early 1346 (her mother was reported as being pregnant in the former year and Maud was the only known child of the marriage), and was younger than five years old when, by June 1350, she was contracted in marriage to Thomas, the second but eldest surviving son of John de Vere, seventh earl of Oxford. Thomas, approximately eight years older than Maud, became earl in 1360, and the couple's only child, Robert, later ninth earl of Oxford and duke of Ireland, was born in 1362 at Earls Colne priory in Essex.[5] Earl Thomas died in 1371 when Maud was in her mid-twenties; she was to be a dowager countess for forty-two years, and never remarried.

Earl John, Maud's father-in-law, had licence to settle three manors in jointure on Thomas and Maud at the time of their wedding.[6] To this jointure, probably specified in their marriage contract, her husband added a great deal of his own volition. First, on 2 September 1369, just before setting out to campaign in France, he added the manor of Wigston Magna in Leicestershire, and probably two manors in Essex and another in Suffolk.[7] A grant by feoffees in April 1370 of the manor of Market Overton in Rutland to the earl's retainer Sir William Wingfield for life, with reversion to Thomas and Maud and the heirs of Thomas, added a further estate that would fall to them in the future.[8] Yet another grant of jointure, made in April 1371, some five months before Thomas's death, added seven more manors in Herefordshire, Hertfordshire, Kent and Sussex, and a reversionary interest in another.[9] In 1369, Earl Thomas showed real consideration to his wife, ensuring on the eve of his departure on campaign that she would be fully provided for. The 1371 enfeoffment was probably made in expectation that he would not live much longer, as he had been in poor health for some time since the end of the 1369 campaign – writs of *diem clausit extremum* ordering an inquisition *post mortem* were erroneously issued in July 1370 – so he was clearly looking to provide generously for Maud's widowhood,

---

(pp. 26–8): 'Seditious Activities: the Conspiracy of Maud de Vere, Countess of Oxford, 1403–4', in *The Fifteenth Century III. Authority and Subversion*, ed. Linda Clark (Woodbridge, 2003), 25–42. See also, James Ross, 'Vere [*née* Ufford], Maud de, Countess of Oxford (1345?–1413), *Oxford DNB*.

[5] *CIPM*, xv. no. 889. For Thomas, whose date of birth is uncertain, see James Ross, 'Vere, Thomas de, eighth Earl of Oxford (1336x8–1371)', *Oxford DNB* (revised version published online December 2022).

[6] *CPR*, 1348–50, p. 511; CP25/1/287/43, no. 449B; *Feet of Fines for Essex, III (1327–1422)*, ed. R.C. Fowler and S.C. Ratcliffe (Colchester, 1899), 99.

[7] The enfeoffment of Wigston is known from lawsuits of 1396 and 1409: *CCR, 1392–6*, p. 465; JUST1/477/3, rot. 6d. The latter states the grant included besides Wigston 'other manors and tenements', without specifying details. The two Essex manors, Frating and Hedingham Vaux, and Preston in Suffolk, were in Maud's hands by (and probably well before) 1386 and were not part of her dower. Hedingham Vaux and Preston (though not Frating) were the subject of the same lawsuit of 1396 and it seems probable they formed part of the same enfeoffment.

[8] LR14/562.

[9] CP25/1/288/49, no. 719; E326/12895; *Sussex Feet of Fines*, ed. L.F. Salzman (3 vols, Sussex Record Society, ii, vii, xxiii, 1903–16), iii. 173; *CCR, 1369–74*, pp. 271–2. The transfer of Lyonshall in Herefordshire to Maud noted in the enfeoffment did not take place as Sir John Burley had custody of the manor during Earl Robert's minority in the 1370s at an annual farm of 50 marks (*CPR, 1377–81*, p. 137) and it came into Robert's hands at his majority. The manor of West Dean in Sussex was held for life following a grant by the seventh earl (see below, n. 14).

and perhaps anticipating a long minority for his son.[10] To all of this, smoothly and just three months after Earl Thomas's death, dower was added, comprising nine manors and three smaller holdings in Buckinghamshire, Cambridgeshire, Essex, Kent, Hertfordshire and Suffolk.[11] The two dower manors in Essex, Earls Colne and Great Bentley, contained high-status residences, and Bentley had been the favourite seat of the comital couple during their marriage. Besides the lands, Maud received significant bequests in her husband's will, of plate, religious items and household goods, and she was one of the five executors appointed for its administration.[12]

Two accounts survive from the administration of Maud's estates during the forty-two years of her widowhood: a receiver-general's account covering 1385–8 and a brief household account dated 31 July–30 September 1389.[13] Both are rather odd in their chronological coverage. The short duration of the household account probably reflects a change of official: Robert de Feriby was the steward of Maud's household in 1385–8, but by 1389 John Pollard, parson of Lavenham, was both steward of the household and treasurer, so the two-month account was probably drawn up to complete the accounting year before Michaelmas. The receiver-general's account is very unusual in that it is a composite record of receipts from each manor Maud held over as many as four regnal years, 9–12 Richard II, but only the tenth year (1386–7) contains one or more receipts from every manor. While it does also include foreign receipts, there is no *summa* of income nor detail of outgoings and may therefore be a view of the official's account or some form of working document. The accounting official, William Sesille, was also replaced shortly afterwards, as John Broke was named as receiver-general in the household account of 1389. Changes in administrative personnel were not uncommon, but the replacement of two of the three most senior officials in the same year – and the two rather unusual documents – suggest a degree of upheaval rather than efficiency or reform.

Totalling the receipts recorded for the tenth regnal year in Sesille's account provides Maud with an income of £568 7s. 2½ d., but in estimating the overall value of the estates for the purposes of valuing her dower and jointure a number of adjustments need to be made. Certain extraordinary expenses should be discounted, including an annuity of £20 donated by the countess to the nunnery of Bruisyard from the manor of Aldham, and another of £10 granted to John de Pelham, parson of West Wickham, from the manor of Welles in Hertfordshire. Three other manors generated only half their expected revenue in 10 Richard II compared to other years; whether this was because they were in part accounted for elsewhere or as a result of administrative issues or problems of revenue collection is not clear.[14] When all these

---

[10] *CFR*, viii. 112.
[11] *CCR, 1369–74*, pp. 272–3. For a full list of Maud's dower and jointure estates, see the Appendix below, and for surveys of dower and jointure in the later Middle Ages, see Jennifer Ward, *English Noblewomen in the Later Middle Ages* (Harlow, 1992), ch. 2; Michael Hicks, 'Crossing Generation: Dower, Jointure and Courtesy', in *The Fifteenth Century Inquisitions Post Mortem. A Companion* (Woodbridge, 2012), 25–46, which suggests that, to some degree, Maud was unusual and lucky in having both a substantial jointure and a full dower assignment.
[12] *Registrum Simonis de Sudbiria*, ed. R.C. Fowler and Claude Jenkins (2 vols, Canterbury and York Society, xxxiv, xxxviii, 1927, 1938), i. 4–6.
[13] BL, Harleian Roll N3; Longleat House, Wiltshire, MS 442.
[14] The manor of Wigston generated £33 in 1385–6 and £32 in 1387–8, but only £19 in 1386–7, so a value of £33 has been used for the overall estimate, and the same principle has been applied for Great Bentley, where only half the annual sum seems to have been handed over in 1386–7 (£6 6s. 8d., com-

adjustments are made, Maud's optimum annual income, before any extraordinary expenditure is taken into account, can be calculated at £649 per annum.

The household account is mainly a stock account but does contain a summary of cash income and expenses. Payments and wages for those two months in 1389 totalled £105 9s. 1d. – a rate that, multiplied across the year, would have seen her household expenses consume almost all of her ordinary income.[15] However, the figures were skewed by the fact that Maud then appears to have had her daughter-in-law, Philippa, duchess of Ireland, staying with her, probably for an extended period. Certainly, in the course of that year Philippa contributed £113 6s. 8d. for her expenses, and the two-month period of the account saw half of that sum handed over to the steward of Maud's household. Yet even with Philippa's contribution taken into account, and making a big assumption that this rate of spending was typical for her, if Maud's household was consuming 75–80 per cent of her income, this was much higher than the normal aristocratic rate of approximately 60 per cent, and may have contributed to the financial problems Maud was to suffer.[16] By comparison, although Margaret of Brotherton received an income of nearly £3,000 p.a. her household expenditure in 1385–6 was just £1,116.[17] Additional evidence from the dorse of the account supports this hypothesis of excessive expenditure.[18] Scribbled on it are daily lists of members of the household present, probably at mealtimes, for a Sunday through to a Thursday – no day or month is given. On each day, the household is divided into four ranks (young ladies,[19] gentlemen, valets and grooms), and numbers provided. With the exception of the Tuesday, when the numbers were very low (perhaps the countess was out for the day with her travelling household), the numbers are extremely high. The ladies vary from four to seven, gentlemen from eighteen to twenty-three, valets from eighteen to twenty-three and grooms from fifteen to twenty-two. Daily totals range from seventy-one on the Sunday, fifty-five on the Monday, twenty-nine on the Tuesday, seventy-one on the Wednesday and sixty-four on the Thursday. These are explicitly members of the household; occasional guests are noted, such as Lady Stafford's valet, who was present on the Thursday. Caution must be taken as to how far these figures are representative of Maud's normal household; it is not impossible that for these purposes Duchess Philippa's retinue would have been counted

---

pared with £11 13s. 4d. for the previous year). The figure of £55 has been used for Aldham as that was the farm, although the farmer did not pay the full sum in the year 10 Richard II. The manor of West Dean generated nothing for the countess in 1386–7, as it had been granted by the seventh earl of Oxford to William Notebeem for life, and she held only the reversion until Notebeem's death at Pentecost 1387 (E326/12895). The following year the manor was farmed out at £10, so this sum has been used instead. Bentley, Maud's primary residence, seems to have been consistently undervalued in the account: together with Cruswiche (in Weeley) it produced £11 13s. 4d. in the accounts, but Bentley alone was valued at £15 in Maud's inquisition *post mortem* (*CIPM*, xvii. no. 1049) and £22 in that of Richard, earl of Oxford, in 1417 (*CIPM*, xx. no. 648), and Cruswiche at £6 13s. 4d. in *Cal. Inq. Misc.* v. no. 116. It seems likely that the lower revenue from Bentley was because cash, crops or livestock were sent directly to the household and are therefore hidden in the account.

[15] Longleat MS 442, mm. 2d–3d.
[16] Christopher Given-Wilson, *The English Nobility in the Late Middle Ages* (1987), 94, estimates 50–60 per cent, and it was probably at the higher end of the scale by the close of the fourteenth century.
[17] Archer, 'Estates and Finances of Margaret of Brotherton', 274–5.
[18] Longleat MS 442, m. 1d.
[19] The word given is '*janc*', or similar, which is probably '*jonencel*' in middle French, although it lacks an ending so possibly refers to young men, or henchmen, rather than ladies. I am grateful to Drs Hannes Kleineke and Stephen O'Connor for their advice and suggestions on this point.

as part of the household if she was present on this unspecified date. If, however, this did reflect Maud's standard entourage, such numbers would be excessive, and perhaps unsupportable, on her level of income. Comparisons emphasise this point. Christopher Woolgar has calculated that in the mid-1380s Edward, earl of Devon, on an income of approximately £1,000 p.a., maintained a household of forty-six persons, and Thomas Arundel, bishop of Ely, employed just over eighty servants while enjoying annual revenues of £2,500.[20] A little later, Cecily, duchess of York, with an income of 5,000 marks, probably had a household numbering over 100, yet this was not only affordable, but her household was regulated and ordered, if the extant ordinances are a reliable guide.[21]

The year 1388 proved something of a watershed for Maud. Before that date, she ranked as one of Rowena's 'rich ladies' (although by no means yet old). With an income of around £650 p.a., she was certainly not the wealthiest widow of the time, but this was primarily because she was only a very minor heiress; she inherited just one manor from her parents. Furthermore, the de Veres, while far from poor, were not the richest of peerage dynasties. However, Maud had done very well from her marital family. Excluding other endowments taken from the de Vere estates, notably the dower for Elizabeth Courtenay, widow of the eldest son of the seventh earl, John (d. 1350), most of which was earmarked to form after her death an endowment for Aubrey, the third son of the seventh earl, she held twenty-five of the fifty-four manors that were intended to descend after her death to her son, Robert. The latter, by contrast, held only twenty manors when he came of age. Yet it was Robert's downfall at the hands of the Lords Appellant at Radcot Bridge in December 1387, his forfeiture in the 'Merciless Parliament' of 1388 and ultimately his exile and death overseas in November 1392 that made a huge difference to Countess Maud's financial position. Various factors in consequence of these events changed her prospects. Some of the estates she held for life were granted in reversion after her death to others, and several of these were transferred during her lifetime, probably with her connivance, since after 1392 no child of hers would inherit them. She also set out to sell others. As a consequence, Maud's relations with her brother-in-law, Aubrey (d. 1400), who succeeded to the earldom in January 1393, and with his son and successor Earl Richard (d. 1417), became very poor, leading to a string of lawsuits between her and the male line of de Veres.

II

What happened after Robert's exile between his mother, Maud, and his uncle and eventual successor in the earldom, Aubrey, is a very rare example of a deliberate attempt by a dowager countess to defraud the right heirs and damage estates she held in dower, jointure and at farm to the detriment of the noble family she had married into, as well as to dispose of them in contravention of the spirit – if arguably not the letter – of the law and of social conventions amongst the aristocracy.[22] Unpicking the

---

[20] C.M. Woolgar, *The Great Household in Late Medieval England* (1999), 12–13.
[21] J.L. Laynesmith, *Cecily Duchess of York* (2017), 86, 102–7.
[22] For another example, the sale by Lady Mohun of Dunster, of property which had been put into the hands of feoffees to her use, and was thus legal but also against the social mores of the day and led to a

extent to which Maud chose to alienate particular estates is difficult in some cases, but overall a clear policy emerges.

There were a number of aspects to Maud's actions. The first related to Duke Robert's estates in which Maud held an interest simply through royal grant; these were farmed out to her by November 1389 for a term of twenty years.[23] However by May 1392 commissions had been appointed to inquire into waste on the manors she held in dower or in farm,[24] and the results show that a great amount of destruction had been committed by her officials: on eight of her son's farmed estates that destruction had cost in total between £113 and £137.[25] Such waste was not unheard of – John, Lord Mowbray had been awarded £1,000 in damages in 1366 to compensate for that committed by his mother-in-law – but it was not common.[26] On investigating Maud's dower lands the commissioners found that on three estates (Great Bentley, Ramsey and Earls Colne), the waste amounted to between £227 and £308 according to differing inquisitions, because of the sale of wood 'at unfit and unseasonable times', buildings falling down through lack of repair, and other examples of bad management.[27] This was waste on a large scale, often one or two times the average annual income from the property. It is also worth noting that only the returns from the Essex and Hertfordshire commissions survive; those issued for Cambridgeshire, Kent and Suffolk have not. The scale of the waste on Maud's dower estates is even more difficult to explain, not only as it deprived her of future income from those manors, but also laid her open to prosecution, as the statute of Gloucester of 1278 laid down that waste on dower estates would be punishable by loss of dower and payment of compensation to the right heir, who, in Maud's case in 1392, was the king.[28] Also puzzling was that until Robert's death in November 1392 there had remained a possibility that he would eventually have his exile reversed and be restored to his inheritance.

Part of the reason behind the waste may have been Maud's support for her son. On 10 May 1391 she received a pardon for visiting Robert overseas and relieving him with certain gifts, although a favour from the king ought to have allowed her to recoup some or all of her financial outlay on this front, for on the same day as the pardon she received a licence to sell wood on her Oxfordshire dower estates to the value of 400–500 marks. The obvious implication is that she could sell wood to recoup the cost of her gifts to her son. The licence contained the specific instruction that no waste was to be committed; two months later she surrendered it in return for another that allowed her to sell wood to the value of 400 marks on her dower lands 'for her maintenance, provided that she causes wood so felled to be enclosed',[29] and the clause relating to waste was omitted. However, the licence related only to lands in Oxfordshire, a puzzle in itself as she held no land in that county and it is

---

'near-inevitable' legal dispute, see S.J. Payling, 'Legal Right and Dispute Resolution in Late Medieval England: the Sale of the Lordship of Dunster', *EHR*, cxxvi (2011), 17–43 (quote on p. 17).

[23] *CPR*, 1388–92, p. 151.
[24] *CPR*, 1391–6, p. 87; *Cal. Inq. Misc.* v. no. 342.
[25] *Cal. Inq. Misc.* vi. nos 12–14. Different juries gave differing estimates. These are maximum and minimum figures for the manors of Helions Bumpstead, Great Canfield, Castle Hedingham, Cruswiche, Downham, Doddinghurst, Fingrith and Stansted Mountfichet.
[26] Archer, 'Rich Old Ladies', 21.
[27] *Cal. Inq. Misc.* vi. 12–14.
[28] Archer, 'Rich Old Ladies', 20.
[29] *CPR*, 1388–92, pp. 404, 407, 462.

possible it was a clerical error for Essex.[30] Nonetheless, the scale of waste was far in excess of either the wood sales or of acceptable management of estates that she held in dower or at farm. Maud received a respite for all actions regarding the waste on 1 September 1394, though only until the king's return from Ireland; she received a pardon for all trespasses at the same time.[31] This may or may not have ended the matter, but no further pardon or action was noted in the patent rolls.[32] While none of this was initially aimed at Aubrey, nevertheless it seems unlikely that many of the estates that Aubrey inherited shortly afterwards would have been as productive as they ought to have been.

Aubrey claimed the title and the oldest estates of the earldom of Oxford in January 1393, presumably shortly after he received news of the death of Maud's son. In a separate petition, perhaps a little later, he also laid claim to the office of great chamberlain of England, and an early hint of the issues which were to arise between him and his sister-in-law, Maud, can be seen there. Aubrey claimed the office despite the fact that, as the petition stated, most of the documentary evidences were not in his possession, for some were kept by the countess of Oxford, some had been removed from Hedingham Castle when the estates had been taken into the king's hands, and some for other causes.[33] Either Maud had refused access to relevant documentation or this was simply a more generalised snipe at her. The estates which Aubrey claimed after the death of his nephew were very limited and based upon entails settling them on Earl Thomas and Maud and the right heirs of the seventh earl: indeed, they consisted of only twelve manors in three counties, comprising the most ancient estates of the earldom, which had been in Robert's possession at his forfeiture (and were mainly held in farm by Maud in 1393); they excluded all those held by Maud in dower and jointure.[34]

Trouble between Maud and Aubrey did not take long to bubble to the surface. The first evidence of this came during Hilary term 1395, when in the exchequer of pleas Maud sued Earl Aubrey for the £20 he had received from Robert's lands during the period she held them at farm, and in a separate suit for a trespass.[35] Matters were to get more serious. During 1395–6 two cases were brought in the court of common pleas by Aubrey, one relating to the manor of Fleet in Kent, the other to Wigston in Leicestershire, Hedingham Vaux in Essex and Preston in Suffolk, all of which Maud held in jointure.[36] Aubrey's claim was that the manors had been enfeoffed to the seventh earl John and his wife, who died seised, had descended to Earl Thomas and then, startlingly, that Thomas had died without any heir of his body; thus Aubrey,

---

[30] Yet the county is clear in both the patent roll and the warrant for the great seal: C66/322, m. 19; C81/525, no. 7226.
[31] *CPR, 1391–6*, p. 491.
[32] It has not been possible to locate any crown prosecution against the countess in the king's bench controlment rolls or the exchequer of pleas: KB29/39–42; IND1/7034 (the contemporary repertory roll to E159, checked for 16–19 Richard II).
[33] SC8/22/1054A, printed in *Rot. Parl.* iii. 326.
[34] *Cal. Inq. Misc.* vi. no. 31; *CCR, 1392–6*, pp. 41–3. Aubrey's success regarding the core estates was briefly noted by C.D. Ross, 'Forfeitures for Treason in the Reign of Richard II', *EHR*, lxxi (1956), 563, but not the wider portfolio of other estates discussed below. As Ross noted, lands in fee tail were not confiscated by virtue of the parliamentary judgment.
[35] E13/112, rot. 14d. This contains only notation of process and no pleadings have been found.
[36] CP40/537, rot. 108 (Fleet); 551, rot. 349d (Wigston); *CCR, 1392–6*, p. 465 (Wigston, Hedingham Vaux and Preston).

as Thomas's brother and heir, should have possession. Maud, in her defence, cited the transactions of 1369 and 1371 by which Earl Thomas had granted the manors to feoffees, who had returned them to him and Maud in jointure, with reversion to the right heirs of Thomas. In the case relating to Wigston, she called Alice Wotton, the daughter and heir of Walter de Wotton, one of the feoffees of 1369, to give warranty, and claimed that the reversion belonged to the king. In the case regarding Fleet she noted the fact that Duke Robert was Thomas's son, that in 1388 he had forfeited the manors to the king, who had granted their reversion to Thomas, duke of Gloucester, and that Gloucester had granted them to feoffees. An order by the king to the justices of common pleas to proceed in the case of Wigston, Hedingham Vaux and Preston – the justices had deferred proceeding as Maud had begged the king's aid – was enrolled on the close roll in May 1396;[37] and a similar order to proceed in the Fleet case, albeit not to reach judgment without advising the king, was enrolled in November 1398.[38] Nevertheless, process was still ongoing in Hilary term 1400 and the next date given to the parties was the octaves of Trinity. Neither case ever reached a judicial verdict because of Aubrey's death on 23 April that year. Aubrey's plea that Maud should never have had the manors neatly sidestepped the forfeiture of Robert, duke of Ireland, but was peculiar on two levels: the contention that Robert effectively had not existed and the manors should have descended to Aubrey on Thomas's death, and that Maud had not been granted them in jointure, despite the fact that, certainly in the case of Fleet, the conveyance was done through a final concord in common pleas and thus easily evidenced.[39] Maud also found herself in a peculiar position; she was effectively arguing at the start of the case that one of her estates ought to belong to the duke of Gloucester, the man perhaps most responsible for the downfall of her son in 1387–8.

The reversal of Duke Robert's forfeiture in the parliament of September 1397 not only changed the legal situation but emboldened Earl Aubrey. There are payments by Aubrey noted in the court of common pleas to levy final concords in Easter term 1399 regarding five estates Maud held in jointure, one concerning the manors of Chesham in Buckinghamshire, Market Overton in Rutland and Whitstable in Kent, the second over Bockingfold, also in Kent, and Laughton in Sussex.[40] The first was a conveyance to Thomas Shelley and William Tasburgh, trusted servants respectively of John Holand, duke of Exeter, and Aubrey, the second to these two and to the duke of Exeter, Robert Braybrooke, bishop of London, and Walter, Lord Fitzwalter.[41] By 1399, Aubrey's son and heir, Richard, had married a daughter of the duke of Exeter, and by associating the influential Holand with his cause, he may have been seeking allies, or it is not impossible that some or all of these manors were intended to form

---

[37] *CCR, 1392–6*, p. 465.
[38] *CCR, 1396–9*, p. 350.
[39] CP25/1/288/49.
[40] CP40/553, rot. 381d.
[41] Shelley was the steward of the household of the duke of Exeter, and may well have been working in the duke's interests here, although he was highly acquisitive in his own right: *The History of Parliament. The House of Commons, 1386–1421*, ed. J.S. Roskell, Linda Clark and Carole Rawcliffe (4 vols, Stroud, 1993), iv. 353–5. He may also have had some connection with Earl Aubrey, who had lands in Buckinghamshire where Shelley lived. Tasburgh, parson of Rayleigh in Essex (a manor Aubrey held for life), had been a business associate of his since the late 1380s (*CCR, 1385–9*, p. 485; 1389–92, p. 288). He was named as a feoffee in a major settlement of Aubrey's estates in 1397 (*CIPM*, xviii. 57–8) and was granted administration of Aubrey's goods after he died intestate.

the couple's jointure.[42] The final concords seem never to have been levied; the deposition of Richard II just a few months later made Holand, who fled to Aubrey at Rayleigh castle after participating in the failed Epiphany rising of January 1400, an ally of little use, and the reimposition of Duke Robert's forfeiture in Henry IV's first parliament changed the legal position again.

The timing of Aubrey's legal challenges from 1395 onwards is probably not a coincidence, and was seemingly not an opportunistic attempt to acquire manors from his sister-in-law. It was in that year that Maud started to dispose of estates she held in jointure by selling the manor of Westwick, and in the following year disposing of the manor of Bockingfold. While relations may have been cool already, Aubrey's legal challenge was surely in response to her actions and an attempt to reverse such alienations, or stop any future ones, of estates to which he would have seen himself entitled to as heir-male of his brother. While Maud was surely entitled to hold the estates during her lifetime, whatever Aubrey claimed, the question of whether she was entitled to dispose of those she held in jointure is more complicated. If the king was entitled to the reversions, then if – as in some cases – she acquired his permission alienation would have been lawful. Yet only estates held in fee simple should have been forfeited in the parliament of 1388, and three of Maud's jointure estates were held in fee tail.[43] The first settlement in 1350 had conveyed three manors to Thomas and Maud jointly and to the heirs of their bodies, and then in reversion to the right heirs of Earl John; Maud disposed of two of these manors. The jointure settlement of 1369, as far as Wigston in Leicestershire was concerned (the only manor whose terms are known) conveyed the property to the right heirs of the earl, rather than to the heirs of his body, as did the jointure settlement of 1371 of eight manors, which meant that Maud held these in fee simple.[44] Richard II certainly treated the reversions of the manors as his to dispose of, and duly granted a number to the duke of Gloucester. This legal position would have changed between 1397 and 1399, when Aubrey's position as heir-male was unchallengeable. Maud also later sold several dower estates, though this was also covered by a licence from the king; Aubrey and Richard apparently never challenged this in court. Indeed, that Aubrey's cases in 1395–6 related to just four manors can be explained by the fact that these were almost all of Maud's jointure manors not yet licensed by the king to be passed to feoffees or granted in reversion by the king to the duke of Gloucester.

As the appendix demonstrates, Maud alienated nearly half of the manors she held, but not in any systematic way. The first group of manors that were lost were those granted by Richard II in reversion to Thomas, duke of Gloucester, who intended to use them to endow his newly founded college of Pleshey. These were West Dean and Laughton in Sussex, Welles in Hertfordshire, and Whitstable and Bockingfold in Kent, all of which Maud held in jointure.[45] However, Maud granted Pleshey the manor of Bockingfold in July 1396, so the college had seisin during her lifetime;[46] Whitstable and Welles came into the possession of the college after her death in 1413, while the valuable manor of Laughton and that of West Dean nearby eventu-

---

[42] For the marriage, known only through the reference in the parliament of 1399 to Richard having married the daughter of the new king's sister Elizabeth, duchess of Exeter, see *PROME*, viii. 67–8.
[43] Ross, 'Forfeitures for Treason', 560–75.
[44] JUST1/477/3, rot. 6d; E326/12895; *CCR*, 1369–74, pp. 271–2.
[45] *CPR*, 1391–6, pp. 98, 347; see also *Sussex Feet of Fines*, iii. 202.
[46] *CPR*, 1391–6, p. 512; *CCR*, 1413–19, pp. 1–2; *CIPM*, xix. 379.

ally ended up in the hands of others.[47] What happened to Laughton and West Dean is complicated. Having earmarked Laughton to go to Pleshey after her death, in 1401 Maud granted the estate to Sir John Pelham and John Colbrooke for her lifetime, in return for a rent of £60 p.a., and either at the same time or later she probably farmed out West Dean to Pelham for £10 p.a.[48] While this was a reasonable sum for the lease of West Dean it may have undervalued Laughton.[49] Pelham's tenure of Laughton was noted in an account of 1403, while according to the subsidy return of 1412 West Dean was also held by him by that date. West Dean was noted in Maud's inquisition *post mortem* while Laughton was not, despite it being in Pelham's hands only for term of her life. Neither ended up in the possession of Pleshey college. A series of original documents and a later roll of evidences created for the Pelham family trace initially the reversion and then the possession of the manor of Laughton through a series of enfeoffments starting with the duke of Gloucester in 1397 to a grant in 1428 by a fourth set of feoffees to Sir John, his wife Joan and the heirs of their bodies.[50] As the original enfeoffments never specified the duke's intention to grant the manors to Pleshey and in the chaos of the duke's forfeiture and death in 1397, Richard II's deposition in 1399 and the troubles of Henry IV's reign, the future of Laughton seems to have been in limbo until Pelham judged it time to acquire it outright. The postscript to this came at the reversion of Robert de Vere's forfeiture in 1464, when John de Vere, the thirteenth earl of Oxford, immediately launched legal proceedings against the Pelham family over Laughton, and eventually agreed to quitclaim his rights in the manor in return for the very substantial payment of 1,000 marks.[51] The fact that it was not until Robert de Vere's forfeiture was reversed that the then earl launched a legal challenge suggests that Pelham's acquisition of the manor had long been perceived as lawful. Meanwhile, West Dean, noted in Maud's inquisition *post mortem* as being held with reversion to the archbishop of Canterbury and others (by a licensed fine of 1394),[52] came by 1436 into the possession of William Halle of Ore in Sussex and was mentioned in his will of 1449; how Halle acquired it is unclear. Again, the thirteenth earl of Oxford seems to have challenged the title and was perhaps, again, bought off.[53]

In July 1393 Maud paid 1,000 marks to Richard II for a licence for him to grant the reversions of seven further estates – Old Romney, Charlton, Ringwold and Kingsdown, all in Kent, Westwick in Hertfordshire, and Ramsey and Frating in

---

[47] *CIPM*, xix. 376, 379.
[48] BL, Add. Chs 30362, 31577 (10); see also *CPR, 1396–9*, p. 207. Sir John Pelham was probably related to the John de Pelham, clerk, who had acted as executor to Maud's father-in-law, and was in receipt of a pension of £10 a year from Welles: E.G. Pelham and David Maclean, *Some Early Pelhams* (Hove, 1931), 47–8. For Sir John, see *House of Commons, 1386–1421*, iv. 39–44.
[49] While the subsidy returns of 1412 stated the manors were worth no more than £70 combined and Maud had farmed them out in the mid-1380s for exactly these sums, an account of Pelham's in 1403 suggests Laughton produced £100 in that year and another account of 1405–6 saw income of over £80. The 1403 valor is transcribed in *Collins's Peerage of England; Genealogical, Biographical and Historical* (9 vols, 1812), v. 494–5; BL, Add. Ch. 32143 (1405–6 account); BL, Harl. Roll N3, m. 4; *Calendar of Feudal Aids* (6 vols, 1899–1920), vi. 521.
[50] BL, Add. Chs 30362, 30374, 30375, 31577 (nos 6–13).
[51] J.A. Ross, *The Foremost Man of the Kingdom. John de Vere, Thirteenth Earl of Oxford, 1442–1513* (Woodbridge, 2011), 53–4.
[52] CP25/1/290/57, no. 274; *CPR, 1391–6*, p. 512.
[53] For Halle's possession, see *The History of Parliament. The House of Commons, 1422–61*, ed. Linda Clark (7 vols, Cambridge, 2020), iv. 715–16, and for the later challenge Ross, *John de Vere*, 54, n. 25.

Essex – to a group of feoffees, headed by Thomas Percy, and their heirs and assigns. The patent roll notes that Maud held some of these properties for life and some in fee tail, after the possibility of issue had ended, and states that the reversions belonged to the king by reason of the judgment in parliament against Duke Robert, so Maud had to pay for them to be diverted elsewhere. Four were held in jointure – presumably the 'fee tail' of the patent roll – while three were dower estates. The timing of Maud's purchase of the licence – just over six months since the death of Robert de Vere – is significant, and while no purpose is stated she then or later saw the conveyance as being to enable her to sell the properties.[54] A later law suit suggests that Maud had access to cash reserves or to sources of credit at this point – 800 marks was paid to the king at the time of the issuing of the licence, and 100 marks each at the following Easter and Michaelmas.[55]

John Hende, a wealthy merchant and former mayor of London, purchased five of the seven (those at Charlton, Kingsdown, Old Romney, Ramsey and Ringwold), together with Wrabness, the only manor of Maud's own inheritance. This seems to have happened in two stages, as Charlton, Old Romney and Ringwold were in his possession by April 1407, when they were enfeoffed to joint tenure with his wife along with other property; Kingsdown and the manor of Ramsey changed hands at an unknown date; while Wrabness was sold to Hende after Maud's death.[56] The sale of Wrabness was conducted in accordance with her will, and the profits donated to the minoresses of Bruisyard abbey in Suffolk, where she was to be buried.[57]

Westwick is a different case. It had been part of the possessions of the abbey of St Albans in the mid-twelfth century, but had been granted by Abbot Geoffrey de Gorham to his brother-in-law without the consent of the convent,[58] came to a cadet branch of the de Veres by the 1270s, and in 1331 the scion of that cadet line became the seventh earl of Oxford.[59] The abbey had apparently regretted the loss of the manor and while it was in the possession of Countess Maud, who was holding it for life with (apparent) reversion to the crown, the opportunity arose to reacquire it. Nor was this simply a pious gift, it was a sale: 800 marks was agreed upon and the manor changed hands in 1395 in a complicated series of conveyances.[60] The abbot and

---

[54] *CPR*, 1391–6, p. 305; C81/542, no. 8929.
[55] CP40/738, rot. 529d.
[56] CP25/1/290/61/114. In 1408 Hende was granted free warren in his manor of Ringwold; *CPR*, 1405–8, p. 468. In two separate grants made on 13 November 1413, he conveyed the old de Vere estates to feoffees headed by Sir William Bourgchier: *CCR*, 1413–19, pp. 370–2, 374–5. Richard de Vere quitclaimed his rights in Ringwold, Charlton and Old Romney on 24 February 1410 to a large group of men including Hende: *CCR*, 1409–13, p. 78. It has not been possible to trace what happened to the moiety of the manor of Kingsdown. For Wrabness and Ramsey, see *CIPM*, xxi. 31–2.
[57] Philip Morant, *History and Antiquities of the County of Essex* (2 vols, 1768), i. 491; *Testamenta Vetusta*, ed. N.H. Nicolas (2 vols, 1826), i. 182. While this was a (limited) pious gesture, for a sceptical take on historians' assumptions about the devoutness of medieval noblewomen, see Archer, 'Piety in Question', 118–40. Little evidence of intense devotion can be found in Maud's career, land sales or brief and functional last will.
[58] *VCH Hertfordshire*, ii. 392–3.
[59] Alice, countess of Oxford, a relation of the Gorham family, purchased the manor for the use of her third son, Alphonso de Vere: Bodl., MS Rawlinson B 248, f. 28v; *Collectanea Topographica et Genealogica* (8 vols, Society of Antiquaries, 1834–43), v. 193–4.
[60] *Gesta Abbatum Monasterii Sancti Albani*, ed. H.T. Riley (3 vols, RS, 1869), iii. 376, 400, 455, 456–7; *CPR*, 1391–6, pp. 305, 637, 644; *CCR*, 1392–6, pp. 242, 479. See also *Collectanea Topographica et Genealogica*, v. 193–7, although there are obvious errors.

convent felt their title was insecure enough to pay Earl Richard a further 100 marks for a quitclaim in 1411, and following a legal challenge to their tenure in the court of common pleas by the twelfth earl of Oxford in 1444 to seek an out of court settlement in a final concord in 1446 with a payment of as much as £300.[61]

There may have been yet another manor of which Maud attempted to dispose, to the detriment of Aubrey and Richard de Vere. She held a reversionary interest in the manor of Market Overton in Rutland, which her late husband's retainer Sir William Wingfield held for the term of his life. Wingfield died in May 1398, and a year later Maud granted the manor to two feoffees. Then, on 4 August 1399, as Henry of Bolingbroke, supported by the Percys, was in the midst of seizing power and the throne from Richard II, the feoffees regranted it to Maud along with Henry Percy, earl of Northumberland, Thomas Percy, earl of Worcester, and Sir Henry Percy ('Hotspur').[62] The source does not record the purpose of the transaction, but this might have been to provide a tenancy for life for Maud with a reversion to a member of the Percy clan. Maud might also have been trying to ingratiate herself with those who looked likely to be key supporters of a new regime.[63] In this case, it was the crown which challenged her tenure; by Michaelmas 1402, the manor had been seized into the crown's possession under colour of the judgment of forfeiture against Duke Robert in 1388. Although in February 1403 a local jury decided in favour of upholding Maud's tenure and conveyance,[64] whatever plans she held for the manor were then thrown into disarray by the rebellion of the Percys later that year, and the death of Worcester and Hotspur at the battle of Shrewsbury. Together with the earl of Northumberland, she was forced to petition again in February 1405, rehearsing the same complaint but also adding that it had been agreed by the parliament assembled in January 1404 that none of the manors held by Worcester and Hotspur to the use of others should be forfeited.[65] It was not until 1406 that she was confirmed in her tenure, and if she did have plans to dispose of Market Overton these were evidently abandoned as the manor descended to Earl Richard at her death.[66]

Lands in which a widow held an interest for life were not allowed to be sold or otherwise diverted away from the right heir; this had been the case since Edward I's reign.[67] The fact that only seven out of nine dower manors and six out of fifteen estates held in jointure ultimately passed to Earl Richard at Maud's death reveals a piecemeal, opportunistic dispersal of property, made easier by the death of Earl Aubrey in 1400, followed by a six-year minority which not only ended the legal challenges in the short term, but allowed Maud to continue the process.[68] Indeed, her

---

[61] *Gesta Abbatum*, iii. 512–13; CP40/738, rot. 529; CP25/1/91/115, no. 131.
[62] C44/22/12.
[63] Maud may already have had connections with the Percy family, for her clerk had signed an acquittance at the Percy seat at Leconfield in Yorkshire in October 1376, raising the possibility that she was then staying there as well: *Calendar of the Plea and Memoranda Rolls of the City of London: Volume 2, 1364–1381* (1929), 251. The acquittance was produced by Sir William Berland to defeat the countess's claim that he owed her £10, leading to a judgment that she should take nothing by her plea and be in mercy.
[64] *CPR*, 1401–5, pp. 69–70 (C66/366, m. 11d.); C44/22/12.
[65] *CPR*, 1401–5, p. 512 (C66/372, m. 6d.).
[66] *CCR*, 1405–9, pp. 155–6; *CIPM*, xix. 377.
[67] For a discussion of this issue, see Archer, 'Rich Old Ladies', 21.
[68] That Earl Aubrey's affairs were in disarray is suggested by the fact that he died intestate: CP40/578, rot. 161; *CCR*, 1409–13, p. 305.

disposal of many estates was confirmed by a complex set of arrangements enforced on Richard on 21 December 1406, the same day that he was granted livery of his inheritance. Although he agreed to confirm Philippa, duchess of Ireland, in possession of her dower, and was rewarded with a grant of several properties and reversions then in the king's hands, he was forced to accept the validity of all the grants made by Richard II and Henry IV before that date, thus agreeing to the loss of a number of estates, notably those earmarked for Pleshey college and those conveyed to feoffees under the terms of Richard II's licence of 1393. With regard to two manors, Chesham and Market Overton, which were intended to pass to Philippa after Maud's death before transferring to Earl Richard, the parliamentary act of 1406 notes that the grant should stand 'notwithstanding that the said countess has made any demise or alienation of the manors', which suggests that she might have tried to dispose of Chesham as well as Market Overton.[69] The benefit of the act was that it stopped Maud making any further piecemeal alienations. Yet it was damaging to Richard, and one wonders whether Henry IV was aware of how damaging it was or whether he – one of the victors at Radcot Bridge against the duke of Ireland fifteen years earlier – chose to proceed regardless.

That Earl Richard clearly resented what Maud had done with his familial estates is demonstrated in the proceedings of an action of novel disseisin taken against him for seizing her manor of Wigston Magna in Leicestershire in 1409.[70] Maud had made an enfeoffment of the manor in 1403–4 to Thomas Langley, then keeper of the privy seal and later bishop of Durham and chancellor of England, and others, including her kinsman by marriage, William Danvers.[71] Whether this enfeoffment was arranged to provide better security of her tenure or whether she intended to use or dispose of the manor for a particular purpose is not clear. The case was brought by Langley and the other feoffees stating that at an unspecified date the earl and others had seized the manor, and they rehearsed the countess's title based on the settlement of jointure in 1369. Earl Richard entered a plea that ignored the settlement entirely, stating that Earl Thomas had held it in his demesne as of fee, as had Duke Robert and Earl Aubrey, and that it was only in the aftermath of the Percy revolt and the countess's conspiracy that Wigston Magna had mistakenly been assumed to belong to her: therefore, it ought to belong to him.[72] He also referred to the parliamentary acts relating to Philippa's rights in the duke's forfeited lands as additional evidence of title.[73] The earl lost and was fined 40 marks. His pleading had been peculiar, since by 1409 Maud had held the manor for forty years on the basis of the settlement of 1369,

---

[69] *CPR*, 1405–8, p. 314, and see also pp. 297, 299, 311; *PROME*, viii. 377.

[70] JUST 1/477/3; Ross, *John de Vere, Thirteenth Earl of Oxford*, 75–6; idem, 'Vere, Richard de, eleventh earl of Oxford (1385–1417)', *Oxford DNB*.

[71] JUST1/477/3, rot. 7 (no date other than the regnal year is given). For Langley, see C.M. Fraser, 'Langley, Thomas (c.1360–1437), *Oxford DNB*; for Danvers, who married Joan Leget, see *House of Commons, 1386–1421*, ii. 748–9. In 1408 Maud released all actions against Danvers and his wife: F.N. McNamara, *Memorials of the Danvers Family* (1895), 511 (citing Magdalen College, Oxford, Staneswyke, 41). I am grateful to Dr Hannes Kleineke for his help in tracking down this reference. In her will of 1453, Joan left money for prayers for the soul of Maud, countess of Oxford, together with her own soul and that of her husband: PROB11/4/212. One of the other feoffees was a Richard Wakefield, perhaps a son or brother of Thomas Wakefield of Leicester (*House of Commons, 1386–1421*, iv. 731), who may have been the bailiff or farmer of the manor, which is just south of the town.

[72] JUST1/477/3, rot. 6.

[73] JUST1/477/3, rot. 7; *PROME*, viii. 112–13, 377.

but the damages awarded make it unlikely to have been a collusive case designed to prove Richard's title. On this reading, the case shows both the hostility of Earl Richard to the countess and the ongoing threat to her tenure of some of her manors.

What happened in 1393 in particular, when Richard II licensed the grant of certain manors to Maud's feoffees with the likelihood that they would be sold, suggests the king's connivance in allowing her, the mother of his close friend, to act against the terms of the original legal conveyances of property to her by her father-in-law and husband. While the grant by Gloucester of the reversion of Maud's manors to Pleshey college was out of her control, her own grant of Bokingfold to the college during her lifetime and her actions as defendant in suits regarding some of these and other manors against Earl Aubrey suggests that she had no desire to counter the arrangement. The sale of other manors in 1395 and in or before 1407 was even more blatant. Taken together, this seems to have been a deliberate policy by Maud, albeit implemented in a sporadic and opportunistic way, to ensure at least a partial disinheritance of the de Veres. The scale of the disposal of manors – more than would be expected for pious reasons and not in a number of cases to religious institutions – combined with the vast amounts of waste committed by Maud on de Vere manors in the 1390s suggest very strongly that she had little liking for her marital relations. It is interesting to note that in accordance with her will she was buried at Bruisyard abbey in Suffolk and not next to her husband (and son) at Earls Colne, even though, given the size of her husband's tomb, it was clearly intended to have two effigies resting upon it.[74] She no longer had any links by blood to the de Veres, and after 1392 no child of hers would inherit the earldom. Yet it was very unusual, and of dubious legality, for such a deliberate attempt to be made by a dowager to disinherit a noble family of part of its lands.[75] The property sold to John Hende and St Albans abbey, and Bockingfold, granted to Pleshey during Maud's lifetime, were together worth around £140 annually; the value of the lands involved in the first round of legal process which Maud claimed belonged to the king and not the de Veres was just over £113 a year; while other evidence suggests she tried to dispose of two more manors worth a further £62 p.a.[76] Lands lost to Pleshey College or other recipients after Maud's death, perhaps with her connivance and certainly without resistance during her lifetime, totalled a further £125 p.a.[77] On a conservative estimate, taking the lowest valuation for the amount of waste committed by Maud by 1392, she had cost the estate £364 11s. 4d. (the highest possible estimate being nearly £506); and this related to the Essex manors alone. It is clear just how much damage was done to the de Veres' patrimony: no wonder that Aubrey's son Richard was in financial difficulties at the start of Henry V's reign.

---

[74] Lambeth Palace Library, Reg. Arundel II, f. 161; Geoffrey Probert, 'The Riddle of Bures Unravelled', *Essex Archaeology and History*, 3rd series, xvi (1984), 61. Maud made a payment of 6s. 8d. on the anniversary of the death of her husband in 1389: Longleat MS 442, attachment 1.

[75] Archer, 'Rich Old Ladies', 22, 25 provides examples of Katherine Neville, dowager duchess of Norfolk, conveying Mowbray estates she held in dower to Joan, her daughter by another husband, in 1468, and of Joan, Lady Mohun, selling estates which ought to have descended to her daughters in 1374, although this was at least with the agreement of Lord Mohun and through a fresh enfeoffment (for the latter, see the detailed account in Payling, 'Legal Right and Dispute Resolution').

[76] Annual values of the properties sold, as given in BL, Harl. Roll N3: Bockingfold (£16), Kingsdown (£2), Old Romney (£21), Ramsey (£30), Ringwold and Charlton (£16), Westwick (£38), and Wrabness (£17); legal case valuations: Fleet (£40), Frating (£11 13s. 4d.), Hedingham Vaux (£10), and Wigston (£51 9s. 8d.); and the two further manors were Chesham (£42) and Market Overton (£20).

[77] Laughton (£60), Welles (£15), West Dean (£10), Whitstable (£40).

III

However, Maud's actions in disposing of many of her estates had another consequence, in that they deprived her of revenue during her lifetime, and there is considerable evidence from the law courts that suggests she was in financial trouble from the 1390s onwards, caused by her dealings with citizens of London. As early as September 1394 she forfeited goods and chattels by waiver in the husting court in London at the suit of Richard Storm, in a plea of debt for £17 7s. 11d. However, the goods were granted to Nicholas Brayham and William Ayllesswy, a servant of the countess, and she herself was pardoned in November for her non-appearance.[78] The pace of suits quickened after this date: in 1396, alongside her receiver-general, John Pollard of Lavenham, and two others, she was sued for a debt of 100 marks by William Oliver, a London skinner, and in the same term a further case was brought by a draper, William Spray, for the much less serious debt of £4 8s.[79] Also in 1396 the skinner William Fremlyngham sued Maud for a debt of £114 12s. 4d., most of which, £112, Maud acknowledged by 1398, when she agreed to a schedule of repayment: £90 in two instalments, at the following Easter and Michaelmas, and the remainder later, all secured on the revenues of the manor of Fleet in Kent. She also allowed Fremlyngham the power to enter the manor and distrain her goods if she should fall into arrears. Fremlyngham claimed that she was £12 short at Michaelmas 1399 and £22 10s. 6d. short at Easter 1400, and that she therefore owed him £34 10s. 6d., and he also claimed damages of £100. Maud responded that he had been paid in full because he had entered Fleet and levied distraint there for the arrears; but Fremlyngham denied that he had been able to make good on what he was owed in the manor. The fact that he had entered Fleet to levy a distraint on her property was surely embarrassing for a countess and lady of the manor and more so if he had not been able to raise the money he was owed. The case was postponed and no verdict appears to have been reached.[80] Similarly in 1398, Simon Casteleyn, citizen and mercer of London, had three separate ongoing debt cases against Maud, for £10, £29 12s. 5d. and £44 13d. respectively.[81]

The situation did not ease with the change of dynasty. There were two cases in progress in Easter term 1401 in the court of common pleas, where Roger Gosselyn of West Firle, Sussex, was the plaintiff for debts of £78 in Essex and £24 in Sussex, and two further cases for debt in Trinity term 1403 brought against Maud by the abbot of Bury St Edmunds for £34 and by John Bishop of Aston in Suffolk for £13 4s. 4d.[82] By 1405 the last seems to have nearly doubled to a debt of £25 4s. 4d.[83] Late in Henry IV's reign two more suits, one for a debt of £15 Maud owed to a Colchester chandler for goods supplied a decade earlier, the other brought in 1412 by Agnes Feriby (probably the widow of the former steward of Maud's household, Robert Feriby) for a debt

---

[78] *CPR*, 1391–6, p. 479.
[79] CP40/541a, rots. 55d, 219d (Oliver), 54d (Spray).
[80] CP40/541a, rot 143d; 567, rot. 405; Jonathan Mackman and Matthew Stevens, 'CP40/567: Michaelmas term 1402', in *Court of Common Pleas: The National Archives, CP40 1399–1500* (2010), via *British History Online*, www.british-history.ac.uk/no-series/common-pleas/1399-1500/michaelmas-term-1402#h2-0055; CP40/570, rot. 241.
[81] CP40/549, rots 400d, 448d.
[82] CP40/561, rots 9d, 191 (Gosselyn), 570, rots 166d, 200d, 234.
[83] CP40/578, rot. 389d.

of £69, suggest Maud's position had not eased.[84] Even after her death there was no respite: John Sumpter sued her executor, Robert Boleyn, for a debt of £26 13s. 4d. very soon after her decease.[85] Sumpter and his father had been closely associated with the countess a decade before, and both had been tried for treason in connection with her conspiracy.[86]

There is evidence that Maud was also owed money and chased it through the law courts. In Easter term 1396, she had suits in progress against John Barberd for a debt of £20, John Colman of Polstead and John Rosche for an identical sum, and Henry Robyn of Westwick for £40.[87] For the first two Maud had associated with her as a plaintiff Edward Pichard, a household servant and probably a member of her estate administration, and the suit against Robyn was brought very shortly after the sale of Westwick.[88] Given that the annual farm of Westwick was £38 and that Robyn had been the farmer of the manor in 1387–8 and may well have continued in the role in the 1390s, the sum of £40 was probably unpaid arrears from the preceding year, while the first two debt cases may also have been an attempt to secure manorial income.[89] These suits perhaps suggest that Maud and her servants were struggling to ensure her landed revenues were paid on time. In 1408 Maud was suing Thomas Helwedyn of Kent for a debt of £20.[90] In 1403, she brought a case relating to the farm of one of Duke Robert's estates which she had not held since January 1393.[91] More significantly, in 1402 she brought a case of debt for £300 against her former receiver-general, William Sesile, on an obligation dated 5 September 1388, probably about the time he was dismissed from his office, and which presumably related to the arrears from his account. Sesile claimed he had a quitclaim from the countess dated 23 March 1392 and produced it in court; the countess denied it was of her making. The case went to trial by jury but no verdict is recorded in the pleading of the case on the roll.[92]

Even so, these cases, many of which may simply have been brought to realise expected income or arrears, were fewer in number and, excluding the Sessile case, dwarfed in size by the suits for debt where Maud was a defendant. The frequency with which she was sued seems to have been exceptional. While comparative figures for noblewomen are hard to come by, men of equivalent status were rarely defendants in the court of common pleas where comparisons can be drawn over long

---

[84] CP40/589, rot. 349d; 603, rot. 417 (I owe this reference to Dr Simon Payling); for Feriby: CP40/605, rot. 55.
[85] CP40/609, rot. 50; 618, rot. 312; 621, rot. 73. By 1402 Boleyn had been granted for life Maud's manor of Cruswiche, worth 10 marks p.a.: C131/55/14.
[86] Ross, 'Seditious Activities', 31, 35. The younger John Sumpter, found not guilty at trial, had subsequently built a successful career in Colchester and as an Essex landowner: *House of Commons, 1386–1421*, iv. 532–3.
[87] CP40/541, rots 64, 281. Colman was pardoned for his non-appearance to answer the countess in 1398: *CPR*, 1396–9, p. 302.
[88] Pichard supplied goods to Maud's household in 1389 and was pardoned in 1391 as her servant: Longleat MS 442, rot. 1; *CPR*, 1388–92, p. 407.
[89] For Robyn, see BL, Harl. Roll N3, mm. 2–3.
[90] CP40/589, rots 9d, 237. Two entries appear against the same man for the same sum, one in Essex and one in London. There may therefore have been two separate suits for a total debt of £40.
[91] E13/119, rot. 25. She claimed damages of £40.
[92] CP40/567, rot. 407d.

periods. To take one example, Ralph, first earl of Stafford, was sued only twice in the court between 1334 and 1372.[93]

Further evidence for Maud's financial difficulties can be discerned from the contents of her will.[94] She made few cash bequests: 20 marks to Robert Roueyte, 40 marks each to Joan, a recluse at Westminster, and Katherine, wife of John Cook, £40 to William Aylleswy and 100 marks to her cousin Joan Lucy.[95] Nor were there any specific legacies of valuable goods or objects. All the rest of her possessions were to be disposed of for the benefit of her soul, and the souls of her parents, ancestors and all faithful departed. Cash bequests totalling £173 are far less than one would expect a countess to have accumulated after a widowhood of more than forty years. By comparison, Joan, Lady Abergavenny, disposed of over £4,000 in her will of 1435.[96]

As far as the male de Veres were concerned, Maud did significant damage to their landed holdings, and joins a very small group of dowagers who defrauded their marital families. In 1371 she held twenty-five manors, twenty-four of which were granted to her in dower and jointure and would, in normal circumstances, have descended to the future earls of Oxford, but after her death in 1413, just fourteen of these manors passed to the right male heir.[97] Given that a significant number were alienated in her lifetime, this clearly had a significant impact on her finances. Evidence suggests that this was compounded by extravagance. In the 1380s – at the height of her prosperity – she seems to have been overspending relative to her income and may well have continued to do so despite declining receipts, given the number of debt cases brought against her by London merchants. Really serious financial difficulties amongst the elites, and particularly elite women, were rare.[98] K.B. McFarlane noted that 'there is no sign whatever that even a single one of the comital houses, though a few like those of Vere and Courtenay had never been over-rich, came to disaster by any other road than political miscalculation'.[99] The financial man-

---

[93] Stafford was twice a defendant and eleven times a plaintiff. Figures from *Collections for a History of Staffordshire* (William Salt Arch. Soc. xi–xiii, 1890–2), xi. 78, 85, 114; xii. 11, 23, 45, 65, 83, 86, 87, 94, 117, 164, 173; xiii. 22, 34–5, 38, 88. I am grateful to Dr Matthew Hefferan for extracting and sharing these references with me. The third duke of Buckingham brought dozens of suits for debts, mainly unsuccessfully: Carole Rawcliffe, *The Staffords, Earls of Stafford and Dukes of Buckingham, 1394–1521* (Cambridge, 1978), 164–70, 244–51.

[94] Lambeth, Reg. Arundel II, f. 161.

[95] Aylleswy, Maud's household servant, was pardoned with her in 1391 for travelling overseas to visit Robert, duke of Ireland, without licence: *CPR*, 1388–92, p. 407. This is a huge sum to bequeath to a servant, however, and one wonders if the payment related to his involvement in the conspiracy of 1403–4: Ross, 'Seditious Activities', 31.

[96] For this and other examples, see Archer. 'Piety in Question', 131. Joan, Lady Dinham, made cash bequests of over £500 in her will of 1497 from an income of between £300 and £350 p.a., having also played an important role in supporting her family over the previous forty years: Hannes Kleineke, 'Lady Joan Dinham: A Fifteenth-Century West-Country Matriarch', in *Social Attitudes and Political Structures in the Fifteenth Century*, ed. Tim Thornton (Stroud, 2000), 69–87, esp. 83, 86.

[97] Hedingham Vaux, Preston and Cruswiche are not mentioned in her inquisition *post mortem*, but may have been omitted in error (*CIPM*, xix. 376–80); they did descend to the de Veres. Frating, also omitted, did not.

[98] For another lady suffering significant financial difficulties in reduced circumstances during the same period, see D.L. Biggs, 'Patronage, Preference and Survival: the Life of Lady Margaret Sarnesfield, c.1381– c.1444', in *The Ties that Bind. Essays in Medieval British History in Honor of Barbara Hanawalt*, ed. L.E. Mitchell, K.L. French and D.L. Biggs (Farnham, 2011), 143–58, esp. 154–7.

[99] K.B. McFarlane, *The Nobility of Later Medieval England* (Oxford, 1973), 48–9 (and more generally 15–16). For a more recent discussion of the ways the aristocracy in general made ends meet, see

agement of Maud, countess of Oxford, is not fully counter-evidence to this; political miscalculation of Robert, duke of Ireland, played its part, and Maud did not sink to the level of 'disaster'. However, the de Veres had grown increasingly rich by the mid-fourteenth century, and it was, in part, Maud who reversed that trend, and if she was not in a disastrous position by the first decade of the fifteenth century, she was perhaps not too far from it. Barbara Harris has argued that historians should not look upon widows from the point of view of the family they married into, and that widows managed the property in their possession profitably and carefully.[100] Yet, while the historian should certainly not solely look at a widow from the marital family's point of view, equally that perspective should not be ignored, and in terms of a widow managing her estate profitably and carefully Maud, countess of Oxford, absolutely exemplifies the reverse. Maud was a rich lady in the 1370s and 1380s; by the first decade of the fifteenth century, she was an old lady but no longer rich.

Christopher Dyer, *Standards of Living in the Middle Ages. Social Change in England c. 1200–1520* (Cambridge, 1989), 86–108.

[100] B.J. Harris, *English Aristocratic Women, 1450–1550* (Oxford, 2002), 127–8. See also J.T. Rosenthal, 'Aristocratic Widows in Fifteenth-Century England', in *Women and the Structure of Society. Selected Research from the Fifth Berkshire Conference on the History of Women*, ed. B.J. Harris and J.K. McNamara (Durham, NC, 1984), 36–47, 259–60, esp. 37.

APPENDIX: ESTATES HELD BY COUNTESS MAUD

Manor/holding	Source of acquisition	Recipient/next owner	Date
Wrabness, Essex	Inheritance	John Hende/Bruisyard	sale 1413
Chesham, Bucks.	Jointure 1350	Earls of Oxford	1413
Ramsey, Essex		John Hende	sale bef. 1413
Westwick, Herts.		St Albans Abbey	sale 1395
Wigston Magna, Leics.	Jointure 1369	Earls of Oxford	1413
Frating, Essex	Jointure ?1369	?duchy of Lancaster/crown	?by 1402–3[101]
Hedingham Vaux, Essex		Earls of Oxford	1413
Preston, Suffolk		Earls of Oxford	1413
Market Overton, Rutland[102]	Jointure 1370	Earls of Oxford	1413
Bockingfold, Kent	Jointure 1371	Pleshey College	1396
Fleet, Kent		Earls of Oxford	1413
Laughton, Sussex		Feoffees, then Sir John Pelham	bef. 1413
Old Romney, Kent		John Hende	sale bef. 1407
Welles, Herts.		Pleshey College	1413
West Dean, Sussex		Pleshey College/William Halle	1413
Whitstable, Kent		Pleshey College	1413
Aldham, Suffolk	Dower 1371	Earls of Oxford	1413
land in Charlton, Kent		John Hende	sale bef. 1407
land in Cowley, Bucks.		Earls of Oxford	1413
Earls Colne, Essex		Earls of Oxford	1413
Great Abingdon, Cambs.		Earls of Oxford	1413
Great Bentley, Essex		Earls of Oxford	1413
Great Hormead, Herts.		Earls of Oxford	1413
land in Kingsdown, Kent		John Hende	sale bef. 1413
Lavenham, Suffolk (two manors)		Earls of Oxford	1413
Ringwold, Kent		John Hende	sale bef. 1407
Cruswiche, Essex	Unknown	Earls of Oxford	?1413

[101] It is difficult to trace the ownership of this manor. It is not included in Maud's inquisition *post mortem* nor in later de Vere accounts, which suggests that Maud disposed of it. A Philip de Frating held a knight's fee in Frating of the duchy honour of Tutbury in 3 Henry IV, and Frating is noted among duchy court rolls in 1410–11, so this seems a likely possibility: DL30/122/1858A, p. 29; DL30/77/979.

[102] In reversion after the death of Sir William Wingfield (d. 1398).

THE ADOPTION OF THE ENGLISH LANGUAGE BY HENRY V[1]

Samuel Lane

In 1513, the anonymous author of *The First English Life of Henry V* sat down to translate Titus Livius' *Vita Henrici Quinti* from Latin into English. In his *Prohem*, he declared that he did so in order to 'reduce it into our naturall English tongue', and thus to make it 'more fruitefull, open and pleasant to the readers and hearers hereof'. Even at this stage of the sixteenth century, doubts remained as to the status and prestige of English; the self-styled Translator of Livio himself referred to 'rude and holme [sic] English, from whome all pratique and famous inditinge is farr exiled'.[2] Nonetheless, English had come a long way as a written language, from being rarely deployed in formal documents in the early fourteenth century, to being the 'naturall English tongue' to which the Translator referred, and which his decision to translate from Latin into the vernacular for reasons of accessibility tacitly acknowledged.[3] So much is plain. However, the reasons for this growth of written English are altogether more contentious. In particular, Henry V has long been ascribed a central significance in the process: J.H. Ramsay averred that his adoption of the vernacular marked the 'transition from Late Medieval English to Early Modern English'; Albert Baugh asserted that his employment of the vernacular helped to make his reign 'the turning point in the use of English in writing'; and

---

[1] This chapter began life as an MSt essay written under the supervision of Rowena E. Archer and John Watts. Like everything that I have written, it owes so much to Rowena's support, kindness and encouragement. When reading through past drafts, she suggested further examples in support of the points I made, pointed out areas in which my arguments could be developed, and applied a characteristically sharp pruning knife to the flabbier parts of my prose. I hope that relatively little verbosity has returned in the interim.

[2] *The First English Life of King Henry the Fifth Written in 1513 by an Anonymous Author Known Commonly as the Translator of Livius*, ed. C.L. Kingsford (Oxford, 1911), 3.

[3] M.H. Keen, *English Society in the Later Middle Ages, 1348–1500* (1990), 223–4; Tim Machan, *English in the Middle Ages* (Oxford, 2003), 161–78; Helen Wicker, 'Introduction', in *Vernacularity in England and Wales*, ed. Elisabeth Salter and Helen Wicker (Turnhout, 2011), 5, 9. To observe that English linguistically played very much second fiddle to Latin and French in the early fourteenth century is of course not to doubt the importance or quality of the texts which were produced in the language, not least the work of Robert Mannyng and the pieces compiled in the Auchinleck manuscript. These are discussed fruitfully in Thorlac Turville-Petre, *England the Nation: Language, Literature, and National Identity, 1290–1340* (Oxford, 1996), 108–38.

J.H. Fisher argued that his 'use of English marks the turning point in establishing English as the national language of England'.[4] More recently, in his splendid work on the monarch, Malcolm Vale contended that Henry's 'enduring legacy' was 'the creation, adoption, and stabilisation – for the first time – of an English language and idiom of government, politics, and administration'.[5] However, other scholars have cast doubt on Henry's personal contribution, and insisted that English achieved prominence through more structural, 'grass-roots' factors, such as how it was the most widely understood language in the realm.[6] In the context of this historiographical controversy – which has rendered the subject, in John Watts' words, 'a hot topic for historians and literary scholars alike' – this essay shall consider afresh the adoption of English by the Translator's great hero, 'this most noble prince, Kinge Henrie the Fifthe'.[7]

Henry's major step to embrace the vernacular came in August 1417, when he embarked on his conquest of Normandy, and the language of his signet letters changed from Anglo-Norman to English. Although a smattering of royal documents had been penned in the vernacular before this point – including a handful of signet letters and several proclamations – this was the first government department since the eleventh century systematically to prefer English.[8] Three overarching reasons, each with their own variants and developments, have been put forward for this change of practice. First, it has been suggested that Henry adopted the vernacular because it was more widely understood than French, with Anne Curry

---

[4] J.H. Ramsay, *Lancaster and York: A Century of English History (A.D. 1399–1485)* (2 vols, Oxford, 1892), i. 308–9; Albert Baugh, *A History of the English Language* (2nd edn, New York, 1957), 184; John Fisher, *The Emergence of Standard English* (Lexington, KY, 1996), 22. See also Malcolm Richardson, 'Henry V, the English Chancery, and Chancery English', *Speculum*, xl (1980), 738–41; John Fisher, 'A Language Policy for Lancastrian England', *Publications of the Modern Language Association*, cvii (1992), 1171–8; Christopher Allmand, *Henry V* (1992), 419–22; and Giedrius Subačius, 'Two Types of Standard Language History in Europe', *Res Balticae*, viii (2002), 133–4.

[5] Malcolm Vale, '"With mine own hand": The Use of the Autograph by English Rulers in the Later Middle Ages, c. 1350–c. 1480', in *Manu Propria: Vom eigenhändigen Schreiben der Mächtigen*, ed. Claudia Feller and Christian Lackner (Vienna, 2016), 186. See also idem, *Henry V: The Conscience of a King* (2016), 124–5.

[6] For instance, John Watts suggested that 'the really significant development [the greater 'administrative use of English'] was driven by a wider set of social and pragmatic changes; the individual [Henry V] and his conscience weren't so important after all': 'He Who Must Bear All: Review of *Henry V: The Conscience of a King* by Malcolm Vale', *London Review of Books,* xxxix (2017), 31–2. See also Michael Benskin, 'Chancery Standard', in *New Perspectives on English Historical Linguistics: Lexis and Transmission*, ed. Christian Kay, Carole Hough and Irene Wotherspoon (Glasgow, 2004), 1–40; Anne Curry, Adrian Bell, Adam Chapman, Andy King and David Simpkin, 'Languages in the Military Profession in Later Medieval England', in *The Anglo-Norman Language and its Contexts*, ed. Richard Ingham (York, 2010), 83; Gwilym Dodd, 'The Rise of English, the Decline of French: Supplications to the English Crown, c.1420–1450', *Speculum*, lxxxvi (2011), 143; idem, 'The Spread of English in the Records of Central Government', in *Vernacularity in England and Wales*, 263–4.

[7] Watts, 'He Who Must Bear All', 32; *First English Life*, ed. Kingsford, 5.

[8] See, for instance, *English Medieval Diplomatic Practice, Part I*, ed. Pierre Chaplais (2 vols, 1975–82), i. 98–101; *A Book of London English, 1384–1425*, ed. R.W. Chambers and Marjorie Daunt (Oxford, 1931), 64–6; Vale, *Henry V*, 35, 121–2. In addition to the handful of English governmental texts from the early fifteenth century, Henry III's use of the vernacular almost two centuries previously in his letters of 1258 has also attracted a substantial literature: see, for example, Alexander Ellis, 'On the Only English Proclamation of Henry III', *Transactions of the Philological Society*, xiii (1869), 1–17; Machan, *English in the Middle Ages*, 21–69; and David Matthews, *Writing to the King: Nation, Kingship, and Literature in England, 1250–1350* (Cambridge, 2010), 27–8.

and others arguing that Henry assumed the language to reach 'as wide an audience as possible'.[9] Second, it has been proposed that English was embraced because of its greater clarity; in his excellent work on the 'rise of English', Gwilym Dodd remarked that 'the early adoption of English in the king's signet letters under Henry V is a useful reminder of the importance attached to the English language by the monarchy as a means of conveying the king's will in the clearest and most unambiguous way possible'.[10] Finally, a number of historians and literary scholars have suggested that the king employed the vernacular because of its ability to inspire nationalistic sentiments, appeal to a nascent sense of English identity, and stir support for Henry's foreign campaigns. In particular, Derek Pearsall remarked that Henry made 'strenuous efforts to encourage the use of the English language in official documents as part of a programme to promote a sense of English national identity', and Malcolm Richardson claimed that Henry's 'motive for using the vernacular was undoubtedly to win support for the war'.[11] However, while these factors might well have lain behind the increasing prominence of English in the fifteenth century more broadly – and, indeed, might well have played some part in Henry V's own decision-making – they fail to explain fully his decision to adopt the vernacular. When the audiences and purposes of Henry's signet letters are considered in some detail, more practical and rudimentary explanations for their adoption of English emerge: the king's own aptitude for the language, and the relative indecipherability of the vernacular, should his letters be intercepted and read by his French foes.

The argument that Henry adopted the vernacular in his signet correspondence because it could be comprehended by a wider portion of England's population rests on suspect foundations. Of course, there is a variety of evidence that suggests a broader swathe of society understood English. Thus, in the mid-fourteenth century, William of Nassington pondered how 'somme understonden Englysch/ that can nother Latyn or Frensch/ But lerned and lewed, olde and yonge/ Alle understonden Englysch tonge'.[12] More famously, the oft-quoted 1422 memorandum of the London Brewers averred (in Latin) that 'there are many of our craft of Brewers who have the knowledge of writing and reading in the said English idiom, but ... Latin and French, before these times used, they do not in any wise understand'.[13] Nevertheless, even if these statements about the wide understanding of English are accepted at face value, something which has been cautioned against, they still fail to provide a satis-

---

[9] Curry *et al.*, 'Languages in the Military Profession', 83. See also K.B. McFarlane, *Lancastrian Kings and Lollard Knights* (Oxford, 1972), 119; Allmand, *Henry V*, 421–2; and Anne Curry, *Henry V* (2015), 117.

[10] Dodd, 'Rise of English', 141. See also Gerald Harriss, *Shaping the Nation: England, 1360–1461* (Oxford, 2005), 46; Curry *et al.*, 'Languages in the Military Profession', 83–5; and Dodd, 'Spread of English', 259.

[11] Richardson, 'Henry V, the English Chancery, and Chancery English', 740; Derek Pearsall, 'Chaucer and Englishness', *Proceedings of the British Academy*, ci (1999), 91. See also Fisher, *Emergence of Standard English*, 16–35; W.M. Ormrod, 'The Use of English: Language, Law and Political Culture in Fourteenth-Century England', *Speculum*, lxxviii (2003), 784–7; Vale, *Henry V*, 122–5; and Juliane Werlin, *Writing at the Origin of Capitalism: Literary Circulation and Change in Early Modern England* (Oxford, 2021), 27, n. 19.

[12] HMC, *Reports on the Manuscripts of Lord Middleton* (1911), 239.

[13] *London English*, ed. Chambers and Daunt, 139.

factory explanation for the adoption of the vernacular in Henry's signet letters.[14] This becomes apparent when the recipients of Henry's 114 known English signet letters from August 1417 to the end of his reign are assessed.[15]

The vast majority of the surviving letters (88 out of 114) were addressed to the chancellor, Thomas Langley, bishop of Durham.[16] These included a variety of directions and instructions, ranging from the more mundane, such as an order of 19 January 1418 to summon the justices to enquire into a case touching the earl of Huntingdon, to the more overtly significant, including a command of 30 January 1419 to proclaim news of the truce with Brittany.[17] There can be no question of Langley's ability to understand French. He had become chancellor on 23 July 1417, a fortnight before the adoption of the vernacular in Henry's signet correspondence, and had received at least two signet letters in the interim that were both written in Anglo-Norman.[18] Indeed, Langley had previously served as chancellor between March 1405 and January 1407, during which period he had received at least 227 signet letters in French.[19] Moreover, as chancellor, he necessarily had to deal with much Anglo-Norman correspondence, even after the adoption of English in Henry's signet letters.[20] Of course, Langley was not only proficient in French, but also adept in Latin, which was the pre-eminent language of both the Church and the chancery; English did not feature in documents such as the patent, close and fine rolls until the later fifteenth century, and Latin in fact continued to predominate and not to be abandoned until 1731.[21]

---

[14] J.B. Trapp, 'Literacy, Books and Readers', in *The Cambridge History of the Book in Britain III, 1400–1557*, ed. Lotte Hellinga and J.B. Trapp (Cambridge, 1999), 39–40; Ormrod, 'Use of English', 784; Simon Horobin, *Chaucer's English* (2nd edn, Basingstoke, 2013), 22.

[15] For the purposes of this article, the letters which are 'known' are taken as those included in *Calendar of the Signet Letters of Henry IV and Henry V*, ed. J.L. Kirby (1978), which contains all those found by the editor in the public records and several other depositories (such as the British Library, the Bodleian Library and the London Record Office). While, as the editor acknowledged, other letters may have survived (and may have been subsequently found) in public record 'classes which have not been systematically explored', or indeed elsewhere, Kirby's edition remains – in the words of Gwilym Dodd – 'the main published collection of this material', and offers at least a reasonably large sample from which to consider the characteristics of the signet letters, the types of message they conveyed and the people to whom they were written: *Calendar of Signet Letters*, ed. Kirby, 5; Dodd, 'Spread of English', 231. It must be noted, however, that while the signet letters calendared by Kirkby are probably the vast majority of those which survive, they likely represent less than a tenth of all those written in the period: *Calendar of Signet Letters*, ed. Kirby, 5.

[16] *Calendar of Signet Letters*, ed. Kirby, 165–201.

[17] *Ibid.*, nos 818, 853.

[18] *Ibid.*, pp. xii, 165.

[19] *Ibid.*, pp. xii, 64–143.

[20] See, for instance, *PPC*, ii. 292–3, a French petition from John Mosdale of July 1421, regarding his position as keeper of Scarborough castle, which was addressed to the chancellor.

[21] Benskin, 'Chancery Standard', 36–8; Dodd, 'Spread of English', 234. Of course, much of the correspondence addressed to Langley would have ultimately been dealt with by chancery clerks, rather than by Langley himself. However, such clerks would also have necessarily understood French and Latin: T.F. Tout, 'Literature and Learning in the English Civil Service in the Fourteenth Century', *Speculum*, iv (1929), 368; John Fisher, 'Chancery and the Emergence of Standard Written English in the Fifteenth Century', *Speculum*, lii (1977), 870–99; Kitrina Bevan, 'Clerks and Scriveners: Legal Literacy and Access to Justice in Late Medieval England' (PhD thesis, University of Exeter, 2013), 244–5.

In addition, Henry wrote eight surviving vernacular signet letters to English cities, principally to London,[22] nine to his brothers,[23] seven to his officers in France,[24] and four to his council.[25] It seems clear that all his recipients were capable of understanding French. The civic elites of London appear to have had few difficulties with Anglo-Norman. They received royal correspondence in the language, both before and after the adoption of the vernacular by Henry's signet clerks,[26] and used it for their own documents: almost all texts issued under the mayoralty seal remained in French throughout the early fifteenth century, as did almost all bills of complaint and petitions for remedy in the city's law courts.[27] The dukes of Bedford and Gloucester also clearly understood French; both men held positions which required them to read and speak the language, such as when Bedford was made regent of France after Henry's death;[28] both owned French works, with Gloucester owning a French translation of Vegetius' *De Re Militari*;[29] and both could write in the language.[30] Similarly, the officials in France whom Henry addressed necessarily had a grasp of French to perform their roles, and indeed William Bardolf wrote a letter in Anglo-

[22] Henry wrote seven surviving letters to London – which publicised news of his military successes at Touques, Caen and Pont-de-l'Arche – and one to Bath, which concerned a dispute over the ringing of bells in the city: *London English*, ed. Chambers and Daunt, 67–84; *Calendar of Signet Letters*, ed. Kirby, no. 811. While less material survives from the corporation of Bath than that of London, it suggests that the city's elites had little difficulty with foreign tongues: the majority of its fifteenth-century records are in Latin, with a handful in French (including grants of land and agreements regarding rents), and the city received royal correspondence in Latin: *The Municipal Records of Bath, 1189–1604*, ed. A.J. King and B.H. Watts (1885), p. xx; *Ancient Deeds Belonging to the Corporation of Bath*, ed. C.W. Sickle (Bath, 1921), pp. viii, 138; *CPR*, 1416–22, p. 447.

[23] Henry wrote five surviving letters to the duke of Bedford, and four to the duke of Gloucester (two of which were addressed to the council as well). These touched on a range of matters, from the truce between England and Brittany to a petition from a yeoman usher of the chamber: *Calendar of Signet Letters*, ed. Kirby, nos 851, 886; *PPC*, ii. 243–4.

[24] Henry wrote letters to Sir John St John, mayor of Bordeaux, Sir John Radcliffe, constable of Bordeaux castle, William Bardolf, lieutenant of Calais, and Richard Buckland, treasurer of Calais: *Calendar of Signet Letters*, ed. Kirby, nos 883, 909, 917. In addition, he wrote three surviving letters to an officer in Calais and one to a commander in France, whose identities are unknown.

[25] These letters date from October 1418, when Henry instructed his councillors to liaise with the ambassadors of the duke of Bavaria, to May 1420, when he enclosed copies of the treaty of Troyes, and ordered that the peace be proclaimed throughout the kingdom: *Calendar of Signet Letters*, ed. Kirby, nos 848, 894.

[26] For instance, Henry wrote in French to the city in September 1415, boasting of his capture of Harfleur, and the duke of Clarence wrote similarly in September 1417 and July 1418, notifying Londoners of the capture of Caen and fall of Louviers respectively: *Memorials of London*, ed. H.T. Riley (1868), 618–20; *Calendar of Letter-Books Preserved Among the Archives of the Corporation of the City of London at the Guildhall*, ed. R.R. Sharpe (11 vols, 1899–1912), ix. 131, 185, 200. Indeed, the Londoners deployed French in their reply to Henry's first English signet letter to them from Touques, reporting their pleasure at his capture of the town, and that the city remained in a state of tranquillity: *Calendar of Letter-Books*, ed. Sharpe, ix. 184.

[27] *Calendar of Plea and Memoranda Rolls Preserved Among the Archives of the Corporation of the City of London at the Guildhall* (6 vols, Cambridge, 1926–61), iv. pp. xv, xvii–xviii.

[28] Jenny Stratford, 'John, duke of Bedford', in *Oxford DNB*. Gloucester was also made governor of Rouen in 1419: Gerald Harriss, 'Humphrey, Duke of Gloucester', in *Oxford DNB*.

[29] L.C.Y. Everest-Philipps, 'The Patronage of Humphrey, Duke of Gloucester: A Re-Evaluation' (D.Phil. thesis, University of York, 1983), 171–2; Jenny Stratford, 'The Manuscripts of John, Duke of Bedford: Library and Chapel', in *England in the Fifteenth Century: Proceedings of the 1986 Harlaxton Symposium*, ed. Daniel Williams (Woodbridge, 1987), 346–7.

[30] Everest-Philipps, 'Patronage of Humphrey, Duke of Gloucester', 52; Stratford, 'Manuscripts of John, Duke of Bedford', 347.

Norman to the duke of Bedford in October 1415.[31] Furthermore, Henry's councillors appear to have been literate in French; the council received, and responded to, petitions in Anglo-Norman, and its own minutes were principally written in that language until May 1421.[32]

What is more, Henry's recipients also appear to have comprehended Latin. The government regularly wrote in Latin to the mayor and commonalty of London, and citizens' bonds, bills of obligation, property deeds and wills remained overwhelmingly in that language throughout the early fifteenth century.[33] Likewise, both Bedford and Gloucester seem to have been proficient in Latin: an elementary Latin grammar was purchased for Bedford when he was seven or eight; both men's official positions required them to deal with Latin correspondence; both brothers' extensive libraries contained books in the language; and both men commissioned the translation of works into the tongue, as Gloucester did with Aristotle's *Politics* in 1434.[34] In a similar vein, the officials in France that Henry addressed in English could seemingly understand other letters in Latin. Thus, the crown wrote in Latin to William Bardolf and Richard Buckland in June 1419, instructing them to negotiate with the Burgundians, and to Sir John St John and Sir John Radcliffe in June 1420, ordering them to inspect the company mustered by the seneschal of Aquitaine.[35] Moreover, Henry's council was also familiar with the language, and tellingly, after their minutes ceased to be written in French in May 1421, they were penned not in the vernacular, but rather in Latin.[36]

In this light, the fact that a wider portion of the population might have understood English fails to explain satisfactorily the adoption of the vernacular by Henry's signet clerks. The majority of these letters were private communications, written to royal officials with a mastery of Anglo-Norman. Even the handful of letters which were penned for broader audiences – namely Henry's dispatches to the Londoners, which publicised news of royal successes – did not require the use of the vernacular, for similar letters had been sent to the city in French, by Henry himself and the duke of Clarence. This suggests either that there was a sufficiently broad understanding of the language among the sectors of London society which the king sought to reach, or that Henry had no objection to his words being translated for the masses by other

---

[31] *Foedera*, ix. 314–15. Bardolf, Buckland, St John and Radcliffe were all involved in negotiating – with the French, Burgundians and Gascons – which would have necessitated some knowledge of French: *ibid.*, 422, 449, 591, 754, 760, 804; *Calendar of Signet Letters,* ed. Kirby, nos 797, 877, 879, 883.

[32] See, for example, *PPC,* ii. 280–2, 282–3. See also Dodd, 'Spread of English', 265–6, n. 102. There might, however, have been some decline in the learning of French among England's elites in the late fourteenth century, for in the 1380s John Trevisa remarked that 'gentil men haueþ now moche i-left for to teche here children Frensche': *Polychronicon Ranulphi Higden, Monachi Cestrensis, together with the English Translations of John Trevisa,* ed. Churchill Babington and J.A. Lumby (2 vols, 1869), ii. 161. See also Philip Ziegler, *The Black Death* (1969), 252–3; Ardis Butterfield, *The Familiar Enemy: Chaucer, Language, and Nation in the Hundred Years War* (Oxford, 2009), 325–8; Vale, *Henry V*, 94–6.

[33] See, for instance, *CPR*, 1416–22, p. 67; *CCR*, 1413–19, p. 466; Malcolm Richardson, *Middle-Class Writing in Late Medieval London* (2011), 65–6, 74, 98–9, 114.

[34] Nicholas Orme, 'The Education of the Courtier', in *English Court Culture in the Later Middle Ages,* ed. V.J. Scattergood and J.W. Sherborne (1983), 81; Stratford, 'Manuscripts of John, Duke of Bedford', 346–7; Everest-Philipps, 'Patronage of Humphrey, Duke of Gloucester', 182.

[35] TNA, C61/118, m. 4; *Foedera,* ix. 760.

[36] See, for example, *PPC,* ii. 286–92; Dodd, 'Spread of English', 265–6, n. 102.

hands or mouths.[37] Yet not only could the recipients of Henry's letters comprehend French, but they also appear to have had a knowledge of Latin. Accordingly, even if there had been a diminishing understanding of French, there was another language that the king's signet clerks could have turned to, rather than embracing the vernacular.[38] Indeed, it is noteworthy that Henry's correspondents resisted the lure of their native language in their own texts, such as the urban muniments of London, the bureaucratic records of the chancery and council, and the libraries of Bedford and Gloucester. It would therefore have been surprising had Henry assumed the vernacular to cater for their linguistic frailties and predilections.

The second argument, that it was the government's need to communicate as clearly as possible which drove the king's adoption of English, also sits awkwardly with the evidence.[39] It is implausible that English, a language in its administrative infancy, would have been better suited to conveying the crown's instructions than French: a language which had been honed for this very purpose for generations.[40] Numerous documents reveal Anglo-Norman's capacity for clarity and precision, even after Henry adopted the vernacular for the majority of his signet correspondence. For instance, Henry's letter of 26 September 1419 to the council at Bordeaux told it to give full credence to Sir John St John and Sir John Radcliffe in clear and succinct terms. Likewise, his letter of 11 October 1419 to two merchants in Bristol commanded them to allow his officers to select a portion of the goods which they had taken from the Genoese in an exact and incontrovertible manner.[41]

Conversely, it appears that it was English which was perceived (at least by some) as inconvenient and imprecise. The first problem with the vernacular was the existence of a number of dialects which might have been imperfectly understood by those from other areas of the country.[42] This was emphasised in successive translations of

[37] This sets Henry and Clarence apart from, for example, the Wycliffite translators, who rendered sermons into English in order to create a stable theological language from which preachers could preach without excessive deviation, and implies that they did not share their concern to control the precise choice of words used: Jeremy Catto, 'Written English: The Making of the Language, 1370–1400', *Past & Present*, clxxix (2003), 51–2.

[38] For broader work regarding the widespread understanding of French during this period, see, for example, Richard Ingham, *The Transmission of Anglo-Norman: Language History and Language Acquisition* (Amsterdam, 2012), 162–3; Butterfield, *Familiar Enemy*, 316–28; Jocelyn Wogan-Browne, 'General Introduction: What's in a Name: The "French" of "England"', in *Language and Culture in Medieval Britain: The French of England, c. 1100– c. 1500*, ed. Jocelyn Wogan-Browne, Carolyn Collette, Linne Mooney, Ad Putter and David Trotter (York, 2009), 1–3, 9–13. For work concerning the continued vitality of Latin, see, for instance, Norman Blake, 'Introduction', in his *Cambridge History of the English Language, 1066–1476* (Cambridge, 1992), 5–9, 15–16, 18; Benskin, 'Chancery Standard', 4, 30, 34; and Robert Swanson, '*Elephants in Camera*: Latin and Latinity in 15th-and Early-16th-Century England', in *Latin in Medieval Britain*, ed. Richard Ashdowne and Carolinne White (Oxford, 2017), 106–30. See also Machan, *English in the Middle Ages*, 163–4.

[39] See, for instance, Dodd, 'Rise of English', 141.

[40] Richard Britnell, 'Uses of French Language in Medieval English Towns', in *The French of England*, 88; Michael Clanchy, *From Memory to Written Record: England 1066–1307* (3rd edn, Chichester, 2013), 221–3; Jocelyn Wogan-Browne, '"Invisible Archives?" Later Medieval French in England', *Speculum*, xc (2015), 654–5.

[41] *Calendar of Signet Letters*, ed. Kirby, no. 875; *PPC*, ii. 263, 266–7.

[42] Marilyn Corrie, 'Middle English – Dialects and Diversity', in *The Oxford History of English*, ed. Lynda Mugglestone (Oxford, 2006), 97–116; Robert Epstein, '"Fer in the north; I kan nat telle where": Dialect, Regionalism, and Philologism', *Studies in the Age of Chaucer*, xxx (2008), 95–124; Gabriele Stein, *Sir Thomas Elyot as Lexicographer* (Oxford, 2014), 100–19.

Ranulph Higden's *Polychronicon*. Writing in the 1380s, John Trevisa claimed that the 'men of myddel Engelond, as it were parteners of þe endes, understondeþ bettre þe side languages, norþerne and souþerne, þan noþerne and souþerne understoneþ eiþer oþer', and that 'al þe longage of þe Norþumbres, and specialliche at York, is so sharp, slitting, and frotynge and unschape, þat we souþerne men may þat longage unneþe understone'.[43] Although the language became somewhat more standardised in the last decades of the fourteenth century,[44] major differences still remained to the extent that William Caxton, writing in his 1480 edition of the *Polychronicon*, observed that 'a man of Kente, southern, western, and northern men speken Frensshe al lyke in sowne and speche; but they can not speke theyr Englyssh so'.[45]

Yet the more substantial issue was the imprecision of English. This was highlighted by contemporaries. Thus, Sir John Fortescue described how lawyers were used to pleading in French:

> until the custom was much restricted by force of a certain statute; even so, it has been impossible hitherto to abolish this custom in its entirety, partly because of certain terms which pleaders express more accurately in French than in English, partly because declarations upon original writs cannot be stated so closely in the form of these writs as they can in French, in which tongue the formulas of such declarations are learned.[46]

It is telling that the provisions of the 1362 Statute of Pleading were apparently still resented when Fortescue wrote his *In Praise of the Laws of England* between 1468 and 1471, over a century after the statute had been enrolled. This is most sensibly explained by the legal classes' opposition to the English tongue, on account of both its perceived imprecision and their attachment to their profession's customs, as well as a possible desire to ensure that their profession was not opened up to those who had failed to learn law French.[47] Their frustration might well have been shared by clerks more generally, who had also learnt relevant formulae in French; while the Grocers' Company of London began keeping their records in English in 1418, they reverted to mainly using French in 1432, presumably because their clerk was trained to write financial accounts in that language.[48] Rather than applauding the clarity of English, a number of fifteenth-century commentators therefore criticised the vernacular's inaccuracy and regional diversity.

---

[43] *Polychronicon*, ed. Babington and Lumby, ii. 163.
[44] Nicholas Watson, 'The Politics of Middle English Writing', in *The Idea of the Vernacular: An Anthology of Middle English Literary Theory 1280–1520*, ed. Jocelyn Wogan-Browne, Nicholas Watson, Andrew Taylor and Ruth Evans (Exeter, 1999), 333; Catto, 'Written English', 24–59.
[45] *Polychronicon*, ed. Babington and Lumby, ii. 161.
[46] John Fortescue, *On the Laws and Governance of England*, ed. Shelley Lockwood (Cambridge, 1997), 67.
[47] See, for example, Ormrod, 'Use of English', 773; Serge Lusignan, 'French Language in Contact with English: Social Context and Linguistic Change', in *The French of England*, 21; Sebastian Sobecki, *Unwritten Verities: The Making of England's Vernacular Legal Culture, 1463–1549* (Notre Dame, IN, 2015), 45–54; Gwilym Dodd, 'Languages and Law in Late Medieval England: English, French and Latin', in *The Cambridge Companion to Medieval English Law and Literature*, ed. Candace Barringon and Sebastian Sobecki (Cambridge, 2019), 24–5.
[48] Richardson, *Middle-Class Writing*, 110. See also José Miguel Alcolado Carnicero, 'Dating the Shift to English in the Financial Accounts of Some London Livery Companies: A Reappraisal', *Multilingua*, xxxiv (2014), 383–5.

Indeed, there seems to have been a certain reluctance among Henry V's own signet clerks to abandon French, perhaps arising from their long experience with the language. They continued using Anglo-Norman in their formulas of address on the reverse side of letters – preferring, for example, '*Au reverend pere en dieu, levesque de Duresme, nostre chancellor Dengleterre*' to 'to þe worshipful fader in God our[e] ryht trusty and wellbeloved þe bysshop of Duresme, our[e] Chancellor' – until May 1418, nine months after English had been adopted for the main text.[49] They also continued using French phrases and formulae, and simply translated them word-for-word into English. Thus, '*Dar par le Roy*' became 'By þe kyng'; '*Donne soubz nostre signet*' became 'Yeven under oure signet'; and '*volons et vous mandons*' became 'we wol and charge yow'.[50] Most strikingly, they occasionally lapsed into both French and Latin, either because they absent-mindedly reverted into the language to which they were accustomed (as when one clerk employed the French phrase '*en due forme*' in a letter of 12 August 1417), or because an English equivalent for a technical term had not yet been developed, as when a clerk specified that the warrant given to Richard Whittingdon and Robert Harroweden should be with '*clause preferramento decem milium librarium regi in parliamento suo nuper facto non obstante*' in a letter of 18 January 1418.[51] In these circumstances – when signet letters were manifestly based on Anglo-Norman models, when they retained French formulae, merely rendered into the vernacular, and when they periodically lapsed into foreign tongues, either because of habit or the inability of English to convey a particular instruction – it seems unlikely that Henry's signet clerks adopted English because of its greater clarity and lucidity.

It seems equally doubtful that Henry principally adopted the vernacular in his signet correspondence for its patriotic potential. That the English language could be used to inspire nationalistic sentiment, which could in turn be harnessed to drum up support for the war in France, is plain.[52] For instance, in the parliament of 1344, it was alleged that Philip VI intended to 'destroy the English language and occupy the land of England'; in the parliament of January 1377, it was said that the French conspired 'to destroy our lord the king and his realm of England, and to do away with the English language entirely'; and in the parliament of January 1380, it was claimed that England's enemies strove 'to destroy our land ... and oust the English tongue'.[53] This rhetoric continued to be deployed in the fifteenth century: in 1400, Henry Percy averred that the Scots plotted to 'make war against the language and people of England', and an indictment of 1407 referred to the desire of the Welsh 'to destroy the English tongue as far as they can and turn it into the Welsh tongue'.[54] However,

---

[49] *Calendar of Signet Letters*, ed. Kirby, 165; Vale, *Henry V*, 113.
[50] *Calendar of Signet Letters*, ed. Kirby, 17–18; Vale, *Henry V*, 113–14.
[51] *Calendar of Signet Letters*, ed. Kirby, no. 817; Vale, *Henry V*, 113.
[52] Allmand, *Henry V*, 419–20; Butterfield, *Familiar Enemy*, 388–9.
[53] *PROME*, iv. 362; v. 397; vi. 153. See also Allmand, *Henry V*, 420; Dodd, 'Rise of English', 133; Andrea Ruddick, *English Identity and Political Culture in the Fourteenth Century* (Cambridge, 2013), 162–3; and S.J. Drake, *Cornwall, Connectivity and Identity in the Fourteenth Century* (Woodbridge, 2019), 84.
[54] J.E. Messham, 'The County of Flint and the Rebellion of Owen Glyndwr in the Records of the Earldom of Chester', *Flintshire Historical Society Publications*, xxiii (1967–8), 11–12, 33; Allmand, *Henry V*, 420.

the ironic fact that these remarks were recorded in Latin or French shows that one by no means needed to use English itself to draw upon its potential emotive power.[55]

Still more problematic is the manner in which Henry's signet letters made their transition to English. Unlike the royal posturing about the English tongue in 1344, 1377 and 1380, Henry's decision was not announced in parliament, or even in a proclamation. Instead, his correspondence simply assumed the language, without comment, justification or explanation. If Henry had really embraced the vernacular to inspire nationalistic sentiment, it seems unlikely that he would have passed over such an opportunity to declare how he would defend his kingdom's tongue by assuming it himself. Furthermore, it is at least open to question whether Henry had an unambiguously nationalistic view of the English tongue. While his ambassador, Master Thomas Polton, explained to the Council of Constance in 1417 that language was 'the chief and surest proof of being a nation', he considered the multiplicity of British languages a great strength, remarking that:

> where the French nation, for the most part, has one vernacular which is wholly or in part understandable in every part of the nation, within the famous English or British nation, however, there are five languages, you might say, one of which does not understand the other. These are English, which the English and Scots have in common, Welsh, Irish, Gascon and Cornish.[56]

Polton's evidence must be viewed with caution, since he was performing a challenging rhetorical task in arguing that England was not only a single nation, but also sufficiently large to represent a host of other nations.[57] Nevertheless, his remarks still raise doubts about the straightforwardness of the connection between the English language and the English nation. This issue has also been discussed by Andrea Ruddick, who doubted the existence of 'a direct and emotionally charged connection between English identity and the English language' in the fourteenth century,[58] and Ardis Butterfield, who demonstrated the complexity of the English tongue's relationship with nationalism during the fifteenth century itself.[59] Considering that French was capable of expressing nationalistic sentiments, that Henry declined the opportunity to boast about his adoption of the vernacular, and the difficulties of assuming that the English language had intrinsically patriotic overtones, one hesitates to ascribe this great importance in the crown's assumption of English.

In a subtler development of this idea, Malcolm Vale has suggested that Henry's assumption 'of the English language to express his will and intentions when dealing

---

[55] Dodd, 'Rise of English', 133; Drake, *Cornwall, Connectivity and Identity*, 84.
[56] C.M.D. Crowder, *Unity, Heresy and Reform, 1378–1460: The Conciliar Response to the Great Schism* (1977), 121.
[57] This perhaps led to him making claims which were sometimes astonishing, such as France only having one vernacular, which neglects the predominance of Occitan south of the Loire. See also Aubrey Gwynn, 'Ireland and the English Nation at the Council of Constance', *Proceedings of the Royal Irish Academy*, xlv (1939–40), 217–21; Christopher Linsley, 'Nation, England and the French in Thomas Walsingham's *Chronica Maiora*, 1376–1420' (PhD thesis, University of York, 2015), 51–3; Andrea Ruddick, 'The English "Nation" and the Plantagenet "Empire" at the Council of Constance', in *The Plantagenet Empire*, ed. Peter Crooks, David Green and W. Mark Ormrod (Donington, 2016), 109–27.
[58] Ruddick, *English Identity*, 162–3.
[59] Butterfield, *Familiar Enemy*, 390–1.

with English matters' ensured that both his French and English subjects 'retained their separate identities'.[60] Vale identified considerable concern among Englishmen that the king's successes in France might lead to their subjugation to French practices, and the dilution of English political culture and customs. These fears lay behind the Commons' petition in 1420 for Henry to confirm a statute of March 1340, which promised that neither 'the kingdom of England, nor the people of the same ... shall at any time in the future be placed in subjugation or obedience to him [Henry V], his heirs and successors, as heir, regent and king of France'. Henry sought to assuage this concern; he granted the petition, and the treaty of Troyes provided that the crown 'would keep the laws, customs, usages and rights' of the English kingdom, and that neither France nor England would be subjected to the others' 'rights, laws, customs, and usages'.[61]

Nevertheless, although Vale makes a compelling case that Englishmen were anxious about their potential subordination to the French kingdom, his claim – albeit with a telling acknowledgement that 'this argument should not be overstated' – that this anxiety stirred Henry's adoption of the vernacular is altogether less convincing.[62] First, it is notable that neither the Commons' petition nor the treaty of Troyes make explicit mention of the English language. Second, it appears that English fears about the possible loss of their customs and rights only became apparent in 1420, following Henry's martial successes and the opening of viable negotiations with the French.[63] Had a wish to mitigate these worries lain behind Henry's assumption of English in his signet letters in 1417, he would have had to have accomplished the masterful political feat of anticipating and acting to avert his subjects' fears three years before they had even been articulated.

Third, and most importantly, the uniqueness of Henry's signet letters means that it is difficult to see their employment of the vernacular as part of some grand plan to use English to express the royal will when dealing with English matters. These were the only major set of government documents to be penned in the vernacular in Henry's reign. The records of the common law courts continued to be largely written in French throughout the later medieval period, and parliamentary statutes persisted in that language until 1489. Likewise, the records of the exchequer remained predominantly in Latin throughout the fifteenth century, as did the rolls of the chancery until 1731.[64] Most strikingly, the documents most often used for communicating with Henry's English subjects directly – namely the 'original writs' issued by the crown to instigate court proceedings, the 'judicial writs' issued in the course of legal actions, and the broader array of royal mandates, instructions and announcements issued under the great seal – continued to be written in Latin throughout Henry V's reign. In contrast, English was assumed in Henry's signet letters alone: letters used primarily for facilitating internal communication within the royal administration.[65] If Henry wished to adopt English to appease his subjects' fears that their customs might be subordinated to those of the French kingdom – or indeed to exploit his subjects' nationalistic tendencies, to harness the language's clarity, or to tap into the

---

[60] Vale, *Henry V*, 125.
[61] *Ibid.*, 123; *English Historical Documents IV, 1327–1485*, ed. A.R. Myers (1969), 220–2.
[62] Vale, *Henry V*, 125.
[63] *Ibid.*, 122–3.
[64] Dodd, 'Spread of English', 234; Richardson, *Middle-Class Writing*, 109.
[65] Dodd, 'Spread of English', 230, 234.

broader understanding of the vernacular – it is hard to see not only why this linguistic shift did not occur throughout all branches of central government, but also why it was limited to the signet office, a royal department which communicated far less with the commonalty than many others.

The question of why Henry's signet letters suddenly changed from being entirely in French to almost entirely in English thus remains. On 26 July 1417, in Portsmouth, the signet office was united with every other part of the royal bureaucracy in its preference for French or Latin; less than two weeks later, in Touques, the signet office became the only part of central administration systematically to prefer the vernacular. What changed? What happened in that fortnight to the signet office, but did not happen to every other branch of government? Once asked in those terms, the answer is obvious. While all the other branches of government remained in England, the signet office travelled with the person of the king to France.

This had two important ramifications. First, it meant that Henry was absent from the seat of the royal bureaucracy.[66] This had mattered less when Henry had crossed to France in 1415, when his letters had remained in French, because he was on campaign for just three months, rather than three years. Although the council in Westminster had been able to supervise royal administration without extensive personal involvement from the king between mid-August and mid-November 1415, this was impossible for the much longer period between July 1417 and February 1421.[67] Consequently, Henry needed to retain greater contact with his domestic administration.[68] Since he could not meet and discuss matters with his ministers, his signet correspondence constituted his closest direct link with them.[69] It is therefore likely that he sought to involve himself more closely with the authorship of his signet letters than beforehand.[70] This is suggested by how evidence of Henry's personal involvement with royal documentation, including his signet correspondence, both through the use of his autograph sign manual and through writing letters in his own hand, blossoms after 1417.[71]

---

[66] *Calendar of Signet Letters*, ed. Kirby, 1–5; A.L. Brown, *The Governance of Late Medieval England, 1272–1461* (1989), 43–60.

[67] Allmand, *Henry V*, 360–3; Christine Carpenter, 'War, Government and Governance in England in the Later Middle Ages', in *The Fifteenth Century VII: Conflicts, Consequences and the Crown in the Later Middle Ages*, ed. Linda Clark (Woodbridge, 2007), 7–8; Vale, *Henry V*, 43–4.

[68] This is suggested by the fact that 102 signet letters survive from the period of his 1417–20 campaign, compared to just two from the period of his Agincourt campaign: *Calendar of Signet Letters*, ed. Kirby, 161–99. The maintenance of contact with his council and ministers was especially important for Henry V, as a king who was concerned with involving himself in the everyday business of kingship: McFarlane, *Lancastrian Kings*, 117; G.L. Harriss, 'Conclusion', in *Henry V: The Practice of Kingship*, ed. G.L. Harriss (Oxford, 1985), 206–10; Vale, *Henry V*, 15–61. For instance, even while abroad, Henry reserved to himself matters of prerogative and grace, as well as higher appointments: E.F. Jacob, *The Fifteenth Century, 1399–1485* (Oxford, 1961), 430–1; Allmand, *Henry V*, 358–9; Harriss, *Shaping the Nation*, 593. Of course, while Henry was, in Christine Carpenter's words, 'a micro-manager', he nevertheless delegated some powers (such as calling parliament and authorising ecclesiastical elections) to a lieutenant to act in his stead (principally John, duke of Bedford), and allowed the council in Westminster to direct much of the routine business of government: Jeremy Catto, 'The King's Servants', in *Henry V: The Practice of Kingship*, 81; Allmand, *Henry V*, 343–4, 358, 363; Carpenter, 'War, Government and Governance', 8.

[69] Jocelyn Otway-Ruthven, 'The King's Secretary in the Fifteenth Century', *TRHS*, xix (1936), 88; Allmand, *Henry V*, 362–3; Vale, *Henry V*, 44–57.

[70] Allmand, *Henry* V, 362; Vale, *Henry V*, 80.

[71] Vale, *Henry V*, 74–87; *Calendar of Signet Letters*, ed. Kirby, nos 4, 180.

Second, Henry's journey to France meant that he was now writing letters from inside hostile territory, from inside a land that he was trying to conquer, and from inside a warzone. Although Henry's two surviving signet letters from the period of his 1415 campaign may have been of limited interest to the French – since they only describe how Henry was besieging Harfleur and how he had captured it respectively, rather than mentioning any information of strategic importance – this can hardly be said of his later correspondence.[72] Henry's letters from his 1417–21 campaign reported matters which could prove disadvantageous if they fell into enemy hands. This included the locations to which he wanted supplies directed, namely 'as fer as they may vp þe Riuer of Seyne to Roan-ward'; details regarding military logistics, such as a direction to an anonymous recipient 'þat in al þe hast ye may sende unto our cofrer to Rouen all þe gonne stones þat been at oure tounes of Caen and Harefleur wiþ al þe salt pietre, cole, and brymstoon þat is at Harefleu'; and instructions regarding the keeping of French prisoners, with him exhorting the chancellor to 'see and Ordeyne that good Heed be taken unto the seure Keping of our Frensh Prisonners withynne our Reaulme of England; And in especiall of the Duc of Orleins ... for their Eschaping might never have been so harmful ner prejudicial unto Us, as hit might be Now'.[73] The risks of relaying such sensitive matters by letter were clear; Henry suspected that the bearer of his missive to London of 27 August 1419 had been 'by our enemys taken in to Crotey', which caused him to 'renouelle hem here at Trye the Castell' almost a month later.[74] Ensuring the security of his letters would therefore have been a priority for Henry in 1417, and a much higher priority than it had been two years previously.

Henry's desire to compensate for his distance from his ministers by taking a more direct role in his signet correspondence might well have lain behind its adoption of English. While some evidence survives for Henry's ability to converse in French, evidence of his ability to write in that language is scarce.[75] He customarily used the vernacular when writing in his own hand, even when French or Latin might have been the more natural choice. For instance, although the letters written on Henry's behalf to his father were typically in French, his holograph missives to Henry IV were all in English.[76] Likewise, the king's autograph responses to petitions were

---

[72] *Calendar of Signet Letters*, ed. Kirby, nos 964, 965.
[73] *London English*, ed. Chambers and Daunt, 73–4, 83–4; R.A. Newhall, *The English Conquest of Normandy, 1416–24* (1924), 264; *Foedera*, ix. 801.
[74] *London English*, ed. Chambers and Daunt, 83.
[75] In his discussion of the king and his captains' linguistic abilities, Malcolm Vale gives two examples of Henry speaking French: his conversation with Raoul le Gay (when he asked le Gay who had captured him, where he was from, if he was the prisoner of those who escorted him, and whether he had been armed when he was taken), and the fact that he thanked Jean Fusoris with the words with '*Grans mercis* [many thanks]': Vale, *Henry V*, 116–19 and L. Mirot, 'Le Procès de Maitre Jean Fusoris. Episode des négociations anglo-francaises Durant le Guerre de Cent Ans', *Mémoires de la Société de l'Histoire de Paris et de l'Ile de France,* xxvii (1900), 212–13, 244, 256–8. That some of the best evidence of Henry speaking French comes from conversations he had with Frenchmen does little to assuage suspicions that he might have been more comfortable with the vernacular. Indeed, there is some evidence that Henry's ability to understand French left something to be desired; Cardinal Orsini's letter to the French ambassadors at Pont de l'Arche in December 1418 claimed that Henry 'says that he does not understand French perfectly' (although how literally this remark should be interpreted is open to question): *Foedera*, ix. 658. See also Pierre Chaplais, *English Diplomatic Practice in the Middle Ages* (2003), 129.
[76] See, for example, W.J. Hardy, *The Handwriting of the Kings and Queens of England* (1893), 19–24;

consistently in the vernacular, even when the petitions themselves were in French. Thus, while John Kingsley's petition for the restoration of the Cheshire revenues granted to him by Thomas, duke of Clarence, before his death was in Anglo-Norman, Henry used English when endorsing it in his own hand: 'R.H. In the fo[r]me and man[er]e that our brother's l[ett]res p[ur]poten whil us lust'.[77] Indeed, Henry even used the vernacular in the subscriptions to his wills. For example, the will he made on 24 July 1415 was entirely in Latin, aside from its concluding lines, which read:

> *Haec scripta sunt propria manu Regis*, viz [These [words] are written in the king's own hand, that is to say]: This is my last will subscribed with my own Hand, R.H. Jesu Mercy and Gremercy, Ladie Marie help.[78]

Yet perhaps the most striking example of Henry writing in English, when a foreign tongue might well have been expected, was his correspondence with Pope Martin V of June 1422, which concerned an alleged slight suffered by Thomas Polton, then bishop of Chichester, his representative at the papal court. The pope's reply to Henry referred to 'certain letters, which are said to be in your own hand, and in the English tongue, [which were] explained to us through an interpreter'.[79] That Henry communicated directly with the pontiff in the vernacular – when the pope was customarily addressed in Latin, and evidently had little knowledge of the language (hence his need for an interpreter) – was most unusual.[80] This is perhaps best explained by how, in Pierre Chaplais' words, 'the king ... chose the language which he knew best and perhaps the only one which he could write himself unaided'.[81] Nevertheless, even if Henry *could* write unaided in French, his consistent use of English when writing in his own hand reveals a clear preference for composing in the vernacular. This, alongside his apparent wish to involve himself more in the composition of his signet letters, plausibly explains their adoption of the English tongue.

Henry's decision to write in English, a language much less familiar to the French than their native tongue, may also be read in the light of his concern to ensure the secrecy of his letters. There is a variety of anecdotal evidence to suggest that there was a limited understanding of English on the continent: Geoffrey le Baker wrote of a French knight who was killed while sacking Southampton in 1338 because he could not ask for quarter in English; Jean Froissart described how English soldiers mocked a group of Galicians in 1386 for not being able to 'speak good French or English'; and Henry VI wrote to the duke of Silesia in 1452 to explain that he had rejected the offer of assistance from one Silesian noble since he could not speak any English whatsoever.[82] Even in the parts of France most closely associated with England, knowledge of English was slight; the king's secretary Thomas Bekynton recorded that the archbishop of Bordeaux had to translate a vernacular letter from

---

Frederick Solly-Flood, 'Prince Henry of Monmouth – His Letters and Dispatches During the War in Wales', *TRHS*, iv (1889), 125–38.

[77] Hardy, *Handwriting*, 28. See also Vale, *Henry V*, 79.
[78] *Foedera*, ix. 293. See also Vale, *Henry V*, 82–6.
[79] J. Haller, 'England und Rom unter Martin V', *Quellen und Forschungen aus italienischen Archiven und Bibliotheken*, viii (1905), 294–6; Vale, *Henry V*, 70.
[80] Vale, *Henry V*, 69–71.
[81] Chaplais, *English Diplomatic Practice*, 133.
[82] *Ibid.*, 131; *Chronicon Galfridi Le Baker de Swynbroke*, ed. E.M. Thompson (Oxford, 1889), 63; Butterfield, *Familiar Enemy*, 163.

Henry VI into Gascon for the benefit of the local community.[83] Indeed, as Anglo French diplomacy and trade was almost exclusively conducted in French, it is hard to see why many Frenchmen would have felt any need to learn the English tongue at all.[84] Adopting it therefore added an additional layer of security to Henry's letters. While of course the French could have found someone to translate any English letters that they intercepted, not least English hostages and prisoners, these were few and far between compared to Frenchmen who could read Anglo-Norman and Latin, which would have provided Henry and his forces with valuable time and breathing space before his plans were revealed.[85]

Both Henry's concern with the secrecy of his correspondence and the limited knowledge of the vernacular on the continent are evident in the capture and treatment of Raoul le Gay, a twenty-eight-year-old French priest, during the Agincourt campaign of 1415.[86] Le Gay was captured on 16 August by seven English scouts, who evidently thought that they had caught a spy. Nevertheless, they were unable to converse with him, since they knew no French and he no English. Two days later, a young Englishman was able to talk to le Gay in Latin. However, when the young man turned to speak to le Gay's guards in the vernacular, the only word that the le Gay could understand was 'drinch'. Thereafter, le Gay was taken to the earl of Dorset, who questioned him in French.[87] On 27 August, le Gay was then passed on to Richard Courtenay, bishop of Norwich, who two days later gave him a letter in Latin to take to Jean Fusoris, an astrologer in Paris. The letter told Fusoris that the English had landed with 50,000 men and sufficient victuals to sustain a six-month siege of Harfleur, adding that Fusoris was not to mention his own or Courtenay's name in his reply, as the matter was a secret from everyone except the king, 'who is most discreet, as you know'.[88] However, le Gay was an ineffective agent, and was caught by the French on the following day in Montivilliers, where they realised that he was carrying secret correspondence for Fusoris. Accordingly, Fusoris was arrested on 6 September, thrown into the gaol at Little Chatelet, and the next day

---

[83] *Official Correspondence of Thomas Bekynton, Secretary to King Henry VI and Bishop of Bath and Wells*, ed. George Williams (2 vols, 1872), ii. 185.

[84] Butterfield, *Familiar Enemy*, 165–71.

[85] The importance of deploying a relatively unknown language as a form of quasi-encryption was furthered because the use of ciphers did not take root in England until the final years of the fifteenth century: Ian Arthurson, 'Espionage and Intelligence from the Wars of the Roses to the Reformation', *Nottingham Medieval Studies*, xxxv (1991), 150.

[86] For the entirety of the story in this paragraph, see Mirot, 'Le Procès de Maitre Jean Fusoris', 255–9 and J.H. Wylie and W.T. Waugh, *The Reign of Henry the Fifth* (3 vols, Cambridge, 1914–29), ii. 25–9. For further discussion of the episode, see also Juliet Barker, *Agincourt: The King, the Campaign, the Battle* (2005), 171–3; Anne Curry, *Agincourt: A New History* (Stroud, 2006), 51–2, 91; Ian Mortimer, *1415: Henry V's Year of Glory* (2009), 339–40, 346–7, 349–50; and Vale, *Henry V*, 117–19. For broader literature about medieval secrecy and espionage, and the concern of late medieval English monarchs (including Henry V) to ensure the security of their communications, see, for instance, Newhall, *Conquest of Normandy*, 267–8; J.R. Alban and C.T. Allmand, 'Spies and Spying in the Fourteenth Century', in *War, Literature, and Politics in the Late Middle Ages*, ed. C.T. Allmand (Liverpool, 1976), 73–101; Christopher Allmand, 'Intelligence in the Hundred Years War', in *Go Spy the Land: Military Intelligence and History*, ed. B.J.C. McKercher and Keith Neilson (1992), 31–47; and Margaret Harvey, *England, Rome and the Papacy, 1417–1464* (Manchester, 1993), 86–7.

[87] Mirot, 'Le Procès de Maitre Jean Fusoris', 257–8.

[88] *Ibid.*, 258. Courtenay also tasked le Gay with relaying a verbal message to Fusoris, asking him to obtain certain 'pumpkins, melons, almonds, and other fruits' from the prior of Celestines in Paris, and to send them back to Courtenay.

The Adoption of the English Language by Henry V

charged with high treason. On 18 September, an official was dispatched to bring le Gay himself to Paris, where he was imprisoned for three months, and examined on 14 and 21 December.[89] The whole episode reveals Henry's belief in the importance of secrecy and discretion; the inability of Latin to provide that secrecy, since Courtenay's letter to Fusoris was easily read when intercepted; and the seriousness of indiscretion's consequences, with English agents being imprisoned.

Indeed, although such speculation must remain tentative, it is possible that the le Gay affair itself might have encouraged Henry to adopt English in his signet letters. While le Gay was in the earl of Dorset's custody on 25 August, he was taken before the king for questioning. It appears that Henry suspected that le Gay was a French spy, since he asked the priest whether he had been taken in arms, and notwithstanding his answer that he had not been – rendering his capture in contravention of the king's own military ordinances – still refused to release him.[90] It is possible that Henry was struck by how someone like le Gay – who was an educated priest, and appeared to be a French agent – knew no English. He might also have been struck by how one of his most secret plans – which had apparently been kept between himself and Courtenay – fell apart the very day after le Gay was given the Latin letter, with it being intercepted, read and acted upon by the local authorities in Montivilliers. It is therefore not implausible that this episode remained in Henry's mind, and contributed to his resolve when returning to France that his letters should be penned in a language which – unlike Latin and French – was incomprehensible to a large proportion of his foes.

That the relative indecipherability of the vernacular and Henry's personal preference for the language lay behind the adoption of English in his signet correspondence is further suggested by the king's letter to Sir John Tiptoft of 25 January 1417. This is one of the handful of documents under the signet to have been written in the vernacular prior to the summer of that year. The missive informed Tiptoft, Henry's envoy at the Council of Constance, of secret negotiations which Henry had conducted with the duke of Bourbon, his Agincourt prisoner, regarding his potential release and its terms. These discussions had consequences for his war in France, a war in which he also perceived a role for Sigismund, the Holy Roman Emperor.[91] The letter was therefore highly secret, as is made explicit in the text itself, which refers to how Tiptoft must 'kepe þis matere ... secre, save from my broþer þemperour owne personne', because this is 'oon of þe secreest thing[es] þat touchis me'.[92] Since the letter would have travelled across continental Europe, and risked falling into other hands, its use of a language that was unknown to many can only have bolstered its security. Yet the missive was also written in Henry's own hand, and was therefore penned in the language with which Henry felt most comfortable. This rendered it unlike the other surviving signet letter sent on the same day – an order to the chancellor to issue a 'warrant for license for Raoul de Gancourt to go to France' – which was written by a signet clerk in Anglo-Norman.[93] Indeed, the confidential nature of the letter and the fact that it was written by Henry himself went hand-in-hand, with it concluding:

---

[89] Wylie and Waugh, *Reign of Henry the Fifth*, ii. 28–9.
[90] Mirot, 'Le Procès de Maitre Jean Fusoris', 212–13; Barker, *Agincourt*, 172.
[91] *English Medieval Diplomatic Practice I*, ed. Chaplais, 98–100; Vale, *Henry V*, 76–7.
[92] *English Medieval Diplomatic Practice I*, ed. Chaplais, 98.
[93] *Calendar of Signet Letters*, ed. Kirby, no. 800.

And for þe secrenesse of þis matere I have written þis instruccion [wyth myn owne] hande and seled hit with my signet of þegle þe xxv day of ja[nuary, that is the] day of Conversion of seint Poole.[94]

While Henry's signet clerks might thus have adopted English because of the king's preference for the vernacular and its security advantages, it may be that they retained the language for the duration of his reign – even after his return to England in February 1421 – because they had become accustomed to using it.

A very different reason for the assumption of English in royal records can thus be posited. The adoption of the vernacular in Henry's signet correspondence cannot be adequately explained by either of the grand narratives used to explain the spread of English in the fifteenth century: that of a sweeping Lancastrian scheme to embrace the vernacular, because of its nationalistic resonances, or that of a gradual shift throughout the period, in consequence of the wider understanding of the language and its clarity. That the use of English in these letters was not part of some triumphant royal design is clear in how the only department of government affected in Henry V's reign was the signet, and how even the signet clerks reverted to using French on his death.[95] Yet it seems equally clear that the letters' adoption of the vernacular was not the product of some slow, structural shift; there was no gradual change, in which English emerged, became the language of a significant minority of letters, before becoming the language of the majority of letters, before finally becoming the language of all letters. Rather, in the space of two weeks, Henry's signet clerks switched from writing almost all correspondence in French to writing almost all correspondence in English. This was clearly the result of a royal decision. Nevertheless, this is not to deny that the broader factors identified by historians and literary scholars – such as the ability of English to reach a broader audience – helped the vernacular to develop in the longer term, and indeed explain why the language took root slowly and incrementally in every other branch of the royal bureaucracy.[96] But the use of English in the signet letters of Henry V stemmed from a short-term, short-lived decision by the crown, and appears not to have principally been the outcome of either structural factors or a grandiose royal masterplan.

In these circumstances, it appears that the adoption of the vernacular in these letters might not have represented a momentous 'turning point' in the development of English. Instead, it appears that this was primarily a particular response to a particular set of issues at a particular time: the king's need to involve himself more directly in his correspondence while on a lengthy campaign, and his wish to add a further layer of security to his letters. Such a change could be – and indeed was – easily reversed. Ultimately, this reminds scholars that the 'triumph of English' in the fifteenth century was not some relentless march of progress for the language, but rather a fragmented, complex and disjointed series of gains and losses, which eventually and over time led to the vernacular becoming increasingly visible in society.[97]

---

[94] *English Medieval Diplomatic Practice I*, ed. Chaplais, 100–1.
[95] Dodd, 'Rise of English', 129.
[96] Machan, *English in the Middle Ages*, 161–5; Watts, 'He Who Must Bear All', 32–3. Of course, the possibility that such factors also weighed on Henry V's own mind cannot be excluded.
[97] Dodd, 'Rise of English', 142–6; Richardson, *Middle-Class Writing*, 108–10.

THE ORIGINS AND DEVELOPMENT OF THE BODY CORPORATE IN LATE MEDIEVAL ENGLAND[1]

Edward Powell

The theme of this essay is the emergence during the late Middle Ages of the body corporate as a legal entity, having the rights and obligations of a natural person. Such an entity is also known in the legal literature as a *persona ficta* or a fictitious person. By the late fifteenth century the outlines of the body corporate were well established in English law, and were frequently discussed in the Year Books, but its early development remains obscure. The argument I propose is that the birth of the body corporate as a legal concept in England can in fact be pinpointed specifically to a London case report in the Year Book for 1375, and that it took a century of legal debate and decision-making to work through the implications of that case.

What, then, are the common characteristics of a legal person (natural or fictitious)? Each natural person has a unique identity, indicated by name, date of birth and other defining factors.[2] Flowing from the possession of legal capacity are the power to own land and property and to sue and be sued in a court of law. Bodies corporate have additional attributes necessitated by their artificial status; having no natural existence, they must be created by a process of incorporation. It was already clear by the fifteenth century that incorporation could only be put into effect by the

---

[1] It is a real pleasure to be able to offer a small tribute to Rowena. We first met in the late 1970s when we were both research students in Oxford studying under Gerald Harriss. Gerald was a lovely man and a very conscientious supervisor, but he was also painfully shy, so in my final year I was astonished to be invited to a party he was giving for his students. Later I discovered that Rowena had a hand in this – she has a great gift for friendship and bringing people together. Our paths then diverged: I went to Cambridge and she built her career in Oxford. Years later, after I had left academic life, I was thrilled when my daughter Helena told me that Rowena was teaching her for the 'Wars of the Roses' special subject. We re-established contact, and I was touched that she still regarded me as part of the academic community and asked me to return to teaching at the Cambridge Summer School. There, she ruled with a rod of iron – woe betide any student who was a minute late for classes! Her students were devoted to her, returning year after year for another fortnight of Medieval Studies. After the final course she invited me to a feast at Brasenose on 14 March 2020, an event which was later dubbed 'The Last Supper', for obvious reasons. I was seriously outranked by Rowena's other guest, no less than Jonathan Sumption, former justice of the Supreme Court, then completing his monumental history of the Hundred Years' War. What follows is offered in thanks to a generous colleague, a fine scholar and an excellent teacher.

[2] In the fifteenth century these would include the addition – the place and county of residence and status or profession of the individual: Statute of Additions 1413: 1 Henry V c.5: *Statutes*, ii. 171.

monarch (or, until the Reformation, the pope). They enjoyed perpetual succession, that is they did not die when the original members of the body died. In order to provide a means of validating and authenticating its actions, a body corporate was required to have a unique common seal.[3] Finally, a company had the power to make statutes in order to regulate the conduct of its business. By the late fifteenth century these attributes are clearly set out in the incorporation document: a good example is the foundation charter given by Edward IV in 1475 for St Catharine's College, Cambridge.[4] It is important to note that in its mature form the body corporate has a legal personality separate from its members. In this respect it contrasts with a trust, an enfeoffment-to-use, or a partnership, none of which has a separate legal personality from its trustees or members.

Perpetual corporations were of course a familiar feature of medieval life long before the fifteenth century, the most obvious examples being religious houses holding land in perpetual alms. What we are considering here, however, is an entirely new phase in the development of the law of corporations, centring in particular on the manner in which they were created and the legal consequences which flowed from their creation. It was this development which led ultimately to the evolution of the modern limited company.

We may start with the comparative certainty of the late fifteenth century. In the words of F.W. Maitland, 'if for a moment we take our stand in Edward IV's reign, we can say that the idea of a corporation is already in the minds of our lawyers'.[5] The contemporary terms most frequently used were 'commonality', 'corporation', 'body corporate' or 'body politic'.[6] The corporate person was already a mature legal concept: its primary characteristics were settled and defined. It possessed a unique name, it could own property, it was capable of suing and being sued in the king's courts, and it could enjoy existence in perpetuity. There is much discussion of corporations in the Year Books, especially after 1470, but these concerned second order issues, mainly in relation to the wider characteristics of a corporation: the questions which arose included whether a body corporate could commit trespass, whether it could be imprisoned, and whether individual members could be held liable for its debts. Sir John Fortescue also discussed the concept extensively in his various treatises, making no distinction between the body corporate in private law and the wider public concept of the body politic.[7]

We can push back further into the fifteenth century without too much difficulty. In 1440 we find the charter of incorporation of Kingston-upon-Hull, conventionally taken as the first example of municipal incorporation in England. That charter includes many of the standard attributes of a corporation. The clause of incorporation, which has a strong emphasis on perpetuity, runs as follows: 'The town of the mayor and burgesses shall be corporate, and the mayor and burgesses shall be a perpetual corporate commonality of the town so incorporated under the name of

---

[3] The requirement for a company to have its own seal was abolished by the Companies Act 1989.
[4] Edward Powell, 'Body Politic and Body Corporate in the Fifteenth Century: the Case of the Duchy of Lancaster', in *Political Society in Later Medieval England: A Festschrift for Christine Carpenter*, ed. Benjamin Thompson and John Watts (Woodbridge, 2015), 181–3.
[5] F.M. Pollock and F.W. Maitland, *The History of English Law before the Time of Edward I* (2 vols, Cambridge, 1898), i. 489.
[6] At this early date the terms 'body corporate' and 'body politic' were interchangeable.
[7] Powell, 'Duchy of Lancaster', 175–6.

the mayor and burgesses of that town and shall have a perpetual succession.'[8] Going further back beyond 1440 matters begin to get hazier. In Maitland's words, 'we go back a little way in the Year Books and the idea that we have been watching begins to disappear. The figure of the ideal person vanishes or rather it seems at times to become a mere mass of natural persons.'[9]

Here, I must respectfully disagree with Maitland. It is true that the evidence is sketchier in the first half of the fifteenth century, but in fact there are plenty of signs of development, and quite rapid development at that. The earliest evidence dates from the late fourteenth century, and relates to the foundation of perpetual chantries for the celebration of masses for the dead. Through the work of Katherine Wood-Legh in her book *Perpetual Chantries in Britain* it becomes clear that there was a sudden burst of development in corporation law from the late 1370s into the early fifteenth century.[10] This is evident through the evolution in the form of mortmain licences, which were required for the foundation of chantries, and suggests that something occurred to prompt these developments. Lawyers are cautious professionals who rely on tried and trusted precedents; they do not adopt change unless it is forced upon them, either by legislation or through the determination of a 'leading case' – an authoritative legal decision. It is reasonable to assume therefore that the rapid evolution in the forms of corporate chantries identified by Dr Wood-Legh must have resulted from a change in the law. A search of the Year Books of Richard II's reign yields no results, but near the end of Edward III's there were two related cases arising from inquiries in the court of chancery about the purported creation of a perpetual chantry in the form of a body corporate. These are the Whittawers cases of 1374 and 1375, which turned on the question of whether the Whittawers, a London guild specialising in the production of high-quality leather goods such as purses, straps and harnesses, had the power to set themselves up as a body corporate. The first, arising from the will of Nicholas Rumbold, whittawer, of London, survives among the chancery common law pleadings for 1374. The second, arising from the will of Ralph Jordan, also a London whittawer, survives as a law report from 1375 in the *Liber Assisarum*, the collection of reports on pleas of the crown dating from Edward III's reign. The two cases are so similar in their facts that one might suspect they were variant accounts of the same matter, yet the parties involved in the two cases are clearly distinct, so that this seems unlikely.

The case of Nicholas Rumbold is comparatively well documented.[11] Nicholas died in January 1364 and his will was proved in the London court of husting the following month. He devised all his property to his wife Agatha, provided that she should find a chantry chaplain to celebrate masses for his soul and the souls of all the faithful in the church of All Hallows London Wall. Rumbold's will further stipulated that after Agatha's death the property was to pass to two 'good men' (*probi homines*) of the Whittawers' fraternity to maintain the chantry in perpetuity. When Agatha died in May 1374, William Dawe and Roger Rudd, as the *probi homines*, entered the property and continued to administer it according to the provisions of Nicholas's

---

[8] Martin Weinbaum, *The Incorporation of Boroughs* (Manchester, 1937), 63–8, 93–6; *English Historical Documents, IV, 1327–1485*, ed. A.R. Myers (1969), 570–3.
[9] Pollock and Maitland, *History of English Law*, i. 492.
[10] K.L. Wood-Legh, *Perpetual Chantries in Britain* (Cambridge, 1965), 315–30.
[11] For the proceedings in chancery, see TNA, C44/7/10 (Mich. 1374); see also C135/238/15 – inquisition *post mortem*, 1374.

will. The case was summoned into chancery as the result of the mortmain inquiry initiated by the crown earlier, in 1364, when the mayor and chamberlain of London had been ordered to search their records and to make returns of all land and property amortised in the city without licence, by devise or otherwise, since the date of the Statute of Mortmain (1279). The returns were duly made in January 1365, and one of the last items included, out of a total of over 400, was the will of Nicholas Rumbold.[12] Over the next quarter of a century the crown slowly but steadily worked its way through the cases on the returns, finally attending to Rumbold's case in 1374. Following an inquisition *post mortem* before the mayor of London, the case was summoned into chancery in the Michaelmas term. Dawe and Rudd appeared on behalf of the Whittawers claiming that Rumbold's will was valid under the ancient custom and usage of the city as confirmed by royal charters. They alleged that the same practice had been followed by other city guilds such as the Goldsmiths, Saddlers and Fishmongers. Michael Skilling, who was the king's attorney in the court of common pleas, acted for the crown. He rejected the basis of the Whittawers' claim, arguing that the men of the Whittawers' craft were not a commonality (*communitas*); they were merely a number of persons belonging to the commonality of London who lived separately and not as a community. In consequence they did not have the power to make a fraternity, as one body capable of holding land and pleading in the courts, without a royal charter confirming the same. Rumbold's bequest to the Whittawers was therefore invalid because no legal person existed which was capable of taking the gift. The chancellor found in favour of the crown and the property escheated to the king.[13]

Pausing there for a moment, we may note two points arising from Rumbold's case. The first is that the legal device employed to set up a chantry seems to have been a fairly standard procedure at that time – the Whittawers cited other London guilds which had also used it. Second, the crown lawyer Michael Skilling accepted the idea that a community of individuals could be a commonality or legal person; the members of the Whittawers' guild were, he argued, members of the commonality of London, which had long been recognised as a body corporate, but they could not create a separate commonality of their own without a royal charter. The chancellor confirmed this was the correct legal position.

The second Whittawers' case followed a year later. The only record we have of it is the report in the *Liber Assisarum*, of which there are two versions.[14] The facts were as follows. Sometime in the reign of Edward III or perhaps earlier, Ralph Jordan, being seised of certain tenements in the city of London, devised his property to Agnes Lawe for life, on condition that she would find a chaplain to sing masses for the souls of Ralph and his ancestors in the church of All Hallows London Wall. After Agnes's death the property was to pass to two of the 'best men' (*meliours homes*) of the guild of the fraternity of Whittawers in London for ever (*a toujours*), on condition that they found a chantry chaplain. In effect, Ralph Jordan, like Nicholas Rumbold was attempting to set up a perpetual chantry in association with the fraternity of Whittawers. As with Rumbold's case the matter was called into the common law side

---

[12] TNA, JUST 1/556, final membrane.
[13] For the later history of the estate, see W.H. Black, *The History and Antiquities of the Worshipful Company of Leathersellers* (1831), 83–5.
[14] *Les Reports del Cases en Ley* (1678–80), Year Book, Hil. 49 Edward III, pl. 7, pp. 3–4; *Le Livre des Assises et Pleas del Corone* (1679), *Liber Assisarum*, 49 Edward III, pl. 8, pp. 320–1.

of chancery following an inquest before the mayor of London. The mayor's inquest had found that Ralph's devise was invalid, and that the property therefore escheated to the crown. The reasoning for the decision was not given, but it was probably on the grounds that Ralph's gift was void because of uncertainty: he had not specified a person with legal capacity in whom the gift could take effect following Agnes's death. The guildsmen were summoned into chancery to show cause why the property should not be forfeit to the crown. Unusually, the case was heard by a panel of at least four judges, including the chancellor and the chief justices of king's bench and common pleas. Thomas A and William B, the two 'best men' of the Whittawers, came into court and offered a very interesting defence. They argued that they had entered the property in question 'as custodians of the Guild of the Fraternity aforesaid to the use [*al oeps*] of the said Commonality [*comminaltie*] of the fraternity'.[15] The reference to three overlapping entities – the fraternity of Whittawers, the guild and the commonality, perhaps reflects the vagueness of the legal status of the transaction. Whether they were different terms in use for what was essentially the same group of men is not clear. The guildsmen seemed to have regarded the arrangements as a form of enfeoffment-to-use, under which they acted as custodians of the property for the use of the Whittawers' fraternity. They argued furthermore that by the usage and custom of the city of London, as confirmed by royal charters, the men of each craft could make a commonality of a guild or fraternity, and individual members, as citizens of London, could make a devise to it. In summary, the Whittawers claimed that under the liberties of the city they could set up their own guild as a commonality or perpetual body corporate. This was essentially the same argument as the Whittawers had made in Rumbold's case. In reply, the king's serjeant, Henry Percy, rejected the Whittawers' argument, asserting that the members of a guild could not create a commonality within the city of London without express authority under a royal charter. The existing charters of the city were not sufficient to confer such powers upon individual guilds.

The leading judgment was given by Chief Justice John Cavendish. He agreed with Percy that the Whittawers did not have the power to set themselves up as a perpetual commonality having separate legal capacity, without a royal charter. The judge confirmed that the city of London was a perpetual commonality, that is a body corporate of long standing which was a distinct entity in and of itself (*un gros a par luy*).[16] A guild within the city could not set itself up as a body corporate without a specific charter from the king, because otherwise it would be a legal person capable of holding property, and to sue and be sued in the courts, and this required royal authority.[17] Moreover, the fraternity of Whittawers and other such bodies were not perpetual, but were instituted by the guildsmen of their own free will, and an individual member of the fraternity could leave it if he chose, whereas a citizen of London remained perpetually a member of the commonality of the city because the city existed in perpetuity. Cavendish drew an analogy with the priory of Westminster, whose property had been severed from that of the abbey, so that the abbot could not intermeddle in it. The property division had been made by royal charter because

---

[15] '*Come Gardiens de la dit Gild al oeps de la Comminaltie de la Fraternite avantdit*'.
[16] *Liber Assisarum*, 49 Edward III, pl. 8, pp. 320–1.
[17] Ibid.: '*Car si ils auront action devers autres come Comminalty, et respond' a autr' suit come Cominalty et ceo ne puit estre sans special charter du Roy*'.

otherwise the abbey, which was a distinct entity body (*un gros et un corps*), could not have been divided in such a way as to create two such fraternities.[18] Summing up, Cavendish concluded, 'This fraternity which was made by themselves by the craft of Whittawers could not by law be adjudged a body [*corps*] to have freehold estate by purchase or devise because if so they could have an action against others as a commonality and would answer to the suit of another as a commonality and this could not be without a special charter of the King.'[19]

A mystery remains as to the relationship between the two Whittawers' cases. Their occurrence in consecutive years cannot be coincidental; but whereas Nicolas Rumbold's case is well documented in central and local government records, it has not been possible to trace any other sources relating to Ralph Jordan's case, apart from the Year Book reports themselves. Most significantly, Jordan's case does not appear among the London mortmain returns of 1365. This suggests that Jordan's chantry may have been ancient one, possibly preceding the 1279 Statute of Mortmain. Perhaps the hearing of Rumbold's case in Chancery prompted wider discussion among the judges of the powers claimed by London livery companies to establish commonalities or bodies corporate, leading to a review of Jordan's case in chancery in 1375. A striking feature of the 1375 case, as reported in the *Liber Assisarum*, was the composition of the court. The report indicates that there were at least three judges present – John Knyvet, the chancellor, John Cavendish, chief justice of the court of king's bench, and Robert Belknap chief justice of the court of common pleas – as well as John Holt, a king's serjeant who later became a justice of common pleas. This was a most unusual and very high-powered tribunal, for the chancellor usually sat alone, and in itself suggests that the Whittawers' case was one of some significance, meriting particularly careful deliberation. One commentator has described the case as being heard in the court of the exchequer chamber, which in later centuries acted as the authoritative court of final decision:[20] Sir Edward Coke described in the early seventeenth century how 'all cases of the greatest difficulty in Kings Bench or Common Pleas are and of ancient time have been adjourned and there debated, argued and resolved by all the judges of England and Barons of the Exchequer'.[21] Can we justifiably label the Whittawers' case as an early example of an exchequer chamber decision, and thus one carrying particular weight and authority? The law reports do not refer to it as such, and the earliest identifiable cases of the exchequer chamber date back only to the reign of Henry IV.[22] However, the case does exhibit some of the characteristics of fifteenth-century exchequer chamber cases: notably the presence of the chancellor and judges from both benches, the determination of a significant uncertain point of law, and issues relating to crown grants or the royal prerogative.

[18] Ibid.: '*Et il est issint que le Prior de Westm' ad ses possessions severes del Abbe, issint qe l'Abbe ne mellera rien de ses possessions ... et ceo fuit a commencer par la charter le Roy, car autrement l'Abbe que fuit un gros et un corps, ne purra ny avoir etre mis en division de leur possessions a tiel entent a doner a chescun several fraternity*'.
[19] Ibid.
[20] See D.J. Seipp, in *Legal History: The Year Books*: www.bu.edu/phpbin/lawyearbooks/display.php?id=14766.
[21] *Select Cases in the Exchequer Chamber before all the Justices of England, 1377–1461*, ed. M. Hemmant (Selden Society, li, 1933), p. xiii.
[22] *Ibid.*, pp. i–v.

There can be little doubt that this was regarded at the time as a major legal decision – a 'leading case'. There are two lengthy reports of the case in the Year Books, going into great detail on the arguments, and it is cited several times under different headings in Brooke's *Abridgement*, the mid-sixteenth-century collection of legal authorities.[23] Most importantly, the case had an immediate impact on the law, as is evident from a number of sources. The reaction to the decision was extremely rapid, as courts and litigants attempted to come to grips with its implications. The judges' decision in the Whittawers' case sent ripples of uncertainty across the legal world. It created difficulties for founders and administrators of chantries, who now found their legal arrangements thrown into doubt, but also opportunities for lawyers to generate additional business. The immediate problem thrown up by the case was its rejection of the previous practice adopted by London craft guilds to establish perpetual chantries, on the grounds that it did not create a *persona capax* – a person with legal capacity to hold the land in perpetuity. In 1378 the common council of the city of London attempted to remedy this defect by means of a declaration that 'for the avoidance of doubt' (*pro dubio removendo*) a devise of property to chantries by freemen of the city was not to be invalidated by the absence of a specific *persona capax*.[24] A few weeks after that declaration two chantry priests of the London parish of St Michael Paternoster, John Chamberlain and Thomas Bilk, brought an action before the city's possessory assizes against four tenants for non-payment of rent. The defendants alleged among other things that at the time of the death of the founder of the chantry, Walter Waldeschef, there was no *persona capax* designated to receive the estate under the will; therefore, they claimed, the devise was void in law. They made this argument notwithstanding royal letters patent of 1367 which provided for the presentation of priests pursuant to William's will.[25] A jury was summoned which found in favour of the plaintiffs on the strength of the will and the royal letters patent.

A similar problem emerged a few years later, in 1386, when John Leicester, the priest of the chantry of Nicholas Bole, citizen of London, obtained royal letters patent confirming the effect of Bole's will, which had devised an annual rent of ten marks for the endowment of a chantry chapel in the parish church of St Anthony. The background was that the tenant subject to the devise, William Aldeburgh, having paid rent to John Leicester for several years, had refused to continue paying after his death. This was on the grounds that Bole had not bequeathed the rent to a person with legal capacity (*redditus predictus alicui persone capaci non fuit legatus*).[26] This was not an isolated case: the Whittawers decision had the effect of encouraging the tenants of chantries to withhold rent. This made good sense from the tenant's point of view, because if he was not certain who his landlord was, then he risked paying rent to the wrong person, and potentially having to pay twice over. The problem was raised in a Commons' petition to Parliament in 1394, which complained that two chantry priests of St Mary Aldermary in London had submitted a petition requesting that a statute be enacted to give effect to chantry legacies created with insufficient words, that is, lacking a *persona capax*. The Commons rejected this, and requested

---

[23] Robert Brooke, *La Seconde Part du Graunde Abridgement* (1573), Prescription, pl. 12, p. 149.
[24] *Calendar of Letter-Books of the City of London, H, 1375–99*, ed. R.R. Sharpe (1907), 106.
[25] *London Possessory Assizes: A Calendar*, ed. H.M. Chew (London Record Society, i, 1965), no. 142.
[26] *CPR*, 1385–89, pp. 161–2.

the existing law to remain in force.[27] The ruling also created problems for more established institutions. In 1393 the guild of Goldsmiths found it necessary to obtain royal letters patent granting it a licence to own property. In the reign of Edward III, the guild had been granted the right to acquire land to the value of £20 for charitable purposes, but had not been able to take advantage of it because the grant had failed to specify a *persona capax* to hold the land. The king granted the Goldsmiths the status of a 'perpetual commonality', allowing them to hold land, and marking the first steps on the road to incorporation.[28]

It is evident from these cases that in the final quarter of the fourteenth century there was a phase of disruption and confusion following the Whittawers' decision. Lawyers and institutions sought to come to terms with the changed legal position, uncertain as to how to respond to it. There then followed a phase of reformulation, as new precedents came into use and the new rules were embodied in corporate foundation documents. The evidence from mortmain licences for chantries from the turn of the century onwards shows that donors were beginning to make express provision for legal capacity. For example, in 1398 a licence granted to Thomas Hawley of Lincolnshire to found a chantry for three chaplains includes express words providing for legal capacity: 'one of the chaplains shall be named master, and the said master and chaplains shall be capable of holding lands for themselves and their successors in perpetuity'.[29] Although the chantry chaplains were not incorporated by express words the key power of legal capacity was clearly established. The endowment of John of Gaunt's chantry in 1403 went a step further, reflecting perhaps the expertise of the duchy of Lancaster's lawyers: 'and the said chaplains and their successors shall be persons perpetually capable, corporate and fit to acquire land ... for the use of the said chantry in perpetuity'.[30] Three years later a mortmain licence was granted for the collegiate charity in Chalgrave, Bedfordshire, founded by Robert Braybrooke, bishop of London. The drafting is lengthy and elaborate, and includes all the key elements of a corporation found later in the fifteenth century: the name by which the charity should be known, express words of incorporation, the capacity to acquire and hold land, the right to sue and be sued in the courts, perpetual succession of the chaplains, and a common seal.[31] Thus, barely thirty years after the Whittawers' case, we see the essential outlines of the modern corporation in its mature form.

The real test of the fully developed legal concept of a corporation is the 'one member' company, that is a body corporate which has only a single member but enjoys separate legal personality. Such an entity may seem counterintuitive, and even today it remains controversial in certain circumstances, but its validity in modern company law was upheld in the leading case of Salomon versus A. Salomon and Company.[32] Already in the fifteenth century donors of limited means, who could only afford to endow a chantry with a single chaplain, nevertheless wanted the

---

[27] Wood-Legh, *Perpetual Chantries*, 317.
[28] *English Historical Documents, IV, 1327–1485*, p. 563.
[29] '*Idem magister et capellani sint persone habiles ad percipiendum et adquirendum sibi et successoribus suis in perpetuum terras et tenements*', Wood-Legh, *Perpetual Chantries*, 318.
[30] Ibid.: '*Et quod prefati capellani et successores sui sint persone perpetue capaces corporati et habiles ad perquirendum terras ... ad usam et utilitatem cantarie predicte imperpetuum*'.
[31] Thus, the only omission by comparison with the mature form of incorporation was the power to make statutes.
[32] Salomon v. A. Salomon & Co. Ltd [1897], Appeal Cases, 22.

benefits of incorporation to establish the chantry in perpetuity. The law soon accommodated them and from early on in the century we find examples of one-chaplain chantries receiving licences to incorporate. For example, in 1409 a mortmain licence was granted for the foundation of a chantry for the soul of Robert Chepe, to be served by a single chaplain. He and his successors were to be named 'the chaplains of the chantry of Robert Chepe in the said chapel [of St Thomas the Martyr] in the suburb of Bristol', and were given the capacity to own land and property in perpetuity.[33] By mid-century the legal status of the one-chaplain chantry was well established, and the wording of such mortmain licences had acquired a settled form very similar to that of larger chantries.[34]

From around 1450 therefore, after seventy-five years of evolution, we can speak with confidence of the maturity of the concept of incorporation in English law. During the next phase under Edward IV, as Maitland described, there was considerable discussion in the Year Books working through the detailed implications of the new legal definition of corporate status. A mark of its maturity and acceptance is that older forms of corporate entity were becoming increasingly assimilated into the new model. In 1458, for example, Merton College, Oxford, which had been founded in 1264 and therefore lacked the new corporate formulae in its foundation charter, was sued in the court of common pleas in a property dispute. The plaintiff impleaded the college by the name of 'the warden of Merton College', but the college's lawyer argued that the action was not good because the correct name of the college by which it was incorporated, was 'the warden and scholars of Merton College'. In view of the lacuna in the college's charter he claimed that the college had been corporate by that name since time immemorial, and that it had always been sued and been sued in that form. This was a minor point, advanced in an attempt to have the case thrown out on a legal technicality, but it is likely that such a point would not have been made a hundred years earlier.[35]

---

[33] *CPR*, 1409–13, pp. 87–8; TNA, C66/381, m. 14: '*idem Capellanus et successores sui capellani cantarie Roberti Chepe in capella predicta in suburbia ville predicte nuncupentur. Quod idem Capellanus et successores sui predicti persone capaces et habiles ad perquirendum terras, tenementa ... existat in perpetuum*'.
[34] Wood-Legh, *Perpetual Chantries*, 319–21.
[35] Anthony Fitzherbert, *La Graunde Abridgement* (1577), Briefe, f. 146v.

'THE PRINCIPAL PLACE OF HONOUR ABOUT THE PERSON OF THE QUEEN.' MARGARET OF ANJOU AND ALICE CHAUCER, DUCHESS OF SUFFOLK: THE MAKING OF A FRIENDSHIP[1]

Diana Dunn

Can a medieval queen be thought to have formed friendships in any modern sense of that word? Studies of medieval queenship over the past forty years have tended to focus on the relationship between the queen and the sovereign in the broader context of the operation of the court and royal household,[2] and queens have conventionally been judged a success or failure by reference to perceived queenly duties, in particular the capacity to bear children, and especially the ability to produce male heirs. Other duties identified as essential have been to provide companionship to the king, to preside at court at his side, to bestow charity and hospitality to worthy recipients and to maintain a dignified and discreet presence without indulging in extravagant behaviour of any kind, especially not lavish expenditure.[3] While it is often possible to trace through official government records the activities and lifestyle of the queen as she accompanied the king around the country, any evidence of her personal daily routines and social contacts is far more difficult to find and tends to survive only haphazardly. Such close social contacts were most likely to be with immediate members of her own family and the extended royal family, as well as with members of the royal household serving her in a range of positions, some official but others more personal. Historians have rarely considered whether, or how, queens formed close relationships outside their immediate family circle or what factors may have

---

[1] The quotation is from Agnes Strickland, *Lives of the Queens of England* (6 vols, 1864), i. 553. This essay is written in celebration of fifty years of friendship shared with Rowena, and in recognition of the truth of the words of Cicero's maxim, translated from his *De Amicitia:* 'Friendship improves happiness and abates misery, by the doubling of our joy and the dividing of our grief.'

[2] The most recent studies of Margaret of Anjou both adopt this approach: H.E. Maurer, *Margaret of Anjou: Queenship and Power in Late Medieval England* (Woodbridge, 2003); B.M. Cron, *Margaret of Anjou and the Men Around Her* (2021). I would like to thank Bonita Cron for her enthusiastic and helpful response to my initial ideas for this essay and for her useful comments on an earlier draft.

[3] Anne Crawford, 'The King's Burden? the Consequences of Royal Marriage in Fifteenth-century England', in *Patronage, the Crown and the Provinces in Later Medieval England*, ed. R.A. Griffiths (Gloucester, 1981), 33–56.

influenced their choice of friends other than the obvious commonality of elite social status and high birth.

This essay explores the relationship between the young Queen Margaret of Anjou and Alice Chaucer, duchess of Suffolk, one of the leading noblewomen of fifteenth-century England, from the time of their first meeting, which probably took place in Rouen in March 1445, until May 1450 when Alice was widowed for the third time by the death of her husband, William de la Pole, duke of Suffolk, and considers how it continued thereafter.[4] What factors affected the relationship between these two women of such significantly different ages and backgrounds? One was of effectively regal status, as the daughter of René, duke of Anjou, and Isabelle of Lorraine; the other was a commoner, the grand-daughter of the poet Geoffrey Chaucer and daughter of an outstanding servant of the English crown, Thomas Chaucer.[5] This study assesses the divergencies and commonalities in the experiences of these two women who shared much misfortune, albeit with markedly different outcomes. The pivotal role played by Alice's husband in the negotiations for the marriage of Henry VI to Margaret of Anjou in 1444 must clearly have been a significant factor in determining the nature of the relationship between the two women.[6] Later sources, invariably hostile to both William de la Pole and Margaret of Anjou, implausibly accused the pair of adultery, blamed them for the loss of English territories in France and, ultimately, held them responsible for the downfall of the Lancastrian monarchy.[7] Had there been any truth in the malicious charges of improper relations made against Suffolk, this would undoubtedly have affected the relationship between Margaret and Alice. Yet if, as seems more credible, these accusations are disallowed as scurrilous and hostile propaganda, and Suffolk's role in the marriage negotiations is viewed more positively, it may be possible to construct a very different basis for their longer-term relationship. It is feasible to argue that the Valois princess, having left her familial home, and facing an uncertain future as the young and inexperienced wife of the king of England, should find solace in the company of a noblewoman, at least twice her age, with a wealth of life-experience. During the few weeks Margaret spent in the company of the lords and ladies who made up Suffolk's entourage in Rouen, and on the drawn-out journey back to England, she had much to learn about the man,

---

[4] For an overview of the life of Alice Chaucer, see Rowena E. Archer, 'Chaucer, Alice, duchess of Suffolk (c.1404–1475)', *Oxford DNB*, and for a flavour of her strong personality, *eadem*, '"How ladies … who live on their manors ought to manage their households and estates": Women as Landholders and Administrators in the Later Middle Ages', in *Woman is a Worthy Wight: Women in English Society c.1200–1500*, ed. P.J.P. Goldberg (Stroud, 1992), 153–7. See also Diana Dunn, 'Margaret of Anjou, Queen Consort of Henry VI: A Reassessment of her Role, 1445–53', in *Crown, Government and People in the Fifteenth Century*, ed. R.E. Archer (Stroud, 1995), 133–4, for a brief overview of the relationship between Margaret and the duke and duchess of Suffolk.

[5] *The History of Parliament. The House of Commons 1386–1421*, ed. J.S. Roskell, Linda Clark and Carole Rawcliffe (4 vols, Stroud, 1993), ii. 524–32.

[6] The career of the duke of Suffolk and his role in the negotiations for the marriage are discussed in the ground-breaking essay by C.L. Kingsford, 'The Policy and Fall of Suffolk', in *Prejudice and Promise in Fifteenth Century England* (1962), 146–76, first published in 1925. For a more recent detailed examination of Suffolk's role in the marriage negotiations, B.M. Cron, 'The Duke of Suffolk, the Angevin Marriage, and the Ceding of Maine, 1445', *Journal of Medieval History*, xx (1994), 77–99. An extremely negative view of the marriage and its consequences is provided by M.L. Kekewich in *The Good King: René of Anjou and Fifteenth Century Europe* (Basingstoke, 2008), 8, 80–1, where Margaret is described as being 'sacrificed' for both Anjou and the kingdom of France.

[7] Kingsford, 'Policy and Fall of Suffolk', 174–5.

already her husband, whom she had never met, and the customs of the English court.[8] Who better to educate and prepare her for her new role as queen-consort than the worldly-wise and politically astute duke and duchess of Suffolk? This initial period of intense social contact could very plausibly have resulted in a long-lasting friendship between Margaret and Alice which endured even after 1450 when both women faced challenges to their position and status in an increasingly threatening political environment.[9]

Despite the limitations of the sources available, it is possible to make a plausible assessment of the personal relationship between these two women in the context of later medieval European aristocratic society. One of the few historians to consider how friendships between noblewomen were formed in this period is Jennifer Ward, who while acknowledging that it can be difficult to define the difference between a woman's friends and her business and social acquaintances, the friends are likely to have been those with whom contact was regularly maintained, who visited each other frequently or over a considerable period, and who exchanged substantial gifts or bequests. Few women, even those of high social status, have left more than the most limited records of their activities in either the public or private sphere and even less evidence of their feelings and personal responses to events and the people around them.[10] Nowadays we would expect to find a plethora of material which might be used to document relationships: letters, diaries, photographs, and tokens of friendship including cards, books and other gifts, often accompanied by explicit messages of affection. By contrast, although some personal records survive for each of the women (Margaret's letters, household and jewel accounts and Alice's estate records, accounts and household inventories), it is difficult to reconstruct a meaningful relationship between them from the meagre documentary evidence alone.[11]

---

[8] The composition of the entourage that escorted Margaret to England is documented in the accounts of expenditure incurred from 17 July 1444 to 16 October 1445, printed in *Letters and Papers Illustrative of the Wars of the English in France during the Reign of Henry the Sixth*, ed. Joseph Stevenson (2 vols in 3, 1861–4), i. 443–64. The particulars on which the account was based are now BL, Add. MS 23938.

[9] The idea that Margaret and Alice established a lasting friendship has been expressed repeatedly by historians from Tout in 1909 to Cron in 2021, but the evidence for the basis of this friendship has not been discussed in any detail: T.F. Tout, 'Margaret of Anjou', *DNB*, xii (1909), 1026; Kingsford, 'Policy and Fall of Suffolk', 163; J.J. Bagley, *Margaret of Anjou, Queen of England* (1948), 54; R.A. Griffiths, *The Reign of King Henry VI* (1981), 256; B.P. Wolffe, *Henry VI* (1981), 348; *Letters of the Queens of England 1100–1547*, ed. Anne Crawford (Stroud, 1994), 124; Maurer, *Margaret of Anjou*, 80–1; J.L. Laynesmith, *The Last Medieval Queens. English Queenship 1445–1503* (Oxford, 2004), 171, 210; Cron, *Margaret of Anjou*, 61–2, 236, 319, 453–5.

[10] J.C. Ward, *English Noblewomen in the Later Middle Ages* (1992), 93, 103–4. For a rare example of a lady whose relationship with other women is well documented, see F.A. Underhill, *For Her Good Estate: The Life of Elizabeth de Burgh, Lady of Clare* (Basingstoke, 1999), esp. ch. 3.

[11] All known letters written by, or to, Margaret of Anjou have recently been published in *The Letters of Margaret of Anjou*, ed. H.E. Maurer and B.M. Cron (Woodbridge, 2019), but they shed little light on the personal relationship between Margaret and Alice. Of more value are her jewel accounts – TNA, E101/409/14, 17; 410/2, 8 and 11, of which the last, for 1452–3, is transcribed in A.R. Myers, 'The Jewels of Queen Margaret of Anjou', *BJRL*, xlii (1959–60), 113–31 – and her household accounts for 1452–3 (TNA, DL 28/5/8), published by Myers in 'The Household of Queen Margaret of Anjou, 1452–3', *BJRL*, xl (1957–8), 79–113, 391–431. Of value to an understanding of Alice's lifestyle are the inventories – Bodl. Ewelme Muniments A 47 (1–6) – included as Appendix VII in J.A.A. Goodall, *God's House at Ewelme: Life, Devotion and Architecture in a Fifteenth-Century Almshouse* (Aldershot, 2001), 281–90. No will for Alice survives, and Margaret's is very brief: A. Lecoy de la

It could be argued, however, that a strong determinant of friendship between them was a shared cultural background rooted in common linguistic and literary interests, evident in the books they inherited or acquired at different stages of their lives.[12] Another shared personal experience was their religious life, demonstrated not only in their daily routines of worship, both in private and in public, and their patronage of religious institutions, but also in their ownership of devotional and liturgical books such as personal prayer books, books of hours and psalters, and texts aimed at the improvement of the individual's spiritual life.[13]

Margaret and Alice's probable first meeting at Rouen in March 1445 was at a time when the capital of Lancastrian Normandy functioned as an important economic and administrative centre as well as a military stronghold, as it had done from the time of the rule of John, duke of Bedford, from 1422 to 1435, and especially after the fall of Paris to the French in 1436. Richard Beauchamp, earl of Warwick, Richard, duke of York, and Edmund Beaufort, duke of Somerset, successively held the position of lieutenant-general and governor in France and took up residence in Rouen. It had been Henry V's intention to build an English colony in Normandy, and integration between the native population and settlers was encouraged for mutual benefit. English soldiers, merchants, administrators and clerics bought land, rented property and set up businesses to supply the needs of a population which required the services of skilled artisans and craftsmen.[14] A tradition of service to the crown in France ran through certain noble families from the earliest phases of the Hundred Years' War to the campaigns led by Henry V and his brother the duke of Bedford. The de la Poles were one such family whose leading members served as soldiers over several generations, although the campaign of 1415 took its toll on them when Michael, second earl of Suffolk, was killed at the siege of Harfleur and his eldest son, also Michael, lost his life at Agincourt. Following their deaths, William de la Pole, third earl of Suffolk, continued to serve in France in the expedition of 1417 and until

---

Marche, *Le Roi René: sa vie, son administration, ses travaux artistiques et littéraires* (2 vols, Paris, 1875), ii. 395–7.

[12] Cron, *Margaret of Anjou*, 61–2. There has been a surge of interest in the study of medieval women as book-owners since the publication of *Women and Literature in Britain, 1150–1500*, ed. C. M. Meale (Cambridge, 1993); *Women, the Book and the Worldly: Selected Proceedings of the St Hilda's Conference, Oxford, Volume II*, ed. Lesley Smith and J.H.M. Taylor (Cambridge, 1995) and *Women and the Book: Assessing the Visual Evidence*, ed. Smith and Taylor (1997). Two essays on Alice Chaucer and her books have informed my consideration of the links between Alice and Margaret as book-owners: C.M. Meale, 'Reading Women's Culture in Fifteenth-Century England: The Case of Alice Chaucer', in *Mediaevalitas: Reading in the Middle Ages*, ed. Anna Torti and Piero Boitani (Cambridge, 1996), 81–101, and K.K. Jambeck, 'The Library of Alice Chaucer, Duchess of Suffolk: A Fifteenth-Century Owner of a *Boke of La Cité des Dames*', *Misericordia International* (1998), 106–35. For books owned by Margaret of Anjou, see R.L. Radulescu, 'Preparing for her Mature Years: The Case of Margaret of Anjou and her Books', in *Middle-aged Women in the Middle Ages*, ed S.A. Niebrzydowski (Cambridge, 2011), 115–38.

[13] For a succinct overview of the devotional books owned by Margaret, see Laynesmith, *Last Medieval Queens*, 253, and for her piety, see Cron, *Margaret of Anjou*, 42–3, 193. For devotional books owned by Alice, see Jambeck, 'Library of Alice Chaucer', and for a more general discussion of female piety and book-ownership, see Felicity Riddy, '"Women talking about the things of God": a Late Medieval Sub-culture,' in *Women and Literature*, ed. Meale, 104–27.

[14] C.T. Allmand, *Lancastrian Normandy, 1415–1450: The History of a Medieval Occupation* (Oxford, 1983), 41, 50–7, 88–9; Jenny Stratford, 'John, Duke of Bedford, as Patron in Lancastrian Rouen', in *Medieval Art, Architecture and Archaeology at Rouen*, ed. Jenny Stratford, *British Archaeological Association Conference Transactions, XII* (1993).

the siege of Orleans in 1428–9 when he was taken captive by the French. His ransom of £20,000 was eventually raised through the sale of lands in England and France and, on his release, he returned to England in 1430. There he was licensed to marry Alice Chaucer, dowager countess of Salisbury,[15] whose previous husband, Thomas Montagu, earl of Salisbury, killed at the siege of Orleans, had left her an extremely wealthy widow in possession of half of his moveable goods together with 1,000 marks in gold, jewellery and plate worth 3,000 marks, the revenues of his lands in Normandy,[16] and valuable assets in Oxfordshire and Berkshire. Furthermore, the marriage brought Suffolk important connections, most significantly with Cardinal Henry Beaufort, a leading figure in Henry VI's minority government, who was the cousin and close associate of Alice's father. By the time the young king assumed his majority in 1437, Suffolk had proved himself a loyal and versatile royal servant both at home, sitting on the king's council and serving as steward of his household, and abroad, acting as an ambassador with Beaufort in missions to Calais in 1433 and Arras in 1435, as well as joining the duke of York in an expedition to Normandy in the aftermath of Bedford's death. Thereafter, he successfully strove to establish himself at the heart of the government, becoming the central figure in the household of a young and immature king who lacked either the capacity or the will required to meet the complex demands of government not just as king of England but also as crowned king of France.[17]

Historians have long debated Suffolk's role and motives in the determination of royal policy and the direction of foreign diplomacy in the early 1440s, which eventually led both to the truce of Tours agreed with France in May 1444 and the marriage of Henry VI to Margaret of Anjou.[18] Suffolk claimed that he was sent to France to negotiate for peace reluctantly, appreciating the high stakes involved in this strategy, and an awareness of the split in opinion and attitude to the 'problem' of the war with France among members of the royal council.[19] As far as the French were concerned, a marriage between the king of England and one of Charles VII's daughters was out of the question and therefore Margaret, daughter of Duke René of Anjou, whose sister Marie was queen of France, was the next best thing; but for the English the marriage proposal had its drawbacks and Suffolk would have been aware of the probability of opposition from those English noblemen who still favoured war. The details of Suffolk's embassy to Tours in 1444 and the subsequent marriage ceremony held in the church of St Martin there on 24 May, when he stood proxy for Henry VI, have been rehearsed many times, most convincingly by Bonita Cron who has untangled the confusing evidence from both French and English sources, establishing a convincing chronology for the events of 1444–5.[20] The long delay in the departure of Margaret from her homeland has been explained in various ways, most of the sources reflecting a bias against the young queen, or Suffolk, or both. Hostility to Suffolk is most pronounced in the publications of nineteenth-century English writers who, with hindsight, interpreted and embroidered the accounts of

---

[15] John Watts, 'Pole, William de la, first duke of Suffolk (1396–1450)', *Oxford DNB*.
[16] Archer, 'Chaucer, Alice', *Oxford DNB*.
[17] John Watts, *Henry VI and the Politics of Kingship* (Cambridge, 1996), esp. 153–254, for a detailed discussion of Suffolk's role in government.
[18] Kingsford ascribed to Suffolk a consistent peace policy from as early as 1433: 'Policy and Fall of Suffolk', 146–9.
[19] *PPC*, vi. 32–5 (wrongly dated 1445); Wolffe, *Henry VI*, 174.
[20] Cron, 'The Duke of Suffolk', 77–99.

earlier French historians.[21] Charges levelled against Suffolk after his fall from power in 1449 look back to his mission to France in 1444, and accuse him of colluding with Margaret to make promises to Charles VII which were later enforced by the French, thereby putting pressure on the malleable Henry VI. It was alleged that Suffolk took advantage of a young and naïve queen to force her into an irregular relationship, later using her to manipulate the unworldly Henry VI during further negotiations for the surrender of Maine and Anjou to the French after her arrival in England.[22] These accusations reached their extreme level in the criticism of Suffolk's policy in France by his political opponents after the ignominious surrender of Rouen in October 1449. Blame for the failure of the English war effort was laid firmly on his shoulders, with additional charges amounting to treason being brought against him in the parliamentary session of January to March 1450. Despite Suffolk's efforts to remind the Commons of his family's service to the crown, he was charged with conspiring with the French to replace the king of England with his own son and heir, John, after arranging John's marriage to his ward Margaret Beaufort, heiress to John, duke of Somerset (d. 1444).[23] These accusations of treason against Suffolk, as well as the charges of improper relations with Margaret, have been convincingly dismissed by historians as the outpouring of hostile political opponents seeking to find a scapegoat for the inadequacies of Henry VI and the disastrous misconduct of the war.[24] Yet if we regard Suffolk as working towards a resolution to the long-standing and, by the early 1440s, hopeless conflict with France, it is possible to construct a different, and more positive, relationship between him, Alice his wife, and Margaret, founded upon a strong mutual desire to bring about a permanent peace settlement.[25] In building this relationship, from the first meeting of William de la Pole with Margaret in Tours in May 1444, to the arrival of the young queen in England almost a year later, the few weeks spent together in Rouen in March and April 1445 were likely to have been seminal to any longer-term friendship forged between Margaret and Alice.

It was once thought that Alice accompanied her husband to Tours in the spring of 1444, but historians now agree that it was not until Suffolk, then newly created marquess, set out again, in the following November, to escort the young queen to her marital home in England, that he was accompanied not only by his wife but by a large and costly retinue. It is evident from the allowances made to him, his wife and their entourage, that they were regarded as the most senior representatives of the king.[26] They were kept waiting in Rouen for five months before Margaret was escorted to Normandy from Pontoise by members of her family and representatives

---

[21] James Ramsay, using Thomas Gascoigne, an Oxford theologian described by Griffiths as 'the arch-rumour-monger of late-Lancastrian England' (*Reign of Henry VI*, 487), as his source, thought that the delay was deliberate in order to force concessions relating to the surrender of Maine out of Suffolk before the marriage was agreed: J.H. Ramsay, *Lancaster and York* (2 vols, 1892), ii. 62.

[22] Kingsford, 'Policy and Fall of Suffolk', 161–3, 166, 170–1. Tudor chroniclers' accounts were followed by Shakespeare in *Henry VI, part 2*, act III, scene 2, presenting Suffolk and Margaret as lovers in league against the naïve king, a negative view of Suffolk dismissed by Tout, 'Margaret of Anjou', 1026; Kingsford, 'Policy and Fall of Suffolk', 174–5; and Bagley, *Margaret of Anjou*, 53–4.

[23] *PROME*, xii. 92–106; Griffiths, *Reign of Henry VI*, 677–83.

[24] Despite Tout's unflattering portrayal of Margaret as 'precocious' and 'unscrupulous', he dismissed the idea that she had improper relations with Suffolk as absurd: 'Suffolk was an elderly man, and his wife was very friendly with Margaret during his life and after his death': 'Margaret of Anjou', 1026.

[25] For a more favourable interpretation of Suffolk's regime, see Watts, *Henry VI*, 205–25.

[26] Cron, 'The Duke of Suffolk', 79–80, 88; *Letters and Papers*, ed. Stevenson, i. 443–60; Griffiths, *Reign of Henry VI*, 256, 315–16.

of Henry VI, headed by Richard, duke of York, for her journey was delayed by the marriage celebrations for her elder sister Yolande, at Nancy in February 1445,[27] and broken by a stay in Paris as a guest of Charles, duke of Orleans. She only reached Rouen around 18 March. The strain of the long journey, exacerbated by the emotion of bidding farewell to her close family members at Nancy, in full knowledge that she was unlikely to see them again for many years, caused her to fall ill on her arrival at Rouen, where she celebrated her fifteenth birthday (on 23 March), and as a result of her indisposition she was unable to participate in her ceremonial entry into the city; her place in the procession was taken by Alice, marchioness of Suffolk.[28] The wives of other noblemen most closely associated with the recent conduct of the war also played an important part in the procession: they included Margaret, countess of Shrewsbury, and Alice, countess of Salisbury (step-daughter to the marchioness),[29] and alongside them were the most senior ladies assigned to the new queen's household: Beatrice, Lady Talbot (the Portuguese-born wife of William Talbot, and sister-in-law to the earl of Shrewsbury), Ismania, Lady Scales (wife of Thomas, Lord Scales, seneschal of Normandy), Elizabeth Grey (widow of Sir Ralph Grey, captain of Mantes) and Margery Hull (wife of Sir Edward Hull, who had accompanied Suffolk to bring home Henry VI's bride and was assigned to her household as one of her carvers).[30] According to John Benet's chronicle, Margaret was accompanied by only a small number of Angevin servants, which attracted adverse comment from those who felt that her high status required a larger and more prestigious entourage.[31] She was thenceforth reliant on this elite group of English ladies for advice and guidance on the customs of the English court as she prepared for her new life among strangers. In this unfamiliar environment, Suffolk and his wife must have played a crucial role in preparing her for her first meeting with the king and his courtiers. It is unlikely that Margaret spoke English with any fluency whereas the noblewomen who became her closest companions would have been conversant in French, having spent long periods of time living in Normandy while their husbands were undertaking governmental or military service.

During this time of readjustment for the new queen in Rouen, it is likely that John Talbot, earl of Shrewsbury, presented Margaret with his wedding gift of the finely illuminated manuscript, now known as the 'Shrewsbury Book' and the messages contained within it may have shaped her thinking in the early years of her mar-

---

[27] Cron, 'The Duke of Suffolk', 89–90.
[28] Mathieu d'Escouchy, *Chronique*, ed. Gaston du Fresne de Beaucourt (3 vols, Paris, 1863–4), i. 86–7; Cron, 'The Duke of Suffolk', 90; *eadem, Margaret of Anjou*, 28–9. There is a record of payments to 'Master Francis, the queen's physician' for the provision of medicines to treat her: *Letters and Papers*, ed. Stevenson, i. 452.
[29] Although Cecily, duchess of York, was the highest-ranking noblewoman in Rouen to welcome the queen, she did not take part in the procession. Laynesmith speculates that, as 'hostess', she may have taken responsibility for looking after the sick queen for its duration: J.L. Laynesmith, *Cecily Duchess of York* (2017), 47.
[30] Cron, *Margaret of Anjou*, 29; *History of Parliament. The House of Commons 1422–61*, ed. Linda Clark (7 vols, Cambridge, 2020), v. 1029–34. These ladies remained in Margaret's household after she reached England and the queen regularly made gifts to them: Myers, 'Household of Queen Margaret', 404–5; *idem*, 'Jewels of Queen Margaret', 113–31. Lady Scales received an annuity of £40.
[31] 'John Benet's Chronicle for the Years 1400 to 1462', ed. G.L. and M.A. Harriss, *Camden Miscellany*, XXIV (Camden Soc. 4th ser. ix, 1972), 190; Kingsford, 'Policy and Fall of Suffolk', 157–8; Griffiths, *Reign of Henry VI*, 255.

riage.[32] The manuscript had probably been originally intended for the personal use of the earl himself and his wife, but once the royal marriage had been arranged, and in the expectation that the new queen would pass through Rouen en route to England, it was quickly adapted for its new purpose.[33] Made up of an eclectic mix of texts in French and Latin, the volume contains many messages to the queen indicating the hopes and expectations not just of Talbot himself but of many of the soldiers whose lives had been inextricably bound up with the war over the previous thirty years. The dedicatory verse, perhaps penned by Talbot himself, expressed these expectations as he addressed Margaret and her yet unborn son, destined to be heir to the thrones of both England and France.[34] Recent analysis of both the text and the illuminations has drawn out their distinctive features while emphasising their principal message: the claim of Henry VI to the French throne through his descent from St Louis, as illustrated in the magnificent genealogical tree on folio 3, with the importance of his marriage to Margaret of Anjou as a means of reinforcing this claim shown in its marginalia.[35] Talbot's support for the couple is shown through depictions of heralds holding their arms.[36] The texts chosen for inclusion in the volume demonstrate the messages Talbot wished to convey to the queen, and given the impressive record of military service of a significant number of the nobility to the Lancastrian monarchy in support of the English claim to the French throne, it seems reasonable to assume that his views reflected the outlook of many of them, including those of Suffolk himself. In her insightful discussion of the contents of the 'Shrewsbury Book', Catherine Reynolds observed that some of the texts of a chivalric and militaristic subject matter, which she describes as 'masculine texts', were not obvious choices for a queen. These included Honoré Bonet's *Arbre des batailles*, Christine de Pizan's *Le Livre des fais d'armes et de chevalerie* and the statutes of the Order of the Garter.[37] Andrew Taylor sees it as a 'programme of instruction for a future heir and implicit bid for the position of his tutor',[38] and, echoing this view, Craig Taylor notes the wide-ranging set of writings on warfare and chivalric culture.[39]

There is a strong emphasis in the 'Shrewsbury Book' on the expected role of Queen Margaret as educator of the heir to the thrones of England and France, acknowledging the importance of noblewomen as teachers of their children. In this role, Margaret had something in common with Alice Chaucer, who in 1442, at the age of thirty-eight,

---

[32] BL, Royal MS 15 E. VI.
[33] Catherine Reynolds, 'The Shrewsbury Book, British Library, Royal MS 15 E.VI', in *Medieval Art ... at Rouen*, ed. Stratford, 109–16; Andre de Mandach, 'A Royal Wedding-Present in the Making: Talbot's Chivalric Anthology (Royal 15 E VI)) for Queen Margaret of Anjou and the Laval-Middleton Anthology of Nottingham', *Nottingham Medieval Studies*, xviii (1974), 56–76. For a more recent discussion of the manuscript, see the chapters by A.D. Hedeman, Andrew Taylor, Craig Taylor and Karen Fresco which make up Part II, 'Networks of Texts, Book Producers, and Readers: The Case of the Shrewsbury Book', in *Collections in Context: The Organization of Knowledge and Community in Europe*, ed. Karen Fresco and A.D. Hedeman (Columbus, OH, 2011), 99–188.
[34] Reynolds, 'The Shrewsbury Book', 112–13; A.J. Pollard, *John Talbot and the War in France, 1427–1453* (1983), 128.
[35] Anne Hedeman, 'Collecting Images: The Role of the Visual in the Shrewsbury Book' and Craig Taylor, 'The Treatise Cycle of the Shrewsbury Book', in *Collections in Context*, 99–119, 134–50; Reynolds, 'The Shrewsbury Book', 113.
[36] Hedeman, 'Collecting Images', 113–14.
[37] Reynolds, 'The Shrewsbury Book', 111.
[38] 'The Time of an Anthology', *Collections in Context*, 122–3, 131.
[39] 'The Treatise Cycle', 142, 146.

had at last given birth to a son, her only surviving child from her three marriages.[40] Carol Meale has suggested that one of the factors affecting Alice's acquisition of books was her role as mother and teacher of her son which may well have overlapped with her interest in French court culture, including some more 'masculine' elements.[41] The 'Shrewsbury Book' contained a French version of one of the most popular educational manuals or 'mirrors for princes', Henri de Gauchi's translation of *De regimine principium*, originally written by Giles of Rome in 1281, offering advice on government, household management, education of children and the conduct of individuals, including queens.[42] This can be compared with one of Alice's own books (listed in the Ewelme inventory of 1466): 'a boke of latyn of the morall Institution of a prince conteynyng xxvij[ti] chapters covered in rede lethere', which Meale identifies as the mid-thirteenth-century *De moralis principis instutione*, a didactic treatise by the Dominican friar Vincent de Beauvais, possibly acquired from John Courteys of Exeter College, Oxford, who, following his appointment as rector of Ewelme in 1455, may have been made a tutor to Alice's son, John.[43] By then, when John was aged thirteen, the widowed Alice had sole responsibility for his education. This same role and responsibility would in due course be shared by Margaret as Henry VI became increasingly ineffective as king, and the queen perforce shifted her focus and hope for the future to her son, Prince Edward, born in 1453.[44]

Despite their different backgrounds and nationalities, it may also be argued that William de la Pole and his wife Alice shared with Margaret of Anjou the same cultural tastes and influences, essentially deriving from French writers and artists reflected conspicuously in the books they owned.[45] The cities of Paris and Rouen were at the heart of book production and the luxury book trade, and their highly skilled artists and craftsmen served the demands of both French and English royal and aristocratic patrons, notably those living in Rouen as representatives of the king and leaders of the English armed forces. Besides the earl of Shrewsbury, they included Richard, duke of York, Thomas, Lord Scales, Sir John Fastolf and Sir Thomas Hoo (later Lord Hoo), chancellor of Normandy and France from 1443 to 1449. These English noblemen maintained a lifestyle appropriate to their high status which required regular expenditure on their residences, not just for their own benefit but as places of hospitality for visiting dignitaries such as foreign ambassadors. Among the luxury items purchased by the English nobility from Rouen craftsmen were books, jewels and gold and silver plate.[46] Catherine Reynolds has argued for

---

[40] Archer, 'Chaucer, Alice', *Oxford DNB*.
[41] Meale, 'Reading Women's Culture', 91, 98–9.
[42] For a discussion of the French clerics, Vincent of Beauvais, Bartholomew Glanville and Giles of Rome, as authors of political and educational treatises, see Nicholas Orme, *From Childhood to Chivalry: The Education of the English Kings and Aristocracy, 1066–1530* (1984), 90–7. Orme also states that 'in educational literature France generally led and England followed': 110.
[43] Meale, 'Reading Women's Culture', 87, 98–9.
[44] Diana Dunn, 'Margaret of Anjou, Chivalry and the Order of the Garter', in *St George's Chapel Windsor in the Late Middle Ages*, ed. Colin Richmond and Eileen Scarff (Windsor, 2001), 39–40. See also Laynesmith, *Last Medieval Queens*, 150, for Margaret's responsibility for the education of her son and the didactic literature associated with her, and Radulescu, 'Preparing for Mature Years', 229–30.
[45] Radulescu, 'Preparing for Mature Years', 226–7.
[46] During Margaret's stay in Rouen in 1445, the wedding gifts presented to her by the citizens included twelve '*chargeurs*', twelve '*plats*' and twelve '*ecuelles*' contained in a decorated leather case bearing

the importance of English patrons to the high-end Rouen book trade, identifying a distinctive Rouen style of manuscript illumination linked to specific patrons including Shrewsbury, Fastolf and Hoo and their wives. While providing a new market for luxury books, the English did not depart from local artistic style, for both English and French buyers patronised the same artists, whose strongest stylistic influences came from the Netherlands.[47]

As the expedition to accompany Margaret of Anjou to England lasted far longer than had been anticipated, the noblemen and women in the royal escort found themselves over-wintering in Rouen with ample time for making purchases of locally produced luxury items; for example, Cecily, duchess of York, took the opportunity to order a new wardrobe of clothes to impress the new queen on her arrival.[48] This prolonged stay in Rouen also provided opportunities for Alice to patronise the local producers of books, and this may be the source of some of the volumes later in her library. Carol Meale's analysis of the twenty-two books listed in the inventory of 1466 of items brought to Ewelme from Wingfield in Suffolk, has shown that this well-travelled and intelligent lady owned a number of French books, indicating her exposure to a range of cultural influences through travel.[49] The inventory includes 'a frensh boke of quaterfilz Emond', a popular epic verse;[50] 'a frensh boke of le Citee de dames covered with rede lethere clasped with latoun newe', popular with French and English female readers from the time of its composition in about 1405 right through the century,[51] and 'a frensh boke of temps pastoure … containing divers stories', possibly Christine de Pizan's *Le Dit de la Pastoure*, completed in 1403, a text known to be in circulation in England during Alice's lifetime.[52]

The importance of queens and noblewomen as patrons and book-collectors in the fourteenth and fifteenth centuries has long been recognised.[53] There is a suggestion that their knowledge of Latin may have been limited to the understanding and use of liturgical texts and books of piety,[54] and French was the preferred language of secular books purchased for, or by, English aristocratic women such as the duch-

---

Rouen's emblem of an *agnus dei* and Margaret's emblem of a marguerite. The city also bestowed gifts on the marchioness of Suffolk and members of her household: BL. Add. MSS 26805–8.

[47] Catherine Reynolds, 'English Patrons and French Artists in Fifteenth-Century Normandy', in *England and Normandy in the Middle Ages*, ed. David Bates and Anne Curry (1994), 299–313.

[48] Laynesmith, *Cecily Duchess of York*, 46–7. Laynesmith points out that Cecily's dressmaker, Margaret Chamberlayne, came to the young queen's attention while in Rouen, and was brought from London to Southampton soon after Margaret reached England in April 1445 'for diverse business touching the said lady queen'. She received New Year's gifts from the queen on a number of occasions: *ibid.*, 47–8; *Letters and Papers*, ed. Stevenson, i. 452; TNA, E101/410/8.

[49] Bodl., Ewelme Muniments A 47.3; Goodall, *God's House at Ewelme*, 285–8; Meale, 'Reading Women's Culture', 93–5, 100.

[50] A prose version of this text was included in 'The Shrewsbury Book': BL, Royal MS 15 E.VI, ff. 155–206v (*Romance Quatre fils Aiman*).

[51] Meale, 'Reading Women's Culture', 86. The duchess of York also owned a copy of *Le Livre de la Cité des Dames* (BL, Royal MS 19. A. XIX), adapted for her use with her husband's emblems of the white rose and fetterlock added to f. 4: Laynesmith, *Cecily Duchess of York*, 42–3.

[52] It is included in BL, Harley 4431 (Collected Works of Christine de Pizan); Meale, 'Reading Women's Culture', 88–9.

[53] S.G. Bell, 'Medieval Women Book Owners: Arbiters of Lay Piety and Ambassadors of Culture', in *Women and Power in the Middle Ages*, ed. Mary Erler and Maryanne Kowaleski (Athens, GA, 1988), 149–79; C.M. Meale, '"… alle the bokes that I haue of latyn, englisch, and frensch": Laywomen and their Books in Late Medieval England', in *Women and Literature*, ed. Meale, 128–58.

[54] J.L. Laynesmith, '"To please … dame Cecely that in Latyn hath lityll intellect": Books and the

esses of York and Suffolk. From her examination of a range of evidence (rare book catalogues, wills and inventories and dedications to patrons), Susan Bell has established the important role played by high-ranking women book-owners in promoting cultural change, which could be achieved most effectively through their marriages to foreigners.[55] As the daughter of a highly cultured, book-loving aristocrat, Margaret of Anjou may well have played some part in the dissemination of French texts following her marriage to Henry VI.[56] It is very likely that she brought some books to England with her in 1445, including the 'London Book of Hours', also known as the 'Egerton Hours' (now British Library Egerton MS 1070) and *Les Grandes Chroniques de France* (Royal MS 20 C. VII).[57]

Once in England, and needing to adapt to her new way of life in the absence of any close family members, the question arises as to whom Margaret turned for advice and reassurance, as well as companionship.[58] The only reference to a relative who may have accompanied her from her homeland is to her niece, Marie, illegitimate daughter of Charles, count of Maine, who in 1457 married Thomas Courtenay, the son of Thomas, earl of Devon.[59] 'Parve Marione' was a recipient of gifts from the queen, and the queen paid for her cream and gold wedding gown. Widowed in 1461 following the battle of Towton, Marie was to accompany Margaret into exile in France in the 1460s.[60] Ralph Griffiths has commented on the close connection between the king's and the queen's households in the early years of their marriage, when they appear to have been in one another's company for much of the time. Although their households were distinct administrative organisations, they overlapped in their personnel, and Margaret's household was staffed by a number of people who had earlier served the king or had been engaged on Suffolk's mission to

---

Duchess of York', in *The Fifteenth Century XV. Writing, Records and Rhetoric*, ed. Linda Clark (2017), 37–56.

[55] Bell, 'Medieval Women Book Owners', 167–8. See also Radulescu, 'Preparing for Mature Years', 225–7.

[56] René of Anjou inherited a substantial library from his parents, housed in their castle at Angers, and he was also a book collector and patron of the arts, presiding over a magnificent court: Kekewich, *The Good King*, 19–20, 155–97. De la Marche compiled a list of René's books using an inventory from Angers (1471), the books that Charles, count of Maine, inherited from his uncle in 1480, and books that were mentioned as acquisitions in the king's accounts, totalling 202 items: Kekewich, *The Good King*, 19 n. 28; Lecoy de la Marche, *Le Roi René*, ii. 182–97. Radulescu emphasises the importance of Yolande of Aragon, Margaret's grandmother, as a commissioner of books and shaper of Margaret's political thinking: 'Preparing for Mature Years', 219–33. For an alternative view of Margaret's formative years and her book ownership, see Anthony Gross, 'A Mirror for Princes: Antoine de la Sale and the Political Psyche of Margaret of Anjou', in *The Fifteenth Century XVII. Finding Individuality*, ed. Linda Clark (Woodbridge, 2020), 61–80.

[57] Cron, *Margaret of Anjou*, 42; *Royal Manuscripts: The Genius of Illumination* (British Library Exhibition Catalogue, 2011), ed. Scot McKendrick, John Lowden and Kathleen Doyle, 404; Anne F. Sutton and Livia Visser-Fuchs, *Richard III's Books: Ideas and Reality in the Life and Library of a Medieval Prince* (Stroud, 1997), 289–90. For suggestions of other books brought by Margaret to England, see Radulescu, 'Preparing for Mature Years', 226–7.

[58] Margaret also lacked a mother-figure from the king's side of the family as a source of guidance, for Henry VI's mother, Katherine de Valois, having married a Welsh squire (Owen Tudor) in 1430, had died in 1437. Anne Crawford notes Henry VI's isolation from the age of eight, and that he was 'brought up by ageing, distinguished soldiers': *Letters of the Queens of England*, ed. Crawford, 119.

[59] Historians frequently confuse the two Thomas Courtenays, the senior of whom died in 1458. See Griffiths, *Reign of Henry VI*, 802, 847 n. 175.

[60] Cron, *Margaret of Anjou*, 239, 379, 534 n. 61; *CPR*, 1446–52, p. 240; Laynesmith, *Last Medieval Queens*, 194 n. 64; TNA, E101/410/14, 19.

France. Griffiths notes that 'This brotherhood of household service was very much of Suffolk's achievement'.[61] Margaret's five jewel accounts, for 1445–6, 1446–7, 1448–9, 1451–2 and 1452–3, together with her only surviving household accounts (for 1452–3), provide us with evidence about some of the people close to her in those years.[62] They included many of the female members of her personal escort from Rouen to England. The highest-ranking ladies were Alice, now duchess of Suffolk, who 'held the principal place of honour about the person of the Queen',[63] Jacquetta of Luxembourg, dowager-duchess of Bedford, who had secretly married Richard Wydeville, son of Bedford's chamberlain, Lady Talbot, Lady Scales, and Lady Grey. All received gifts of jewels. It is significant that another recipient of gifts from the queen in the years 1445–7 was John de la Pole, the young son of the duke and duchess of Suffolk, and servants of the duchess of Suffolk were also beneficiaries of her generosity in 1445–6 and 1452–3.[64] In addition, in 1448–9 Margaret made a gift of a golden 'armill' to Anne Wroughton *'camerar' domine ducisse Suff'* on her marriage, and another present to Robert Bulkeley, *'valetto camera ipse domine'*.[65] This surely can be taken as evidence of a continuing closeness of relationship between Margaret and Alice after their shared journey from France.

Suffolk's influence can be seen in some of the appointments made to the queen's household, and it is feasible that Alice also played a part in the selection of those appointed to look after Margaret's personal welfare. The couple's chaplain, Walter Lyhert, who accompanied them to Rouen in 1444–5, was officially assigned to the queen's household as her confessor soon after her arrival in England. He received New Year's gifts from Margaret in 1446 and 1447.[66] Other members of Suffolk's embassy to bring the queen to England included George Ashby, who became her clerk of the signet, and Sir John Wenlock, who served as usher of her chamber and later her chamberlain. Slightly more at a distance, John Norris, successively keeper of the queen's jewels and of her wardrobe in the years 1445–57, and whose wife was one of her ladies-in-waiting, was associated with Suffolk in the establishment of the king's new college at Eton, and Suffolk acted as a feoffee for him.[67] Yet while these connections reinforced amicable relations between duke, duchess and queen, this close association between members of Margaret's household and Suffolk's intimates did her no good in the longer term, damaging her reputation long after Suffolk was dead.[68]

The royal court in fifteenth-century England is not an easy institution to define.[69] An idealised image of it is depicted on the dedicatory page of the 'Shrewsbury Book'. On either side of the enthroned king and queen are gathered their courtiers, segregated by gender, men to the right of the king and two women to the left of the queen.[70] The women's fashionable costume and elaborate head-dresses indicate

[61] Griffiths, *Reign of Henry VI*, 257, 360–1.
[62] Myers, 'Jewels of Queen Margaret', 113–31; *idem*, 'Household of Queen Margaret', 79–113, 391–431.
[63] Strickland, *Lives of the Queens*, i. 553.
[64] TNA, E101/409/14, 17; 410/2, 8, 11.
[65] TNA, E101/410/2.
[66] *Letters of Margaret of Anjou*, ed. Maurer and Cron, 45; BL, Add. MS 23938; TNA, E101/409/14, 17; R.J. Schoeck, 'Lyhert, Walter', *Oxford DNB*.
[67] *House of Commons 1422–61*, ed. Clark, iii. 93–6; v. 670–7; vii. 417–30.
[68] Laynesmith, *Last Medieval Queens*, 230.
[69] *Ibid.*, 220–1.
[70] BL, Royal MS 15 E.VI, f. 2.

their high status. The leading lady's left hand rests on the dais upon which the royal couple are seated, perhaps signalling a direct connection with the kneeling earl as he presents her with his book; this may well represent the countess of Shrewsbury, and perhaps the lady behind her is Alice, marchioness of Suffolk. The court had effectively been in abeyance since the death of Henry V, but the arrival of Margaret, and the confirmation of the king's maturity by his marriage, became the occasion for its revitalisation. It had an important part to play in the projection of a positive image of the monarchy, and the queen was expected to be present for such formal state occasions as the ennoblement of peers and the observance of religious festivals. She was also the subject of certain royal rituals in her own right, some of which were closely connected with the legitimacy of the monarchy, when the most important audience was the high nobility upon whose support the king was most dependent.[71] A queen's major rites of passage were her marriage, coronation, the birth of heirs to the throne and the churching ceremonies that followed their births. These rituals of queenship provided opportunities for her to bond with her female peers whose role was to support and counsel her on the etiquette of each occasion, based on English custom and their own personal experiences.

Following Margaret's arrival in England, a private ceremony of matrimony had been held in Titchfield Abbey on 22 April 1445, conducted by William Aiscough, bishop of Salisbury, the king's confessor. Her first major public ceremony and rite of passage was her coronation, preceded by her state entry into the city of London celebrated with a series of lavish pageants staged at key points on her route through the city to St Paul's Cathedral, and on the day of her coronation from the Tower of London to the palace at Westminster and thence to Westminster Abbey. The pageants emphasised Margaret's role as the bringer of peace with France,[72] while the coronation brought together the highest-ranking members of the clergy, the nobility and the knights of the realm. Other ceremonial occasions that are likely to have brought the queen into direct contact with some of her leading ladies, including Alice, duchess of Suffolk, are those associated with the Order of the Garter. A copy of its statutes was written in the 'Shrewsbury Book',[73] and the gift ensured that Margaret had access to a text linking the English monarchy back to the glory days of chivalry and military prowess embodied in the founder of the Order, Edward III. As James Gillespie revealed, from early on ceremonies associated with the Order were not entirely masculine affairs, for a small number of highly favoured women (up to a maximum of fourteen) were granted the robes of the Order from its earliest days until the end of the reign of Henry VII.[74] These ladies included the queens of England from Philippa of Hainault to Elizabeth of York, and it is likely that the selection of others so honoured rested with the king.[75] Although Henry VI showed little personal interest in chivalric ideals and in the Order, during his reign each female recipient was closely related to him and was the wife, daughter or widow

---

[71] Laynesmith, *Last Medieval Queens*, 72–3, 221, 242, 250–1.
[72] *Ibid.*, 82–110. See also Cron, *Margaret of Anjou*, 32–9.
[73] Dunn, 'Margaret of Anjou ... and the Order of the Garter', 39–56.
[74] James Gillespie, 'Ladies of the Fraternity of Saint George and the Garter', *Albion*, xvii (1985), 259–78.
[75] *Ibid.*, 264; Dunn, 'Margaret of Anjou ... and the Order of the Garter', 44–8; Hugh Collins, 'The Order of the Garter, 1348–1461: Chivalry and Politics in Later Medieval England', in *Courts, Counties and the Capital in the Later Middle Ages*, ed. D.E.S. Dunn (Stroud, 1996), 155–80.

of a Knight of the Garter.[76] Alice Chaucer had first received her robes as early in the reign as May 1432, not long after her marriage to William de la Pole, then earl of Suffolk, and at the same time as Isabel, second wife of Richard Beauchamp, earl of Warwick,[77] and the importance with which she regarded her membership of the Order is evident from her tomb effigy in the parish church of Ewelme where she is depicted wearing her garter on her left arm.[78] Although women were excluded from the formal chapter assemblies held annually on the eve of the feast of St George, they attended high mass and evensong held on St George's Day in the chapel at Windsor castle, seated in their own closet in the rood loft.[79] Their presence at the feast itself would have added to the spectacle and sociability of the occasion. Queen Margaret herself was granted robes for life on 12 April 1447.[80] The grant may have been made at the behest of Margaret and her friends, perhaps by William de la Pole, rather than on the initiative of the king himself,[81] but whatever the circumstances of Margaret's admission to the Order, the annual garter ceremonies attended by both the duke and duchess of Suffolk in the later 1440s provided useful opportunities for socialising.

Of necessity both Margaret and Alice led peripatetic lifestyles, moving from one residence to another as circumstances demanded. The queen's principal residences in the early years of her marriage were at Westminster, Windsor, Greenwich (given to her after the death of Humphrey, duke of Gloucester, in 1447), Sheen and Eltham. We know that she liked to hunt and can imagine her enjoying the freedom to exercise provided by the extensive royal park at Windsor.[82] Alice's wealth from lands inherited from both sides of her family (Chaucer and Burghersh) and her right to dower and jointure from her first two husbands, Sir John Phelip (d. 1415)[83] and Thomas, earl of Salisbury, provided her with the means to enjoy an extremely comfortable lifestyle in emulation of the royal family.[84] She also travelled regularly between her principal residences of Wingfield in East Anglia, and Ewelme in Oxfordshire, as well as spending time in London each year in order to attend on the queen and participate in ceremonial occasions. Although it is difficult to calculate how much time she spent at court during Suffolk's ascendancy, records of occasional payments indicate her continued attendance on the queen after 1445. Notable among these was the enormous sum of £200 authorised in January 1447 for her doing so 'for much

---

[76] Gillespie, 'Ladies of the Fraternity', 262–4. See also P.J. Begent and Hubert Chesshyre, *The Most Noble Order of the Garter: 650 Years* (1999), 100.

[77] John Anstis, *The Register of the Most Noble Order of the Garter* (2 vols, 1724), ii. 124. Thereafter Alice was a regular recipient of garter robes, certainly in 1434–6, 1439–46, 1448 and 1449: R.E. Archer, 'Alice Chaucer, Duchess of Suffolk (d.1475), and Her East Anglian Estates', in *Wingfield College and its Patrons: Piety and Patronage in Medieval Suffolk*, ed. Peter Bloore and Edward Martin (Woodbridge, 2015), 189.

[78] H.A. Napier, *Historical Notices of the Parishes of Swyncombe and Ewelme* (Oxford, 1858), 102; Archer, 'Alice Chaucer and Her East Anglian Estates', 187; Goodall, *God's House*, 175–91, plate 82; C.B. Newham, *Country Church Monuments* (2022), 331, series of images, 198.

[79] Anstis, *Register*, i. 197; ii. 123; Dunn, 'Margaret of Anjou ... and the Order of the Garter', 45–7.

[80] TNA, E101/409/19; Dunn, 'Margaret of Anjou ... and the Order of the Garter', 45. There appears to have been some delay between the grant of robes to the queen and the first occasion on which she wore them, according to the great wardrobe accounts for 1449, TNA, E101/409/18.

[81] Gillespie, 'Ladies of the Fraternity', 273.

[82] *Letters of Margaret of Anjou*, ed. Maurer and Cron, 158–70.

[83] *House of Commons 1386–1421*, ed. Roskell et al., iv. 68–70.

[84] For an evaluation of Alice's estates and her wealth at death, see Archer, 'Chaucer, Alice', *Oxford DNB*.

of the year'.[85] These records can be supplemented by evidence of the close relationship between Margaret and Alice provided by the queen's gifts to the duchess, her son and her servants in 1446–7: six large gold plates each to Alice and Suffolk, worth £90, and 'an armlet like a horn decorated with pearls' and three diamonds worth £12 to their three-year-old son.[86] The location of the manor of Ewelme, in the Thames valley, upstream from Windsor, provided further opportunities for the two ladies to meet. The king is recorded as being in this locality during the first two weeks of August 1447 when he toured the area, leaving Windsor castle at the start of the month, travelling to High Wycombe, Tetsworth, Islip, Woodstock, Osney, Dorchester, Ewelme, Reading and Maidenhead before returning to Windsor,[87] and it is very likely that he was accompanied by Queen Margaret on this summer break which included being entertained by the duke and duchess of Suffolk at their newly rebuilt and palatial Ewelme residence. Ewelme had been the seat of Alice's father, and had come into her possession in 1437, following the death of her mother. John Goodall describes the work undertaken at Ewelme from September 1444, to create a magnificent new residence commensurate with de la Pole's new rank as a marquess, noting that the design of the house, constructed in brick, within a moat and arranged around a courtyard, had much in common with other major building projects of this date associated with the king and queen, in particular the cloister court at Eton College, begun in 1441 and erected under Suffolk's supervision, and the buildings of Queens' College, Cambridge, largely built by Margaret of Anjou in 1448–9.[88]

Conjecture surrounds Margaret's part in the negotiations for a permanent peace with France. Such negotiations had been started by Suffolk at Tours in 1444, but talks with a French embassy in the following year led only to an extension of the truce until November 1446.[89] Charles VII, encouraged by René of Anjou, then decided to work through the queen to persuade her susceptible husband to hand over the county of Maine to the Angevins as part of the final peace deal,[90] and Suffolk pursued this course, believing that Maine would be the price of Angevin goodwill.[91] Although Margaret had no formal role in the negotiation process, her actions have been deduced from a series of letters written by her to her uncle Charles VII between December 1445 and December 1446 in which she promised to help obtain the cession of Maine by putting pressure on her husband.[92] It is impossible to know the extent of Margaret's influence over her husband in these discussions, but even

---

[85] TNA, E404/63/14; E403/767, m. 11 (July 1447); Cron, *Margaret of Anjou*, 62.
[86] TNA, E101/409/17; Cron, *Margaret of Anjou*, 488.
[87] Wolffe, *Henry VI*, 94–5, 366.
[88] Goodall, *God's House*, 12–18. Griffiths regards Suffolk's involvement in the decision-making connected with Henry's educational establishments of Eton and King's College, Cambridge, in the later 1440s as 'paramount' (*Reign of Henry VI*, 246), and it is likely that he encouraged Margaret in her decision to found her own college: *CPR*, 1446–52, pp. 143–4. A copy of the foundation charter of Queen's College bearing the queen's personal seal is noted in W.G. Searle, *The History of Queen's College of St. Margaret and St. Bernard in the University of Cambridge, 1446–1560* (Cambridge, 1867), 15–16.
[89] Cron, *Margaret of Anjou*, 48–52; Griffiths, *Reign of Henry VI*, 490–3; Wolffe, *Henry VI*, 184–8.
[90] Kingsford, 'Policy and Fall of Suffolk', 158–63; Cron, *Margaret of Anjou*, 53–4.
[91] Watts, *Henry VI*, 221–6.
[92] *Letters of Margaret of Anjou*, ed. Maurer and Cron, 175–85. See also, *Letters and Papers*, ed. Stevenson, i. 164–7, 183–6; ii. 639–42; Griffiths, *Reign of Henry VI*, 494–5; Wolffe, *Henry VI*, 184–5; Maurer, *Margaret of Anjou*, 32–8.

though ultimately the decision was the king's,[93] her role was emphasised by those who became increasingly hostile to her after the loss of territories to the French in the final disastrous phases of the Hundred Years' War. One of the most vocal and persistent critics of both Suffolk and the queen in their pursuit of a peace policy was the Oxford theologian, Dr Thomas Gascoigne,[94] who in a series of notes written around 1457 accused Suffolk of agreeing to give up Maine and Anjou in 1444 in return for the safe conduct of Margaret to England. The deeply hostile Gascoigne accused Margaret of complicity in the promise made to the French 'at the urging of William Pole, duke of Suffolk, and his wife' thus, emphasising the malign influence of the duke and duchess of Suffolk over the queen.[95] Margaret's reputation was tarnished forever by Gascoigne and others, and Henry VI's marriage to a French woman came to be regarded as the root of all the troubles that befell the English from 1445 onwards.[96]

Despite many attempts to arrange a meeting between the kings of England and France, it became evident by 1448 that a permanent peace treaty was no closer, and the English cause was not helped by the arrival in Rouen of the arrogant Edmund Beaufort, duke of Somerset, to take over as lieutenant-general and governor of France. Beaufort alienated Charles VII by his uncompromising stance and 'discourteous tone', eventually provoking him to declare war on 31 July 1449.[97] The surrender of Rouen on 29 October, after a siege directed by Charles VII himself, ultimately sealed the fate of the duke of Suffolk.[98] The mood of the parliament that met eight days later was angry and hostile to the king's closest ministers, but it was not until the second session, which opened on 22 January 1450, that Suffolk came to face the Commons to defend himself and his conduct in France over the past fifteen years.[99] The charges brought against him hinged on the promises he had made to Charles VII in 1444 in Tours while negotiating the marriage of Henry VI to Margaret of Anjou, and he was accused of plotting with the king of France to put his young son on the throne.[100] Despite Suffolk's declarations of loyalty to Henry VI and denial of all the charges made against him, the king could not save his chief minister and it was agreed that, in lieu of a trial, Suffolk would be banished from all territories held by the English for five years. The strength of feeling against the king's favourite was evident from the way in which he met his violent death at the hands of sailors

---

[93] Cron, *Margaret of Anjou*, 53–4; *eadem*, 'Duke of Suffolk', 77–99. This view is supported by Wolffe who places responsibility for the surrender of Maine firmly on the king himself: *Henry VI*, 188–9, while Kekewich believes Margaret to have been very badly disposed towards her husband's subjects, and remaining loyal to the house of Valois: *The Good King*, 81–2, 100.
[94] Maurer, *Margaret of Anjou*, 29–38; Kingsford, 'Policy and Fall of Suffolk', 154–8.
[95] Gascoigne, *Loci e Libro Veritatum*, ed. J.E.T. Rogers (Oxford, 1881), 221. See the comments on Gascoigne's accusations against Suffolk in Wolffe, *Henry VI*, 181.
[96] Maurer, *Margaret of Anjou*, 25–30. Gascoigne, *Loci et Libro*, 204.
[97] Griffiths, *Reign of Henry VI*, 509, 514.
[98] *Ibid.*, 516–17; Kingsford, 'Policy and Fall of Suffolk', 166. See also the verdict on the end of Suffolk's political career in Archer, 'Alice Chaucer and her East Anglian Estates', 196.
[99] *PROME*, xii. 92–106; Kingsford, 'Policy and Fall of Suffolk', 167; Griffiths, *Reign of Henry VI*, 676–84; Wolffe, *Henry VI*, 219–29.
[100] Griffiths, *Reign of Henry VI*, 679; Kingsford, 'Policy and Fall of Suffolk', 167–71; Cron, *Margaret of Anjou*, 124–5; Archer, 'Alice Chaucer and her East Anglian Estates', 197; *Calendar of Papal Letters*, x. 472–3.

manning the *Nicholas of the Tower* who boarded the ship taking him into exile in the Low Countries on 2 May.[101]

The duke's estimation of his wife's qualities is clear from the letter he wrote to his young son while preparing for his exile, and in anticipation of his death. He commended John to God and the king, and instructed him 'to love, to worshepe youre lady and moder, and also that ye obey alwey hyr commaundements, and to beleve hyr councelles and advises in alle your werks'.[102] Suffolk's murder left Alice a widow for the third time, with a seven-year-old son to protect from his father's political enemies. The vulnerability of noblewomen widowed in times of war or political turmoil is well-known and Alice was especially vulnerable because of the powerful position previously held by her husband in the government and the violence of the backlash against him.[103] The vitriol in the personal attacks directed against her supports the view that she too was perceived as a powerful force at court. In the first session of the next parliament, which met in November 1450, the Commons demanded the removal of twenty-nine allegedly corrupt individuals, mostly former associates of Suffolk and members of the royal household perceived as having a malign influence on the king. At the top of the list, after the duke of Somerset, was the dowager duchess of Suffolk, a sure indication that Alice, in her own right, was regarded as a potentially dangerous and potent influence on the queen, and thereby on the monarch and not simply 'guilty by association' through the opprobrium heaped upon her late husband.[104] However, the attempt of the Commons to put her on trial for treason along with other prominent members of the Suffolk faction was overturned by the Lords.[105] That Alice should have succeeded both in defending herself against charges of treason and securing the de la Pole estates into her keeping during the minority of her son, is testimony to her strength of character and determination.[106] It may also reflect the continued importance of her connection with the queen, and a desire by Margaret to ensure that Alice was protected from the consequences of the

---

[101] Suffolk's death is described in a letter written by William Lomner to John Paston: *The Paston Letters and Papers of the Fifteenth Century*, ed. Norman Davis (2 vols, Oxford, 1971, 1976), ii. 35–6, no. 450.

[102] *The Paston Letters*, ed. Richard Beadle and Colin Richmond (Oxford, 2005), 82–3, no. 980, quoted in Archer, 'Alice Chaucer and her East Anglian Estates', 197–8. Archer describes the impact of the death on his widow: 'The death unleashed a battery of problems that were especially acute in East Anglia where the intense dislike of the dead duke rapidly became apparent ... Alice's survival now depended on her political wit and skills.'

[103] J.T. Rosenthal, 'Other Victims: Peeresses as War Widows, 1450–1500', *History*, lxxii (1987); M.A. Hicks, 'The Last Days of Elizabeth Countess of Oxford', *EHR*, ciii (1988), 76–95; Anne Crawford, 'Victims of Attainder: The Howard and de Vere Women in the Late Fifteenth Century', in *Women in Southern England* (Reading Medieval Studies, xv, 1989), 59–74. For a consideration of the consequences of Suffolk's death on the widowed duchess, see Archer, 'Alice Chaucer and her East Anglian Estates', 196–8, and for a wider discussion of the impact of widowhood on land-owning women, see Archer, 'Women as Landholders', 162–73.

[104] *PROME*, xii. 184–6; Griffiths, *Reign of Henry VI*, 308–9; Archer, 'Alice Chaucer and Her East Anglian Estates', 198. Laynesmith considers that 'the Commons' perception of the duchess's undue influence is a stronger indicator of friendship with the queen' than the evidence of Margaret of Anjou's New Years' gifts alone: Laynesmith, *Last Medieval Queens*, 210 n. 156.

[105] Griffiths, *Reign of Henry VI*, 309–10; Watts, *Henry VI*, 275 n. 60; Archer, 'Alice Chaucer and Her East Anglian Estates', 198. Many of the twenty-nine named individuals had close connections with the queen as members of her household since 1445 and it is likely that she would have been as keen as her husband to protect them from attack.

[106] Watts, *Henry VI*, 289 n. 125, points out that she had paid for the privilege of keeping her husband's lands by advancing 3,500 marks out of the proceeds before 8 October: *CPR*, 1446–52, p. 431.

violent assault on her husband. That some members of the queen's household with close links to the duke of Suffolk had left Margaret's service in 1450 to join Alice's household, perhaps indicates a genuine concern on the queen's part for the welfare of her friend as she faced an extremely difficult future.[107]

Margaret's failure to produce an heir to the throne had been the subject of adverse comment since 1448.[108] It is tempting to think that she and Alice conferred regularly about her failure to conceive a child since Alice seems to have experienced the same difficulty, and although, frustratingly, no letters between the two women survive, the queen's gifts to the servants of the duchess in 1452–3, post-dating the death of the duke of Suffolk, indicate a continuing closeness between the two women despite Alice's change in circumstances. At last, in the spring of 1453, Margaret made a pilgrimage to Walsingham to give thanks for her successful pregnancy and to pray for the safe delivery of a son.[109] In an undated letter to her from Cecily, duchess of York, the queen was asked to act as an intermediary between Cecily's husband, the duke of York, and the king, indicating Margaret's perceived political power. Cecily referred to Margaret's pregnancy, describing the child carried by her as 'the most precious, most ioyfull, and most comfortable ertheley tresor that might come unto this land and to the people therof'.[110] On 13 October Margaret gave birth to a healthy son, Prince Edward, who was baptised at Westminster Abbey by William Waynflete, bishop of Winchester. The role of the godparents (the chancellor, Cardinal John Kemp, the duke of Somerset, and Anne, duchess of Buckingham) was especially important as the king had collapsed into a catatonic state the previous August and there was no way of knowing when, or if, he would recover his senses.[111] The ceremony of churching, or purification, which customarily took place between thirty and sixty days after the birth, was an occasion for women to come together to support the new mother,[112] and the writ of summons issued under the privy seal for attendance at the

---

[107] Alice, the wife of Edward Grimston, a retainer of the duke and in royal service in the late 1440s, left court in 1450 to serve the dowager duchess: BL, Egerton Roll 8779, mm. 1, 8; and Grimston himself, who had been indicted in July 1450 for having plotted in 1447 with the late duke to put the duke's son and heir on the throne (KB27/762, rex rots 8, 15; R.L. Storey, *The End of the House of Lancaster* (1966), 74) long remained in Alice's service. Jacques Blondel, a Norman who was Margaret's avener and also in the service of the duke, was on board the ship taking Suffolk into exile; having escaped the same fate as his lord, he joined Alice's household: D.A.L. Morgan, 'The King's Affinity in the Polity of Yorkist England', *TRHS*, xxiii (1973), 14. I am grateful to Bonita Cron for these references.

[108] TNA, KB9/256/12, 260/40a; Dean and Chapter of Canterbury Archives, M. 239 (1448); Griffiths, *Reign of Henry VI*, 255–6; Laynesmith, *Last Medieval Queens*, 133–4.

[109] She made a gift of a gold tablet, with an angel holding a crucifix garnished with rubies, sapphires and pearls, worth £29, to the shrine of the Virgin Mary: TNA, E101/410/11; Myers, 'Jewels of Queen Margaret', 115, 124.

[110] Margaret's pilgrimage to Walsingham is also referred to in the letter, now Huntington Library, San Marino, California, Battle Abbey MS 937. See Carole Rawcliffe, 'Richard Duke of York, the King's "obeisant liegeman": A New Source for the Protectorates of 1454 and 1455', *HR*, lx (1987), 232–9; and for a more recent commentary, *Letters of Margaret of Anjou*, ed. Maurer and Cron, 195–9. Cecily Neville may have been a reassuring source of advice to the queen on the problems of conception, having herself waited ten years before her first pregnancy when she was aged twenty-four, and thereafter giving birth to twelve children: Laynesmith, *Cecily Duchess of York*, 35–53, 60–1.

[111] Griffiths, *Reign of Henry VI*, 715–18; Wolffe, *Henry VI*, 270–3.

[112] Laynesmith, *Last Medieval Queens*, 115–18. The queen's household accounts for 1452–3 record payments for a 'chrisom-robe', a white robe put on a child at baptism as a token of innocence and given as an offering at the mother's purification (TNA, E101/410/11), and the king gave his wife the cost of an embroidered chrisom-cloth, with 20 yards of russet cloth of gold, called 'tisshu', and 540 'broun

ceremony of purification of Queen Margaret to take place at Westminster Abbey on 18 November lists those ladies of rank expected to attend: ten duchesses, eight countesses, a viscountess, and seventeen of lesser rank. The inclusion of Alice, dowager duchess of Suffolk, three years after the death of the duke, is an indication of her continuing relationship with the queen.[113]

Despite the vulnerability of her position and the continued enmity expressed against anyone with close personal connections to the late duke of Suffolk, Alice showed herself a resolute fighter and a politically astute operator. Sensing the tide gradually beginning to turn against Henry VI and his queen, she began to look elsewhere for allies in high places, earning her the reputation of a 'trimmer'.[114] Embroiled in disputes over the de la Pole estates in East Anglia, she needed to work hard to make potentially beneficial alliances to secure her son's future. Historians have generally considered that, in the longer term, the relationship between Margaret and Alice did not work in the queen's favour and that Margaret's reputation was permanently damaged by her friendship with the duke and duchess of Suffolk.[115] Laynesmith also considers that the connection impacted in a negative way on Margaret's role as queen, preventing her from being impartial in the way that historians have implied she should have been.[116] Yet it is possible to see the relationship in a more positive light, and to regard Alice as a worldly-wise pragmatist who provided the queen with sage advice during the early years of her marriage and an example to follow as the king's health and capabilities failed and political circumstances changed. It could be argued that Margaret demonstrated the same qualities of determination and strength of character in the face of adversity as Alice had shown, when she was forced to fill the power vacuum left by her husband's fragile mental state after 1453. In 1456 she withdrew the court from an increasingly pro-Yorkist London to Coventry, in her search for support for the king and Prince Edward from retainers with connections to their duchy of Lancaster estates in the midlands and the north-west.[117] Just as Alice fought to protect her young son's interests from her late husband's enemies, Margaret took the initiative to defend Prince Edward's position as heir to the throne against his rival Yorkist supporters. There is no conclusive evidence to link either Margaret of Anjou or Alice Chaucer to any surviving copies of Christine de Pizan's *Livre des trois vertus*, but this book was readily available to high-status women in the mid-fifteenth century,[118] and they both owned other texts written by her, so it is very likely that they were both familiar with Christine's words of advice addressed

---

sable bakkes' worth altogether the enormous sum of £554 16s. 8d.: Frederick Devon, *Issues of the Exchequer* (1837), 748. Presumably, the sables and gold cloth attired the queen and dignitaries present at the christening.

[113] Lincoln's Inn, Hale MS 12, item 75, cited in Joseph Hunter, *Three Catalogues describing the Contents of the Red Book of the Exchequer, of the Dodsworth Manuscripts in the Bodleian Library* (1838), 277.

[114] For an overview of Alice's life after 1450, see Archer, 'Alice Chaucer and Her East Anglian Estates', 198–205.

[115] Tout, 'Margaret of Anjou', *DNB*; Kekewich, *The Good King*, 116; *Letters of the Queens of England*, ed. Crawford, 123.

[116] Laynesmith, *Last Medieval Queens*, 230–1.

[117] Griffiths, *Reign of Henry VI*, 772–90; Wolffe, *Henry VI*, 302–12; Cron, *Margaret of Anjou*, 230–41.

[118] Laynesmith, *Last Medieval Queens*, 3–4, 150; Meale, 'Reading Women's Culture', 100–1; C.C. Willard, 'Christine de Pizan and "The Manuscript Tradition" of the *Livre des Trois Vertus* and Christine de Pizan's Audience', *Journal of the History of Ideas*, xxvii (1966), 433–44; idem, 'A Fifteenth-Century View of Women's Role in Medieval Society: Christine de Pizan's *Livre des Trois Vertus*', in *The Role of Woman in the Middle Ages*, ed. R.T. Morewedge (Albany, NY, 1975), 90–120.

to 'all princesses, empresses, queens, duchesses and high-born ladies ruling over the Christian world, and generally to all women'.[119] They responded to Christine's advice in their own ways by adjusting their behaviour according to circumstance and remaining strong in the face of adversity.[120]

In 1458, through the marriage of her son John, duke of Suffolk, to the duke of York's daughter Elizabeth, Alice, dowager duchess of Suffolk, was brought into York's orbit, and when Queen Margaret was captured by the Yorkists following the Lancastrian defeat at the battle of Tewkesbury in 1471, Elizabeth's brother Edward IV decided to place her in the custody of John and his mother, at Wallingford castle and nearby Ewelme. Though unknown, the reason for this decision must surely be significant.[121] Following the deaths of both Margaret's husband in the Tower of London and their son at Tewkesbury, Margaret was no longer a threat to the Yorkists and, as with all widowed queens, she was more of an expensive encumbrance than a political liability.[122] Alice, albeit now an elderly lady, was still in control of extensive and valuable estates inherited from her parents, through her rights to jointure and dower from her three husbands, and through the acquisition of yet more land in the 1450s and 1460s, while also acting as a creditor of the crown.[123] An inventory of goods and books compiled in 1466 when Alice had left Wingfield to return to her own family home at Ewelme provides an insight into the lifestyle enjoyed by the dowager in the closing years of her life, when she spent some of her time in the company of 'her old friend' Margaret. The inventory provides information about the layout and opulent furnishings and decoration of the principal rooms at Ewelme which would have certainly provided accommodation fit for a former queen.[124] This may have been the time when the two ladies experienced the benefits of a true friendship going back over thirty years, enjoying each other's company and sharing their common interests. They may have spent long hours seated in 'my lady's closet' reading some of the books in French and Latin collected by Alice over her lifetime and attending daily worship in her private chapel where a priest conducted services using 'the masse boke covered with white leather' listed in the Ewelme inventory alongside other high quality and richly bound service books.[125] The precise duration of Margaret's stay is unclear, although regular payments for her 'diets' made to John,

---

For a discussion of the application of Christine de Pizan's advice to women as landholders in general, and to Alice Chaucer in particular, see Archer, 'Women as Landholders', 148–81.

[119] Christine de Pisan, *The Treasure of the City of Ladies*, trans. Sarah Lawson (Harmondsworth, 1985), 35.

[120] C.C. Willard, 'Christine de Pizan's *Livre des Trois Vertus*: Feminine Ideal or Practical Advice?', in *Ideals for Women in the Works of Christine de Pizan: A Collection of Essays*, ed. Diane Bornstein (Detroit, MI, 1981), 93–113.

[121] On 8 January 1472 Sir John Paston reported to his mother, 'As for Qween Margrett, I vndreston þat sche is remeuyd from Wyndeshor to Walyngfforthe, nyghe to Ewhelme, my lady of Suffolk place in Oxenfforthe schyre': *Paston Letters*, ed. Davis, i. 446, no. 266; Napier, 'Historical Notices', 101. By this time Alice's son held the custody of Wallingford castle jointly with his wife: *CPR, 1461–7*, p. 45. Elizabeth was given an allowance of £5 6s. 8d. a day to feed Margaret and her ladies: C.L. Scofield, *The Life and Reign of Edward the Fourth* (2 vols, 1923), ii. 23. For Alice's expenses incurred looking after the former queen: E405/56, rot. 3.

[122] *Letters of the Queens of England*, ed. Crawford, 124; Laynesmith, *Last Medieval Queens*, 170–1.

[123] Archer, 'Chaucer, Alice', *Oxford DNB*; eadem, 'Alice Chaucer and Her East Anglian Estates', 187–205.

[124] Goodall, *God's House*, Appendix VII, 282–9.

[125] Ibid., 287; Bodl. Ewelme Muniments A 47 (3). See also Meale, 'Reading Women's Culture', 82–101.

Lord Dudley, the constable of the Tower of London from Easter 1473, indicate that she was placed in more secure accommodation at a time coinciding with a rising against Edward IV led by John de Vere, earl of Oxford.[126] Perhaps it was feared that she might be a figurehead for the rebels, although it is hard to believe that the king regarded her as any serious threat, and it is likely that she enjoyed considerable freedom of movement while living either in royal apartments within the Tower or at Windsor castle.[127]

Alice died at the age of seventy, on either 20 May or 9 June 1475.[128] Shortly afterwards a permanent peace settlement between England and France was finally negotiated by Edward IV with Louis XI following their meeting at Picquigny on 25 August, and arrangements were subsequently made for the return of Queen Margaret to her homeland, as part of a financial package favourable to the English.[129] Margaret spent the last seven years of her life in France, initially in her father's castle of Reculée near Angers and then, after his death in 1480, at the chateau de Dampierre near Saumur, as a pensioner of the king of France.[130]

---

[126] TNA, E405/56–9.
[127] She was admitted to the London Skinners' fraternity of the Assumption of the Virgin in July 1475 at the same time as her lady-in-waiting Dame Katherine Vaux, two of Queen Elizabeth's ladies and one of her household officers, indicating that she was enjoying the lifestyle appropriate to her status: Laynesmith, *Last Medieval Queens*, 171–2.
[128] Archer, 'Chaucer, Alice', *Oxford DNB*. Her monumental inscription has 20 May, her inquisition *post mortem* 9 June.
[129] Charles Ross, *Edward IV* (1974), 231–8.
[130] Cron, *Margaret of Anjou*, 454–60; Griffiths, *Reign of Henry VI*, 892. She was accompanied to France by Katherine Vaux, who witnessed Margaret's will on 2 August 1482 shortly before her death aged fifty-two on 25 August.

'BROKEN BY AGE AND REDUCED BY POVERTY': CARE FOR THE ELDERLY IN LATE MEDIEVAL ENGLISH ALMSHOUSES[1]

Carole Rawcliffe

In about 1500, Joan Lunde, 'widoo, being of greate age', began a lawsuit in the court of chancery against the master of St Giles's hospital, Beverley. Her case hinged upon a contract that she and her late husband had allegedly made with his predecessor some twelve years earlier on their retirement from 'the bysynesses of the world'. In return for free board and lodging in the hospital for life, the couple surrendered £12 in cash, along with jewels and goods of even greater value, and a reversionary title to all their remaining possessions. Their corrody was to comprise a cell or private chamber in the south part of the infirmary, the sole use of a nearby garden, an allocation of two loaves of bread and two gallons of ale every fortnight, three meals a year at the master's table and all the other unnamed benefits to which the resident brothers and sisters were then entitled.[2] Earlier regulations suggest that these last – or their monetary equivalent – may have been generous, since the poor men and women for whom the hospital had originally been founded had been promised a regular supply of eggs, poultry, cheese, mutton, beef and pork, as well as a daily helping of potage, a nutritious porridge made of oatmeal, peas and sometimes bacon.[3] Joan's grievance had nothing to do with the paucity of her rations, but with the fact that she had recently been evicted from the garden upon which she had lavished considerable sums of money and threatened with the loss of her remaining privileges should she object. Reformers who had spent decades campaigning for the removal of affluent pensioners from institutions that were supposed to assist the sick and destitute are unlikely to have sympathised with her predicament.[4] On the other hand, however,

---

[1] Pride of place among the 'rich old ladies' about whom Rowena Archer has written during her long and distinguished career goes to Alice Chaucer, duchess of Suffolk, co-founder with her husband of one of England's most celebrated medieval almshouses, at Ewelme in Oxfordshire. Having known Rowena since her days as a postgraduate student, long before my attention turned from members of the political elite to their sick and destitute dependents, I am delighted to contribute an essay on our shared interest to this *festschrift* in her honour.

[2] TNA, C1/242/72.

[3] *The Register of William Wickwane, Lord Archbishop of York, 1279–1285*, ed. William Brown (Surtees Society, cxiv, 1907), 137–8.

[4] Carole Rawcliffe, 'A Crisis of Confidence? Parliament and the Demand for Hospital Reform in Early-15th- and Early-16th-Century England', *Parliamentary History*, xxxv (2016), 85–110.

Bishop Deane of Salisbury, the chancellor to whom Joan addressed her petition, would almost certainly have appreciated the extent of her loss and the beneficial effects that a garden would have had upon her health and emotional well-being. Being by then a man of at least sixty, and thus in contemporary medical terms elderly, if not aged, he too would have derived 'greate yertheley comfort' from access to green space, or, at the very least, have been encouraged to do so by his physicians.[5]

The ubiquity of gardens in late medieval English hospitals and almshouses reflects a practical need to grow produce as cheaply as possible for communal use. Yet the therapeutic value of gentle outdoor activity and the positive outlook that it engendered were also widely recognised, especially in institutions for the elderly.[6] Each resident of John Barstaple's almshouse in Bristol tended his own individual plot, while those at Gregg's almshouse in Hull shared a common garden where they could take daily exercise and grow herbs in pots 'for the welefare of them alle'.[7] The lack of such facilities at St Anthony's hospital, London, was solved by royal letters patent of 1429 permitting the acquisition of land 'for the recreation of the inmates', who included almsmen.[8] Elsewhere, horticulture assumed a moral dimension as an antidote to the corrosive effects of inertia or depression.[9] At St Mary's hospital, Yarmouth, the warden could compel anyone who was still fit enough 'to worke or digg in theire gardens or to dresse them' in return for an appropriate reward.[10] That well-kept grounds devoid of unsightly overgrowth, 'unclene water or any filth' would create a healthier environment was impressed upon the thirteen inmates of God's House, Ewelme, who had to 'kepe clene the closter and the quadrate abowte the welle fro wedis and all odyr unclennesse and theyr gardeyns and aleis [paths]' on pain of lost wages.[11] Setting aside the assumption that anyone 'ybroke with age or any other maner ympotence' should be fined for neglecting his responsibilities, these arrangements may strike the reader as surprisingly modern, given the emphasis currently placed in geriatric care upon exposure to green spaces and the need to encourage mobility.[12] A long and influential tradition of Greco-Arabic medicine

---

[5] See *Oxford DNB*, xv. 634–6, for Deane's biography.

[6] Carole Rawcliffe, '"Delectable Sightes and Fragrant Smelles": Gardens and Health in Late Medieval and Early Modern England', *Garden History*, xxxvi (2008), 3–21. In 1440 the resident bedesmen at the hospital of St Mary in the Newarke, Leicester, complained that land assigned by the founder a century earlier for their garden had been wrongfully appropriated: A.H. Thompson, *The History of the Hospital and New College of the Annunciation of St Mary in the Newarke, Leicester* (Leicester, 1937), 109.

[7] Elizabeth Prescott, *The English Medieval Hospital, 1050–1640* (1992), 99; John Tickell, *The History of the Town and County of Kingston-upon-Hull* (Hull, 1798), 758. The foundation charter of William Wynard's almshouse in Exeter also refers to a communal garden: Devon RO, Exeter, ED/WA/2.

[8] *CPR*, 1422–9, pp. 517–18.

[9] At the earl of Arundel's almshouse in Arundel, gardening and weeding the churchyard were believed to 'guard against idleness, the parent and fomenter of every other disorder': M.A. Tierney, *The History and Antiquities of the Castle and Town of Arundel* (2 vols, 1834), ii. 666.

[10] 'The Cartulary of St Mary's Hospital, Great Yarmouth', ed. Carole Rawcliffe, in *Poverty and Wealth: Sheep, Taxation and Charity in Late Medieval Norfolk*, ed. Mark Bailey, Maureen Jurkowski and Carole Rawcliffe (Norfolk Record Society, lxxi, 2007), 187, 229. The residents of Archbishop Chichele's almshouse at Higham Ferrers were likewise expected to cultivate the communal garden: BL, Lansdowne MS 846, f. 79.

[11] J.A.A. Goodall, *God's House at Ewelme* (Aldershot, 2001), 241.

[12] As an example of a significant and growing academic literature, see T.L. Scott, B.M. Masser and N.A. Pachana, 'Positive Aging Benefits of Home and Community Gardening Activities: Older Adults Report Enhanced Self-Esteem, Productive Endeavors, Social Engagement and Exercise', *SAGE*

maintained similar priorities, albeit for reasons based upon ideas about human physiology and the ageing process that are very different from our own.[13]

Advice about the preservation of health from the cradle to the grave derived from a genre of medical writing known as the *regimen sanitatis*, which developed in western Europe from the early thirteenth century onward.[14] On the basis that, once lost, a sound constitution would be hard, if not impossible, to recover, the conventional *regimen* explained how six external factors known as 'non-naturals' might be managed to avoid illness and postpone the onset of old age. Diet, 'the first instrument of medicine', played a vital role in fending off disease and prolonging youth. So too did a salubrious environment in which the air remained free of the pollutants and miasmas associated with disease, invigorating rather than infecting those who breathed it. Stress, a source of both physical and spiritual sickness, could be relieved through recourse to activities such as gardening that dispelled anger, depression, anxiety and other negative emotions ('accidents of the soul'). The other non-naturals addressed the balance between exercise and rest ('movement and repose'), the hygiene of sleep and the procedures and practices that could purge potentially dangerous matter from the body ('expulsion and repletion').[15]

Initially produced for, or dedicated to, prominent individuals, such as Beatrice of Savoy and her four daughters (who included Henry III's queen, Eleanor of Provence), these guides grew increasingly popular as the demand for self-help manuals spread among the general public.[16] The vernacular French regimen dedicated to Beatrice, which contains a carefully organised chapter on 'how to delay ageing and keep oneself young', was composed by the Italian physician Aldobrandino of Siena in about 1257 and circulated widely during the later Middle Ages.[17] In response to this burgeoning demand, the authors of *regimina* began to target designated audiences, such as urban magistrates and the parents of young children. Although comparatively few texts focused specifically upon the health of the elderly before the end of the fifteenth century, an awareness of the basic recommendations involved, and of the importance of the 'non naturals' at all stages of human development, was widespread.[18] Research undertaken over the last few decades has confirmed that the

---

    Open Medicine, viii (2020), 1–13: https://journals.sagepub.com/doi/pdf/10.1177/2050312120901732 [accessed October 2021].

[13] Daniel Schäfer, trans. Patrick Baker, *Old Age and Disease in Early Modern Medicine* (2011), 11–39.

[14] Pedro Gil Sotres, 'The Regimens of Health', in *Western Medical Thought from Antiquity to the Middle Ages*, ed. M.D. Grmek (Cambridge, MA, 1998), 291–318; Marylin Nicoud, *Les régimes de santé au moyen âge* (2 vols, Rome, 2007).

[15] L.J. Rather, 'The Six Things Non-Natural: A Note on the Origins and Fate of a Doctrine and Phrase', *Clio Medica*, iii (1968), 337–47.

[16] Carole Rawcliffe, 'The Concept of Health in Late Medieval Society', in *Le interazioni fra economia e ambiente biologico nell' Europa preindustriale secc. XIII–XVIII*, ed. Simonetta Cavaciocchi (Florence, 2010), 331–2.

[17] BL, Sloane MS 2435, ff. 31–2v. For an edition of the text, see *Le Régime du corps de Maître Aldebrandin de Sienne: texte français du XIIIe siècle*, ed. Louis Landouzy and Roger Pépin (Paris, 1911), and for its dissemination, Françoise Fery-Hue, 'Le Régime du corps d'Aldebrandin de Sienne: Tradition manuscrite et diffusion', in *Santé, médecine et assistance au moyen âge: Actes du 110e congrès national des sociétés savantes, Montpellier, 1985* (Paris, 1987), 114–15.

[18] Luke Demaitre, 'The Care and Extension of Old Age in Medieval Medicine', in *Aging and the Aged in Medieval Europe*, ed. M.M. Sheehan (Toronto, 1990), 3–22. The *De retardatione accidentum senectutis*, erroneously attributed to Roger Bacon, included a popular regimen for the elderly: Roger Bacon, *De retardatione accidentum senectutis*, ed. A.G. Little and Edward Withington (Oxford, 1928), 90–5. For an English version produced c. 1458–68, see 'On Tarrying the Accidents of Age', ed. C.A.

better managed late medieval leper houses and open ward hospitals for the sick poor sought to apply these principles, notably with regard to hygiene, diet and the creation of an atmosphere conducive to the spiritual welfare of patrons and patients.[19] Did the founders of almshouses for the accommodation of the old and vulnerable follow suit? Is it, indeed, even possible to speak of a coherent policy of care in the context of institutions that have been compared to Victorian sweatshops, and their residents to 'secular workhorses of prayer'?[20]

Levels of support

Throughout the later Middle Ages, and especially in the years following the arrival of plague in 1348, a 'privileged sub-group' of elderly men and women ended their days in charitable institutions.[21] Those who survived successive epidemics enjoyed a better diet and healthier living conditions than before, and therefore tended to live longer, but a combination of stagnant birth rates and high mortality meant that they often lacked family support in their old age. As a result, the need for residential care became more pressing. Affluent corrodians like Joan Lunde and her husband paid handsomely for places in established hospitals,[22] while others gained free – or almost free – admittance to the almshouses that were springing up across England in growing numbers for the support of the deserving poor.[23] The focus in what follows is inevitably upon the wealthier, better documented and more tightly regulated of these establishments, many of which were purpose built by senior clergy, aristocrats, merchants and urban communities as conspicuous statements of personal piety and philanthropic intent. Others either developed as adjuncts to hospitals for the sick poor or were re-foundations of hospitals and leper houses that no longer served a

---

Everest and M.T. Tavormina, in *Sex, Aging and Death in a Medieval Medical Compendium*, ed. M.T. Tavormina (2 vols, Tempe, AZ, 2006), i. 133–247.

[19] Peregrine Horden, 'A Non-natural Environment: Medicine without Doctors in the Medieval European Hospital', in *The Medieval Hospital and Medical Practice*, ed. B.S. Bowers (Farnham, 2007), 133–45; Christopher Bonfield, 'Therapeutic Regime for Bodily Health in Medieval English Hospitals', in *Hospital Life: Theory and Practice from the Medieval to the Modern*, ed. Laurinda Abreu and Sally Sheard (Oxford, 2013), 21–48; Carole Rawcliffe, 'Medicine for the Soul: The Medieval Hospital and the Quest for Spiritual Health', in *Religion, Health and Suffering*, ed. J.R. Hinnells and Roy Porter (1999), 316–38.

[20] Colin Richmond, 'The English Gentry and Religion c. 1500', in *Religion, Belief and Ecclesiastical Careers in Late Medieval England*, ed. Christopher Harper-Bill (Woodbridge, 1991), 139; *idem*, 'Victorian Values in Fifteenth-Century England: The Ewelme Almshouse Statutes', in *Pragmatic Utopias: Ideals and Communities, 1200–1630*, ed. Rosemary Horrox and S.R. Jones (Cambridge, 2001), 237.

[21] M.K. McIntosh, *Poor Relief in England 1350–1600* (Cambridge, 2012), 59.

[22] The indiscriminate sale of 'private' accommodation to people who lived so long that they eventually became a financial burden not only plunged many hospitals into debt but also prompted a move toward the foundation of almshouses under stricter lay management: Rawcliffe, 'Crisis of Confidence?', 88–90.

[23] Few almshouses catered for the completely destitute. Some assumed that new entrants would bring with them possessions, such as 'pottis, pannys, pewter vessel, beddyng, and other necessaries', which would revert to the community when they died: Canon Jackson, 'Ancient Statutes of Heytesbury Almshouse', *Wiltshire Archaeological and Natural History Magazine*, xi (1869), 289–308, at 301. See also BL, Lansdowne MS 846, f. 77.

viable purpose.[24] They formed the tip of an iceberg, below which were an unknown number of more basic and often short-lived refuges for the elderly and infirm, sometimes comprising no more than a couple of small rooms or dwellings, with little, if anything, in the way of further assistance.[25]

Since the founders of higher status institutions frequently drew upon existing models, the regulations that they devised contain many common elements. It is hardly surprising that Elias Davy should borrow heavily from the statutes of the almshouse endowed by his fellow mercer, the celebrated Richard Whittington (d. 1423), when setting up a more modest establishment in Croydon during the 1440s.[26] But so too did the duke and duchess of Suffolk: several of the eighty-nine precisely worded ordinances that governed God's House at Ewelme from 1448–50 employ identical phrasing to those devised by Whittington's executors.[27] Yet despite the striking similarities between them, and the possibility that 'a widely recognized formula' or blueprint was already in circulation, the rules adopted in English almshouses were far from uniform.[28] Financial considerations clearly determined the scale and longevity of any new institution, while a founder's administrative or commercial expertise might prompt a greater degree of managerial control. Awareness of, and sensitivity to, the needs of elderly residents could likewise vary considerably from one place to another.

In their anxiety to avoid abuses, many founders imposed strict criteria regarding the marital status, financial circumstances, previous employment and reputation of those they intended to help, there being a general consensus that admission should be confined to individuals who could no longer work or otherwise fend for themselves.[29] The old were not automatically accorded priority and might have to compete with younger, needier candidates. Perhaps for this reason, both Archbishop Henry Chichele's almshouse at Higham Ferrers and Henry VII's prodigy foundation for 'menial servants' of the crown at Westminster excluded anyone under fifty.[30] Significantly, one of the illuminated miniatures in Henry's richly decorated

---

[24] McIntosh, *Poor Relief in England*, 59–94. For two excellent regional studies, see E.M. Phillips, 'Charitable Institutions in Norfolk and Suffolk, c. 1350–1600' (PhD thesis, University of East Anglia, 2001), and Sarah Lennard Brown, 'Almshouses of London and Westminster: Their Role in Lay Piety and the Relief of Poverty, 1330–1600' (PhD thesis, Birkbeck College, University of London, 2021).

[25] P.H. Cullum, '"For Pore People Harberles": What Was the Function of the Maisondieu?', in *Trade, Devotion, and Governance: Papers in Later Medieval History*, ed. D.J. Clayton, R.G. Davies and Peter McNiven (Stroud, 1994), 36–54.

[26] G.S. Steinman, *A History of Croydon* (1834), Appendix VII, 267–88; Jean Imray, *The Charity of Richard Whittington* (1968), 109–21. In 1472 Margaret, Lady Hungerford, in turn, incorporated passages from Davy's statutes in the revised regulations of her family's almshouse at Heytesbury: see below, note 113.

[27] Goodall, *God's House at Ewelme*, 219–21.

[28] Goodall, *ibid.*, 221, argues that the duke and duchess worked from 'a common model' and are unlikely to have seen the statutes of Whittington's almshouse. But the duke must have known Whittington's chief executor, John Carpenter, who drew them up, through their mutual involvement in the affairs of Norwich during the 1430s: *The History of Parliament: The House of Commons 1422–61*, ed. Linda Clark (7 vols, Cambridge, 2020), iii. 754–60. It was in July 1437, just four months after Suffolk imposed order in the city, that Henry VI licensed the almshouse at Ewelme: Philippa Maddern, 'Order and Disorder', in *Medieval Norwich*, ed. Carole Rawcliffe and Richard Wilson (2004), 190; Goodall, *God's House at Ewelme*, 1.

[29] Carole Rawcliffe, 'Institutional Care for the Sick and Aged Poor in Later Medieval England', in *The Routledge History of Poverty c. 1450–1800*, ed. David Hitchcock and Julia McClure (2021), 209–33.

[30] BL, Lansdowne MS 846, f. 77; Harley MS 1498, f. 41v. See also, C.M. Fox, 'The Royal Almshouse at

foundation charter depicts grey-haired and heavily lined bedesmen clutching their rosaries.[31] Such precise restrictions reflect a tendency in the medical literature to define different stages of the ageing process chronologically by calendar years rather than biologically in terms of physical or mental capacity. From a Galenic standpoint, *senectus* began at some point between thirty-five and forty and lasted until fifty-five or sixty, when advanced old age (*senium*) set in.[32] The burgesses who re-founded St Mary's hospital, Yarmouth, as an almshouse in 1386 may have been prompted by these ideas to adopt what at first glance seems a surprisingly low threshold of thirty for admissions.[33] At the other end of the spectrum, William Ford's almshouse in Coventry was by 1528 making special provision for its 'very ancient' residents of sixty or above, believing 'persons at that age to be impotent and not well able to keep themselves in good honest order and clean of their bodies'.[34]

When endowing his almshouse at Hythe in 1336, Bishop Hamo Hethe made a more typical and inclusive provision for 'ten aged and infirm poor of both sexes, preferably such as have fallen into poverty from no fault of their own'.[35] Eight years later, James de Kyngeston of Hull widened his net to include 'poor men and women broken by age, misfortune or toil, who cannot gain their own livelihood'.[36] Richard, earl of Arundel (d. 1397), offered lodgings for twenty poor unmarried men who 'from age, sickness or infirmity [were] unable to provide for their own sustenance', but expected that some would be too old to participate in the religious round, preferring to concentrate upon their own impending mortality.[37] The 'lowly, devout and poor' inmates of the domus Dei in Stamford founded by the wealthy clothier William Browne (d. 1498) had simply to be incapable of earning a living, although here, too, the assumption that many would be decrepit and weak suggests that the elderly would predominate.[38] The fact that almshouse accommodation was generally assigned for life unless residents persistently misbehaved, came into money or contracted repellent diseases meant that, once sure of a reasonable level of care, a significant proportion of them would have grown old and eventually been replaced through a natural process of attrition.[39] An analysis of the accounts of Bishop

---

Westminster c. 1500–c. 1600' (PhD thesis, Royal Holloway, University of London, 2012) and *CCR*, 1500–9, nos 389 (xi), 390, for a printed calendar of its regulations.

[31] BL, Harley MS 1498, f. 59.

[32] Demaitre, 'Care and Extension of Old Age', 8; J.M. Cummins, 'Attitudes to Old Age and Ageing in Medieval Society' (PhD thesis, University of Glasgow, 2000), 14–42.

[33] 'Cartulary of St. Mary's Hospital', ed. Rawcliffe, 187, 229.

[34] John Cleary and Michael Orton, '*So Long as the World Shall Endure*': *The Five-Hundred Year History of Bond's and Ford's Hospitals* (Coventry, 1991), 45.

[35] *Registrum Hamonis Hethe Diocesis Roffensis, A. D. 1319–1352*, ed. Charles Johnson (2 vols, Oxford, 1948), i. 393. John Plumptre's almshouse in Nottingham was established in 1392 for thirteen poor widows 'broken by age and reduced by poverty (*senio confractis et pauperitate depressis*)': *CPR*, 1391–6, p. 116. After its refoundation in 1495, St John's hospital, Lichfield, accommodated a similar number of 'honest poor men upon whom the inconveniences of old age and poverty, without any fault of their own, have fallen': Bodl., MS Ashmole 855, ff. 150v–61.

[36] *CPR*, 1343–5, p. 239.

[37] Tierney, *Castle and Town of Arundel*, ii. 664, 666.

[38] H.P. Wright, *The Story of the "Domus Dei" of Stamford* (1890), 37.

[39] Residents of St Mary's hospital, Great Yarmouth, were, for instance, assured on admission that, unless they persistently broke the rules, they would 'a byde in the sayd place on to hyre lyues ende': 'Cartulary of St Mary's Hospital', ed. Rawcliffe, 227.

Walter Stapleton's almshouse for infirm priests at Clyst Gabriel reveals that, of those inmates whose age can be determined, the majority were, indeed, over fifty.[40]

Elderly or otherwise incapacitated clergy without the means for survival had long been given preferential treatment, in part because they lacked the network of family support available to laymen.[41] Bishop Walter Suffield (d. 1257) was sufficiently concerned about the problem to earmark permanent accommodation for poor diocesan priests who were 'broken with age or bedridden with constant sickness' in the new hospital for the sick poor that he was building in Norwich.[42] Having housed a declining number of elderly women as well as men, the hospital of St Saviour, Bury St Edmunds, was reformed and re-founded by Abbot Northwold in 1294 as a refuge for 'aged and sick priests', some of whom had previously served his own charnel house.[43] The presence in major urban centres of a sizeable clerical proletariat composed of underpaid chantry chaplains and other hirelings raised the unedifying spectacle of 'decayed' clergy begging in the streets and demanded an appropriate response, notably on the part of their more affluent brethren. Established in London during the early 1440s, a religious fraternity composed largely of local clergy secured the necessary support and funding for a hospital attached to the church of St Augustine Papey, where 'poor priests in their old age' could end their days in comfort with access to a garden.[44]

Since the concept of retirement was ill-defined in later medieval England, especially for those of lower social status, it was widely assumed that the fitter residents of almshouses would shoulder a variety of tasks, including the care of others.[45] Reflecting a common practice in single sex establishments, the regulations of God's House at Ewelme decreed that the brothers 'beyng holer in body, strenger and mightier' would 'faver and soccoure and diligently minister to them that be seke and febill'.[46] In mixed houses, such as the domus Dei in Stamford, the task of the female inmates was 'to bear themselves in washing and other things befitting honest women, and, so far as is decent, be altogether attentive and useful to the ... poor men in their necessities'.[47] A ruling at Roger Thornton's almshouse in Newcastle upon Tyne

---

[40] Nicholas Orme, 'A Medieval Almshouse for the Clergy: Clyst Gabriel Hospital near Exeter', *Journal of Ecclesiastical History*, xxxix (1988), 1–15, at 8.

[41] J.T. Rosenthal, *Old Age in Late Medieval England* (Philadelphia, PA, 1996), 107–12; Nicholas Orme, 'Suffering of the Clergy: Illness and Old Age in Exeter Diocese, 1300–1540', in *Life, Death and the Elderly: Historical Perspectives*, ed. Margaret Pelling and R.M. Smith (1991), 62–73.

[42] Carole Rawcliffe, *Medicine for the Soul: The Life, Death and Resurrection of a Medieval Hospital* (Stroud, 1999), 27–8, 243.

[43] *Charters of the Medieval Hospitals of Bury St Edmunds*, ed. Christopher Harper-Bill (Suffolk Records Society, Charters Series, xiv, 1994), 14–17.

[44] *CPR*, 1441-6, pp. 3, 87; BL, Harley MS 604, f. 12; Cotton MS Vitellius F XVI, ff. 113–23; Thomas Hugo, 'The Hospital of Le Papey in the City of London', *Transactions of the London and Middlesex Archaeological Society*, v (1877), 183–221.

[45] On retirement in general, see Rosenthal, *Old Age*, ch. 7.

[46] Goodall, *God's House at Ewelme*, 241. Similar rules obtained at the earl of Arundel's almshouse in Arundel (Tierney, *Castle and Town of Arundel*, ii. 666), at St Katherine's hospital, Heytesbury (Jackson, 'Ancient Statutes of Heytesbury Almshouse', 298–9), and at St John's hospital, Lichfield (Bodl., MS Ashmole 855, ff. 150v–61). Seven of the thirteen almsmen at Isabel Pembridge's college at Tong were to be 'so weak and worn in strength that they can scarcely help themselves without the assistance of another': J.E. Auden, 'Documents Relating to Tong College', *Transactions of the Shropshire Archaeological and Natural History Society*, 3rd series, viii (1908), 169–244, at 184.

[47] Wright, *Story of the "Domus Dei"*, 39, 47. See also Imray, *Charity of Richard Whittington*, 117, and Steinman, *History of Croydon*, Appendix VII, 277.

that one of the thirteen inmates should be capable of looking after all the rest, who were to be too old or debilitated to support themselves ('*que propter debilitatem aut grandem senectutem pro sustentatcione sue nequit laborare*'), would inevitably have called upon the services of a younger and more robust female.[48]

Paid care was, however, sometimes available. Among the many weekly outgoings of his almshouse at Westminster, Henry VII assigned 4*s*. for three reputable women to 'wasshe the napry [linen] … and the clothes of the … thretene pore men, make their beddes, kepe theym in their siknesse, dresse their mete, as well for their dyners as soppers, and serue theym with the same'.[49] Such a high level of support was beyond the means of most founders, who could at best afford to engage a single 'keeper'.[50] Thus, for example, a female servant was employed to cook, clean and perform rudimentary nursing duties for the residents of St John's hospital, Sherborne.[51] Gregg's almshouse in Hull and the almshouse endowed by the townspeople of Saffron Walden in 1400 likewise retained a 'suster huswiff'.[52] To avoid any hint of scandal, these women were themselves often supposed to be at least forty or fifty and would therefore have ranked among the elderly whom they were required to serve. Mixed establishments, such as Ford's in Coventry, might well set aside the next available place for them when they could no longer work as a guarantee of security.[53]

Applying the regimen

The recommendations set out in medieval *regimina* drew upon entrenched assumptions about the human body that derived from the work of Galen of Pergamum (d. 216) and other classical authorities. Their teachings were, in turn, developed and synthesised by Muslim scholars such as Avicenna (Ibn-Sīnā, d. 1037), whose *Canon* formed the bedrock of the medical syllabus in north European universities.[54] Put simply, the effectiveness of all physical and mental processes depended in the first

---

[48] J.C. Hodgson, 'The "Domus Dei" in Newcastle: Otherwise St Katherine's Hospital on the Sandhill', *Archaeologia Aeliana*, 3rd series, xiv (1917), 181–220, at 206.

[49] BL, Harley MS 1498, ff. 73v–4.

[50] Two Lancastrian institutions founded in the 1440s furnish notable exceptions. Cardinal Henry Beaufort appointed three female servants to tend the thirty-five *generosi* whom he planned to support at the hospital of St Cross, Winchester, in accommodation envisaged on collegiate lines as 'a house of noble poverty': G.L. Harriss, *Cardinal Beaufort: A Study of Lancastrian Ascendancy and Decline* (Oxford, 1988), 370–1. The ratio of staff to inmates was higher at the almshouse established by Henry VI's physician, John Somerset, at Brentford, where two 'sober industrious men' cared for nine 'blind, lame and withered' inmates: *CPR*, 1446–52, p. 29.

[51] C.H. Mayo, *A Historic Guide to the Almshouse of St John the Baptist and St John the Evangelist, Sherborne* (Oxford, 1933), 33–6.

[52] Tickell, *Town and County of Kingston-upon-Hull*, 758; 'The Statutes of the Saffron Walden Almshouse', ed. F.W. Steer, *Transactions of the Essex Archaeological Society*, new series, xxv (1955–60), 161–221, at 166–7, 172–3. St Katherine's hospital, Heytesbury, had originally recruited two female servants to tend the twelve poor almsmen, but on its refoundation in 1472 the number was halved: Jackson, 'Ancient Statutes of Heytesbury Almshouse', 302–3; M.A. Hicks, 'St Katherine's Hospital, Heytesbury: Prehistory, Foundation and Refoundation', *Wiltshire Archaeological and Natural History Magazine*, lxxviii (1984), 62–9, at 67–8.

[53] Cleary and Orton, '*So Long as the World Shall Endure*', 45.

[54] Gil Sotres, 'Regimens of Health', 291–6; *Medieval Medicine: A Reader*, ed. Faith Wallis (Toronto, 2010), 486; Luke Demaitre, *Medieval Medicine: The Art of Healing from Head to Toe* (Santa Barbara, CA, 2013), ch. 1.

instance upon what one ate. Having been cooked in the oven of the stomach, partially digested food was conveyed to the liver, where it was converted into humoral matter: blood (hot and wet), yellow bile or choler (hot and dry), phlegm (cold and wet) and black bile (cold and dry). From the liver, all this matter – which constituted the natural spirit – travelled along the veins to the organs and extremities, providing the nourishment essential for survival and growth.[55] In a healthy individual any surplus would be excreted, leaving a slight imbalance in favour of the humour which determined their personal temperament or complexion.

Since, according to contemporary medical opinion, people grew progressively cooler and drier (melancholic) with age, the elderly were advised to adopt a warm, moist (sanguine) diet that would restore some measure of equilibrium.[56] Their bodies would ultimately be consumed 'like the charred wick of a lamp' as their reserves of innate heat and natural moisture dwindled, but a prudent regimen could delay the process, while keeping them relatively fit and active.[57] We should, nevertheless, bear in mind the French physician Bernard Gordon's belief that the elderly ought to observe the dietary habits to which they had grown accustomed ('some people survive well even though they follow a bad regimen and make a mockery of physicians') rather than risking sudden change.[58] The dangers of adopting an unduly rich and unfamiliar diet after years on simple commons were well known, not least through the medium of sumptuary legislation.[59] In offering their patients nourishing and affordable foodstuffs such as potage, herring, fresh bread, eggs, milk, cheese, bacon and home-brewed ale, the more affluent hospitals for the sick poor implemented this advice.[60]

Lacking the resources and staff of these large monastic or quasi-monastic institutions, most late medieval almshouses either provided a weekly cash allowance for residents to purchase their own food or assumed that they would support themselves, if necessary by recourse to charity.[61] Rates varied considerably: each of Henry VII's almsmen at Westminster pocketed a regal 17½d. a week, over and above the 7½d. assigned for their midday meals, while residents of God's House at Ewelme and the retired priests at the hospital of Le Papey received 14d.[62] They ranked among the most fortunate. Like many founders, Archbishop Chichele reckoned that 7d.

---

[55] Rawcliffe, 'Concept of Health', 318–22.

[56] O. Cameron Gruner, *Treatise on the Canon of Medicine of Avicenna* (1930), 432–6; Nicoud, *Régimes de santé*, i. 204; Demaitre, 'Care and Extension of Old Age', 15.

[57] Although old age was quintessentially melancholic (cold and dry), gradual loss of heat meant that, as death approached, moisture levels would eventually rise again because they could no longer be burnt off. As a result, the body would become 'accidentally' phlegmatic (cold and wet): Michael McVaugh, 'The "humidium radicale" in Thirteenth-Century Medicine', *Traditio*, xxx (1974), 259–83.

[58] Nicoud, *Régimes de santé*, i. 207. The ordinances of Richard Whittington's almshouse ruled that any inmate who fell ill should 'be provided with a suitable diet out of his or her weekly pension according to his or her usual commons': *CPR*, 1429–36, p. 215.

[59] Carole Rawcliffe, *Urban Bodies: Communal Health in Late Medieval Towns and Cities* (Woodbridge, 2013), 242.

[60] Bonfield, 'Therapeutic Regime', 41–2.

[61] Begging was forbidden in many elite institutions but could hardly be prevented when payments fell into arrears or were withheld by avaricious masters: *The Fifteenth-Century Cartulary of St Nicholas' Hospital, Salisbury, with Other Records*, ed. Christopher Wordsworth (Salisbury, 1902), pp. lxii, 8.

[62] BL, Harley MS 1498, ff. 42, 73; Goodall, *God's House at Ewelme*, 231; Hugo, 'Hospital of Le Papey', 187. Residents of Whittington's almshouse also received 14d. a week: Imray, *Charity of Richard Whittington*, 118.

a week, supplemented by donations from 'well-disposed people', would feed his almsmen, who were to buy their rations every Saturday for the keeper to cook, any leftovers being added to the potage that she made for them on alternate days.[63] A ruling of 1356 allocating the bedesmen at the hospital of St Mary in the Newarke, Leicester, an extra half penny a day when wheat prices rose proved so unworkable that they, too, were eventually permitted to share all the offerings made in the poor box instead.[64] Donations in both cash and kind may have been substantial, especially in conveniently situated houses like St John's hospital, Lichfield, whose residents enjoyed 'a fair degree of comfort' thanks to the generosity of clergy at the nearby cathedral.[65] The elderly almswomen housed at the London hospital of St Katherine by the Tower did particularly well in this regard, benefiting from a combination of royal, aristocratic and civic largesse.[66]

Some of their peers could rely on regular allocations of bread, ale and other dietary staples to supplement their cash stipends, although few were as well provisioned as the residents of Isabel Pembridge's foundation at Tong in Shropshire. Here, according to the 'order and use accustomed of the almes house', the master had to supply his thirteen charges with meat worth 6*d*. and liberal quantities of rye (for bread) and malt (for ale) every week. They were also promised two 'fat kyne' and eight 'fat swyne' for their larder, four bushels of wheat, cheese worth 13*s*. 4*d*., a milch cow and 450 eggs a year. During the penitential season of Lent, when meat-eating was forbidden, their allowance comprised 450 herring, three bushels of peas (for potage) and six 'cowple' of salted and dried fish.[67] Precept did not, of course, always accord with practice. Each of the twelve men and women at the domus Dei in Portsmouth was entitled to seven high-quality loaves and five gallons of home-brewed ale a fortnight on top of their 6*d*. a week stipend. They complained in the mid-fifteenth century of cost-cutting by the master, who had removed all their brewing equipment and obliged them to make do with 'vere cowrse bred and smaller [weaker] drynke, wiche ys contrary to all good consyens and to the foundacion with no charyte'.[68] Because of its warmth, moisture and digestibility, freshly baked 'wele leveyned' bread was one of the foodstuffs recommended in *regimina* for the elderly, which made the quality as well as the quantity of supplies extremely important.[69]

---

[63] BL, Lansdowne MS 846, ff. 77–9. William Wynard's almsmen, who drew 8*d*. a week, also shared the donations left in a 'common box': Devon RO, Exeter, ED/WA/2.

[64] Thompson, *Hospital and New College of the Annunciation*, 79, 109, 132. Doles at St Katherine's hospital, Heytesbury, were similarly pegged to the price of wheat, rising from a basic 8½*d*. a week: Jackson, 'Ancient Statutes of Heytesbury Almshouse', 304–5.

[65] *VCH Staffordshire*, iii. 279–89.

[66] Legacies were paid directly into the women's alms box: Catherine Jamison, *The History of the Royal Hospital of St Katherine by the Tower of London* (Oxford, 1952), 152. In 1463, for example, the mercer Geoffrey Boleyn left them a significant bequest of 50*s*.: TNA, PROB 11/5/12.

[67] Auden, 'Documents Relating to Tong College', 210–11. The almsmen had a servant to prepare their food. More typically, residents of the almshouse at Saffron Walden shared six flagons of ale worth 6*d*. a week, along with four bushels of peas and a quarter of oats a year for potage: 'Statutes of the Saffron Walden Almshouse', ed. Steer, 167.

[68] Wright, *Story of the "Domus Dei"*, 125–6.

[69] Bacon, *De retardatione accidentum senectutis*, 35, 91; 'Tarrying the Accidents of Age', ed. Everest and Tavormina, 175, 213. The almswomen at St Bartholomew's hospital, Sandwich, were expected to bake bread every fortnight 'from the whole produce of the grain, as it comes from the mouth of the sack' to ensure its quality: *Collections for an History of Sandwich in Kent*, ed. William Boys (Canterbury, 1792), 18–19.

During the sixteenth century, the masters of God's House (formerly St Giles's hospital), Norwich, undertook to feed the residents with 'whole wheat bread withowt either rye or barlye to be putt and myxed therein', perhaps also having regard for their poor dentition.[70]

The almsmen at St Anthony's hospital in London were among the select few who qualified for full board. On first sight they appear to have fared badly in comparison with members of the associated college, who enjoyed a far richer and more varied diet.[71] Bearing in mind current assumptions about the importance of habit and status, noted above, as well as the type of food deemed suitable for ageing digestive systems, it is, however, harder to find fault with their regimen as revealed in the annual accounts. The amount of salt fish consumed by the almsmen would have alarmed Avicenna, as would the ribs of beef that regularly appeared on the menu,[72] although their generous weekly allowance of butter, eggs, milk and veal (all of which were considered beneficial for the old and feeble) should have redressed any potential damage.[73] None can have gone hungry: potage was served three or four times a week and mutton on every meat day, along with abundant supplies of bread and ale.[74] It may, indeed, sometimes have been hard to follow the Galenic principle that the elderly should eat sparingly and never consume more food than they could easily digest.[75]

The diet at Henry VII's Westminster almshouse was remarkably similar, being carefully costed by the prudent monarch. As at St Anthony's, the main midday meal was served communally in the hall. It comprised a farthing loaf, a quart of ale and a helping of 'good and holsome' potage for each inmate, followed by 'asmoche of cates, flesshe or fisshe as the season shall require as shall coste and be worthe an halfpenny'. An additional 1*d*. a week was set aside for mustard to offset the cooling effects of the salt fish and herring served on fast days.[76] If late medieval remedy books are to be believed, it also promised to promote the appetite, strengthen the digestion, purify the brain, improve the eyesight and prevent hair loss, being a general panacea against the ravages of time.[77] As the owner of at least one presentation copy of Aldobrandino's regimen of health, Henry understood that older people should be encouraged to take small, nutritious meals when they felt hungry rather than being confined to an institutional timetable with little choice in the matter of food.[78] Accordingly, since 'the said pore men by cause of their great sondry ages' would not be 'of like disposicion and apetite to their soppers', he arranged for them to take their evening meals alone, when they wished, in their rooms. Everyone was

---

[70] Norfolk RO, NCR, 24B/36.
[71] McIntosh, *Poor Relief in England*, 81.
[72] Gruner, *Treatise on the Canon of Medicine*, 432–3. For the dangers posed by 'al grosse metis metyng agenst digestioun', see also 'Tarrying the Accidents of Age', ed. Everest and Tavormina, 214.
[73] Following Galen, the Aragonese physician, Arnald of Villanova (d. 1311), was less enthusiastic about cow's milk, which he believed to be harmful for the elderly, along with fruit and fish: *Here is a Newe Boke, Called the Defence of Age and Recouery of Youth, Translated Out of the Famous Clarke and Ryght Experte Medycyne, Arnold de Noua Uilla* (Robert Wyer, 1540), STC, 777, p. 5.
[74] Bonfield, 'Therapeutic Regime', 35, 41–2.
[75] Schäfer, *Old Age and Disease*, 68; Demaitre, 'Care and Extension of Old Age', 15; Bacon, *De retardatione accidentum senectutis*, 93; 'Tarrying the Accidents of Age', ed. Everest and Tavormina, 214.
[76] BL, Harley MS 1498, f. 73v.
[77] *The Physicians of Myddvai*, ed. John Williams (Llandovery, 1861), 68.
[78] BL, Royal MS 19 A V.

entitled to 'oon potte of ale of suche mesure and price and asmoche brede as ... they shall lyste resonably to name', together with whatever else could 'resonably' be purchased and prepared for them by one of the female carers, if they fancied a particular dish.[79] Henry may have been unusually responsive to the dietary requirements of the elderly, but few founders went to the opposite extreme of demanding a life of monastic privation. None appears to have followed the example of the Coventry draper, Thomas Bond, who expected his almsmen to mark the three weekly fast days (Wednesdays, Fridays and Saturdays) by confining themselves to one small meal 'for the good prosperity of the brethren and sisters of the Trinity Gild, and for the souls that be departed'.[80] His enforced austerity contrasts sharply with the abundant fare enjoyed at the Trinity almshouse in Salisbury, which was supported by the local guild of St George and could thus afford to roast an entire ox during the Christmas festivities of 1522.[81]

In an age haunted by the spectre of epidemic disease, hygiene mattered greatly to founders such as Archbishop Chichele and the duke and duchess of Suffolk, who were keenly aware of the threat posed by corrupt air. The statutes drawn up by the latter for God's House at Ewelme ruled specifically that 'neythir neygh to the cloyster, neythir abowte the welle, neythir neygh any porch dore ... shall any unclene watir or any filth, or any harlotrie [offensive matter] be made, put or leyde, the which shall in any wise cause stenche or orrour [horror]', thereby implementing the recommendations set out in contemporary plague tracts.[82] Ewelme was one of many houses to demand the immediate removal of residents who had contracted leprosy or any other 'infirmytees intollerabill' as a routine sanitary precaution to prevent the spread of noxious miasmas.[83] The importance of fresh air and personal cleanliness in protecting the old from degenerative diseases had already been noted in the *De retardatione accidentum senectutis*, then mistakenly attributed to Roger Bacon (d. 1292), which warned that foul smells and 'stynkkyng vapours' would obstruct the working of the brain and weaken the vital spirits. And how could corrupt humoral matter be expelled from the body if the pores were already clogged with filth?[84] Chichele made detailed and careful provision on this score, insisting that a barber should visit his almshouse every Friday at noon to shave the inmates 'and to dresse their heads and to make them cleane'. The female keeper was expected to provide her charges with 'a pann of faire water and a dish' for washing every morning when they got up, and to 'see the house cleane swept euery daie'. Aware that he was asking a great deal of a woman of fifty, the archbishop agreed that on Mondays a laundress might be hired to help her 'gather all the poore mens clothes togeather' so that they could be picked free of lice and washed.[85] Barbers and laundresses also appear in the

---

[79] BL, Harley MS 1498, f. 74.
[80] William Dugdale, *The Antiquities of Warwickshire* (2 vols, 1730), i. 194. They were, however, permitted to eat 'white meat', which would have been less harmful in humoral terms than salted or dried fish.
[81] McIntosh, *Poor Relief in England*, 80–1; A.D. Brown, *Popular Piety in Late Medieval England: The Diocese of Salisbury, 1250–1550* (Oxford, 1995), 181, 192.
[82] Goodall, *God's House at Ewelme*, 241; Rawcliffe, *Urban Bodies*, 120–7.
[83] Carole Rawcliffe, *Leprosy in Medieval England* (Woodbridge, 2006), 277–8. Confirmed cases would be transferred to the nearest leper hospital and allowed to retain their stipends for life.
[84] Bacon, *De retardatione accidentum senectutis*, 19–20, 28–9; 'Tarrying the Accidents of Age', ed. Everest and Tavormina, 170–1.
[85] BL, Lansdowne MS 846, ff. 78–9. At Ford's almshouse in Coventry, an 'honest good woman' in her forties was engaged in 1528 to keep the five elderly married couples 'clean in their person and

accounts of St Katherine's almshouse in Heytesbury, at the hospital of Le Papey in London, where a husband and wife were employed 'to keepe the house cleane', and, from 1478, at St Nicholas's hospital, Salisbury.[86]

Although many barbers offered phlebotomy among their services, it is unlikely that elderly almsmen would have undergone such a potentially harmful procedure unless they were gravely ill. Regular bloodletting served an important prophylactic function for younger men who were sanguine by temperament, but depleted vital reserves of warmth and moisture as the body became colder and drier.[87] Like most physicians, Aldobrandino of Siena regarded sexual activity as an even riskier proposition for similar reasons, ranking it as 'the thing that ages one above all others' and therefore best avoided altogether by males over thirty-five.[88] He would certainly have endorsed the widespread practice in higher-status English almshouses of admitting only single people who were required under pain of heavy fines or even expulsion to remain celibate.[89] Some institutions, such as Ford's almshouse in Coventry and the prestigious almshouse constructed by the Merchant Tailors of London next to their guildhall, accepted married couples, but those which followed a more structured liturgical round generally forbade cohabitation, condemning even the slightest hint of impropriety.[90] The majority of elite founders were determined to maintain a devotional environment in which nothing disturbed the daily schedule of prayer or undermined its efficacy. Concern about the damaging physiological effects of coitus upon those interceding on their behalf seems, predictably, to have been a lesser priority. A widespread refusal to tolerate 'dronkley glotons', 'tavern-haunters' and 'whore-masters' reflects similar anxieties, which were reinforced by contemporary medical advice regarding the harmful effects of overindulgence upon ageing bodies.[91]

---

houses, and for dressing of their meat [and] washing of them': W.H. Godfrey, *The English Almshouse* (1955), 47. The 'suster huswiff' at St Katherine's hospital, Heytesbury, had likewise to occupy herself with 'wasshing and other like thyngis convenyent and apperteyning to an honeste woman': Jackson, 'Ancient Statutes of Heytesbury Almshouse', 302–3.

[86] *VCH Wiltshire*, iii. 338; Hugo, 'Hospital of Le Papey', 187; *Cartulary of St. Nicholas' Hospital*, ed. Wordsworth, pp. lxii, 8. At St Katherine's each almsman was allowed 3s. 6d. a year to pay his barber: Jackson, 'Ancient Statutes of Heytesbury Almshouse', 306. See also McIntosh, *Poor Relief in England*, 79.

[87] Pedro Gil-Sotres, 'Derivation and Revulsion: The Theory and Practice of Medieval Phlebotomy', in *Practical Medicine from Salerno to the Black Death*, ed. Luis García-Ballester, Roger French, Jon Arrizabalaga and Andrew Cunningham (Cambridge, 1994), 110–55; 'Tarrying the Accidents of Age', ed. Everest and Tavormina, 218.

[88] BL, Sloane MS 2435, f. 32. See also Demaitre, 'Care and Extension of Old Age', 16. According to current medical theory, semen was a biproduct of digestion which contained both radical moisture *and* innate heat and had therefore to be conserved by the elderly at all costs: Schäfer, *Old Age and Disease*, 29. For a more sceptical contemporary response to these ideas, see Shulamith Shahar, 'The Old Body in Medieval Culture', in *Framing Medieval Bodies*, ed. Sarah Kay and Miri Rubin (Manchester, 1995), 162.

[89] See, for example, 'Cartulary of St Mary's Hospital', ed. Rawcliffe, 186, 229; Tierney, *Castle and Town of Arundel*, ii. 664; Tickell, *Town and County of Kingston-upon-Hull*, 758; Hodgson, '"Domus Dei" in Newcastle', 208; Bodl., MS Ashmole 855, ff. 150v–61.

[90] Carole Rawcliffe, 'Dives Redeemed? The Guild Almshouses of Late Medieval England', in *The Fifteenth Century VIII*, ed. Linda Clark (2008), 1–27, at 24.

[91] Steinman, *History of Croydon*, Appendix VII, 281; Goodall, *God's House at Ewelme*, 240; Imray, *Charity of Richard Whittington*, 119; Jackson, 'Ancient Statutes of Heytesbury Almshouse', 298; 'Statutes of the Saffron Walden Almshouse', ed. Steer, 168–9; BL, Lansdowne MS 846, f. 78 (Higham Ferrers).

While extolling the benefits of moderation, regimens of health stressed the need for older people to conserve their diminishing reserves of natural heat by avoiding cold air and keeping warm.[92] Henry VII's assignment of eighty quarters of 'good and sufficient charre coles and oon thousande good and hable fagottes' to be delivered every year in two instalments for use in the kitchen and hall of his almshouse at Westminster reflects a characteristic obsession with micromanagement but was, in principle, hardly novel.[93] When funds allowed, earlier generations of founders had budgeted for adequate supplies of fuel, over and above the weekly doles paid to residents.[94] Archbishop Chichele felt that eight cartloads of wood, fuel to the value of 10s. for laundry and oil worth 5s. for lamps each year would suffice for his almshouse at Higham Ferrers.[95] Since carts varied in size, it is hard to tell if the annual assignment of sixteen loads of wood and one of coal made to residents of St Nicholas's hospital, Salisbury, or of twenty loads of wood to Bond's almshouse in Coventry was the more generous; Isabel Pembridge's bedesmen at Tong would have been extremely snug with no fewer than sixty loads of wood and faggots to burn.[96]

Late medieval English almshouses were notable for the degree of privacy enjoyed by residents, either in partitioned halls, or, more commonly, single rooms or separate dwellings. Frequent references to chimneys suggest that, in theory at least, heating should have been adequate and rooms well-ventilated.[97] Each resident of God's House at Ewelme occupied 'a lityl howse, a celle or a chambir with a chemeney and othir necessarijs in the same, in the whiche euery of them may by hym selfe ete and drynke and rest, and sum tymes among attende to contemplacion and prayoure'.[98] Not only re-founded but also rebuilt by Bishop Smith in 1495, the hospital of St John the Baptist in Lichfield is still recognisable by the eight towering red-brick chimney stacks that warmed the almsmen's rooms.[99] Similar concern for the welfare of inmates is apparent from a contract made in 1486 for the 'warkmanly' construction of the almshouse at Tattershall College. Each of the thirteen chambers was to be well-lit with two windows 'of competent hight', and to be furnished with a chimney and mantelpiece. The residents were to share three privies 'made of tymbre bynethe and aboue in the said chambres, whereas shall seme most necessarye and according'.[100]

The accounts of the hospital of St John the Baptist in Sherborne, which was run by the townspeople after its refoundation as an almshouse in the 1430s, record regular annual disbursements on fuel, as well as smocks, shirts, breeches, stockings, shoes, gowns, robes, and caps for the twelve male and four female residents, who

---

[92] Demaitre, 'Care and Extension of Old Age', 14. Sensitivity to cold is a recurrent and ubiquitous stereotype in late medieval writing about the elderly: Shahar, 'Old Body', 162.
[93] BL, Harley MS 1498, f. 45.
[94] McIntosh, *Poor Relief in England*, 82.
[95] BL, Lansdowne MS 846, f. 79.
[96] *Cartulary of St Nicholas' Hospital*, ed. Wordsworth, pp. lxi, 8; Dugdale, *Antiquities of Warwickshire*, i. 193; Auden, 'Documents Relating to Tong College', 210–11.
[97] Lennard Brown, 'Almshouses of London and Westminster', 158.
[98] Goodall, *God's House at Ewelme*, 230. Whittington's almshouse in London served as a model here and in other respects: Imray, *Charity of Richard Whittington*, 112.
[99] Prescott, *English Medieval Hospital*, 45, 64–5.
[100] L.F. Salzman, *Buildings in England* (Oxford, 1952), 544–5. The thirteen inmates of Henry VII's almshouse at Westminster shared six privies, which disgorged into an adjacent ditch, the design being modelled on Cardinal Beaufort's 'house of noble poverty' at Winchester: Fox, 'Royal Almshouse at Westminster', 153–9.

appear to have been well shod and warmly dressed.[101] Their outer garments were white, the better to display a 'skochen of the armes of Seynt George' that marked the house's hard-won independence from the local abbot, but most almsmen and women were clad in darker fabric that was robust, durable and unostentatious.[102] A device or badge might well denote the special status of the wearer, while advertising the generosity of a patron and bestowing a sense of collective identity.[103] The ten residents and female servant of Thomas Bond's almshouse in Coventry shared an annual allocation of thirty-eight yards of sturdy black fabric, each gown 'having a conusance of the Trinity before and behind', in recognition of the town's Trinity guild, which managed the house.[104] Merchants like Bond, who had made their fortunes through the sale or production of cloth, were understandably concerned that their dependents should be adequately clad. The Shrewsbury draper, Degory Water, catered to the requirements of individual bedesmen such as Richard Browne, who in 1465 received 'a gowne of myne nowne werying' worth 6s. 8d., a new pair of shoes, russet stockings, a doublet, a cap and a black hat from his benefactor.[105] It has been argued that 'charity clothing' carried little stigma until the end of the nineteenth century, and may until then have been a source of self-esteem among members of elite institutions.[106]

From a late medieval perspective, positive emotions of this kind had obvious benefits, given the holistic connection made in *regimina* between 'passions of the mind' and physical health.[107] A calm and cheerful disposition certainly appeared to offer the best protection against the ravages of old age. As an English translation of Arnald of Villanova's early fourteenth-century regimen for the preservation of youth (*De conservanda juventute et retardanda senectute*) explained:

> … amonge all other thynges there is nothynge the which so strongly doth cause a man to loke eldely as feare and desperacion, for because in that passyon and effectyon all the naturall hete of the body doth resort inwarde, and forsaketh the outwarde partes, and the most chefely when the mannes complexion is disposed

---

[101] Dorset RO, Dorchester, D/SHA A1–30. In 1428–9, for example, the keeper purchased twenty-four pairs of shoes, 30 yards of woollen cloth from Devon, 18 yards of Welsh cloth, shirts, smocks, stockings and breeches for the residents: D/SHA A5. Each of the almsmen at St Katherine's hospital, Heytesbury, received two pairs of stockings, two shirts and two sturdy pairs of 'shone with lether and hempe to clowte them' a year and a new gown every two years: Jackson, 'Ancient Statutes of Heytesbury Almshouse', 305.
[102] Rawcliffe, *Urban Bodies*, 347.
[103] McIntosh, *Poor Relief in England*, 83.
[104] Dugdale, *Antiquities of Warwickshire*, i. 193–4. This allowance was slightly more generous than the 3 yards of russet and black frieze that Henry VII gave to each of his almsmen at Westminster, although the latter sported an escutcheon of a crowned Tudor rose embroidered on their left shoulders: BL, Harley MS 1498, f. 42.
[105] I.M. Rope, 'The Earliest Book of the Drapers' Company, Shrewsbury', *Transactions of the Shropshire Archaeological and Natural History Society*, 4th series, iii (1913), 135–262, at 150–1.
[106] Alannah Tomkins, 'Retirement from the Noise and Hurry of the World? The Experience of Almshouse Life', in *Accommodating Poverty: The Living Arrangements of the English Poor, c. 1600–1850*, ed. Joanne McEwan and Pamela Sharpe (2011), 270.
[107] Elena Carrera, 'Anger and the Mind-Body Connection in Medieval and Early Modern Medicine', in *Emotions and Health, 1200–1700*, ed. eadem (Leiden, 2013), 93–146; Stephen Pender, 'Subventing Disease: Anger, Passions, and the Non-Naturals', in *Rhetorics of Bodily Disease and Health in Medieval and Early Modern England*, ed. J.C. Vaught (Farnham, 2010), 193–218.

to the same, and that is the cause that many beynge turmoyled and vexed with this worldly stormes sodaynly theyr heer waxe hore, or whyte.[108]

While conceding that a little excitement or even anger might stimulate their elderly patients, whose melancholic temperaments made them prey to depression and lethargy, physicians warned against anything likely to cause undue stress or agitation.[109] In theory, if not always in practice, the ban imposed in many almshouses on quarrelsome, difficult people helped to preserve the tranquil environment deemed necessary for the conservation of health, enabling residents to navigate the challenges of communal life and perform their religious duties undisturbed. It was also important for them to enjoy a good night's rest, and perhaps take a nap during the day, as the old were advised to do. 'Long sleepe and long taryeng abedde' facilitated digestion and calmed the spirits, being necessary for those with cooler temperaments.[110] Even allowing for the hours spent in prayer, almsmen and women retired early so that they could rest or attend to their private devotions.[111] Peace and quiet were therefore at a premium. When allocating each of his almsmen a room where he could sleep, meditate and pray, Elias Davy was adamant that 'noo persone of them so being in his owen place make any noise or disturbaunce in letting or troubeling any of his felawes, or any of his felawes lette him or distrouble him'.[112] Repeating this admonition almost *verbatim*, the statutes of St Katherine's hospital, Heytesbury, proscribed 'unsufferabill, debatefull or brygous' behaviour, urging the residents, just as Davy had done, to 'lyve and be conversuante togeder in the forsaide hous ... that they may after this liff transsetory come to the hous of the kyngdome of heven'.[113] Shared rituals, such as the drinking of a post-prandial jug of ale every Sunday at St Bartholomew's hospital, Sandwich, were intended 'to promote brotherly affection' and smooth ruffled feathers before disputes got out of hand.[114]

No such palliatives were offered at St John's hospital Lichfield, which simply – and typically – threatened to expel anyone who was persistently loud or argumentative after three separate warnings.[115] Alice, duchess of Suffolk, covered most contingencies when ordering her bedesmen at Ewelme to be 'restfull and pesibill with oute noyse or troubill of here felowship, withowte cryyng and grete noyse makyng ... kepyng them selfe from jaynglyng and chydyng and speciall from fowle bostfull and ribawdise talkyng of thing doon in here dayes thanne afore passed'.[116] It must have been hard to prevent elderly almsmen from bragging about their younger days and even harder to dissuade the deaf and confused from shouting, but persistent troublemakers could, indeed, face eviction. In 1498, for example, Richard Bulkley was ejected after just one year at the domus Dei in Stamford 'for certain incorrigible

---

[108] *Here is a Newe Boke, Called the Defence of Age*, 4.
[109] Demaitre, 'Care and Extension of Old Age', 18; BL, Sloane MS 2435, f. 32.
[110] K.H. Dannenfeldt, 'Sleep: Theory and Practice in the Late Renaissance', *Journal of the History of Medicine and Allied Sciences*, xli (1986), 415–41; Bacon, *De retardatione accidentum senectutis*, 93; 'Tarrying the Accidents of Age', ed. Everest and Tavormina, 175.
[111] The bedesmen at Higham Ferrers, for example, withdrew for the night at 8 p.m.: BL, Lansdowne MS 846, f. 78.
[112] Steinman, *History of Croydon*, Appendix VII, 274.
[113] *Ibid.*, 287; Jackson, 'Ancient Statutes of Heytesbury Almshouse', 298, 308.
[114] *Collections for an History of Sandwich*, ed. Boys, 19.
[115] Bodl., MS Ashmole 855, ff. 150v–61.
[116] Goodall, *God's House at Ewelme*, 240.

offences … committed against the statutes and laudable customs of this house'.[117] The cartulary of St Nicholas's hospital, Salisbury, records admonitions and expulsions for theft, brawling and inebriation, which suggest that almshouse life may sometimes have been a good deal livelier than generally supposed.[118] The great majority of inmates were, however, only too grateful to have found a refuge that would house and protect them, even if, as Marjorie McIntosh observes, their security and peace of mind came at a heavy price.[119]

The generous stipends and comfortable living conditions described above went hand in hand with onerous religious obligations and restrictions on personal freedom. The founders of these prestigious institutions expected a healthy spiritual return on their investments, insisting that all but the moribund should engage in a constant round of intercession, both in the privacy of their own rooms and together in church.[120] We have no means of telling if the almsmen at Ewelme actually recited the scores of Pater Nosters, Aves, Creeds and psalms demanded of them every single day or attended the neighbouring church on five separate occasions between six in the morning and six at night, but each swore that he would do so on accepting his place.[121] Historians vary in their reactions to these and similar expectations. Michael Hicks highlights the stultifying boredom involved in the 'endless repetition of Latin prayers' at St Katherine's hospital, Heytesbury, while for Colin Richmond the 'quasi-industrial' nature of the Ewelme prayer factory seems oppressively Victorian.[122]

Demonstrating greater sensitivity to the religious aspirations of the residents, Sarah Lennard Brown has more recently suggested that almshouse life may have appealed to those who wished to devote their final years to a 'spiritual pilgrimage', and who regarded intercession for others as a means of hastening their own as well as their patrons' salvation.[123] They would have adapted easily enough to the quasi-monastic regimes followed in high-status institutions like Ewelme, whose purpose was to create an environment as uncontaminated by sin as it was by the miasmas of plague, and thus to bestow 'meaning and potency' upon the liturgical round.[124] Theologians and preachers were not alone in stressing the therapeutic value of prayer, or in regarding old age as a unique opportunity for spiritual development.[125] Some physicians believed that regular devotional practices would 'calm the passions', while preparing the individual to face his or her own mortality with fortitude.[126] Nor should we underestimate the reassurance to be gained from membership

---

[117] *The Wardens: Managing a Late Medieval Hospital: Browne's Hospital, Stamford, 1495–1518*, ed. Alan Rogers (Bury St Edmunds, 2013), 8, 83, 99, 303. Another almsman was expelled in 1512 after fifteen years in the hospital: *ibid.*, 82, 253, 303.

[118] *Cartulary of St Nicholas' Hospital*, ed. Wordsworth, 224–5. See, for comparison, complaints about the drunken, disorderly, larcenous and foul-mouthed residents of God's House, Norwich, addressed by their priest to the civic authorities in 1550: *Records of the City of Norwich*, ed. William Hudson and J.C. Tingey (2 vols, Norwich, 1906–10), ii. 387–9.

[119] McIntosh, *Poor Relief in England*, 63–4.

[120] Unusually, residents of the Saffron Walden almshouse were not compelled to pray for their benefactors, being simply urged to attend church 'when they are well or can conveniently manage it': 'Statutes of the Saffron Walden Almshouse', ed. Steer, 167.

[121] Goodall, *God's House at Ewelme*, 145–53, 234–7.

[122] Hicks, 'St Katherine's Hospital, Heytesbury', 68; Richmond, 'Victorian Values', 228–9.

[123] Lennard Brown, 'Almshouses of London and Westminster', 193–6.

[124] Goodall, *God's House at Ewelme*, 153–5.

[125] Shulamith Shahar, *Growing Old in the Middle Ages* (1997), 55.

[126] Schäfer, *Old Age and Disease*, 39.

of a community that could guarantee a Christian burial and appropriate commemoration after death, especially on the part of elderly people who had no close relatives to provide for them. Guild almshouses, such as those run by the Merchant Tailors and Cutlers of London, were especially keen to mark the exequies of former brethren in a fitting manner, with requiem masses as well as lights.[127] Other establishments, including Roger Thornton's hospital in Newcastle, arranged for prayers to be said by all the inmates for specific periods after one of their number died.[128] Comprising a funeral, month's mind and anniversary, the arrangements made for deceased poor sisters at St John's hospital, Canterbury, were attractive enough to prompt donations from outsiders who also wished to be remembered according to 'the custom of the house'.[129] Founders may have demanded the lion's share of post-mortem intercession, but the residents were not forgotten.

On the strength of all this evidence, it might be assumed that – whatever else they could offer in the way of emotional support – late medieval English almshouses rarely echoed with laughter or fostered the 'joye and gladnes' recommended in *regimina* for the well-being of older people.[130] Yet rules could always be broken or ignored.[131] The May games, pageants of Robin Hood and bear-baiting staged at St Mary's in the Newarke clearly delighted the residents, but found less favour with Bishop Longland when he inspected the house in 1525.[132] Seemlier types of entertainment were not, however, entirely forbidden and might even be encouraged. Once their religious duties had been discharged, the sixteen bedesmen and women at St Mary's hospital, Yarmouth, were free to 'dyne & suppyn & etyn & drynkyn with hyr good frendys in towun'. The strict curfew and ban on frequenting taverns, along with the threat of expulsion for drunken or licentious behaviour, would presumably have curbed any tendency to kick over the traces.[133] Archbishop Chichele not only allowed his almsmen to spend one week every three months among their families without losing any wages, but also stipulated that newcomers who needed a gown on arrival should pay 3s. 4d. into a fund for everyone to 'make merry withall'.[134] The major religious feasts at Christmas, Easter and Pentecost were celebrated in many almshouses with 'public dinners' and extra purchases of food and drink.[135] In older hospitals the award of pittances for poor residents to eat at the master's table on specific occasions was intended as a gesture of commensality, whereby those who

---

[127] Rawcliffe, 'Dives Redeemed?', 19. The accounts of the hospital of St John the Baptist, Sherborne, itemise purchases of candles for the funerals and linen for the shrouds of named individuals: Dorset RO, D/SHA A7, A19 and A30. See also 'Statutes of the Saffron Walden Almshouse', ed. Steer, 173–4.
[128] Hodgson, '"Domus Dei" in Newcastle', 208.
[129] Sheila Sweetinburgh, 'Joining the Sisters: Female Inmates of the Late Medieval Hospitals in East Kent', *Archaeologia Cantiana*, cciii (2003), 17–40, at 33. Funeral feasts of bread, cheese and ale were staged on each of these occasions: *eadem*, 'More Continuity than Change: Almshouses in Tudor Kent', *Southern History*, lii (2020), 21–45, at 41.
[130] 'Tarrying the Accidents of Age', ed. Everest and Tavormina, 168, 203; BL, Sloane MS 2435, f. 32. Cheerfulness was associated with the sanguine (hot and moist) temperament of youth and therefore promised to conserve warmth.
[131] As the duke and duchess of Suffolk ruefully noted when drawing up the regulations for their almshouse: Goodall, *God's House at Ewelme*, 154.
[132] Thompson, *Hospital and New College of the Annunciation*, 156.
[133] 'Cartulary of St Mary's Hospital', ed. Rawcliffe, 229.
[134] BL, Lansdowne MS 846, f. 78. Surprisingly, Chichele did not expect his almsmen to wear a distinctive badge or livery.
[135] Dorset RO, D/SHA A1–30; *Collections for an History of Sandwich*, ed. Boys, 19.

shared the same food momentarily enjoyed the same status, although it may often have reinforced rather than dispelled social inequalities.[136] More overtly convivial (but no less ambivalent) gatherings punctuated the lives of the men and women whose institutions were managed by religious or craft guilds, often for the support of elderly or incapacitated members who could no longer work but remained part of the wider community. The London girdler, Andrew Hunt, provided new hoods for his almsmen so that they would be properly dressed on these important occasions.[137]

Diversions of this kind, which enabled residents to retain their links with the outside world, contrast sharply with the more enclosed and introspective way of life adopted at many institutions associated with chantries or collegiate foundations. They remind us that, despite their common purpose in accommodating the old and vulnerable, even the most prosperous late medieval almshouses differed widely in their practical application of *regimina* for the conservation of physical and spiritual health. The institutions considered here do, nevertheless, demonstrate an awareness, on paper, at least, of contemporary ideas about the dietary requirements of the elderly and of the need to maintain a clean, warm, peaceful and secure environment in which they could enjoy a measure of companionship as they said their prayers and cultivated their gardens.

Almshouses and hospitals discussed in the text

Arundel, Sussex, the earl of Arundel's almshouse, was founded in 1395–6 (as part of a college dedicated to the Holy Trinity) by the fourth earl for twenty poor unmarried men incapable of supporting themselves because of 'age, sickness or infirmity'. Preference was accorded to the earl's own tenants or servants and then to 'the most deserving' candidates from the surrounding area, all of whom were bound by a strict rule (Tierney, *Castle and Town of Arundel*, ii. 662–7; K.J. Evans, 'The Maison Dieu Arundel', *Sussex Archaeological Collections*, cvii (1969), 65–77).

Beverley, Yorkshire, hospital of St Giles. Injunctions for the better management of the hospital issued by Archbishop Wickwane in 1279 ruled that fifteen beds should be maintained for transient sick paupers and generous provision made for ten additional 'poor folks' who had corrodies. In defiance of his instructions, some of this accommodation was later sold to affluent boarders (*Register of William Wickwane*, ed. Brown, 137–8; TNA, C1/242/72).

Brentford, Middlesex, John Somerset's almshouse. Founded in 1446 by Henry VI's physician, along with a fraternity of the Nine Orders of Angels, the almshouse accommodated nine 'blind, lame and withered men' supported by two 'sober and industrious' servants (*CPR, 1446–52*, p. 29).

Bristol, John Barstaple's almshouse, was founded in 1395 by Barstaple, who was then mayor, and his wife, along with a guild in honour of the Holy Trinity to which the almshouse was dedicated. Royal letters patent, re-issued in 1408, con-

---

[136] Jamison, *Royal Hospital of St Katherine*, 52.
[137] Rawcliffe, 'Dives Redeemed?', 19.

firmed an endowment for the support of twenty-four poor people (*CPR*, 1405–8, pp. 410–11; Prescott, *English Medieval Hospital*, 99; Wilfrid Leighton, 'Trinity Hospital', *Transactions of the Bristol and Gloucestershire Archaeological Society*, xxxvi (1913), 251–87).

Bury St Edmunds, Suffolk, hospital of St Saviour. Founded before 1186 for the reception of poor women as well as men, the hospital experienced 'a crisis of management' during the 1290s, when it was reformed by Abbot Northwold. Henceforward, it accommodated only 'aged and sick priests', preference being given to the staff of Northwold's own charnel house (*Charters of the Medieval Hospitals of Bury St. Edmunds*, ed. Harper-Bill, 3–18).

Canterbury, Kent, St John's hospital. Founded before 1089 for the support of 'poor and infirm persons' and staffed by lay brothers and sisters, the hospital increasingly offered permanent places to potential donors or their poor dependents in return for a negotiable entry fee (*VCH Kent*, ii. 211–12; Sweetinburgh, 'Joining the Sisters', 17–40).

Coventry, Warwickshire, Thomas Bond's almshouse. Bond, a wealthy draper, made precise arrangements in his will of 1506 for the foundation of an almshouse for ten poor men from the town's Trinity guild, whose livery they wore. The long, two-storied building was completed within the next two years (Dugdale, *Antiquities of Warwickshire*, i. 193–4; Cleary and Orton, '*So Long as the World Shall Endure*', 10–13).

Coventry, Warwickshire, William Ford's almshouse. Following the example of his father-in-law, Thomas Bond, Ford left money in his will of 1509 for an almshouse for five old men and one woman. William Pisford, his executor, enlarged the endowment to accommodate six poor men over sixty and their wives. Further changes followed in 1528, when new regulations provided for five elderly couples and a nurse to care for them (Cleary and Orton, '*So Long as the World Shall Endure*', 13–15, 23).

Croydon, Surrey, Elias Davy's almshouse. A successful London mercer, Davy drew heavily upon the statutes of Whittington's almshouse (*q.v.*) when compiling the detailed regulations in 1447. He provided accommodation for seven unmarried 'pouer people' of both sexes who had lived in Croydon or its environs for at least seven years and were incapable of work (Steinman, *History of Croydon*, Appendix VII, 267–88).

Clyst Gabriel, Devon, Bishop Stapleton's almshouse, was founded in c. 1310 by Walter Stapleton for poor, infirm and disabled priests who could no longer support themselves. The two chaplains who served the community were themselves promised accommodation when they grew old (Orme, 'Medieval Almshouse for the Clergy', 1–15).

Ewelme, Oxfordshire, God's House, was founded by the earl and countess (later duke and duchess) of Suffolk, following the award of royal letters patent in 1437, for the support of thirteen reputable poor men 'y broke in age or ellys by other maner of feblenesse'. Lengthy statutes of 1448–50 imposed strict standards of discipline and religious observance upon the residents, giving preference to tenants of the lordship of Ewelme and to servants in ducal employment (Goodall, *God's House at Ewelme*, esp. Appendix I).

Exeter, Devon, William Wynard's almshouse, was founded in 1436 by the recorder of Exeter for the accommodation of twelve poor infirm people incapable of supporting themselves, each of whom was allocated a separate dwelling and a garden (Devon RO, Exeter, ED/WA/2).

Great Yarmouth, Norfolk, hospital of St Mary. Having declined into poverty, the once prosperous hospital was re-founded by the townspeople in 1386 as an almshouse for the accommodation of sixteen reputable unmarried paupers of both sexes over the age of thirty ('Cartulary of St. Mary's Hospital', ed. Rawcliffe, 162–6, 181–9, 227–30).

Heytesbury, Wiltshire, hospital/almshouse of St Katherine. Built before 1442 by Walter, Lord Hungerford, for the accommodation of twelve almsmen, the hospital formed part of a larger collegiate foundation. His daughter-in-law, Margaret, obtained the necessary royal licence in 1472, modifying some of the original arrangements and compiling detailed statutes which gave preference to tenants on the family's estates (Hicks, 'St Katherine's Hospital, Heytesbury', 62–9; Jackson, 'Ancient Statutes of Heytesbury Almshouse', 289–308).

Higham Ferrers, Northamptonshire, Archbishop Chichele's almshouse. In 1422–5 the archbishop established a college at his birthplace, adding to it an almshouse for twelve poor men over fifty, who were clearly far from destitute. As was later the case at Ewelme (*q.v.*), the statutes, which survive in a later incomplete copy, paid close attention to physical care and hygiene (*VCH Northampton*, ii. 177–9; BL, Lansdowne MS 846, ff. 77–9).

Hythe, Kent, Bishop Hethe's almshouse, was founded in 1336 by the bishop for the support of ten 'aged and infirm poor of both sexes', preference being given to those whose poverty sprang 'from no fault of their own' and who could repeat the appropriate prayers (*Registrum Hamonis Hethe*, ed. Johnson, i. 393).

Kingston-upon-Hull, Yorkshire, Gregg's hospital/almshouse, was founded in 1414 by the merchant John Gregg and his wife Joan (who oversaw its completion) for the support of thirteen unmarried paupers of both sexes, especially those who had once been 'of most worship' in the town (Tickell, *Town and County of Kingston-upon-Hull*, 756–8).

Kingston-upon-Hull, Yorkshire, James de Kyngeston's almshouse. By 1344 Kyngeston, a royal clerk, had built an almshouse for thirteen poor men and women 'broken by age, misfortune or toil', who could not work for a living. He then entrusted it to the ownership and management of the warden, John le Couper (*CPR, 1343–5*, p. 239).

Leicester, Leicestershire, hospital of St Mary in the Newarke. Founded in 1330 by Henry, earl of Lancaster, the hospital was to support fifty 'poor and infirm folk', of whom twenty were to be 'perpetual inmates ... to dwell forever' in an almshouse adjoining the church. Henry's son issued comprehensive statutes in 1356, doubling these numbers. New regulations were promulgated by Bishop John Russell in 1491 (Thompson, *Hospital and New College of the Annunciation*, 14–20, 41–81, 121–35).

Lichfield, Staffordshire, hospital of St John the Baptist. Having entered a long period of decline, the twelfth-century hospital was rebuilt and re-endowed by Bishop William Smith in the 1490s as an almshouse for thirteen honest, aged and poor men, each of whom occupied his own well-appointed chamber. Smith's statutes of 1495 also made provision for a school (*VCH Staffordshire*, iii. 279–89; Bodl., MS Ashmole 855, ff. 150v–61).

London, Cutlers' almshouse. By 1456, the Cutlers had constructed a company almshouse with individual chambers next to their hall. The male and female residents were expected to attend feasts, processions and funerals, being themselves buried at considerable expense with all the ceremonial accorded to more affluent members (Charles Welch, *History of the Cutlers' Company of London* (2 vols, 1916–23), i. 163, 171–2).

London, Girdlers' almshouse. In his will of 1431, Andrew Hunt left two tenements to the Girdlers' Company, specifying that two accessible rooms on the ground floor were to accommodate two 'decayed persons of the livery', the poorer of whom was to receive 7d. a week (*Calendar of Wills Proved and Enrolled in the Court of Husting, London, 1358–1688*, ed. R.R. Sharpe (2 vols, 1889–90), ii (pt 2), 493; T.C. Barker, *The Girdlers' Company* (1957), 35–7).

London, hospital of St Anthony. Established before 1294 with provision for a school, an infirmary and resident accommodation for twelve poor almsmen, the house was annexed to St George's chapel, Windsor, in 1475. Surviving accounts suggest that from then onward this 'atypically luxurious institution' fed and housed its inmates extremely well (*VCH London*, ii. 581–4; Bonfield, 'Therapeutic Regime', 35, 41–2; McIntosh, *Poor Relief in England*, 81).

London, hospital of St Augustine Papey, was founded in 1441 by a specially constituted religious fraternity for the accommodation of elderly, sick and destitute clergy, 'hauyng nothyng to lyue one, but as well to the great displeasure of God as ... shame to holy churche, do myserably begge' (BL, Harley MS 604, f. 12; Cotton MS Vitellius F XVI, ff. 113–23; Hugo, 'Hospital of Le Papey', 183–221).

London, hospital of St Katherine by the Tower. One of London's oldest charitable foundations, the hospital provided residential accommodation for thirteen poor almswomen, as well as sisters of higher status. By 1377 the former received 20s. a year for their support and a similar sum for their grey tunics and hoods. They occupied the lower floor of a building to the south of the church, with two small halls and individual chambers (Jamison, *Royal Hospital of St Katherine*, 31, 36, 59).

London, Merchant Tailors' almshouse. Completed in 1415 at the remarkable cost of over £150, the almshouse comprised seven separate dwellings 'about a proper quadrant or squared court', where impoverished guildsmen and their wives could live in proximity to the company hall (Matthew Davies, 'The Tailors of London: Corporate Charity in the Late Medieval Town', in *Crown, Government and People in the Fifteenth Century*, ed. R.E. Archer (Stroud, 1995), 161–90).

London, Richard Whittington's almshouse. Whittington had planned a collegiate foundation, including an almshouse for thirteen poor Londoners, before his death in 1423, but the scheme was implemented by his executors, who compiled the lengthy and influential statutes incorporated in the foundation charter of 1432. Preference was given to 'pouer feble men' who had been yeomen members of the Mercers' Company, and then to 'pouer and impotent clerkes' from the nearby college (Imray, *Charity of Richard Whittington*, 9–37, Appendix I).

Newcastle upon Tyne, Northumberland, hospital/almshouse of St Katherine, was completed before 1412 by the merchant and philanthropist, Roger Thornton, for the support of four women and nine men, twelve of whom were to be incapable of work because of debility or great age, while the thirteenth was to care for them. The foundation charter incorporating Thornton's statutes is dated 1425 (Hodgson, '"Domus Dei" in Newcastle', 181–220).

Norwich, Norfolk, hospital of St Giles (later God's House). Founded in c. 1249 by Bishop Walter Suffield with thirty beds for the sick and transient poor, the hospital also offered permanent accommodation for aged and bedridden priests. In 1547 it was re-founded as an almshouse under civic management for forty poor men and women (Rawcliffe, *Medicine for the Soul*, chs 1 and 8).

Nottingham, Nottinghamshire, John Plumptre's almshouse. A wealthy merchant stapler, Plumptre began to plan his almshouse in 1390, obtaining royal permission two years later. It was originally intended for thirteen poor widows 'broken by age', but accommodated just seven from 1415 onward (*The History of Parliament: The House of Commons 1386–1421*, ed. J.S. Roskell, Linda Clark and Carole Rawcliffe (4 vols, Stroud, 1993), iv. 92–3; *CPR*, 1391–6, p. 116).

Portsmouth, Hampshire, God's House. Founded in c. 1212 'for the relief of Christ's poor', the hospital experienced financial difficulties and by the fifteenth century functioned as an almshouse for the support of twelve resident paupers of both sexes, who complained of mismanagement by the master (Wright, *Story of the "Domus Dei"*, 3–177).

Saffron Walden, Essex, almshouse, was established in 1400 by the townspeople for thirteen decrepit, poor and blind local people of both sexes. Unusually for a fifteenth-century foundation, the house also offered facilities for the reception of indigent travellers and pregnant women, while imposing few religious obligations upon the residents ('Statutes of the Saffron Walden Almshouse', ed. Steer, 161–221).

Salisbury, Wiltshire, hospital/almshouse of the Holy Trinity. Founded shortly after 1360 under the auspices of the local guild of St George and a fraternity established for the purpose, the hospital supported twelve resident paupers for life, along with eighteen needy transients (until their exclusion in 1438). The surviving accounts suggest that standards of care were high and dietary provision good (*VCH Wiltshire*, iii. 357–8; Brown, *Popular Piety*, 181, 192).

Salisbury, Wiltshire, hospital of St Nicholas. Founded before 1227, the hospital suffered from maladministration and poverty, having probably become an almshouse by 1442, when aged poor women were already being admitted. Bishop Richard Beauchamp's injunctions of 1478 made formal provision for the permanent support of twelve male and female inmates, who might be married (*VCH Wiltshire*, iii. 343–8; *Cartulary of St Nicholas' Hospital*, ed. Wordsworth, 7–10).

Sandwich, Kent, hospital of St Bartholomew. The hospital was founded in c. 1119, passing into the hands of the rulers of Sandwich during the later Middle Ages, when it became a home for sixteen resident almsmen and women chosen from among the townspeople. Although they had to be 'poor' according to the early fourteenth-century custumal, some inmates paid a negotiable entry fee and, until a prohibition in 1480, might be married (*Collections for a History of Sandwich*, ed. Boys, 17–22; Sheila Sweetinburgh, *The Role of the Hospital in Medieval England* (Dublin, 2004), 224–34).

Sherborne, Dorset, hospital of St John the Baptist and St John the Evangelist. Following a dispute with the abbot of Sherborne, the townspeople re-founded the hospital in 1437 as an almshouse for sixteen poor householders of good character, both male and female. It was financed and run by a fraternity, which raised enough money to rebuild the entire structure, endow a handsome chapel and offer high standards of care (Mayo, *Historic Guide*, 13–27, 34–5, 52–3, 63–8; Dorset RO, Dorchester, D/SHA A1–30).

Shrewsbury, Shropshire, Degory Water's almshouse. Founded shortly before 1457 for thirteen poor local people, the almshouse remained under Water's close supervision until his death in 1477; he bequeathed it to the Drapers' Guild, to which he had belonged (*VCH Shropshire*, ii. 111–12; Rope, 'Earliest Book of the Drapers' Company, Shrewsbury', 150–1).

Stamford, Lincolnshire, God's House. William Browne, a wealthy member of the Calais staple, had already established an almshouse 'at his great costs and expenses' for ten poor men and two women before his death in 1489. Its management devolved upon his brother-in-law, Thomas Stokke, who drew up the detailed statutes six years later (Wright, *Story of the "Domus Dei"*, ch. 2, esp. 31–53).

Tattershall College, Lincolnshire, almshouse. As envisaged by the founder Ralph, Lord Cromwell, in 1439, the college was to include an almshouse for thirteen poor people of both sexes, although it was not until 1486 that a contract was made for the 'warkmanly' conversion of a large property into suitable lodgings for men only (*CPR*, 1436–41, p. 292; Salzman, *Buildings in England*, 544–5).

Tong, Shropshire, Isabel Pembridge's almshouse, was established as part of a collegiate foundation in 1410 for the accommodation of thirteen poor men, seven of whom were to be 'so weak and worn in strength' that they needed assistance. The 'order and use accustomed' of the almshouse allowed for a generous provision of food and fuel (Auden, 'Documents Relating to Tong College', 210–11).

Westminster, Middlesex, Henry VII's almshouse. Intended for the support of thirteen poor men aged over fifty who had been menial servants of the crown, the almshouse formed part of a grandiose commemorative project encompassing the king's tomb and memorial chapel at Westminster Abbey. The statutes, incorporated in a richly illuminated four-part indenture of 1504 between Henry and the monks, reflect concern for the physical welfare of the inmates, who were to be tended by four nurses (BL, Harley MS 1498; Fox, 'Royal Almshouse at Westminster'; *CCR*, 1500–9, nos 389 (xi), 390).

Winchester, Cardinal Beaufort's almshouse at the hospital of St Cross. Founded by Bishop Henry de Blois in c. 1136 for, *inter alia*, the permanent accommodation of 'thirteen poor and impotent men', the hospital suffered repeated scandals until the late fourteenth century when it was reformed. In 1445, Cardinal Henry Beaufort, bishop of Winchester, began construction of a 'house of noble poverty' there, with individual dwellings for thirty-five unmarried and impoverished *generosi*, including former members of his own household. Bishop Waynflete eventually implemented a modified version of these ambitious plans, revising the statutes in 1486 in keeping with a greatly reduced budget (*VCH Hampshire*, ii. 193–7; Harriss, *Cardinal Beaufort*, 370–3).

BUTLERAGE AND PRISAGE: A CINDERELLA TAX? THE BRISTOL EVIDENCE[1]

Margaret Condon

Butlerage and prisage, both levies on imported wine, could be characterised as a 'Cinderella tax', on which little serious work has been done since 1918, when Norman Gras allowed these ancient imposts a few useful pages in his history of England's medieval customs system.[2] With the prevailing decline in the study of administrative history, even the names of the levies have fallen out of any common lexicon. The groundwork was laid by the great legist Matthew Hale (1609–76), whose contributions have proved enduring.[3] Thomas Madox (1666–1727), too, traced the very early history of prisage, and included in his text some well-chosen extracts that among other things traced the lower price paid by the king in Bristol for prise wines back to at least the early thirteenth century.[4] It is true that Margery James (d. 1966) worked her way systematically through the butlerage and prisage accounts, as she did with so many then under-explored sources, but her publications were few. James briefly described the imposts and their levy, and, concentrating especially on the fourteenth century, the changing responsibilities of the chief butler

---

[1] Unless stated otherwise, the manuscript sources cited are in TNA.
[2] N.S.B. Gras, *The Early English Customs System* (Oxford, 1918), 37–48. Accounts of the chief butler, where enrolled, are calendared in *The Enrolled Customs Accounts (E372, E356, E364)*, ed. Stuart Jenks (12 vols, List and Index Society, 2004–13). A few early particulars of account for butlerage in Bristol (the 'new custom' paid by aliens), were edited by Gras or by Eleanor Carus-Wilson: concordance in E.M. Carus-Wilson, *The Overseas Trade of Bristol in the Later Middle Ages* (Bristol Record Society, vii, 1937), 6–7, 30–1; a late exemplar is 'Bristol 1509–10: Particulars of Account of Nicholas Browne, Deputy Butler, for Prisage and Butlerage', ed. M.M. Condon and E.T. Jones (Bristol University, Explore Bristol Research, 2023). For extracts relating to King's Lynn 1346–7, taken from an account of John Wesenham as chief butler, see *The Making of King's Lynn: A Documentary Survey*, ed. D.M. Owen (1984), 449–53. Maryanne Kowaleski is currently editing London entries from 1317–18, 1329–31 and 1333–4 for the London Record Society. Butlerage and prisage accounts from 1509–47 are noticed in *Letters and Papers*, but with the omission of much useful detail, including the nature of the levy: see e.g. i (pt 2), no. 3313. Prise of wine in the port of Chester to 1554 is calendared from local records in K.P. Wilson, *Chester Customs Accounts 1301–1566* (Lancashire and Cheshire Record Society, cxi, 1969). Butlerage and prisage in Cornish ports is included in *The Havener's Accounts of the Earldom and Duchy of Cornwall*, ed. Maryanne Kowaleski (Devon and Cornwall Record Society, new ser., xliv, 2001).
[3] Francis Hargrave, *A Collection of Tracts Relative to the Law of England, from Manuscripts* (Dublin, 1787), 116–31: cf. the caveats of Gras, *Early English Customs System*, 6–7.
[4] Thomas Madox, *The History and Antiquities of the Exchequer* (2 vols, 1769), i. 765–70.

and the variant sources over time. For individual ports, her research was condensed into long tables of annual numbers of wine ships, and totals of tuns of wine imported, some broken down into denizen and alien trade.[5] James's analyses remain important, but they are arid ground in terms of the evidential value and history of the imposts in the fifteenth and early sixteenth centuries.

The collection of butlerage, a monetary tax paid by aliens on their wine imports, and prisage, a levy in kind on the wine imports of denizens, was the responsibility of the chief butler, *capitalis pincerna regis*, known by the mid-fifteenth century, especially after the promotion of Sir Ralph Boteler to the peerage as Lord Sudeley, as *capitalis pincerna Anglie*. Despite the coincidence of title, this was a different and more substantial office than that of the other chief butler of England, who acted and had title only for a coronation banquet. The claims to that privilege were on each occasion subject to verification, and throughout the Middle Ages the coronation office was usually exercised by the earl of Arundel by virtue of precedent, despite occasional challenge on grounds of serjeanty tenure.[6] The *pincerna regis* or *pincerna Anglie* of the so-called butlerage accounts was appointed by letters patent.[7] Many early butlers were appointed 'during pleasure'. Their fifteenth-century successors mostly held office for life, leaving their executors to present their final accounts and to answer for debts and arrears. Local deputies or factors in each port acted for the butler in the collection of the imposts, while purveyors managed much of the purchase of wine. Patronage was a perquisite of office, and deputies, purveyors and menial officers were both appointed by the chief butler and accounted to him. Port deputies were drawn from the same body of men, often themselves merchants, who filled civic, county and customs offices.[8] Indeed, contrary to a statute of 1323, some were concurrently both a port's customer and a deputy butler.[9] Their tenure was 'at pleasure', meaning that they could be replaced at will; over this, they would lose office either on the death or loss of office of the butler who had appointed them, or on the death of the king from whom the chief butler himself derived authority.

The primary responsibility of the chief butler was the provision of wine – in vast quantities – for the royal household.[10] Profits from butlerage and prisage supported this activity, but were supplemented by additional assignments from the exchequer, and sales of surplus wine from an immediately preceding year. Until 1478 the butler was also *ex officio* the king's chamberlain and coroner of London, and surviving

---

[5] M.K. James, *Studies in the Medieval Wine Trade*, ed. E.M. Veale (Oxford, 1971).
[6] C57/2, 3 (Henry IV, Henry V); L.G. Wickham Legg, *Coronation Records* (Westminster, 1901), 138–9 (Richard II), 189; *Cal. Memoranda Rolls 1326–7* (1968), nos 306, 884; cf. *CIPM Edward III*, vii. no. 590, viii. no. 664 (p. 487); see also J.H. Round, *The King's Serjeants and Officers of State* (1911), 142–65; *The Coronation of Richard III: the Extant Documents*, ed. A.F. Sutton and P.W. Hammond (Gloucester, 1983), 245–53.
[7] A partial list of chief butlers, as well as statutes and precedents concerning the office, is in *Reports from the Notebooks of Edward Coke*, ed. J.H. Baker (5 vols, Selden Society, 5th ser., cxxxvi–cxli, 2022–3), iv. 749–52. For a list of the butlers of 1347–1514, see Appendix below.
[8] E.g. Thomas Beaupyne of Bristol and Robert Cache of Wareham: *The History of Parliament: The House of Commons 1386–1421*, ed. J.S. Roskell, Linda Clark and Carole Rawcliffe (4 vols, Stroud, 1993), ii. 164–6, 463–4.
[9] *Statutes*, i. 192. Bristol examples include Walter Derby, Thomas Saundres and Thomas Croft; several others, including Thomas Beaupyne, Robert Russell and John Stapilton, were past or future customs officers.
[10] Robert Blackmore, *Government and Merchant Finance in Anglo-Gascon Trade, 1300–1500* (2020), 228; James, *Medieval Wine Trade*, 177–80.

warrants show him presenting deputies to act for him in this latter office.[11] The early history of the office of the chief butler was traced all too briefly by T.F. Tout, who noted his close association with the merchants of London and his subordination to the steward of the royal household, to whom he accounted prior to the exchequer reforms of 1323–6.[12] The butler's duties are most fully set out, with some anachronisms, in the 'Black Book' and 1478 household ordinances of Edward IV.[13] Fifteenth-century butlers were men of higher social status than the merchant-butlers of previous centuries although they, too, had been both wealthy and men of influence. The distinctions blur. If the butler holding office for much of the first quarter of the century and beyond, Thomas Chaucer, 'remained a mere esquire', he was a man of extraordinary ability, five times Speaker of the House of Commons, and connected to the higher aristocracy by kinship and marriage.[14] His successors were prominent knights and peers, including Edward IV's brother-in-law, Anthony, Earl Rivers, but they had other concerns. Indeed Ralph Boteler, Lord Sudeley, would, from 1447, have been in the peculiar position of being answerable to himself as steward of the household for his office of chief butler.[15]

Early records of the chief butler cover the entire range of responsibilities for which he and his deputies were responsible, including the provisioning of the household at war. The detail is recorded in his particulars of account.[16] Structured entries for prisage listed for each port named ships from which prise had been taken, their dates of entry into port, and associated profits and expenses. The particulars also document the butler's purchases of wines in each port, often naming individual merchants. There is much information on the uses to which both prise and purchased wine was put, including gifts of wine, and on its distribution, storage, sale, disposal and waste, as also on the movement of ships between ports other than their own.[17] These accounts are often more compelling, and capable of wider interpretation, than those of the later Middle Ages, both in general terms and for the history of any port.[18] For Bristol, they confirm that the town was always an important wine port, but would suggest a radically different and changing pattern of both merchantry and shipping from that made familiar by scholars of the later period, such as Eleanor

---

[11] E.g. C81/1644, no. 31; 1647, nos. 2, 70a; cf. *Calendar of Letter-Books of the City of London, K*, ed. R.R. Sharpe (1911), pp. xii, 8, 19, 92, 156, 186–7 (when in 1435 the city refused admission of John Forthey as Boteler's deputy). The city redeemed this appointment from the king in 1478 at a cost of £7,000: *Letter-Book K*, p. xliv.

[12] T.F. Tout, *Chapters in Medieval Administrative History* (6 vols, Manchester, 1920–33), i. 159–60; ii. 261, 264, 266; iv. 85–8, 147, 158–9, 171–2, 202, 211–12.

[13] *The Household of Edward IV: the Black Book and the Ordinance of 1478*, ed. A.R. Myers (Manchester, 1959), 59, 87, 101, 174–6.

[14] Carole Rawcliffe, 'Chaucer, Thomas (c.1367–1434)', *Oxford DNB*; *House of Commons 1386–1421*, ii. 524–32.

[15] A.C. Reeves, 'Boteler, Ralph, first Baron Sudeley (c.1394–1473)', *Oxford DNB*. For the office of steward, *Black Book*, ed. Myers, 142–4.

[16] See also A.L. Simon, *The History of the Wine Trade in England* (2 vols, 1906–7), i. 155–8, 227–337 for early mentions in the close rolls.

[17] E.g. in 1341 ships of Fowey and Cork, and the *Cog John* of Bristol, carried both prise and purchased wine from Bristol to Winchelsea for the king's crossing to France, and in 1343 the *Michael* of Bristol carried 61 tuns of alien-owned wine into London by way of trade: E101/79/5, 10.

[18] James, *Medieval Wine Trade*, used them selectively to study carriage and freightage costs, wine prices and local distribution, and more broadly to explore the convoy system for the import of wine and the role of the butler in victualling for war. Wendy Childs employed them in her many studies of Iberian trade, and Blackmore in his study of English Gascony.

Carus-Wilson and Evan Jones, in which Bristol's own marine and merchants dominated the import trade in wine. Besides much useful detail, they would also highlight the effects, both in terms of trade and in its relations with the crown, of Bristol's proximity to Wales, Ireland and the Atlantic, and the constraints arising from the long sea voyage from Bristol to London, Calais and the north. Emphatically, these butlers' accounts were not just fiscal records of prisage, but had a much wider remit.

In origin butlerage and prisage were a single tax, taken from at least the mid-twelfth century as a form of purveyance. The levy predated by more than a century the more familiar customs duties first granted to the crown in 1275 on a limited range of goods.[19] Prise of wine, in contrast to customs dues, was a prerogative right. Henry VII defined it succinctly as 'belongyng to oure crowne of old inheritance'.[20] Its exercise was enshrined in terms more appropriate to the single-masted cogs in common use in the thirteenth and fourteenth centuries than to the triple-masted ships used later. The king could take one tun from any ship entering England with more than ten tuns of denizen-owned wine, and two tuns from any ship carrying twenty tuns or more. In theory, in the latter scenario, one tun was to be taken before the mast, the other aft of it.[21] The merchant owners of the wine were compensated at the rate of 20*s*. a tun. Even in 1200, this would have been below the market rate for the cost of the wine plus carriage.[22] The compensation was rapidly outpaced by price rises, but approximated throughout the Middle Ages to the cost of the transport of a tun of wine from Bordeaux.[23] Hence it became known as 'freightage'.[24] In Bristol, until the early fifteenth century, the payment was less: 15*s*. a tun.[25]

Early in the fourteenth century prisage bifurcated into two distinct levies. The *Carta Mercatoria* of 1303, a package of privileges and protections for foreign merchants, brought certain new fiscal obligations applicable only to them. Prise of wine was commuted for aliens in return for a 'new custom' of 2*s*. on every tun imported, payable in addition to any other dues.[26] This impost was termed customs or new custom in the accounts, but is commonly known as butlerage from the familiar use of that term after 1500, by which time it had become necessary to distinguish the levy from a new 'new custom' on malmsey wine.[27] Butlerage was due *pro rata* from the individual alien merchant, calculated according to the number of tuns or part tuns

---

[19] M.H. Mills, 'The Collectors of Customs', in *The English Government at Work, 1327–1336*, ed. W.A. Morris and J.R. Strayer (Cambridge, MA, 1947), 168–9; Gras, *Early English Customs System*, 39–42.
[20] E356/23, rot. 75.
[21] Cf. Kenicot v Bogan, *English Law Reports*, lxxx. 132, which, although late evidence, emphasises that this had become a fiction.
[22] Gras, *Early English Customs System*, 41–2.
[23] James, *Medieval Wine Trade*, 125, 144–7, 150–3; E.M. Carus-Wilson, 'The Overseas Trade of Bristol', in *English Trade in the Fifteenth Century*, ed. Eileen Power and M.M. Postan (1933), 239.
[24] Hargrave, *Collection of Tracts*, 117.
[25] Madox, *History and Antiquities*, i. 766; Gras, *Early English Customs System*, 41, 47. Freightage in Bristol stood at 15*s*. until Mich. 1409, but appears to have conformed to the standard rate of 20*s*. thereafter: E101/405/23, 406/3, 5; E361/7, rots 8d–9.
[26] *Munimenta Gildhallae Londoniensis*, ed. H.T. Riley (2 vols, RS, 1859, 1860), ii (pt 1), 207, 209; Mills, 'Collectors of Customs', 169; Gras, *Early English Customs System*, 42–3. A similar agreement had been made with the merchants of Aquitaine in 1302; an attempt to extend the commutation to denizens failed, being part of a wider package intended to increase customs revenues: William Stubbs, *Select Charters*, ed. H.W.C. Davis (9th edn, Oxford, 1921), 496–7.
[27] *PROME*, xvi. 133; cf. E159/283, *brevia directa*, Hil. 20 Hen. VII, rot. 3d. By the 1520s butlerage had alternatively become the 'ancient custom': E101/84/18, rot. 15d.

imported. The chief butler accounted separately for the profits of both imposts, but between the mid-fourteenth century and the reign of Henry VII butlerage, paid in specie by foreign merchants, rather than prisage, taken in casks of wine, figures far more prominently in the extant records.

The reason for this lies primarily in the variant processes of audit. Butlerage, as a levy on alien trade, came under the broad head of 'customs' and indeed was, in some years of the fourteenth century, levied by a port's customers rather than by the butler's deputy. The chief butler accounted at the exchequer rather than in the household for the total receipts of the impost.[28] The enrolment in the pipe office of summaries of the audited accounts has ensured their survival, although many detailed particulars have been lost.[29] In contrast, the chief butler's accounts for wine, including his returns for the levy of prise, were made only in the wardrobe after 1350. The last surviving particulars of account, with their useful record of the movement of ships and other matters concerning the prise and wine purchase, is for 1349–50.[30] Thereafter, until 1485, the accounting record for prise becomes much less coherent.

For both butlerage and prisage there is a watershed period commencing at the mid-point of the fourteenth century that radically affects both the survival, and the utility, of the records of both imposts. It was determined by the iterative grants and progressive implementation of a new subsidy, tunnage, payable *pro rata* on their wine imports by denizens and aliens alike. In what has been called 'the experimental period' for the grants of tunnage and the *ad valorem* duty of poundage, c. 1340–87, the grants were made by consent either in council or in assemblies of merchants, and from 1372 in parliament, to fund the provision of armed shipping for the protection of trade or the safe passage overseas of the king. The subsidies were for strictly limited periods, at stated but variable rates, and ultimately payable to various named accountants including, in 1371–2, the butler.[31] That year the receipts of the Bristol collectors from tunnage were £98 11s. charged on 985½ tuns of wine, approximately 16 per cent of the whole collection. Bristol, in a pattern that would become familiar, was in second place behind London in terms of the value of the levy to the crown.[32] From 1386 grants of tunnage and poundage became increasingly regular and of longer duration, mostly setting a rate of 3s. per tun. As a levy on denizens, tunnage and poundage were intermittently suspended between 1422 and 1431, while continuing to be imposed on aliens who from its first introduction paid (when liable) both tunnage and the new custom on their wines. From 1431 the grants of tunnage and poundage became sequential. From that date also, aliens became subject in addition to a supplement of 3s. per tun *pro rata* on their imports of sweet wine.[33] Henry VI was granted tunnage and poundage for life in 1453 and Edward IV in 1465, although in practice Edward had levied both from the beginning of his reign.[34] In con-

---

[28] The receipts then generally went to the household via exchequer assignment.
[29] The particulars would have been archived by the king's remembrancer, and, like the regular customs accounts, subject to the vagaries of survival of the records of that office.
[30] E101/79/25; James, *Medieval Wine Trade*, 36.
[31] W.M. Ormrod, 'The Origins of Tunnage and Poundage: Parliament and the Estate of Merchants in the 14th Century', *Parliamentary History*, xxviii (2009), 210–15 (quote at 210).
[32] E101/80/22; account of the collectors, whose remit extended to Bridgwater, E122/15/7.
[33] Ormrod, 'Origins of Tunnage and Poundage', 216–17. Sweet wine was generally imported in butts, equated to half a tun, although in practice slightly smaller.
[34] Ormrod, 'Origins of Tunnage and Poundage', 217; *The London Customs Accounts*, ed. Stuart Jenks (Quellen und Darstellungen zur Hansischen Geschichte, lxxiv (3, pt 1), 2016), vii–viii, including

trast, Richard III encountered opposition to the immediate collection of tunnage and poundage; and while the levy of poundage continued without significant interruption the king had to wait until January 1484 and his first parliament before tunnage could be levied. That restriction, the need for prior parliamentary sanction, remained true for subsequent reigns, with the potential to depress in the short term the crown's profit from the wine trade.[35] The enrolled accounts for tunnage collected in each port were expressed in terms both of total numbers of tuns of wine liable to the duty, and in sums of money due. This data has enabled longitudinal studies and comparisons over time that are as accurate as the records themselves allow.[36]

That all-encompassing utility is not true of the fifteenth-century accounts of the chief butler for the collection of the new custom. Not only was butlerage paid only by aliens (and so applied to only a fraction of wine imports), but with rare exceptions the totals recorded in the enrolled accounts were not broken down by port, except to identify null returns – as was true of Bristol in, for example, 1406–8, 1436–8 and 1460–1.[37] Moreover, auditors' notes, which lay behind the innocuous-sounding 'supplement during accounting' of Stuart Jenks's calendars of the enrolled accounts, indicate numerous omissions and errors detected through comparison with customs particulars. For example, exchequer auditors found that forty-two tuns of red and white wine had been omitted from the butler's accounts of 1476–7 for London, Exeter, Dartmouth and Bristol.[38]

Had tunnage and poundage particulars of account survived in quantity, there would have been little reason to pay attention to the butlerage accounts of the fifteenth century, with their partial and imperfect record of the alien import of wine. Even the profits of the new custom, although useful, were relatively insignificant: for much of the fifteenth century they contributed perhaps £100–£250 a year to the financing of the royal household, whereas even in the depressed years from 1455 to 1465 that followed the English loss of Bordeaux in 1453, in Bristol alone alien and denizen merchants together contributed an annual average of around £125 to exchequer coffers from tunnage on wine.[39] But the survival of customers' particulars is dire, even for London, whose port dominated the trade.[40]

---

correction to Ormrod: the grant to Edward IV was made in the second session, opening 21 Jan. 1465, of the 1464 parliament. This and other volumes in the series are e-published: www.hansischergeschichtsverein.de/.

[35] The restriction did not apply to butlerage and prisage, which passed with the crown and continued to be collected: 'Bristol 1509–10: Particulars of Account of a Controller of Customs, 29 September 1509 to c. 14 January 1510: Introduction', ed. M.M. Condon and E.T. Jones (Bristol University, Research Data Repository, 2023), 4–6.

[36] See e.g., James, *Medieval Wine Trade*, 107–15; receipts for individual ports are calendared in *Enrolled Customs Accounts*, ed. Jenks.

[37] The final accounts for the fifteenth century as enrolled are calendared in *Enrolled Customs Accounts*, ed. Jenks, *Part 6*, pp. 1597–1601; *Part 10*, pp. 2598–2601; *Part 11*, pp. 2823–6. The absence of mention of a port in any one account indicates a null return for the period of that account. Blackmore, *Government and Merchant Finance*, 295 appears to be unaware of the enrolments, to the detriment of his data.

[38] *Enrolled Customs Accounts*, ed. Jenks, *Part 10*, pp. 2430, 2505, 2600.

[39] Calculated at 3s. per tun from the figures in Carus-Wilson, *Overseas Trade*, 295.

[40] London tunnage and poundage accounts of the fifteenth century are transcribed in *The London Customs Accounts*, ed. Jenks, lxxiv (2, pts 1–4, 8–10); (3, pts 1–2, 6); (4, pts 1, 3, 9). Rigby's study of Boston's customs accounts includes a brief overview of the general reliability and coverage of both particulars and enrolments, usefully updated to reflect recent literature: S.H. Rigby, *The Overseas Trade of Boston 1279–1548* (Cologne, 2023), 13–22. For a conspectus of published customs accounts,

Where extant, the customs particulars, whether of the customers or a port's controller, provide detailed records of the shipments of individual merchants, the name of the master and (notional) date of entry or exit of the ship on which those goods were laded.[41] Bristol, Hull and sporadically some other ports, supplied additionally the name of the ship itself and its port of origin and departure/destination. A few Bristol particulars survive for the beginning of the century, when denizens were periodically exempt from tunnage. There are no detailed returns at all for the port for the greater part of Henry VI's reign, other than a recently discovered fragment. For the three Yorkist kings, in 1461–85, less than 30 per cent of particulars survive on a census month by month. Those extant are weighted towards the summer, the low period for wine imports, and include just one full year account. The reign of Henry VII is little better, even though five full-year accounts survive.[42] Despite their limitations, details derived from the chief butler's account for the new custom help supply the deficit. Their small fiscal contribution and narrow client base need to be kept in mind, as does the legislative provisions under which the impost was levied. Had the customs particulars for 1477–8 not survived, for example, it would not be obvious that a foreigner, the Basque Juan Arronamendi, had mastered the *Magdalen* of Errenteria on a voyage to Candia (Heraklion), returning with fifty-five tuns of wine for himself and a further 174 tuns, a pipe and a hogshead for Bristol merchants.[43] It was an important voyage that, with another of 1488 under the same master, contradicts the traditional narrative of Bristol's exclusion from the eastern Mediterranean after 1458. A little over ten years after that first voyage, Arronamendi would have paid enhanced customs, tunnage and butlerage as an alien; but under the terms of the treaty of Westminster of 1466–7, enduring until the abrogation of the Castilians' customs privileges in 1489, in October 1477 he paid duties at denizen rates. As the largest shipper after the Bristol merchant Thomas Rowley, he would have been liable as a quasi-denizen for a substantial proportion of the value of whatever two tuns of wine were taken for prise.[44]

The dominance by the fifteenth century of Bristol's own merchants in the port's wine trade means that the butlerage returns for Bristol are less rewarding than those of ports such as London, Southampton, Hull or Exeter, where there was a higher alien presence.[45] All detailed returns included the date of entry of a vessel, the number of tuns shipped and the duty arising, as well as an item of information that positively identified the entry. This might be the name of the ship, or of its master; ideally both, as in the account for 1489–90, although for Bristol such paired entries are in a minority prior to 1500.[46] The name of the alien merchant importer was recorded, occasionally with an extended manifest if there was more than one alien shipper on the same

---

continually updated, see 'Medieval England Maritime Project', ed. Maryanne Kowaleski, https://memp.ace.fordham.edu (hereafter *MEMP*). This includes a list of the London accounts edited by Jenks, with direct links to the online volumes.

[41] E122, *passim*; *The London Customs Accounts, 1445/6*, ed. Jenks, lxxiv, pp. xi–xv.
[42] Editions of the Bristol customs accounts for 1461–1504 are ongoing, and accessible via the University of Bristol's 'Explore Bristol Research' and 'Cabot Project' websites, or *MEMP*.
[43] E122/176/23. This fragment of an account is a recent discovery.
[44] For the effect of the treaties of Westminster and Medina del Campo on Castilian trade, W.R. Childs, *Anglo-Castilian Trade in the Later Middle Ages* (Manchester, 1978), esp. 54–65; eadem, *Trade and Shipping in the Medieval West: Portugal, Castile and England* (Oporto, 2013), 88–9, 153.
[45] Butlers' particulars in E101/81/1–84/3.
[46] E101/83/10. The Bristol entries in this account include, unusually, the continental ports of departure.

vessel, but more usually with variations on the '*et alii*' formula. The supplied details from any port were at the whim of the deputy. Particularly frustrating, given the loss of so many customs accounts, are entries such as those for Bristol in 1462–4 that read merely '*diversi mercatores*' or '*diverse alienigene*', and those particulars for which the date of a ship's entry was omitted despite being required data.[47]

Sample extracts for Butlerage levied in Bristol in 1468.[48]

Navis Ruffian' Inmanus applicuit ibidem vij⁰ die Februarii[49]	Bertillmew Fernandus alienigena	xx dollia[50]	Inde custuma – xl *s*.
Navis Johannis de Burgayne applicuit ibidem xxvij⁰ die Februarii	Johannes Romeneto alienigena	v dollia	Inde custuma – x *s*.
Batella vocata le Cristoffre de Breste applicuit ibidem xxvj^{to} die Maii	Diverse alienigene	v dollia	Inde custuma – x *s*.

Bristol was not the only port whose returns were defective. For any port, there might be omissions of ships and imports, errors in names and dates, and even confusion of months. However, just how and why 257 tuns of wine could be omitted from Bristol's accounts for 1464–6, especially when the deputy butler, Richard Alberton, was a former controller in the port, surpasses understanding.[51] The irregularities in the accounts are symptomatic of a lack of oversight as the office of chief butler became increasingly a sinecure. As a source, the particulars for butlerage come with a caveat for their accuracy. Yet it would be unwise to ignore an archive that, between 1450 and 1500, for Bristol alone documents the movement of at least 145 ships, and trade in over 2,500 tuns of wine, the latter figure being nearly twice the yearly wine import to Bristol in the last years of Edward IV's reign.[52] A similar observation could be made for any other port, even where the evidence proves to be negative or minimal for alien trade in wine.

At the most basic level, the particulars supply sufficient detail to supplement some of the lacunae in the customs accounts. They may trigger broader observations. For example, even if the Bristol customs particulars for 1475–6 and 1492–3 had not

[47] E101/82/7 has '*marcatores*'; E101/82/14 (omitted dates, 1475–6).
[48] E101/82/12, an account for 1466–8, with nine Bristol entries in total, while London has 105. Abbreviations extended.
[49] A Portuguese ship, cf. E122/172/17: *Navicula* (small ship) the *Ruffyan*, Jonyanus (João Eanes) master.
[50] i.e. '*dolia*': 20 tuns [of wine]. Foreign volumetric measures, if present, were recalculated (not always correctly) into conventional units, e.g. E101/82/7, 14, London entries.
[51] E101/82/8. Bristol's enrolled customs accounts do not separate out denizen and alien trade in wine for these years, and there is only a partial overlap with extant particulars.
[52] E101/82/2–84/3. Of the eight surviving particulars of 1400–49 half have no returns for Bristol: E101/81/1–16. The figures for ship movements do not include the sporadic record of Bristol ships trading to other ports, such as the *Gabriel* to Weymouth or Bridgwater in 1407, or John Shipman's vessel in 1500: E101/81/5, 84/3, f. 2.

survived it would still be possible to see, in the butlerage accounts, the spike in the wine trade of aliens that was one outcome of the disruption caused by war, when safe access to Bordeaux became more difficult and some of Bristol's great ships were displaced or engaged in the king's service.[53] As both merchants and carriers, aliens seized a commercial opportunity. The uncluttered presentation of the butlerage particulars highlights the difference between ports in the make-up of their alien trade, and changes over time. The returns as a whole may be coloured by outside factors in help or hindrance, including trade restrictions and licences applicable to particular alien merchant groups or ports. For example, between 1467 and 1489 any Iberian mentioned as importing wine is likely to have been Portuguese since Castilians, notably the Basques, were exempt from the levy. This means that evidence for Castilian merchants trading in wine is lost, unless customs particulars or other sources survive.

With some local knowledge, it is possible to tell stories: of the Castilian Anthony Scalant and his ship the *Mary Gallant* as a regular carrier of wine for the merchants of Bristol; of the Yvos and Evans who are likely to have been Bretons, sailing to Bristol even after the decline in the port's Breton trade from c. 1470; of the *batellae* bringing in small quantities of alien-owned Iberian wine, crossing the Severn from ports such as Chepstow, Cardiff or Tenby, even though the port of departure is not stated and the customs particulars are lost.[54] The Bristol merchant William Weston could realise an attachment for debt on the goods of Martin Denys, a Portuguese resident in London, because in 1490 Denys shipped wine to Bristol, as the butlerage returns reveal.[55]

After 1500 the butlerage records for Bristol are those of Bristol's deputies rather than the chief butler, or the aggregated totals of overview accounts, which sum the receipts of both butlerage and prisage.[56] They conform to a long term trend in which aliens had ceased to be major players in Bristol's wine trade, as Bristol's own merchants not only traded directly with Lisbon and Bordeaux, but also in Andalucia and occasionally further afield, and alien merchants faced an adverse tariff in respect of wine. There were other goods that offered the foreign merchant better returns. Yet wine was still useful portage for a shipmaster, and alien shipment of wine did not cease altogether.[57] Bristol in this respect was very different from London and Southampton, with their trade in high-value eastern Mediterranean sweet wines, a commerce in which Italians in particular were still dominant and encouraged by the crown.

What then of prisage? The short answer is that there is a long near-silence from the last extant particulars for prisage and the purchase of wine (1348–50) until Henry VII's auditors opened a full-scale investigation into the accounts of Sir John Fortescue after that chief butler's death in July 1500.[58] The views that the butler was

---

[53] E101/82/14, 83/13, 16; and see M.M. Condon and E.T. Jones, 'Bristol 1475: Particulars of Account of Thomas Croft and John Langston, Customers, 26 March to 20 July 1475: Introduction' (Bristol University, Explore Bristol Research, 2019), 4–7.
[54] *Batellae*: E101/83/22 (1495), 25 (1497).
[55] E101/83/10; C244/140, nos 46, 62. For Weston, see M.M. Condon and E.T. Jones, 'William Weston: Early Voyager to the New World', *HR*, xci (2018), 628–46.
[56] For the latter, e.g. E101/84/24, 27; E351/454, 455. E36/212, p. 77 conflates the two totals.
[57] See, e.g. E101/85/41.
[58] E101/79/25; see also the summary account for Henry Picard, for 1350–1: E372/196, rot. 44.

supposed to present within the royal household twice a year do not, as far as this author is aware, survive.[59] Nor are records other than those of account particularly helpful. Vintners of the stature of John Stodeye and Henry Picard, the merchant shipowner John Wesenham, or a consummate administrator such as Thomas Chaucer, have left ample evidence of their activity as chief butler not just in the financial records of their office but also in the rolls of chancery, in naval and victualling accounts and in records of litigation.[60] After Chaucer's death in 1434 such men gave way to sinecurists such as John Talbot, earl of Shrewsbury (chief butler from 1458 to 1461), who had, so he said when appointing a deputy to purvey wines, 'no leisure' to perform that office.[61] One side effect of this elevation in status of the holders of the office of chief butler is that for Bristol, at least, it becomes increasingly difficult to construct the sequence of deputies assigned to collect prisage and butlerage within the port. For example, even though the Bristol merchant John Sharpe was joined in 1434 with the customers, controller and searchers of Bristol to enforce the use of legal quays and empowered to seize uncustomed goods, his appointment as a deputy butler is not recorded.[62] For the reign of Henry VII, apart from one chance mention, the names of the deputy butlers in Bristol are unknown prior to 1500. While there are omissions in the tally of fourteenth-century deputies, for the most part in that period the chief butler's requests to the chancellor for the issue of writs of aid (*de intendendo*) for incoming deputies in named ports had resulted in an entry on the patent rolls.

Quantitative evidence for prisage is preserved in summary form within the accounts of the keeper of the wardrobe of the household. These, prior to 1485, noticed income from prisage as revenue, under the head of foreign receipts, in which the chief butler was just one of several accountants.[63] The formulae vary, but the crux of the accounting entries was to record the 'advantage', or profit, from wine taken at prise and then sold. This was the first given figure. The total number of tuns thus sold in 'divers ports', was specified, as was the total freightage – the compensation paid to the merchants. As an outgoing, this was a necessary allowance on both the butler's and the accounting officer's charge. Until 1409 it is possible to establish the number of tuns of prise wine sold in Bristol because of the lower freightage paid by the crown there. In 1402–3, for example, Thomas Chaucer accounted for a total of £153 10*s*., the profit on fifty-three tuns of prise wine sold for £198 15*s*.[64] Thirty-one tuns out of the fifty-three had been taken and sold at Bristol, where the freightage was 15*s*.; the remainder were from other ports, in all of which the standard freightage of 20*s*. applied. The following year, between 1 October 1403 and 6 January 1405, Bristol's contribution was just fourteen out of fifty-two tuns, and the total advantage £155 3*s*. 4*d*.[65] One contributory factor in the significant fall in Bristol's prisage

[59] For the provision of views, a summary declared account, *Black Book*, ed. Myers, 174.
[60] For Picard (also a mayor of London), W.M. Ormrod, *Edward III* (2011), 453; but cf. R.L. Axworthy, 'Picard (Pycard), Henry (*d*.1361)', *Oxford DNB*. For Wesenham, T.H. Lloyd, 'Wesenham, John (*fl*. 1333–82)', *Oxford DNB*.
[61] *CPR*, 1452–61, p. 577. The phrase appears on other warrants and is probably a trope.
[62] *CPR*, 1429–36, p. 468; and see Appendix.
[63] The enrolled accounts are E361/5–7, but in very poor condition after 1400; the ledgers of the keepers and controllers, with many gaps, are in the class of exchequer miscellaneous accounts, E101.
[64] E101/404/21. The difference between the totals was the amount of freightage paid out to merchants via the ships' pursers or masters.
[65] E361/7, rot. 4d.

revenues in such a short space of time might have been the twenty tuns granted by the king to Edward, duke of York, in December 1403, to be taken at Bristol over two years in return for the duke's service at Carmarthen.[66] Prise wine given away was wine not sold, and was for that reason recorded in the accounts. The ledgers listed the names of the recipients and the number of tuns of wine received, valuing the wine for accounting purposes at a median price per tun. It is one of the more interesting uses to which the wine was put. Without supplementary information, however, it is often difficult to distinguish between grants of prise wine, and those drawn from purchased stores. The gifts of wine were the one element of the butlers' wine and prisage accounts that continued to interest the exchequer's auditors, who checked both the validity of the warrants and their execution.[67]

In at least the first part of the century, recipients of grants for life, mandated by warrants dormant under the great seal, seem most usually to have paid freightage on their wine to the butler's factors. Such payments figure separately in the household accounts as an income source. Sir Lewis Clifford, for example, was granted four tuns yearly from the prise wines taken at Bristol 'paying the prise therefore as is customary' in 1392, and regularly paid his 60s. freightage thereafter. In 1393–4, a year in which the price of wine collapsed, he and other recipients of prise wine saw their allowance briefly doubled, but paid the extra freightage at the usual rates.[68] Yet not all such grants triggered payment by the recipient: for instance, there is no indication that in 1386 Elizabeth, prioress of St Magdalen, Bristol, the town's only nunnery, paid freightage on her wine; nor was Joan Howell, Henry VII's childhood nurse, so charged, although in old age and widowhood she was still receiving a tun of wine yearly in Bristol from prise wine taken in the port as late as 1508–9.[69] Gifts were not only assigned on prise wine. For example, John Hampton, king's esquire, received two tuns of wine annually from the Bristol deputy, but had to pay freightage only for the one tun that came from prise.[70] Lay recipients of prise wine were expected to deal directly with the deputies.[71] It is less clear how religious houses receiving wine in alms, for which the king covered the freightage, engaged with the butler or his deputies, but their receipts were usually sealed at the house concerned. For Bristol, this meant primarily the charterhouses of Hinton, Witham and Coventry, to which Edward III had first granted the wines in return for prayers, a spiritual benefit transferred to Edward's successors.[72] Such charitable grants were assigned on geographically appropriate ports, to minimise carriage costs. The livery of this wine

[66] E101/81/2.
[67] The warrants and receipts were, as the auditors occasionally noted, subsidiary to wardrobe accounts: E101/409/16, f. 32v, 410/9, f. 38. Gifts variously entered under Elemosine, Necessaria and Dona.
[68] CPR, 1391–6, p. 119; E361/5, rots 23d–26.
[69] CPR, 1385–9, p. 207, a grant made when the king was at Bristol; E101/83/2, 84/38. After 1485 there is firm evidence only for the payment of freightage by Joan, Lady Dinham (d. 1497), E356/23, rot. 75d. Henry VII's grant to Joan, made shortly before the promotion of her son to be treasurer, renewed grants by Edward IV and Richard III: Hannes Kleineke, 'Lady Joan Dinham: Fifteenth-century West Country Matriarch', in *Social Attitudes and Political Structures in the Fifteenth Century*, ed. Tim Thornton (Stroud, 2001), 77.
[70] CPR, 1436–41, p. 349; 1452–61, p. 48. The duality is very obvious in early accounts of the chief butler, with their huge lists of *dona*, but becomes more difficult to follow in the fifteenth century in the absence of the chief butler's accounts.
[71] The dating clause of receipts for gifts of wine often names the place at which the instrument was sealed.
[72] 'Particulars of Nicholas Browne 1509–10', ed. Condon and Jones, 2.

was recorded in the 'offerings and alms' section of the household books, but without identifying the ports on which it was charged. Aggregated expenses of cellarage and carriage, and losses such as leakage (ullage) and corruption (corrison) were entered as deductions under '*necessaria*', but did not distinguish between purchased and prise wine. It becomes obvious, however, why local sale or gift was long the preferred option for dealing with prise wine. Increased ullage and 'outrageous corrison' was an inevitable result of the carriage of wine from store by cart or ship. The melding of information as described above, the numerous gaps in the evidence and its fragmentation within the accounts makes it difficult to abstract reliable statistics concerning total prisage in any one year, and impossible to table a long sequential series of annual figures for prisage, either for the chief butler or for any one port.

The chief butler's responsibility for the provision of wines for the royal household ended in 1478. The requirement had long been met largely by bulk purchase from the importing merchants, or from London vintners. Increasingly, in the reigns of Edward IV and Henry VII, the king himself also made more direct provision, sending purveyors or chartering ships to acquire wine at source.[73] Ordinances of 1478 discharged the butler of his responsibilities for the purveyance of wine for the royal household, with the king henceforward employing purveyors of wine directly, rather than their appointment falling within the patronage of the butler.[74] Yet as late as the 1460s casual commands given orally by Edward IV to the then chief butler, John, Lord Wenlock, had required Wenlock to provide wine for, among others, the ambassadors of the duke of Burgundy, and the queen's cousin, James of Luxembourg, and similar oral directives of 1467–8 included wines for the king's mother, for Anthony, bastard of Burgundy, and for Burgundian and French ambassadors, as well as a tun for the abbot of Haughmond, to be delivered in Bristol.[75] A warrant under the privy seal, the conventional instrument mandating casual gifts of wine, directed the delivery of a 'butte of Tyre' to the king's godmother, Elizabeth, Lady Say.[76] One unintended side-effect of the abolition of the butler's responsibility for the purchase of wines was that it became more difficult to fulfil assignments made on London, where the deputy's prise of wine was minimal because of the exemption enjoyed by London's citizens. As a result, in 1490 the chancellor commuted his customary twelve tuns of wine for a cash annuity,[77] the prioress of Dartford negotiated a similar arrangement in 1516, and the following year two claimants were referred to Bristol because of the insufficiency of prise in London.[78]

Gifts of wine were one contributory factor reducing the crown's income from prise, although they were an effective way of signalling royal favour, and could be both an act of charity and payment for intercessory prayer. Over and above fluctuations of trade and wine prices, the disruption caused by war and losses through ullage and corruption of the wine itself, there were other significant pressures on revenue. The most important was the long-standing exemption from prisage of the citizens

---

[73] E.g. E101/412/10, f. 4; 412/11, f. 4; Edward's ship, the *Carrigon*, was at Bordeaux in November 1481: E159/258, recorda Hil. 21 Edw. IV, rot. 30d; E101/145/3, ff. 35, 37, 289v, purchase of malmsey by Henry VII. For some earlier and later examples, Simon, *History of Wine Trade*, ii. 128–32.
[74] *Black Book*, ed. Myers, 87, 176.
[75] E159/248, recorda Hil. 11 Edw. IV, rot. 9, 249, recorda Easter 12 Edw. IV, rot. 10.
[76] E101/80/10, no. 319, 19 Feb. 1464. 'Tyre' was a luxury sweet wine.
[77] E101/83/2, f. 27v.
[78] *Letters and Papers*, ii. nos 2021, 2101; E36/183, p. 72.

of London. Granted in 1327, the exemption applied also to their imports through other ports, provided the individual merchant was customarily resident in the capital.[79] A second factor was the greater size of wine ships in the later Middle Ages. In Bordeaux in November 1444 six Bristol ships were loaded with a total of over 1,113 tuns of wine; of these ships two were over 200 tons burden, and even the smallest was over 100 tons.[80] If they all came safely into port, the prisage due would have been just twelve tuns, whereas in the early fourteenth century the yield would have been twenty tuns or more, given the ships' smaller sizes of eighty to 100 tons.[81] Well into the 1490s Bristol's marine included two or three great ships of over 300 tons, in addition to the more numerous *naviculae* of between forty and 150 tons' burden.[82] All these variables mean that, even if it were possible, there would be little benefit in constructing a table of the returns of prisage from 1350 to 1485. It would neither be an indicator of the health of trade, nor useful as a measure of revenue. A sense of proportion is salutary. Bristol alone contributed £800 by way of benevolence to support Edward IV's invasion of France in 1475;[83] in contrast, over the two-year period 1476–8 (the nearest available figure) prisage in all the ports of England raised a mere £165 13*s*. 4*d*. after payment of freightage.[84] Between the 1440s and the late 1460s prisage seldom realised as much as £100 p.a., and often amounted to much less, although in 1478–9, for the first recorded time that century, the butler answered for a profit of over £250 on prise.[85]

When compared to earlier periods, supporting files become more pedestrian. For Bristol, the vouchers are mostly recurrent writs and receipts for the annual delivery of wine. Within the files generally there are still items of note, both regular and exceptional. Agreement for the provisioning of the king's houses prior to a progress, including wine for hunting lodges, was an annual ritual.[86] Provision of wine for the queen was an *ad hoc* arrangement.[87] John Hulle was granted seven tuns of prise wine from either Bridgwater or Bristol to defray his wife's costs for her enforced stay in London awaiting the birth of her child and the confinement that would follow until her churching;[88] and in 1496–7 Henry VII granted nine tuns of wine, presumably from London, to his serjeants at law for their 'common expenses'.[89] Although examples could be multiplied, the loss of many privy seal warrants, combined with the

[79] James, *Medieval Wine Trade*, 4; *The Customs of London, Otherwise Called Arnold's Chronicle*, ed. Francis Douce (1811), 8, 32–3; 'Particulars of Nicholas Browne 1509–10', ed. Condon and Jones, 4. The portsmen of the Cinque Ports were also exempt, but this was rarely relevant to Bristol.
[80] BL, Add. MS 15524, ff. 37–46. The returns for 1448–9 are even more striking, including two ships of around 250 tuns burden: E101/195/19.
[81] The latter metric used by James, *Medieval Wine Trade*, 96–7. See also Ian Friel, 'The Rise and Fall of the Big Ship, 1400–1520', in *The World of the Newport Ship*, ed. E.T. Jones and Richard Stone (Cardiff, 2018), 39–55.
[82] For Bristol's marine in 1503–4, E.T. Jones, 'The *Matthew* of Bristol and the Financiers of John Cabot's 1497 Voyage to North America', *EHR*, cxxi (2006), 786.
[83] E361/7, rot. 39.
[84] E101/412/6. The sum is the charge before deductions for expenses other than freightage.
[85] E101/412/11, f. 5.
[86] E101/80/27, 81/7; *Black Book*, ed. Myers, 59, 174. For early examples, as recorded on the close rolls, Simon, *History of Wine Trade*, i. 340–4.
[87] E101/81/6, June–July 1409.
[88] E101/81/6, 5 Feb. 1409.
[89] E101/83/2, f. 69; perhaps to help defray the huge costs of his serjeants' feast the year before: J.H. Baker, *The Order of Serjeants at Law* (Selden Soc., supp. ser. v, 1984), 99–101, 165.

reduction in the information obtainable from the accounts, severely diminishes the socio-political value of the prisage evidence for the fifteenth century.

Evidence for prise is not, however, confined to accounts, and can be illuminating, either of general practice or of local circumstances. In 1399 a litany of complaints was made against John Stapilton, who was deputy not only in Bristol but also in the port's creeks, and in Wales and Ireland. They can be summed up as allegations of menaces and extortion in respect of merchants, false accounting, adulteration of wine, embezzlement and theft, although one charge, alleging harassment of Bristol's merchants in the port's creeks, could as easily have been an unwelcome investigation by Stapilton into illicit trade.[90] While these allegations of malpractice were on an industrial scale that stretches credibility, it is difficult to see how the deputies could have made money for themselves without at least some under-reporting of seizures and sales.[91] Stapilton came to no lasting harm despite incurring adverse conciliar attention. Successive butlers reappointed him as a deputy in Bristol and, in 1402, in London.[92] Eight years later, Bristol's merchants again figured, not to their credit, when the chief butler, supported by the king's council, successfully opposed their claims that no prise should be taken unless a ship was carrying at least thirty tuns of wine.[93]

Local factors could also come into play. Bristol's proximity to the Severn was one. Merchants could evade prisage if a ship broke bulk in Wales and the wine was then transferred to Bristol or its creeks in small boats whose cargo was kept below the level of prise.[94] To non-resident merchants, Bristol's western location and established trade offered both commercial opportunity and a safer port for access to the Atlantic in times of danger. However, if a London merchant imported wine through Bristol, there was potential for dispute in respect of liability to prise – with the exchequer, with the deputies, or with his fellow merchants.[95] In Bristol and other ports sixteenth-century particulars show the deputies carefully annotating their records to show imports by Londoners in order to facilitate their own discharge from account.[96] The privilege could create difficulties for a body of shippers, as they agreed between themselves the division of compensatory payments for wines taken at prise according to the size of their individual shipments, or attempted to keep a total cargo below the ten-tun liability.[97]

Thomas Chaucer as butler unsuccessfully challenged one exception unique to the port. This was the long-standing privilege of the prior of St James, Bristol, to take

[90] *CPR*, 1396–9, p. 358, from C66/349, m. 3; SC8/213/10625.
[91] While the deputies may have had other legitimate sources of income, and might benefit from privileged purchase of wine for their own use, their annual wage, until it was increased after 1500, was (other than in London) just 40s.
[92] See Appendix.
[93] *CPR*, 1405–8, p. 387; SC8/173/8635; cf. Hargrave, *Collection of Tracts*, 117–18.
[94] E.g. E122/20/9, f. 42; E101/84/18, rot. 9; 'Particulars of Nicholas Browne 1509–10', ed. Condon and Jones, 4–5.
[95] For example, after two and a half years of litigation in the exchequer the grocer William Knolles failed in his plea for exemption, despite providing details of his London shop on Cordwainer Street; his residence, as distinct from his status, was disbelieved, and the allegation that he and his family had relocated to Bristol upheld: E159/202, recorda Trin. 4 Hen. VI, rots 14, 11d; *Coke's Notebooks*, ed. Baker, iv. 751.
[96] E.g. E101/84/15, 85/2, 86/3, 686/13.
[97] See, e.g., E321/25/43; C1/872/13–14; E101/83/2, pt 2, Exeter; 'Particulars of Nicholas Browne 1509–10', ed. Condon and Jones, 7–8.

all prise wines during the *hebdomada* (seven days) of Pentecost, the original period of St James's fair.[98] Several times confirmed by royal charter, the exercise of the prior's right depended on the coincidence of the *hebdomada* and the movable feast of Pentecost with the entry of one or more wine-bearing ships liable to prise. The application of the privilege was thus unpredictable, but it is known from prisage accounts that the prior excrcised his rights at least four times between 1485 and 1509.[99]

When detailed records of prisage re-emerged after 1485 it was a result of a significant failure of an accounting system in which weaknesses had long been evident. As chief butler from 1485, Sir John Fortescue accounted conventionally in the exchequer for the receipts of the new custom, with his accounts being subject to correction at audit.[100] He did not, however, make account for prisage before the treasurer of the household and the board of green cloth, despite that annual audit being a required check on the performance of his office.[101] While the loss of responsibility for the purchase of wine diminished the butler's importance, an aggravating factor might have been the restructuring of the household after 1488, by which the cofferer assumed many of the former responsibilities of the treasurer.[102] The cofferer perhaps lacked the authority, and certainly enjoyed no advantage of precedent, to summon a great officer such as the butler to account. The discovery of Fortescue's default possibly emerged only in the course of an overhaul of household finance and governance that occupied the king and council around the turn of the fifteenth century. These are histories too extensive to explore here; what matters in context is the chain of consequences: the rich archive accumulated in the exchequer concerning both butlerage and prisage from 1485 to 1500, and the ensuing transfer of responsibility for audit from the exchequer to a small group of the king's councillors operating under Henry VII's immediate oversight. This grouping acquired greater permanence after 1509 in the conciliar body that would become known as the general surveyors.[103] One tangible outcome of the transfer of responsibilities is a small sixteenth-century accumulation of particulars of account of individual deputies, in which Bristol, London, Southampton, Exeter and Newcastle are particularly well represented. These give a closer insight than the butlers' accounts into the collection of the imposts within individual ports.

An exchequer audit of Fortescue's prisage accounts was triggered by a writ under the privy seal of 20 November 1498 addressed to the treasurer and barons, ordering them to take Fortescue's accounts and make him due allowances, 'as by the old

---

[98] 'Particulars of Nicholas Browne 1509–10', ed. Condon and Jones, 3; *The Little Red Book of Bristol*, ed. Francis Bickley (2 vols, Bristol 1900), i. 236–46.

[99] E101/83/2, ff. 16v, 32, 37v; 84/18, rot. 4.

[100] *Enrolled Customs Accounts, Part 11*, ed. Jenks, 2823–6. His deputy generally accounted on his behalf. For Fortescue, John Baker, *The Men of Court 1440 to 1550: a Prosopography of the Inns of Court and Chancery and the Courts of Law* (2 vols, Selden Society, supp. ser. xviii, 2012), i. 700.

[101] *Black Book*, ed. Myers, 174, 176. The records were supposed to be delivered into the exchequer yearly. There are no extant records between Mich. 1480 and Mich. 1485, and given the disruption of Richard III's usurpation and violent death the gap in accounting may in practice have been longer. Butlerage accounts are also interrupted from 1481 to 1485.

[102] E404/80, 12 Feb. 1489; E101/413/4, f. 1; A.P. Newton, 'Tudor Reforms in the Royal Household', in *Tudor Studies*, ed. R.W. Seton-Watson (1924), 235 notes only the act of 1495, for which *PROME*, xvi. 219–26.

[103] For conciliar audit, E314/49; E101/517/10; F.C. Dietz, *English Government and Finance 1485–1558* (2nd edn, New York 1964), 69–70; W.C. Richardson, *Tudor Chamber Administration 1485–1547* (Baton Rouge, LA, 1952), 127, 161–2, 176–92, 248–50; Steven Gunn, *Henry VII's New Men and the Making of Tudor England* (Oxford, 2016), 85.

presidentes of suche accomptes which we woll be brought afore you out of oure countinghous for youre further instruccion in that behalf'.[104] It took over two years, possibly longer. Partly this was a result of the size and complexity of the task, and a seven-month delay before Fortescue delivered a digest of his accounts to 1498, his death in July 1500, and a 'contageous sikenesse' in London and Westminster that year, cannot have helped. A second period of audit in 1501–2, unusually overseen by three barons and four auditors rather than just one of each, completed the process up to the date of Fortescue's death.[105] The summary accounts that were the immediate outcome of the audits list the number of tuns of prise wine sold in each of the accounting years, and the prices achieved on sale, further qualified by port and for each port subdivided by region of origin of the wine. By the later 1490s, the monetary figures are suspiciously rounded. The returns from Bristol were higher than any other port, followed by Exeter and Dartmouth.[106] Over fifteen years, the total for all ports (omitting Cornwall and Cheshire) amounted to 1,539 tuns, representing almost 388,000 gallons of wine, and £2,526 16s. 7d. in money, an average of £168 a year.[107] As data, the figures are interesting but of limited utility, but then the primary purpose of the audit was to establish the extent of Fortescue's debt and his money transfers to the household, and the legitimacy of allowances on his accounts. The cumulative deficits found on both the butlerage and the prisage accounts precipitated the committal to the Fleet prison of Fortescue's executor, Thomas Bawde, who was the active accountant.[108]

The enrolled accounts give a sense of the gravity and scale of the audit. The more informative records are the particulars, that is the three ledgers delivered into court by Fortescue and Bawde.[109] For each year, and for each port, they document wine sales and prices, detail cellarage, cooperage, carriage and other costs, and record wine given as gifts and in alms, sometimes adding information derived from warrants. Crucially, there is more. Detailed lists of 'acquittances', ordered by port, record the number of tuns, one or two, taken from every eligible ship entering that year, with each ship's date of entry and the name of her shipmaster. This was sufficient information both to calculate the freightage to be allowed to the butler, and to facilitate a cross-check with the customs accounts for auditing purposes. The names of the ships were not, unfortunately, remarked, but the merest glance at any list of customs accounts shows that, by comparison, such long runs of sequential returns for any port are rare.

The returns for Bristol reflect both the high volume of the port's wine trade, and that the town's marine alone was insufficient for the volume carried.[110] Bristol's merchants laded also on Basque and other foreign ships, despite navigation acts to the

---

[104] E159/275, brevia directa Mich. 14 Hen. VII, rot. 15; copy in E356/23, rot. 75.
[105] E356/23, rot. 75; E101/83/2, 84/4, 5. Numerous draft and copy accounts also survive.
[106] E356/23, rot. 75, tabulated in *Enrolled Customs Accounts Part 11*, ed. Jenks, 2827–33. The low figures for London were not abnormal but a consequence of the exemptions of its citizens.
[107] A full tun of wine was reckoned at 252 gallons.
[108] E356/23, rot. 75; E368/271, states and views, 13 Hen. VII, Easter rot. 7; DL5/4, f. 18; BL, Add. MS 21480, f. 186; *CCR*, 1500–9, no. 218 (sale of lands possibly connected, no. 239); debt paid off by January 1505, BL, Add. MS 59899, ff. 152v, 208v; pardon 1508, *CPR*, 1494–1509, p. 588.
[109] E101/83/2, 84/4, 5.
[110] It should also be remembered that the prise returns do not cover *all* ships entering, since no prise was taken on any ship carrying less than 10 tuns: a condition that applied to three sizeable ships in June 1493: E122/20/9, ff. 47v–48v.

contrary.[111] Some links between named ships and masters can be made, with confidence where prisage and customs accounts overlap, but with great caution where they do not.[112] Notably, the particulars cover three of the prime years of Bristol's voyages of discovery. This is useful. The shipmaster William Claron was consistently associated after June 1504 with John Cabot's *Matthew*, and from 1507 with her eponymous and larger successor. He sailed into port with between ten and nineteen tuns of wine in February, June and early October 1498, which means that he cannot have taken part in the discovery expedition of that year. But while the constant repetition of just one tun taken at prise suggests that his ship was small, it cannot be assumed that she was the *Matthew*, even though the data would fit both with her size, and with the date of a known voyage, under an unknown master, in November 1498.[113]

Fortescue's ledgers were rigorously checked and heavily annotated by the auditors and their clerks. They compared the returns for all ports with archived customers' particulars, finding numerous omissions and errors. Whether these stemmed from the deputies, or from copying mistakes by the butler's clerks, there is no sure way of telling: probably both, although the assumption is that the primary fault lay in the deputies' returns. In addition to marginalia noting agreement or deficit in the returns of prise, a book of extracts was compiled drawing on customs particulars. For each port, the scribe identified those entries omitted from the prisage accounts and supplied the missing information. He copied not just the master's name and entry date of each omitted ship, but frequently also the names and ladings of individual merchants, and sometimes a ship name also. The additional prisage found due was added to Fortescue's charge.

As a resource with sufficient detail to supplement regular customs accounts, this small book appears to be both overlooked and fortuitous.[114] It is less useful for Bristol than for some other ports because after 1494, with one minor exception, the prisage returns conformed to the customers' ledgers, while four full-year customs particulars survive for earlier years.[115] For other ports, including Plymouth and Fowey, whose prise revenues went to the prince of Wales by right of his duchy of Cornwall, the returns are more extensive. As a record of audit, the book shows the exchequer taking an assertive view of the king's rights, claiming prise even when most or all shippers to a port other than London were London citizens, and interpreting ambiguities in the customs accounts in the king's favour.

For four years after Fortescue's death the office of chief butler seems to have been left vacant, until Robert Southwell was appointed to the post on 12 November 1504.[116] It is not clear how the deputies were appointed in the interim, although William Holybrand was made deputy in London in 1500 on the king's verbal man-

[111] Basque shipmasters may be identified on name evidence. If after 1489 prise was taken, then that ship was carrying wine for denizen merchants.
[112] Charter-parties usually covered only a single return voyage, which suggests caution in marrying a shipmaster to a ship without supporting evidence. Some masters, however, were consistently associated over time with a particular ship, e.g. Edward Gibbes and the *Mary Belhouse*.
[113] For Claron, E101/83/2, f. 73, 84/4, f. 2 (and again February 1499); E159/275, recorda Hil. 14 Hen. VII, rots. 2, 4; Jones, 'The *Matthew*', 792–4. No customs ledgers survive for 1498.
[114] Now bound within E101/83/2.
[115] 1485–8 and 1492–3; the omission in 1497–8 was the import of 13½ tuns of wine by the Worcester vintner Gracian de la Place. The improvement in accuracy suggests a change of deputy. In 1492–3 the omissions were the *John Evangelist* of Bristol, the *Marie* of Motrico in which the principal shipper may have been a Londoner, and four small boats incoming from Chepstow and Tintern.
[116] *CPR*, 1494–1509, p. 420; effective from the previous Mich.

date.[117] The accounting system was transformed. At first, individual deputies declared their accounts before a small *ad hoc* committee of king's councillors that included Sir Reynold Bray and Robert Southwell, and paid their receipts directly to the treasurer of the king's chamber.[118] The conciliar audit was regularised by an indenture made on 20 February 1505 between Southwell and Roger Layburne, bishop of Carlisle, on the one part, and the barons of the exchequer on the other. The butlerage and prisage accounts, and various land revenues, were removed from exchequer jurisdiction, although an exchequer auditor assisted the councillors in their work.[119] Once Southwell had become chief butler, the deputies paid over their receipts to him and to his successors, as had been earlier practice. The butler was responsible for the onward transmission of cash to the chamber.

The detailed returns for any port were embodied in the deputies' particulars. Many were informally structured, and as individual as the deputies themselves. In variant ways, each deputy presented his charge: the total revenue arising (on paper) from prise wine and butlerage, and his discharge, the many reasons why he believed the auditors should allow him deductions on his account, including payments of freightage, gifts of wine, cellarage and other expenses, non-payments by merchants, exemptions and monies paid over to the butler, as well an allowance for his own fees and reward, if any. Where the documents are the deputy's own draft ledgers, rather than summary accounts, or the formal parchment estreats that usefully document prisage by ship and master, and individual butlerage, they may present a lively picture of the operation of prise. In 1507–8 John Alston, called out his Bristol predecessor, Hugh Eliot, when Eliot attempted to evade prisage by splitting his wine consignments across several small boats that then sailed in from Wales. That year Alston seems to have paid special attention to Severn traffic, to the detriment of his total returns for butlerage, which are deficient.[120] In 1509 he brought a vintner's eye to his sales of wine, with a notably specific return on its regions of origin.[121] Nicholas Browne reported on the belligerent opposition of masters, a purser and shipowners who prevented his servant from marking wine for the king, incidents that confirm that the deputy had the right to board a ship for this purpose before wine was unloaded on the quay.[122] John Hussey as butler left no doubt as to his displeasure concerning a wayward Exeter deputy, ordering an examination of the customers' ledgers to establish a true record. In different vein he asked his deputy at Boston to procure him two hogsheads of wine 'And let it be good, as my trust is in you.'[123]

Most deputies' particulars list incoming wine ships, often by name, where relevant detail individual Londoners exempt from prise, and indicate or name alien shippers paying butlerage.[124] For any port this is useful information that may not

---

[117] *CPR*, 1494–1509, p. 343.
[118] E101/84/10, 413/2/3 (receipts from the Bristol deputies are on ff. 13, 51).
[119] E101/517/10: heading transcribed in Dietz, *English Government and Finance*, 70; E101/84/38. An earlier writ, 7 November 1503, had exempted the London deputy William Holybrand from exchequer account: E159/282, recorda Mich. 19 Hen. VII, rot. 38d.
[120] E101/84/18, rot. 9 includes, unusually for Bristol, a substantial shipment from Chepstow by a Hansard. In both 1507–8 and 1508–9 Alston's returns for butlerage are below the totals recorded in the enrolled customs accounts.
[121] E101/84/38.
[122] 'Particulars of Nicholas Browne, 1509–10', ed. Condon and Jones, 5, 12–13.
[123] Gunn, *New Men*, 72–3. A hogshead contained around 63 gallons.
[124] There was no obligation to record incoming vessels carrying less than 10 tuns although Roger Dele, deputy in London, habitually did so: E36/183.

be duplicated elsewhere. For example, in 1514–15, a year for which the customers' ledger does not survive, the Bristol deputy listed twenty-three named ships subject to prise, of which three were exempt because the shippers were Londoners, while the prior of St James had claimed the prise wine from one vessel and in a further six ships butlerage only was taken.[125]

Extracts from the prisage and butlerage account of Bristol deputy, 1515.[126]

De Nave vocata Trenite de Bristoll unde Johannes Gorwey est magister venit a Burdeux quinto die marcii	prisagium ij dolia
De Nave vocata Corpus Sanctus de Veana[127] unde Afounso Marouse est magister a Sancto Lucar[128] septimo die marcii De mercatoribus[129] alienigenis pro xlij dolia pipa hogshead	prisagium ij dolia[130] Butteleragium iiij li. vs. vjd.
De Nave vocata Anne de Tewkesbury unde Johannes Bitfeld [est magister] venit a Cardeff xxvij die februarii De mercatore alienigena pro iij dolia	prisagium nulla Butteleragium vjs.

There are at least three reasons why the Bristol returns are particularly significant in this period. The first is self-evident: Bristol's buoyant wine trade, and the heavy involvement of the town's merchants, meant that Bristol prisage was consistently greater than that of any other port, even though the actual volume and value of London's wine trade dwarfed that of Bristol. The second relates to the evolution of prisage as an impost. The third is the information the accounts provide for Henry VII's support for the voyages of discovery. These last can be dealt with only briefly here. From 1500 to 1504 Hugh Eliot and Robert Popham, both Bristol merchants, held the deputyship in Bristol at farm. This was an administrative innovation that must have been agreed, or imposed, by the king's council. The basic principle of a farm was that the lessee agreed a fixed rent payable for a mutually agreed period to the owner of the revenues. Such leases were common in the management of estates but also familiar from royal farms of the exchange or of alnage, a tax on cloth. The arrangement with Eliot and Popham was unusual, not just as the first instance in respect of prisage, but because the farm applied, not as a fixed sum due annually as total revenue, but to a fixed return *pro rata* on a numerically variable commodity, the prise of wine. Each tun was to be valued at £4. The arrangement simplified the accounting, and by being held in joint tenure facilitated Eliot's participation in those continuing voyages of discovery launched from Bristol to the 'new found land' after 1500.[131] It was also hugely risky. Wine prices were both volatile and differentiated by region. Spanish and Gascon wine might yield the farmer a profit on sale; but should

---

[125] E101/85/28.
[126] E101/85/28, f. 2.
[127] Viana do Castelo.
[128] Sanlúcar de Barrameda.
[129] Plural assumed; the MS has '*mercat*'.
[130] Indicates denizen shipment on a foreign vessel.
[131] E.T. Jones and M.M. Condon, *Cabot and Bristol's Age of Discovery* (Bristol, 2016), 60–8.

a significant proportion of the wine imported be the inexpensive Rochelle wine, or should merchants prove recalcitrant, then the farmers would lose heavily. By 1504 Eliot and Popham's account showed arrears of almost £230 over and above claims awaiting the decision of the auditors.[132] For the next two years Eliot, by then in sole occupation of the office, seems to have reverted to more traditional accounting, appraising wine for sale at values that varied by quality and origin, and claiming expenses.[133] Nevertheless, the precedent established, Eliot's successors continued as 'farmer of the prise and deputy of the butler of England for the ancient custom called butlerage'.[134] In the short term, other ports accounted for actual sales, although London, with its minimal prise, seems to have followed Bristol practice by 1520.[135]

The connection between the prisage and butlerage accounts and the Bristol voyages of discovery has been discussed elsewhere. The accounts are the sole source for the very large reward of £100 paid to Eliot towards his costs in sailing with others in two ships towards the 'new found Isle';[136] they are also the source for Henry VII's grant of a pension to him of twenty marks (£13 6s. 8d.) yearly.[137] The warrant for this pension, dated 25 September 1502, closely followed an interview with the king that resulted also in a reward of £20 'to the merchauntes of bristoll that haue bene in the newe founde launde'.[138] A butt of Alicante wine was sent from Bristol to Richmond in October, perhaps as a token of thanks, and seems to have been allowed to Eliot as a deduction on his account.[139] He received his pension for at least three years, but it is unclear whether it continued to the end of his tenure as deputy butler. By then he was at loggerheads with fellow Bristol venturers, in debt to other merchants, and, as importantly, in debt to the king on his arrears.[140] While he had earlier honoured bonds securing the repayment of a loan from the king, before the end of the decade Eliot found himself lodged in a London debtor's prison.[141]

The rewards granted to Eliot for his investment and participation in the voyages of Henry VII's last decade are an extreme example of significant historical evidence that had been missed through general academic neglect of the records of the chief butler.[142] There are other perspectives and insights not addressed here, and other approaches might not focus on a particular port, although local knowledge is a useful

---

[132] E351/454, mm. 41–2.

[133] E101/84/20, f. 3 (2). Eliot's figures for butlerage in 1505–6 are significantly greater than the customers' returns of alien imports of wine; unfortunately the detailed returns, which would facilitate analysis, do not survive.

[134] E101/84/18, rots 1, 5, 7, 10–15 (my translation); E321/8/17; however, John Alston accounted conventionally in 1508–9, perhaps because of uncertainty after the death in April 1509 of Henry VII: E101/84/38.

[135] E351/455; E36/183.

[136] E.T. Jones, 'Henry VII and the Bristol Expeditions to North America: the Condon documents', *HR*, lxxxiii (2010), 452–4.

[137] E101/84/18, rot. 2; E351/454, m. 34.

[138] E351/454, m. 34; E101/415/3, f. 103v.

[139] E351/454, m. 34. The king and queen were at Richmond briefly at the end of October 1502.

[140] Eliot's final account, for 1505–6, E101/84/20, f. 3 (2), is a fair copy declaration that lacks marks of audit. It is not continued, either to any payment to Southwell as butler, or to claims other than the standard costs associated with the management of prise wines. The previous year his outstanding debt represented more than half of Southwell's arrears, and Eliot entered obligations for direct payment to the king's chamber: E36/212, pp. 74–7; 214, f. 247.

[141] E5/5/18.

[142] 'Neither of us [D.B. Quinn and A.A. Ruddock] thought of the Butlerage account …': 'The Quinn Papers', ed. E.T. Jones (Explore Bristol Research, 2009), 5.

1   Grotesque from TNA E351/454, m. 33, '*Summa Totalis*'.

tool. A choice of a different port would have coloured a different narrative, whether regarding the Italians in Southampton, and the close attention paid them by Henry VII, the importance of butlerage in London, and the value of its prisage returns as a tool to analyse the constituency of the port's denizen trade in wine, or the contrasting Low Country trade of east coast ports. An economic historian might test more closely both total revenue and the discrepancies between the deputies' returns of butlerage and the figures derived from customs accounts. Revenue from the imposts increased in the early sixteenth century, but it could not be expanded exponentially.[143] For all the inefficiencies of collection, the more serious block was the exemption of London citizens from prisage, an effect that only increased with time and the overwhelming dominance of London's port.[144]

Butlerage and prisage would have a further 300 years of history. They were farmed out in the sixteenth century, and alienated by the crown after 1660. In the early nineteenth century the revenues were brought back under state control in order to secure the final abolition in 1809 of a long-outdated and debased tax.[145] It would be wrong, however, to end with a downbeat note an essay offered in celebration of the career of Rowena E. Archer. That this essay is about wine is obvious. For royal gardens there is merely the verjuice, suitable only for cooking, supplied to Richard

---

[143] In the sixteenth century, as earlier, both the butler and his deputies ran up significant debts: Gunn, *New Men*, 72.

[144] Southampton obtained similar privileges in 1520: J.S. Davies, *A History of Southampton, Partly from the MS of Dr Speed* (Southampton, 1883), 159, 219–20; *Statutes*, iii. 352 (22 Hen. VIII c. 20).

[145] Gras, *Early English Customs Systems*, 42; 49 Geo. III, c. 98, s. xxxv–vi: *Statutes of the United Kingdom of Great Britain and Ireland*, ed. T.E. Tomlins (1809), 785–6.

II's household, and for music, the coarse sea shanties of Bristol's mariners.[146] But for art, there is a distinctive, if ephemeral, image. The drawing of grotesques, from pattern books or the imagination, was a skill of the accomplished calligrapher. The scribe of an abstract of deputies' accounts for prisage and butlerage of 1500–4 chose to embellish his text – in the sure knowledge that Henry VII would read it closely, and sign off the account.[147]

Although this is a grotesque, the profile, with its hooded eyes and beaked nose, bears more than a passing resemblance to the king. The fanciful hat, with the king's beasts and badges, identifies him. It is perhaps worth asking, somewhat tongue in cheek, whether the ageing Henry VII still had sufficient sense of humour to smile as he viewed himself placed in the text against the total receipts (before deductions) of £2,387 1s. 9¼d.[148] He was no prince charming, and late in life favoured the sweet wines of Wippach (Vipava), which do not figure in the accounts.[149] The reforms he oversaw, however, were briefly transformative in the history of the imposts. If this essay has succeeded in shedding new light on a little studied tax, and persuaded that the records of prisage and butlerage are ripe for further study, it has achieved one basic objective. It is offered to the honerand with deepest respect for her scholarship and her incomparable tutelage.

---

[146] E361/5, rots 18d, 19; Carus-Wilson, 'Overseas Trade', in *English Trade in the Fifteenth Century*, ed. Power and Postan, 191.
[147] '*Computatur cum libro Jhon Heron*' is in the king's hand: E351/454, m. 39.
[148] E351/454, m. 33.
[149] *Cal. State Papers Venetian 1202–1509*, ed. Rawdon Brown (1864), 331.

APPENDIX: CHIEF BUTLERS AND BRISTOL DEPUTIES, 1350–1514

Chief butler	Dates[150]	Bristol deputies	Dates
John de Wesenham	1347–50	John de Wycombe	12 Feb. 1347
		John Hoker[151]	
Henry Picard	1350–9	Unknown	
John Stodeye[152]	1359–61	Walter Frampton	30 Sept. 1359
		John Hakeston[153]	
William Strete[154]	1361–76	Geoffrey Beaufleur	20 Oct. 1361
		Reynold le Frenssh	20 Feb. 1362
		John Stokes[155]	
		Walter Derby	by 1371[156]
Geoffrey Newton[157]	1376–7	Walter Derby	13 Oct. 1376
Thomas Tyle	1377–82	Walter Derby	20 Nov. 1377
John Slegh	1382–94	Walter Derby	28 Oct. 1382
		Thomas Beaupyne	19 Jan. 1387
		Nicholas Derby[158]	
		John Stapilton	18 Oct. 1390, [12 Jan. 1392
Thomas Brounflete[159]	1394–9	John Stapilton	28 Aug. 1395
John Payn	1399–1402	John Stapilton[160]	9 Sept. 1399
Thomas Chaucer	1402–7	Thomas Saundres	9 Nov. 1402
Sir John Tiptoft	1407	Robert Russell	4 June 1407
Thomas Chaucer	1407–18	Thomas Saundres	16 Dec. 1407
		John Stapilton	18 Nov. 1410
		Thomas Saundres	28 Mar. 1413

[150] From *CPR*, unless otherwise specified.
[151] C81/1644, no. 20, but possibly an alias for John de Wycombe.
[152] Previously a deputy in London.
[153] Added in a different ink in C81/1644, no. 31. *CPR*, 1358–61, p. 272 and C81/1644, no. 32 both name Frampton.
[154] Previously a purveyor of wines.
[155] C81/1644, nos 36, 50 (the latter undated). *CPR* has le Frenssh.
[156] E101/80/21.
[157] Previously Strete's deputy in London.
[158] C81/1644, no. 76. Not enrolled. Fiat to bishop of Winchester as chancellor (1389–91).
[159] Keeper of wardrobe of the household 1407–13, previously controller.
[160] Deputy in London 30 May 1402.

Nicholas Merbury	1418–22	John Fish[161]	22 Nov. 1418
Thomas Chaucer	1422–34	John Langley	9 Jan. 1423
		John Piers	20 Nov. 1426
		Thomas Russell	17 Dec. 1431
		William Ludlow	20 Aug. 1433
Ralph Boteler (Lord Sudeley from 1441)	1435–58	John Sharpe	1435–1451 or later[162]
John Talbot, earl of Shrewsbury	1458–61	*Unknown*	
John, Lord Wenlock	1461–71	John Eyton	1461–4[163]
		Richard Alberton	14 Nov. 1464
John Stafford, earl of Wiltshire	1471–3	Richard Alberton	13 June 1471
		John Hawkes	8 March 1473
Anthony Wydeville, Earl Rivers	1473–83	Thomas Croft	13 Dec. 1473
Francis, Viscount Lovell	1483–5	Thomas Croft and William Catesby	14 Sept. 1483
		Philip Ricart	23 Oct. 1484[164]
Sir John Fortescue	1485–1500	*Unknown*	*1485–99*
		Nicholas Browne	before 1500[165]
?*Vacant*[166]	1500–4	Hugh Eliot and Robert Popham[167]	1500–4[168]
Robert Southwell	1504–14	Hugh Eliot	1504–6[169]
		John Alston	1506–9[170]
		Nicholas Browne	1509–14[171]

---

[161] Or Fissher. The sources differ.
[162] E101/81/14, no. 20; 17 (1440–2), 20 (1448–9), 21.
[163] E101/82/6, nos 68, 279, 285.
[164] From Mich.
[165] E101/84/5, f. 9.
[166] The various deputies paid monies directly to the treasurer of the chamber: E101/413/2/3.
[167] Ten year farm from 16 Oct. 1500, E371/266, rot. 20; E372/346, Bristol.
[168] E101/84/10, 18, rot. 2; E351/454.
[169] E36/212, p. 74; E101/84/24.
[170] E101/84/18, rot. 9, 27; 85/12, f. 1. In office until Mich. 1509.
[171] 'Particulars of Nicholas Browne 1509–10', ed. Condon and Jones, 6.

FROM THE WELSH MARCHES TO THE ROYAL HOUSEHOLD: THE LEOMINSTER RIOTS OF 1487 AND UNCERTAIN ALLEGIANCES AT THE HEART OF HENRY VII'S REGIME

S.J. Payling and Sean Cunningham

The early years of any reign provided challenges of leadership as the new monarch sought the unconditional support of the political nation. For monarchs who sat on the throne not through uncontested inheritance but as the victors in dynastic conflict – an all-too-common description of fifteenth-century English kings – these challenges were acute. The most obvious threat to the new king's rule was the unreconciled followers of the defeated party, exemplified by Lancastrian resistance to Edward IV in the north and Wales through the 1460s and the rebellion against Henry VII that ended at the battle of Stoke in June 1487, but, more insidious and elusive, was the threat from within. The new monarch needed to retain the support of those who had helped to win him the crown while resisting their expectations of excessive reward and influence. Such resistance could be costly: Henry IV's alienation from the Percys nearly cost him his throne in 1403, and Edward IV's slow-developing breach from Richard Neville, earl of Warwick, resulted in his deposition, albeit briefly, in 1470.

If such leadership challenges were to be overcome, the new ruler had to extend his support beyond his partisans and develop personal networks to bring his authority to all regions of the realm. Here, however, there were other difficulties. Networks could only be extended through local agents, who, even if wholly committed to the new king, might see opportunities to further their own influence in ways that undermined rather than reinforced his rule. Where these agents had not only local office but also offices within the royal household or central government, the damaging effects of local rivalries could be drawn dangerously close to the king himself. This context links the two narratives in this essay. The one describes major disturbances in the march of Wales, in which the treasurer of the new king's household, Sir Richard Croft, and its chamberlain, Sir William Stanley, were on opposite sides; the other, a conspiracy within the royal household which, seemingly at least, had its origin in the marches. The link between them probably extends no further than the marcher origins of the household conspirators, but both show that the insecurity of Henry VII's early years extended beyond the ranks of the unreconciled Yorkists who brought him to battle at Stoke.

Disturbances in the Welsh marches

Henry VII might have expected disorder in those areas where Richard III's personal lordship, notably the North Riding of Yorkshire, had been strong and where his accession frustrated the political ambitions of leading landholders. There, clashes between disappointed Ricardians and opportunistic supporters of the new regime were an obvious danger.[1] Less predictable was the violent disorder that overtook the Welsh marches in the late 1480s. Although its gentry had stood aside when Henry Stafford, duke of Buckingham, had attempted to raise rebellion there in the autumn of 1483, there had been little positive support for Richard III. Here the trouble arose not between rival political factions but within the ranks of the new king's own supporters.

The principal *dramatis personae* of these disturbances was a short one – two leading Herefordshire gentry, Croft and his neighbour Sir Thomas Cornwall, and one from Shropshire, Sir Richard Corbet – with, waiting in the wings, a more substantial figure, Stanley, who was Corbet's father-in-law. Croft was comfortably the most important of the three principal characters, and his long and remarkable career is already familiar through the work of C.S.L. Davies.[2] Born in the late 1420s into an ancient but fading gentry family settled at Croft, a few miles to the north of Leominster, he took impressive advantage of the opportunities political disturbance gave to a man of ambition. Early in his career he established close ties with Richard, duke of York, whose castle of Wigmore lay not far from Croft, and after a period of equivocation, the first manifestation of the skilful temporising that was to characterise his career, he fought in the victorious ranks of York's son, the earl of March (the future Edward IV), at the battle of Mortimer's Cross, only two miles from his home, in February 1461.[3] Rewarded accordingly, he continued to be active in support of the house of York. During the crisis of Edward IV's reign in the late autumn of 1470 he fled with him to the Low Countries, and in the campaign of the following spring he fought at the battles of Barnet on 14 April and Tewkesbury on 4 May, where he was knighted.[4] Edward IV's restoration brought him new opportunities as the administration of Wales and the marches was reorganised. The hegemony of William Herbert, earl of Pembroke, with whom Sir Richard had never been on close terms, was replaced by a regional council, nominally under the headship of the infant prince of Wales and based at Ludlow, some eight miles north of Croft. First instituted

---

[1] Keith Dockray, 'The Political Legacy of Richard III in Northern England', in *Kings and Nobles in the Later Middle Ages*, ed. R.A. Griffiths and James Sherborne (Gloucester, 1986), 205–27; Sean Cunningham, 'Henry VII and Rebellion in North-Eastern England, 1485–1492: Bonds of Allegiance and the Establishment of Tudor Authority', *Northern History*, xxxii (1996), 42–74; A.J. Pollard, *North-Eastern England during the Wars of the Roses* (Oxford, 1990), 367–86.

[2] C.S.L. Davies, 'The Crofts: Creation and Defence of a Family Enterprise under the Yorkists and Henry VII', *HR*, lxviii (1995), 241–65. A fuller account of Croft's career will appear in *The History of Parliament. The House of Commons, 1461–1504*, ed. Hannes Kleineke.

[3] William Worcestre, *Itineraries*, ed. J.H. Harvey (Oxford, 1969), 204.

[4] TNA, C1/45/10; W.A. Shaw, *Knights of England* (2 vols, 1906), ii. 14. In the latter battle, he may have taken an important role: a Tudor tradition, recorded by the chronicler Edward Hall, identifies him as responsible for the capture of Edward, prince of Wales. The account, the source of which may have been Croft's son, Sir Edward (d. 1547), is careful to clear Croft of all blame, describing him as 'a wyse and valyaut knyght' who surrendered his prisoner trusting to the royal promise that his life would be spared: Edward Hall, *Chronicle*, ed. Henry Ellis (1809), 301; Davies, 'The Crofts', 245–6.

in July 1471, the council was enlarged in February 1473, shortly before the prince took up residence, to include Croft and others. By the autumn of 1480 he was serving as treasurer of the prince's household.[5] This position of prominence was, on the face of it, threatened by Richard III's accession, yet Croft immediately adapted to the diversion of the throne from the natural heir, the prince he had served for ten years. As far as the available evidence goes, he became a trusted servant of the new king; indeed, in May 1484, he was named as treasurer of the royal household, an unthinkable appointment unless he was on close personal terms with Richard. His service to the new king was also manifest outside the household, for in November 1484 he was appointed for his fifth term as sheriff of Herefordshire and in the following February, as the king's sense of insecurity mounted, he was entrusted with the task of repairing the marcher castles of Radnor and Llanelwedd.[6]

The second protagonist, Sir Richard Corbet of Moreton Corbet, was not as important a man as Croft, but he was still a significant figure,[7] coming from one of the longest established and most important gentry families in Shropshire, and one that had seen a major advance in its material fortunes in the previous generation. Sir Richard's mother was Elizabeth, daughter of Thomas Hopton of Hopton castle, about forty miles south of Moreton Corbet. Although when she married his father, in about 1445, she had no expectations, her prospects of inheritance were transformed with the childless deaths of her mother's brother, Sir William Lucy, at the battle of Northampton in July 1460, and of her brother, Walter Hopton, in the following February. These deaths brought her title to both the Hopton patrimony and, much more importantly, a moiety of the Lucy lands, which together extended over eleven counties and may have been worth as much as £200 p.a.[8] Thus, at least in terms of expectations at birth, Corbet was a much richer man than Croft. As it transpired, however, his great maternal inheritance never (in any more than a small part) came into his hands, for his mother survived him, and he had to content himself with the valuable political connexions that came with her remarriage in 1471 to Stanley, a younger brother of Thomas, later earl of Derby. Corbet's brief period in royal wardship brought him another important connexion: on 30 May 1468 his wardship and marriage were granted to the Yorkist servant, Walter Devereux, Lord Ferrers, who married him to his daughter, Elizabeth.[9] The first act of his adult career was, at least on his own later testimony, a very important one. In the first of many military adventures, he numbered among the army which the earl of Pembroke, the husband of his wife's aunt, took north from Raglan (Monmouthshire) to confront the northern rebellion stirred up by the earl of Warwick. At Edgecote near Banbury on 24 July 1469, the royalist army was defeated and Herbert executed by the victors. In the wake of this disaster Corbet, on his own claim, took the initiative, conveying Herbert's twelve-year-old ward, the future Henry VII, from the field to the safety of Hereford and the custody of the boy's uncle, Jasper Tudor.[10] Corbet was again in

---

[5] Davies 'The Crofts', 246; D.E. Lowe, 'Council of the Prince of Wales', *Bulletin of the Board of Celtic Studies*, xxix (1980–2), 281.

[6] Davies, 'The Crofts', 246–7.

[7] A full account of his career will appear in *The House of Commons, 1461–1504*.

[8] TNA, C140/5/42; *CIPM Hen. VII*, ii. 130–1, 155–9, 233–4.

[9] *CP*, xii (2), 845–6; *CPR*, 1467–77, pp. 95–6.

[10] Hugh Owen and J.B. Blakeway, *A History of Shrewsbury* (2 vols, 1825), i. 248. This cannot have been literally true, for in the aftermath of the battle the young Henry is known to have come into the

arms at the end of the Readeption, rallying to the returning Edward IV. Like Croft, he was among those knighted at the battle of Tewkesbury, and, unlike Croft, he went on to serve on the king's expedition to France in 1475.[11] Equally significantly, it was probably during Richard III's reign that he was awarded a royal annuity of £20 assigned on the lordship of Denbigh.[12]

The third of the main protagonists, Sir Thomas Cornwall, was the least important of the three, although he too was a man of some substance. When he was only nine, in 1453, he inherited the family estates, principally the manor of Ashton (in Eye) near Leominster and only five miles from Croft,[13] as a young man, he was knighted on the Yorkist side at the battle of Tewkesbury, like Croft and Corbet, and he went on to enjoy a successful career in the later years of Yorkist rule. In March 1472, perhaps in reward for his service at that battle, he was granted the valuable and prestigious wardship and marriage of William, son and heir of the late earl of Pembroke's brother, Sir Richard Herbert of Coldbrook (Monmouthshire), who like the earl had been executed after Edgcote.[14] Under Richard III Cornwall made further gains: he was granted a life annuity of £40 charged on duchy of York manors in Herefordshire, and along with a knight of the royal body, Sir James Tyrell, he shared the stewardship of the lordship of Builth (Breconshire). Significantly, he was also the first sheriff of Herefordshire during Richard's brief reign, appointed in November 1483 and succeeded by Croft in the following November.[15]

There is nothing in the careers of the three men up to the final days of Richard III's reign to suggest that Croft would find himself at violent odds with an alliance of Cornwall and Corbet. Indeed, the three had much in common, sharing a Yorkist allegiance that had survived the deposition of Edward V. In those last days, however, their dispute had its first documented manifestation. On 8 July 1485 Corbet's servant, John Terry, allegedly raped and then imprisoned at Shawbury, near Moreton Corbet, one Elizabeth Atkins, a widow who was in Croft's service.[16] More seriously and germanely, on the following 1 August, just six days before Henry of Richmond landed at Milford Haven to embark on the campaign that ended in victory at Bosworth, three Welshmen were allegedly murdered by Croft's servants at 'Hagley's Mountain', a rather grand description of the hill above the castle of Hopton, the property of

---

custody of the widowed countess of Pembroke, the Devereux aunt of Corbet's wife, at the castle of Weobley (Herefordshire), but it is entirely possible that it was Corbet who brought him there. In the circumstances in which he presented his story, namely the beginning of Henry's reign, it was politic to say that the boy had been delivered to the custody of Jasper Tudor, then supposedly at Hereford, rather than to Weobley, the lord of which, Corbet's brother-in-law, had died on the Ricardian side at the battle of Bosworth. As it turned out, the boy remained at Weobley until the Readeption, when, in October 1470, he was handed over to Jasper Tudor: M.A. Hicks, *False, Fleeting, Perjur'd Clarence: George, duke of Clarence, 1449–78* (Gloucester, 1980), 57; M.K. Jones, 'Richard III and Lady Margaret Beaufort', in *Richard III: Loyalty, Lordship and Law*, ed. P.W. Hammond (1986), 27.

[11] *Paston Letters and Papers of the Fifteenth Century*, ed. Norman Davis (2 vols, EETS, special ser., xx, xxi, 2004), ii. no. 916 (a contemporary list of those knighted at the battle in which he is mistakenly called 'Robert'); F.P. Barnard, *Edward IV's French Expedition of 1475* (Oxford, 1925), 119–20.

[12] *British Library Harleian Manuscript 433*, ed. Rosemary Horrox and P.W. Hammond (4 vols, 1979–83), i. 202.

[13] TNA, C139/150/38; C.G.S. Foljambe and Compton Reade, *House of Cornwall* (Hereford, 1908), 70.

[14] Shaw, *Knights of England*, ii. 15; *CPR, 1467–77*, p. 335.

[15] *British Library Harleian Manuscript 433*, i. 195; ii. 206; *CFR*, xxi. no. 797.

[16] TNA, KB9/370, m. 38.

Corbet's mother.[17] It is not unreasonable to assume, given the insecurity of the times, that the three unlucky Welshmen belonged to a retinue recruited by Corbet. There are several possible explanations for Croft's violent objection to this gathering. He may have feared that it was to be used against him in what seems, judging by the alleged rape, to have been an existing enmity with Corbet; or perhaps, as sheriff of Herefordshire, he was taking measures, albeit rather heavy-handed ones, to protect public order on the county's border. In the light of subsequent events, which demonstrate the shallowness of his commitment to Richard III, a third possibility can be discounted, namely that he was acting for the king to disperse forces raised to support Henry. In short, he was unlikely to impede Corbet's recruitment on political grounds (unless, improbably, he mistook Corbet's intentions and believed he was recruiting for Richard), and there can be little doubt that the deaths at Hopton castle were an early manifestation of the personal hostility between the two men which was to lead to serious disorder two years later.

Yet although Croft and Corbet were clearly already at odds, they both set aside their outwardly Ricardian loyalties and committed themselves to the Tudor cause. Whether Croft's support for Henry went as far as taking up arms against Richard III at Bosworth is not known, but if he was not there himself, he was represented by both his bastard son, Thomas, and his stepson, John Mortimer, who was knighted on the field.[18] Corbet went further in his support, perhaps motivated by early acquaintance with the young Henry and advance warning that his stepfather, Stanley, was set to abandon the king. He joined Henry at Shrewsbury, bringing with him, at least on his own later testimony, as many as 800 men.[19] If this is true, it is a testament to the effectiveness of his recruiting, despite the violent interruption on 1 August, and shows that, like Stanley, who defected during the battle, he made a significant contribution to Henry's victory. Nevertheless, although both Croft and Corbet supported Henry, it was only the former who received any notable reward. Remarkably, he retained along with his other offices his position as treasurer of the royal household, and it was in this capacity that he was one of those commissioned on 19 October collectively to exercise the office of steward of England at Henry's coronation.[20] It is possible that a personal relationship with the new king underpinned Croft's continued prominence. In January 1486 when he was among those who testified to the degree of kinship between King Henry and his proposed wife, Edward IV's eldest daughter, Elizabeth, he claimed to have known Henry for twenty years. This suggests that they had met at the castle of Raglan, when the future king was in the custody of the ill-fated earl of Pembroke. Although Croft had not been part of the earl's extensive circle, there is nothing unlikely about such a meeting.[21]

Even so, if Croft could claim a prior relationship with Henry, so, even more strongly, could Corbet, having escorted him (if Corbet's word is to be taken at face value) from the field of Edgcote. He, however, gained nothing, and his resentment

---

[17] TNA, KB9/371, m. 14; KB27/915, rex rot. 7d.
[18] Davies, 'The Crofts', 252–3; Shaw, *Knights of England*, ii. 22.
[19] Owen and Blakeway, *Shrewsbury*, i. 248.
[20] Davies, 'The Crofts', 247; *CPR*, 1485–94, p. 49. For his other principal offices, as receiver-general of the earldom of March, first granted to him after the battle of Tewkesbury, and chancellor of Jasper Tudor's lordship of Glamorgan, see Davies, 'The Crofts', 254–5; W.R.B. Robinson, 'A Letter from Sir Richard Croft', *HR*, lxviii (1995), 185, 188–9.
[21] *CPL*, xiv. 17, 20; Robinson, 'A Letter', 178.

can only have been increased by what happened at the hustings for the Shropshire election to the first parliament of the new reign. These were conducted by one of Henry's principal captains at Bosworth, Sir Gilbert Talbot, who returned two local knights, Sir Thomas Leighton of Church Stretton and Sir Richard Ludlow of Stokesay, to the parliament which, summoned on 15 September, met on 7 November 1485. This, however, on Corbet's submission, was a false return, for at the hustings at Shrewsbury on 27 October he had been elected instead of Leighton. One can only speculate as to what lay behind this contest. Since Leighton, like Corbet and Talbot, was among those who had fought for Henry at Bosworth, he had his own claims to election; and, oddly, of the three candidates, it was the election of the least important of them, Ludlow, that was uncontested.[22] Two explanations suggest themselves: Corbet was the legitimately defeated candidate or Talbot set aside his legitimate return. Talbot's evident friendship with Croft might be interpreted as favouring the latter, with Croft prompting the sheriff to exclude his rival from parliament. The fact that he himself was precluded from election for his own county of Herefordshire by his position as sheriff may have made him the more concerned to prevent Corbet's presence there.

While these events were unfolding, Cornwall, whose part in the Bosworth campaign is unknown, was involved in disorderly activities of his own. Their relationship to the rivalry between Croft and Corbet is not clear, but since they involved the town of Leominster, soon to be the focus of the dispute, there seems little reason to doubt that they were related. He is said to have made riotous assemblies at Leominster on both 14 September and 17 October, on the latter occasion assaulting and threatening John Thorne, prior of the abbey of Reading, thereby preventing Thorne from visiting the monks of Leominster priory, a dependency of the abbey. Two weeks later, on 2 November, Cornwall's servants launched an attack on one David Hawksbrook, so grievous that he died four days later.[23] The timing of these offences suggest they may have been related to the Leominster parliamentary election, with Cornwall seeking to impose his own candidates. Further, if Croft was, as seems probable, already steward of the abbot's franchise at Leominster, Cornwall, whether in the context of an election or not, was challenging his local authority, and it is probable that he was doing so as an ally of Corbet. Significantly in this regard, the first direct evidence of the alliance between the two men comes from very soon after these disturbances and relates to the first royal intervention in the dispute. On 5 December, towards the end of the first session of parliament, Cornwall, along with Corbet's servant, Roger Pole, came before the king in chancery and posted bonds in 500 marks each that Corbet, himself bound in twice that sum, would appear before the king and council in the following Trinity term and that, in the meantime, he would behave well to Elizabeth, wife of John Mitton, a servant of Croft's.[24]

There followed another act of violence which cannot be related to the main narrative of the dispute beyond the fact that it involved one of the protagonists. On 12 March 1486, a few days after the dissolution of parliament, a group of Shropshire men headed by Pole and including John Terry (the alleged rapist), mur-

---

[22] TNA, CP40/895, rot. 253; 902, rot. 404. Biographies of both Leighton and Ludlow will appear in *The House of Commons, 1461–1504*.
[23] TNA, KB9/370, m. 41; KB27/899, rot. 30; 906, rex rot. 2.
[24] TNA, KB27/908, rex rot. 18. Mitton was one of Croft's men involved in the deaths at 'Hagley's Mountain': TNA, KB9/371, m. 41; KB27/906, rot. 52.

dered a Welshman, Owen ap Reynold (with the ominous *alias* Owen Glendower), at Westminster. The murderers were variously described as resident at Waters Upton, where Corbet was lord of the manor, and Hopton castle, held by his mother, and it is thus not surprising that he was named as an accessory in indictments taken before both the coroner in the abbot of Westminster's liberty and the Middlesex justices of the peace.[25] Perhaps, although this can be no more than speculation, the unfortunate Welshman was another servant of Croft's. The events of the following month can less speculatively be tied into the narrative of the dispute. On 10 April, when Sir John Harley of Brampton Bryan, as steward of William Fitzalan, earl of Arundel's south Shropshire hundred of Purslow (in which lay Hopton castle), took a view of frankpledge, several of Croft's servants were indicted for the murders of more than eight months before, with Croft and his bastard son, Thomas, named as accessories. A view of frankpledge was an unusual legal setting for so serious an indictment, and it may be that Corbet, despite his inclusion in the first Shropshire bench of the new reign (alongside his stepfather, Stanley), was unable to secure an indictment before the JPs and had thus turned to the lesser court.[26]

In the following Trinity term, at some date between 31 May and 15 June, Croft responded with a proxy legal action of his own: his servant, Elizabeth Atkins, brought an appeal in king's bench, alleging the rape of 8 July 1485 against John Terry and naming Corbet himself as a receiver. The new king recognised in these actions something more than a minor local dispute: on either 15 or 17 June Croft and Corbet were summoned to appear immediately before the royal council. It was probably on this occasion that heavy bonds were taken from them to guarantee their good behaviour. These bonds, said to be in as much as £3,000, are known only from a Year Book case in the following Michaelmas term, when the justices debated whether these bonds were forfeit by the mere fact of both men appearing armed in defensible array, but without open violence, in Westminster Hall and in other unspecified places. The justices equivocated and there is no evidence that the sums were deemed forfeit.[27] Nonetheless, the royal council clearly feared that the dispute would escalate, perhaps because of Corbet's family relationship with Stanley. This fear was soon to be realised, although, on the available evidence, the principal reason for the escalation was Corbet's alliance not with Stanley, but with Cornwall.

That escalation came at the same time as Henry VII's throne was threatened by the rebellion of Lambert Simnel. The story is related in the records of the royal council.[28] If a complaint made by Cornwall is to be credited, on 1 June 1487 Croft

---

[25] TNA, KB9/375, m. 46; KB27/905, rex rot. 3. The appearance of the name of the Welsh rebel leader as the victim's *alias* is as intriguing as it is inexplicable. Such rebel names had a contemporary currency. A month later, the name of another rebel leader, 'Robin of Redesdale', the nominal head of the Yorkshire rising of 1469, was used by Viscount Lovell in an attempt to raise Richmondshire when Henry VII was in the north: Pollard, *North-Eastern England*, 305–6, 371–2, 378–9.

[26] TNA, KB9/371, m. 41; *CPR*, 1485–94, p. 498. There had been an earlier indictment in respect of one of the deaths at 'Hagley's Mountain', but no process was taken on this indictment against Sir Richard Croft (although it was against his eldest son, Edward): TNA, KB9/1060, mm. 20–1; KB27/915, rex rot. 15d.

[27] TNA, KB9/370, m. 38; KB27/900, rot. 7; 901, rot. 15; *Select Cases in the Council of Henry VII*, ed. C.G. Bayne and W.H. Dunham (Selden Society, lxxv, 1956), 9; *Reports del Cases en Ley* (1679), Year Bk. Mich. 2 Hen. VII, pl. 7, ff. 2v–3.

[28] For what follows: *Select Cases in the Council of Henry VII*, 81–7; Davies, 'The Crofts', 255–6; Sean Cunningham, *Prince Arthur: the Tudor King who Never Was* (Stroud, 2016), 93–8.

gathered 200 men at Leominster to kill him as he made his way, in company with his household servants, to join Stanley, no doubt in preparation for the developing campaign that ended at Stoke. Then, after he had departed, Croft and his sons, Edward and Thomas the bastard, proclaimed that Cornwall, along with Corbet and Stanley, were traitors, who gave 'redde Jakettes as all Kynges enemyes and rebelles diden'. There is no reason to suppose that there was any substance to this charge of treachery, even if it was made, but the reference to the distribution of livery reveals the central point at issue. Croft was steward of Leominster for its lord, the abbot of Reading, and his dominance there had been challenged by Cornwall, who, according to a later complaint, had been distributing his own livery and perhaps also that of Stanley in the town. This provoked the next act in the drama, what appears, at least on the complaint of the prior of Leominster, to have been a major riot in the town on 29 June, a market day. Croft's servants had arrested two men for wearing the Stanley livery, presumably given to them by Cornwall, and committed them to the priory gaol. Cornwall took this as a personal affront, and, according to the prior's petition to the royal council, he brought 160 armed men to the priory, smashed his way into the gaol with 'a grete tree as moche as X men mighte bere' and freed the prisoners. The prior also complained against Corbet, who is said to have brought a further 100 men and issued threats against the prior and his brethren.

Croft added his own litany of petitionary complaint against Cornwall and Corbet. This was a rather vague catalogue, alleging that his rivals had lain in wait to kill him, including as he made his way back from the Stoke campaign, and that they had raided the royal park at Gatley, in the immediate vicinity of Croft's castle at Croft and then in his keeping. Corbet made a robust defence to these complaints, portraying Croft as very much the aggressor. He claimed that, as a JP in Herefordshire, he had gathered men to keep the peace after Croft's wife, on her husband's instructions, had raised a gang of felons to murder Cornwall. More seriously, he claimed that this gang had brutally murdered Philip Ruther, a gentleman in Corbet's service, in the church of Rhayader, some forty miles west of Leominster, as 'the prest was at messe soo that the blood of the same Phelipp sprange upon thee habitte and cope'. Whether much reliance can be placed on these accusations is a matter of doubt. Corbet was a Shropshire JP at this time but he was never appointed to the Herefordshire bench and no evidence has been found to substantiate the alleged brutal killing of the priest. If, however, this act cannot be laid at Croft's door, it is easy to credit the claim made by Cornwall, in a petition in his own defence, that Croft was guilty of subverting royal power to his own ends. He accused Croft of making proclamations that 'noo man shuld in places where he was Styward were eny mannys lyverey except his or the lordis to whome they were tennantes', and then asserting that he had royal authority to seize the copyhold lands of contraveners and, on his own part, to retain as many men as he liked.[29] To these claims Cornwall added two others: he accused Croft of exploiting a commission of musters to raise 1,000 men and, more curiously, of having the common bell of Worcester rung 'for multiplyend of his company'.

---

[29] There is independent evidence, admittedly slight and later, to support the first part of this allegation. On 4 November 1490 a Leominster yeoman, John Rawlyns, entered a bond in £40 to Croft, undertaking that he would 'be not reteynyd by clothe promise conisauns nor othe to any lorde knight squyer or Gentilman' save the king or Croft's friends: TNA, CP40/936, rot. 146d.

He concluded that Croft 'soo taketh every thing in his rule as [if] his wylle in every condicion shuld make your lawes'.

Whatever the exact dynamics of the Leominster riots and what followed, the crown, understandably, took measures to end what appeared to be an escalating quarrel. Although there was no repeat of the very heavy sureties that had been taken from Croft and Corbet in 1486, on 28 August 1487 both Croft and Cornwall were bound to appear personally before the king in chancery on the following quindene of Michaelmas and to maintain the peace to each other (and, in Croft's case, to Corbet as well). It seems likely that both parties appeared, although with what result does not appear. Four months later, on 20 December, further bonds were taken, but, on this occasion, not from Croft. Cornwall and Corbet were each bound in 500 marks, with their sureties, Sir Thomas Leighton (who, despite supplanting Corbet as an MP for Shropshire in 1485, was clearly on friendly terms with him) and Corbet's kinsman, Robert Corbet of Wigmore, offering sureties in a further 500 marks each.[30] Again there is no evidence that these bonds were forfeited, and it must be assumed that the parties appeared. Such bonds for appearance before the council were a standard method of restraining disputants, but to them the crown added subtle interventions in the processes of common law to reduce the bones of contention between the parties. On 26 November 1487 a Shropshire jury came into king's bench to try Corbet's servant John Terry in respect of the mysterious murder at Westminster on 12 March 1486. Terry sought to avoid trial by turning approver, but the king personally instructed his attorney-general to repudiate the appeal and Terry was hanged at Southwark two days later.[31] This can be read in two ways, either as a warning to Corbet to curtail his behaviour or as a means of forestalling further divisive litigation. The second is probably to be preferred, for the king soon afterwards showed himself ready to intervene in Corbet's favour. On 17 May 1488, by letters under his sign manual, he told his attorney-general to end process against Corbet for the Westminster murder on the grounds that the relevant indictments had been taken 'by synystre meanes of his aduersaries'; and, three days later, a provisional sentence of forfeiture of office passed against him, was revoked.[32]

With these palliative measures, the government rather proceeded on the assumption that there had been no dispute at all. On 3 July 1490 Corbet and Cornwall were able to sue out general pardons.[33] More significantly, the crown continued to appoint the three rivals to local commissions: in December 1488 Croft and Cornwall had both been entrusted with taking the Herefordshire musters for the Breton expedition, and in July 1491 they were appointed to raise loans in the same county for the invasion of France. Corbet was on the Shropshire commissions for the Breton expedition, on which he served, and Croft retained his place on the peace commissions in Worcestershire and Herefordshire.[34] Thereafter all three of the disputants served on

---

[30] TNA, C54/376, m. 4; C255/8/5/44. Interestingly, a week before he was due to appear before the council, Cornwall came in person into the court of king's bench and belatedly pleaded a pardon of 25 February 1486 against the indictments for the earlier Leominster riots of 1485: KB27/906, rex rot. 2.
[31] TNA, KB27/904, rex rot. 2.
[32] TNA, KB27/905, rex rot. 3d; *Select Cases in the Council of Henry VII*, 19.
[33] TNA, C67/54, m. 5.
[34] *CPR*, 1485–94, pp. 281, 354, 487, 505; Barnard, *Edward IV's French Expedition*, 120; Hall, *Chronicle*, 442.

the French expedition of the autumn of 1492, and with Corbet's death at the end of the year the matter appeared to have come to a natural end.[35]

Yet there was to be one further chapter in the dispute. One can only speculate why this should have been so, but a factor may have been resentment on Cornwall's part that Croft, just as he had done in 1485, was able to regain his dominant place among the local gentry and recreate the position he had enjoyed in the later part of Edward IV's reign. By February 1495 he was in office as steward of Prince Arthur's household (re-established at Ludlow in the spring of 1493), and in April he succeeded Stanley, recently executed for his complicity in the Warbeck rebellion, as constable of Beaumaris castle.[36] This last act is poorly documented. Soon after Stanley's death, Croft presented a petition against Cornwall to the prince's council, no doubt hoping to take advantage of his influence there, but the petition itself does not survive. It is known only that the council, seemingly ready to act even-handedly, examined witnesses before referring the matter to the king's council, which on 3 July 1495 summoned both men to appear at Westminster six days later, and, if an inference can be drawn from later evidence, took heavy bonds from both parties to keep the peace. This, however, did not prove a sufficient deterrent to Cornwall, who appears to have been the aggressor. On 16 August a group of fifty of his servants riotously assembled at Orleton, three miles from Eye, and assaulted a group of Croft's; during the assault two of the latter met their deaths.[37] It was at this point that the crown finally succeeded in bringing the disputants to heel. A memorandum in the account book of the treasurer of the King's chamber dated on 20 October shows that Croft and Cornwall suffered severe financial penalties, presumably on bonds before the royal council. Croft's sureties forfeited 800 marks and he himself £500, and the same penalties were imposed on Cornwall and his sureties, on recognisances forfeited for 'the greate Riott now lately don in Wales'.[38] Regrettably, no evidence survives to illuminate the events in question. If the forfeited bonds were entered into in July, then the offence must have come after that month, but the description of a great riot in Wales hardly corresponds with the clash, serious though it was, at Orleton on 16 August. Further, the common-law records provide no record of any offences on Croft's part, but his forfeiture shows that offences there must have been. In any event, the imposition of these financial penalties appears to have marked the end of a dispute. Whether these penalties – near ruinous one would imagine in Cornwall's case – were ever paid must remain an open question, but it may be that, like many other such fines, the threat that payment would be enforced acted as a restraint on lawless behaviour.

This dispute, beginning with deaths at the beginning of the Bosworth campaign and continuing until the mid-1490s, is difficult to interpret. At the heart of the matter may have been local resentment of Croft's influence, focused on Leominster where he was the abbot of Reading's steward, exacerbated by the increase in that influence after Bosworth when his rivals had every expectation that it would be diminished. Yet, even if the main engine of the dispute was local grievances, the importance of Croft and Stanley (if he did have more of a direct role than the surviving evidence

---

[35] *Letters and Papers Illustrative of the Reigns of Richard III and Henry VII*, ed. James Gairdner (2 vols, RS, 1861–3), ii. 292; TNA, E101/72/5/1124, 6/1160–1; *CIPM Hen. VII*, i. no. 1117.
[36] *CPR, 1494–1509*, p. 29; Edward Breese, *Kalendars of Gwynedd* (1873), 122.
[37] *Select Cases in the Council of Henry VII*, 50; TNA, KB9/408, m. 58; KB27/941, rots 67–8, 91d; 949, rex rot. 11.
[38] TNA, E101/414/6, f. 123; 16, f. 127v.

suggests) meant that the dramatic events in the marches had a dimension within the wider context of national politics. The sudden escalation of the dispute into greater acts of violence in the immediate aftermath of Henry VII's victory at Stoke is likely to have been something more than coincidence. In one sense, the beginning of that escalation is to be explained in practical terms, in that the disputants were at the heads of retinues that they had brought to the campaign. Much more speculatively, it might be suggested that the victory at Stoke removed a restraint upon the local rivalries of the king's supporters now that the threat of a common Yorkist enemy had been removed (for the time being at least), and that this was a factor in the Leominster riots of 29 June. Leaving this aside, there may also have been another context. Even though the king's son, Arthur, born in September 1486, was no more than a baby, it might have been clear that the plan was to place him into the pattern of education and training established for the Yorkist prince of Wales at Ludlow in the 1470s.[39] Both Croft, as treasurer, and Stanley, as steward, had held high office in that Yorkist household, and rivalry between them and their adherents may have intensified in anticipation of a new political dispensation under Prince Arthur.

This latter point invites another speculation. Although the surviving evidence paints Stanley as a peripheral figure in the main narrative of the dispute, it is entirely possible that fuller evidence would show him in a more central part.[40] If so, it is possible that, even early in Henry VII's reign, Stanley was frustrated at what he took to be unjustified restraints upon his local influence and was thus ready to encourage his son-in-law, Corbet, and Cornwall in their opposition to Croft, whom he saw as a rival both locally and in the royal household. This frustration may have amplified in his mind the feeling that the post of king's chamberlain, important as it was, and his other gains from royal patronage were insufficient reward for all he had done to make Henry king.[41] On this reading, the events at Leominster in 1487 marked the beginning of his alienation from Henry, albeit one that did not begin to take on the taint of treason until Perkin Warbeck assumed the persona of Edward IV's younger son, Richard of Shrewsbury, duke of York, in 1491.

The household plot of 1487

Any new king, particularly one who had taken the throne in battle, had the difficult task of winning support in the localities. He also had the seemingly easier one of surrounding himself personally by those in whom he could trust implicitly. Yet, just as in the localities, a new king could not rely upon established friends alone. In the chambers and halls of Westminster, Greenwich or Sheen, service had to be recast in the mould of the new regime, but that mould had to include men with widely

---

[39] Sean Cunningham, 'A Yorkist Legacy for the Tudor Prince of Wales on the Welsh Marches: Affinity-Building, Regional Government and National Politics, 1471–1502', in *The Fifteenth Century XVIII: Rulers, Regions and Retinues: Essays Presented to A.J. Pollard*, ed. Linda Clark and Peter Fleming (Woodbridge, 2020), 125–6.

[40] Davies, 'The Crofts', 255–6.

[41] M.K. Jones, 'Sir William Stanley of Holt: Politics and Family Allegiance in the Late Fifteenth Century', *Welsh History Review*, xiv (1988), 20–1; Ian Arthurson, *The Perkin Warbeck Conspiracy, 1491–99* (Stroud, 1993), 143–6; W.A.J. Archbold, 'Sir William Stanley and Perkin Warbeck', *EHR*, xiv (1899), 529–34.

different political histories, including those, like, in the case of Henry Tudor, Croft and Stanley, who had abandoned the monarch Richard III only at the last moment. The unfortunate and inevitable corollary was that the further Henry looked beyond his own circle to extend his household, the greater the possibility that household would come to include those whose apparent loyalty to him could be subverted by a resurgence of their old allegiances. This was to be strikingly illustrated later in the reign when Stanley entered treasonable correspondence with Warbeck. Nor, to make matters yet more difficult for Henry were resentments within the household confined to those with a Ricardian past. The roll for the parliament of November 1487 describes a conspiracy involving some of the much less august members of the household, at least two of whom had served Henry before his accession.

Six principal conspirators, of varying shades of obscurity, are identified.[42] Two, Maurice ap Hugh and John Spynell, are known to have been yeomen of the crown.[43] The household membership of a third, Thomas Bromhill, is implied by the grant to him on 11 October 1486 for service to the king 'beyond and on this side' of the sea; and the same argument can be made of John Sutton, who, a month after Bosworth, was granted the keeping of the duchy of Lancaster park of Shottle in Derbyshire.[44] The other two – Davy Morice and Piers Gough – are yet more obscure figures, but their inclusion implies that they too were household men. Although, in the act of attainder passed against them, the six are not specifically described as such, the clear link between this act and another, passed in the same parliament, establishing a household court, leaves no doubt that the conspiracy was hatched within the household. A contemporary London chronicler was entirely justified in his remark that there 'was a resistance made in the parlement tyme of men in the kinges howys'.[45] Of the six, Spynell was comfortably the most important. Like Bromehill, he had been in Henry's service before Bosworth, for on 1 June 1486 he had a reward of nearly £7, for his 'grete costis and charges … from the begynnyng of oure reigne and afore'. The grants that had come to him in the first months of the reign, small in themselves but significant in the context of his modest rank, are further evidence of a well-established connexion with the new king. A month after Bosworth he was appointed gauger of Bristol and, on the following 30 December, keeper of the park of Acton Burnell in Shropshire and farmer of the lordship there, forfeited by Francis, Viscount Lovell, still an active rebel.[46] At least some of the six shared something in common, beyond their household membership, namely their geographical origins. Four were certainly from Wales and the marches. Maurice ap Hugh was from Shropshire, judging from the pardon later granted to him, and the Welsh origins of two others, Morice and Gough, as in ap Hugh's case, is strongly suggested by their names.[47] There can be little doubt that Spynell came from Shrewsbury: the

---

[42] *PROME*, xv. 379–80. This conspiracy has largely escaped historical notice, but for the exception, see Paul Cavill, *The English Parliaments of Henry VII* (Oxford, 2009), 54–5.
[43] *CPR*, 1485–94, pp. 58, 257–8.
[44] *CPR*, 1485–94, pp. 30, 558.
[45] R.F. Green, 'Historical Notes of a London Citizen, 1483–1488', *EHR*, xcvi (1981), 589.
[46] *Materials for a History of the Reign of Henry VII*, ed. William Campbell (2 vols, 1873, 1877), i. 406, 445; Cavill, *Parliaments of Henry VII*, 54–5; *CPR*, 1485–1509, pp. 58, 83.
[47] In the pardon granted to ap Hugh on 9 March 1488, he was described as 'of Okeley in the earldom of March': *CPR*, 1485–94, pp. 257–8. This is probably to be identified as Oakley (in Bromfield), just outside Ludlow.

cash reward given to him in June 1486 was charged on the town's fee farm.[48] In respect of the other two, nothing certain can be said. The grant made to Bromehill in 1486 was of a life interest in the royal brewhouse in Fleet Steet known as the 'Signe of the Walshemane', but it is a stretch to argue that this associated him with Wales; and Sutton's only known grant lay in Derbyshire.[49] Although the evidence is not conclusive, it is fair to describe the plot of late 1487 as hatched by a group of minor household men with connexions in the marches.

The only source for the intentions of these plotters is the act of attainder passed against them. It claims that their aim was 'to have slayne, murdred and dystroyed dyvers of the kynges grete officers, and other of his most honorable councell', to which aim they had recruited some eighty men, presumably from outside the household. To execute their purpose, this group, 'not feryng All myghty God ner ther sovereyn lorde' assembled 'in ryottouswyse' at Westminster on 15 December when the king himself was in parliament.[50] Unfortunately, the act is entirely silent about how this ambitious plot was thwarted, but thwarted it certainly was: four of the principal plotters were executed at Tower Hill two days later, a day before parliament's dissolution.[51]

Even in a failure that appears complete and abject, the plot was a dangerous moment for the new king. His person was not the plotters' target, for there is no reason to doubt the act's statement in this regard, but clearly a conspiracy to kill his principal officers posed a serious threat to his government. Measures, or so it was perceived, were thus needed to protect both king and government against plots within the household, and it was to this end that another act was passed in the same parliament. The preamble employs the rather overblown language of crisis: it claimed that hostility to those 'in greate auctorite, office and of councell with kynges of this roialme, hath ensued the destruccion of kynges and the neer undoing of this realme' and, no doubt in reference to late events, it located this hostility in the 'envy and malice of the kings owne howsold servauntes'. As a remedy, the steward, treasurer (Croft) and controller of the royal household were given authority to enquire by a household jury into offences within the household and to prosecute anyone below the rank of lord for any conspiracy there against the king, his lords and officers. If the suspect pleaded not guilty then the officers could proceed to summon a jury from the household to try the suspect for felony. Although this jurisdiction replicated that of the court of the verge, under the steward and marshal of the household, there can be no doubt that it was intended as a new tribunal.[52]

This plot within the household and the new judicial measures are clear illustrations of Henry VII's continued insecurity even after his victory at Stoke. The violent clashes at Leominster in the immediate aftermath of that battle, directly involving the treasurer of the household, Croft, and its chamberlain, Stanley, are further evi-

---

[48] *Materials for a History of the Reign of Henry VII*, i. 445; further, either he, or, if he did not survive the conspiracy, a namesake and probable kinsman, played a modest part in the town's administration in the early 1490s: Shropshire Archives, Shrewsbury recs, assembly book 3365/67, ff. 28v–29.

[49] *Materials for a History of the Reign of Henry VII*, i. 82, 558.

[50] *PROME*, xv. 379–80.

[51] Cavill, *Parliaments of Henry VII*, 54. Ap Hugh was one of the survivors; the other is unknown.

[52] *Pace* W.R. Jones, 'The Court of the Verge: The Jurisdiction of the Steward and Marshal of the Household in Late Medieval England', *Journal of British Studies*, x (1970), 29, who sees it as an extension of the court of the verge's jurisdiction.

dence of his uncertain authority. The marcher links of the plotters make it tempting to draw some link between the local disturbances, continuing at the end of 1487, and events in the household. That temptation is strengthened by Croft's loss of office as treasurer of the household at Michaelmas 1488.[53] Yet the delay of nearly a year rather weakens that temptation, as does his inclusion, as treasurer, as one of the presiding officers of the new court. If some link is to be found between removal from senior household office and the plot of December 1487, there is a more obvious candidate than Croft, namely the steward, John Radcliffe, Lord Fitzwalter. Although he appears not to have been as closely associated with Richard III as either Croft or Stanley, he was certainly from outside Henry VII's circle and had, on the face of it, been a surprising appointment, at the beginning of the reign, to an office so close to the king. Perhaps some doubt as to the wisdom of the move is implied by the nomination as joint steward of one who had shared the king's exile in Brittany, Sir Robert Willoughby de Broke. The uncovering of the plot may have convinced Henry that the risk was no longer worth taking. Radcliffe last appears as a member of the royal council a month before the plot was revealed, and by the end of January 1488 Willoughby was acting as sole steward.[54] Yet, as in the case of Croft, it is hard to argue that Radcliffe's loss of office was related to the plot. The apparent withering of royal trust in him is probably to be explained by local factors: in the previous May he had been equivocal in his response to the demand of the king's friend, John de Vere, earl of Oxford, that the gentlemen of East Anglia follow him to musters in advance of the Stoke campaign. Seemingly he was already advanced on the road that was to lead to his execution in 1496.[55]

On this evidence, the household plot was unconnected with the machinations of Croft, Radcliffe, Stanley or any other senior member of the household. The explanation for the conspiracy, as Paul Cavill has suggested, may have been much more mundane and, from the king's point of view, less threatening, namely resentment at a pending further resumption of certain royal grants. Spyney and Sutton both stood to lose their offices and may have blamed senior royal officers for this impending loss.[56] Nevertheless, to a king already facing several interconnected plots, risings and instances of disloyalty, any manifestations of conspiracy and opposition had the capacity to appear as dangerous challenges to his rule.

The projection of violence and quarrelling from the Welsh marches to Westminster, with the murder of the mysterious 'Glendower' and the appearance of Croft and Corbet with armed followers in Westminster Hall in 1486, and possibly into the royal household, illustrates the weakness of Henry VII in the first years of his reign. The new political dispensation after Bosworth created a febrile atmosphere in local poli-

---

[53] Curiously, the post was not immediately filled. Not until the following Michaelmas did John Payne, cofferer of the household, formally become treasurer, although he did discharge some of the responsibilities of the office in the interim: TNA, E159/266, *brevia directa baronibus*, Easter, rot. 12; E361/8, rot. 17d.

[54] For Radcliffe's last appearance on the council: *Select Cases in the Council of Henry VII*, 15. Willoughby presided over the court of the verge at Southwark as sole steward on 24 January 1488 and appears as such in other contexts in the two following months: TNA, KB9/378, m. 15; E101/412/15, no. 14, 413/2/1, f. 14.

[55] J.A. Ross, *The Foremost Man of the Kingdom: John de Vere, Thirteenth Earl of Oxford, 1442–1513* (Woodbridge, 2015), 126. By July 1488 Radcliffe's loss of royal trust was complete when he was bound in £1,000 to be loyal to the king and serve no other: TNA, C54/376, m. 10.

[56] Cavill, *Parliaments of Henry VII*, 55.

tics as leading landowners, on both sides of the political divide, sought to protect or advance their positions. The actions of Croft, Stanley, Corbet and Cornwall around Leominster in 1487 showed what happened when these tensions were not contained, and in view of the places Croft and Stanley held in the royal household raised the spectre of the contagion of local disorder spreading into the royal chambers. Even so, whether one can draw any wider lessons about the effectiveness of the untried Henry's kingship in this formative period is more difficult. A recent criticism has been forthright in its negativity, accusing Henry of a 'lack of judgement over how to delegate and to whom' and of promoting feuding 'by giving excessive licence to those he trusted'.[57] The Leominster riots might be cited in support of this thesis. Yet this is too harsh a verdict. The riots arose out of local rivalries no king could reasonably hope to contain entirely, and in dealing with them Henry appears to have reacted with a subtle combination of carrot and stick. In intervening in the processes of common law, he prevented litigation driving the rival parties further apart, and he used bonds and fines as breaks on escalation. The local troubles of early in his reign reflect not the limitations of his judgment but the limitations of his options. If he did give 'excessive licence' to some of those leading figures, like Stanley and to a lesser extent Croft, it was because in those early years there were few upon whom he could rely. The Leominster riots and the household plot of 1487 illustrate rather another aspect of these years: a loosening of the ties that had bound his supporters together in 1485.

In terms of the general history of the reign, one further points needs to be made. If Henry was guilty of errors of political judgment in the late 1480s, they were mistakes from which he quickly learned. The sort of violence that overtook the marches in 1487 became less likely there (notwithstanding the ill-documented 'greate Riott' of 1495) as from 1493 the council of the marches and the household of Prince Arthur drew influential local figures, Croft and Cornwall among them, into their orbit. Henry also learnt to trust those from outside the circle of his supporters of 1485, perhaps the clearest example being the establishment of Thomas Howard, earl of Surrey, who had fought against him at Bosworth and had been imprisoned in the Tower of London until 1489, as his regional lieutenant in the north in the 1490s.[58] Henry's skilful adaption to the troubles of his early reign can be said to have laid the basis for the later success of his rule.

---

[57] Christine Carpenter, *The Wars of the Roses: Politics and the Constitution in England, c. 1437–1509* (Cambridge, 1997), 234.
[58] Pollard, *North-Eastern England*, 386–7.

BURIALS AND MEMORIALISATION AT THE COMMAND OF HENRY VII[1]

Ralph A. Griffiths

In the later Middle Ages, noble burials and memorialisation commonly reflected what Nigel Saul has characterised as 'a strong ancestral sense' among the English nobility. This 'sense' was doubtless shared by noble women as well as by their menfolk as they considered the burial and commemoration of deceased relatives. It consequentially contributed to the social, economic and cultural fabric of aristocratic family life which Rowena Archer has described.[2] The choice of burial site and commemoration might also be influenced by crises within families and more broadly. This was certainly so within the English royal family during the later fifteenth century, and particularly during the reign of Henry VII. In the extraordinarily formidable task of establishing his kingship, Henry had an unusually small number of close relatives to support him at his accession in 1485, and he faced a constellation of threats and political uncertainties thereafter. Both factors helped to form his singularly sensitive attitude to the burial and memorialisation of his relatives in the 1490s. The places and circumstances in which burials customarily took place were frequently specified by testators in their wills, unless death occurred unexpectedly or during childhood. Burials were generally arranged within months or at most within a year after death. Memorialisation, on the other hand, might take place much later, and considerations beyond a straightforward desire to commemorate the deceased might play a part in the decision.[3]

In the final chapter of his decisive and authoritative study of Henry VII's reign and government entitled 'The King's Grace', S.B. Chrimes allowed himself some cautious reflections on the king's personal motivations and character, though he was not moved to elaborate on them ten years later when he assessed subsequent

---

[1] I am grateful to R.W. Dunning and James Ross for their comments on an earlier draft of this essay.
[2] Nigel Saul, *English Church Monuments in the Middle Ages: History and Representation* (Oxford, 2009), esp. 130–2. See, for example, R.E. Archer, '"How Ladies ... who live on their Manors ought to manage their Households and Estates": Women as Landholders and Administrators in the Later Middle Ages', in *Women in Medieval English Society*, ed. P.J.P. Goldberg (Stroud, 1997), 149–81, and 'Piety in Question: Noblewomen and Religion in the Later Middle Ages', in *Women and Religion in Medieval England*, ed. Diana Wood (Oxford, 2003), 118–40.
[3] Saul, *English Church Monuments*, 112–13.

research on the king's reign.[4] Yet among Chrimes's observations are two which, taken together, warrant further examination and may help to dispel the fog that obscures the person of the king from the view of historians – from the 'gloom' which G.W. Bernard could still encounter in 1999. Nine years later still, Sean Cunningham, in the most recent study of Henry VII, concluded that while 'It was entirely Henry VII's personality that shaped and directed the course of his reign', 'a true understanding of the man is lost along with the key evidence ... [for] a true biographical picture of him'.[5]

It is worth noting, first, the attention which Chrimes gave to the king's intimate personal relationship with his mother, Lady Margaret Beaufort, countess of Richmond and (from 1485) countess of Derby, as well as with his queen, Elizabeth of York, whom he married in 1486, and indeed to the close relations that existed between all three of them, even to the extent of sharing the king's confidences in family matters. This degree of intimacy – greater than that experienced by Edward IV in similar circumstances – has been substantiated in more recent studies of Lady Margaret and Queen Elizabeth, and it is likely to have helped to frame Henry's decisions relating to his immediate family, not least their burials.[6] Second, Chrimes thought it noteworthy that not only did Henry VII meet the 'doubtless inevitable' costs of the burials of his eldest son, Prince Arthur, in 1502 and of Queen Elizabeth herself in 1503, but that he also (and more surprisingly) paid the bills for the burials of Sir William Stanley in 1495 and Edward Plantagenet, earl of Warwick, in 1499, both executed on the king's orders, as well as the bill for a belated tomb for King Richard III – payments which, Chrimes suggested, he need not have made. Into this latter category, too, may be placed payments for a tomb for the king's father, Edmund Tudor, earl of Richmond, who had died as long ago as 1456, and for the ambitious preparations for the translation of the body of Edmund's half-brother, King Henry VI, to Westminster abbey.[7]

Moreover, with no siblings of his own and with very few immediate male relatives during his lifetime, it is not surprising that the king should have taken a close interest in the burial of his father's brother, Jasper Tudor, earl of Pembroke and duke of Bedford, in 1495, and that of his step-uncle, John, Viscount Welles, the half-brother of Lady Margaret Beaufort, in 1499. Both kinsmen had been staunch supporters of Henry since before the battle of Bosworth and left wills that included arrangements so that the king need not make any financial provision himself for their burials. Nonetheless, Henry took a special interest in the burial of Jasper Tudor and a central role in the choice of site for the burial of John Welles. And the circumstances

---

[4] S.B. Chrimes, *Henry VII* (New Haven, CT and London, 1972; 2nd edn, 1999), 317–20; *idem*, 'The Reign of Henry VII: Some Recent Contributions', *Welsh History Review*, x (pt 3) (1981), 320–33.

[5] G.W. Bernard's assessment is at the end of his Foreword to the second edition of Chrimes's book (p. xix); Sean Cunningham, *Henry VII* (2007), 285.

[6] Chrimes, *Henry VII*, 301–4. See M.K. Jones and M.G. Underwood, *The King's Mother: Lady Margaret Beaufort, Countess of Richmond and Derby* (Cambridge, 1992); Nicola Tallis, *Uncrowned Queen: The Fateful Life of Margaret Beaufort, Tudor Matriarch* (2019); Alison Weir, *Elizabeth of York: The First Tudor Queen* (2013); and J.L. Laynesmith, *The Last Medieval Queens: English Queenship, 1445–1503* (Oxford, 2004), 211–13.

[7] Chrimes, *Henry VII*, 307: his comment is based on published excerpts by Samuel Bentley, *Excerpta Historica* (1831), from the king's and queen's chamber books of payments. The surviving books are now fully transcribed in 'The Chamber Books of Henry VII and Henry VIII, 1485–1521', ed. M.M. Condon, S.P. Harper, Lisa Liddy, Sean Cunningham and James Ross, www.tudorchamberbooks.org

in which these two decisions were made may also have had an indirect connection with the king's proposed reburial at Westminster of the long-dead Henry VI, who had lain at Windsor since Richard III's reign.

Henry VII's involvement in these several burials and memorialisations of the 1490s, between 1495 and 1500, coincided with the continuing security threats to his regime posed by the Yorkist impostor and pretender, Perkin Warbeck, and the allies whom Warbeck attracted in Ireland, Scotland and on the near-continent. The decisions which Henry then took are likely to have involved both his mother (on the Lancastrian side) and his wife (on the Yorkist side), and these decisions seem to have prompted him to attach a renewed importance to Westminster abbey as the appropriate mausoleum for England's kings.[8] In short, these interments at Henry VII's command may reflect both personal and family sentiment alongside political calculation.

* * *

At the beginning of 1495, Henry VII was faced with a major political crisis which had an embarrassing family dimension. The persistent conspiracy (since 1491–2) around the claim of the teenager Perkin Warbeck to be Richard, duke of York, the younger of King Edward IV's two sons who had disappeared in 1483 and had most likely been murdered on the orders of Richard III, acquired heightened seriousness when rumours spread during 1494 that Sir William Stanley had become involved.[9] It also moved uncomfortably close to the king himself. Not only had the duke of York been the younger brother of King Henry's queen, Elizabeth, but Stanley was the younger brother of Thomas, Lord Stanley, who had married Lady Margaret Beaufort as her third husband in 1472. Although both brothers had been erstwhile Yorkist supporters, they were instrumental in ensuring victory for Henry Tudor at Bosworth. Lord Stanley was accordingly created earl of Derby in 1485 while Sir William became chamberlain of the new king's household.[10] If King Henry was reluctant to accept that Sir William Stanley was flirting with treason, and was therefore slow to move against him, the formal creation of the king's second son Henry as duke of York on 1 November 1494, even though he was only three years old, was a signal that potential traitors would no longer be tolerated. Suspicions about Sir William's loyalty had become so compelling by Christmas 1494 that he was widely identified as a likely sympathiser with Perkin Warbeck's claim to be the rightful Yorkist claimant to the English throne. This scandal doubtless shocked both the king and his mother: Stanley was arrested, tried and executed in February 1495, his brother Thomas presiding at the trial as constable of England. Significantly, the commission appointed to hear the

---

[8] S.J. Gunn, 'Warbeck, Perkin (c.1474–1499), *Oxford DNB*. See Ian Arthurson, *The Perkin Warbeck Conspiracy, 1491–1499* (Stroud, 1994), for a full account; and R.A. Griffiths, 'Succession and the Royal Dead in Later Medieval England', in *Making and Breaking the Rules: Succession in Medieval Europe, c.1000–c.1600*, ed. Frédérique Lachaud and Michael Penman (Turnhout, 2008), 97–110, for a context.

[9] For suspicions about Stanley from the early weeks of 1494, and rumours of foreign support in Warbeck's behalf, see Cunningham, *Henry VII*, 77–84.

[10] M.J. Bennett, 'Stanley, Sir William (c.1435–1495)', *Oxford DNB*, and www.oxforddnb.com/. For the close relations between the Stanley brothers and Lady Margaret Beaufort since 1472, see M.K. Jones, 'Sir William Stanley of Holt: Politics and Family Allegiance in the late Fifteenth Century', *Welsh History Review*, xiv (pt 1) (1988), 1–22 (esp. 8–9, 21–2).

indictments laid against Sir William Stanley and his fellow conspirators was headed by the king's uncle, Jasper Tudor, duke of Bedford, and included three of Henry's most trusted councillors, Giles, Lord Daubeney, Sir Reynold Bray and Sir Thomas Lovell, of whom more later.[11]

Not only had the king been slow to conclude that his chamberlain was guilty of treason, but he was nevertheless prepared to pay the costs of Stanley's burial in Syon abbey, just across the Thames from the royal palace of Sheen.[12] Syon had been founded by Henry V for the Bridgettine order of nuns and was one of the largest monasteries in England after its main buildings were completed in 1488. Although a somewhat surprising choice for a nobleman's burial in 1495, it may have been deemed preferable to allowing burial in the Stanley mausoleum in Burscough priory in more distant Lancashire, close to the extensive Stanley estates in north-west England and the Welsh borderland. The decision was likely taken at the urging of Lady Margaret Beaufort and, possibly, her husband, Lord Stanley: both Lady Margaret and Henry VII had a special affection for Syon.[13]

A second death later in the year was a blow of a different and even more personal order, and the burial a natural claim on the king's resources. On 14 September 1495, the king's second daughter, named Elizabeth after her mother, died at the age of three at the royal palace of Eltham, near London. While it would have been a father's duty to arrange, and meet the costs of, the child's funeral, it appears that Henry VII and Queen Elizabeth did not attend the burial in Edward the Confessor's chapel in Westminster abbey even though they were at the palace nearby.[14] If this was the royal couple's custom, it may not have been followed when the king's uncle died at the end of the year. This death had a far greater public, if not private, impact on Henry VII and his family, and was of wider significance. In December 1495, Jasper Tudor, earl of Pembroke and duke of Bedford, died at his wife's manor of Thornbury in Gloucestershire, part of Katherine Wydeville's jointure as the widow of Henry Stafford, duke of Buckingham (d. 1483). Jasper had shielded and then supported his nephew from birth, in Wales, England and France, and after the battle of Bosworth he became one of Henry's closest and most senior noble advisers. He made his will at Thornbury on 15 December, less than a week before he died, and accordingly the king was not faced with meeting the expenses of his uncle's funeral or his tomb, for which Jasper bequeathed 100 marks so that it be 'honourable made after thastate that it hath pleased God to call me to'. And yet, in a rare demonstration of closeness to his uncle, the king may have attended Jasper's burial in Keynsham abbey, not far from Thornbury and near Bristol, or else soon visited the place of his interment, accompanied by Queen Elizabeth and, probably, Lady Margaret Beaufort.[15]

---

[11] Arthurson, *The Perkin Warbeck Conspiracy*, 85–6.

[12] For the burial costs, see 'Chamber Books of Henry VII and Henry VIII', BL, Add. MS 7099, f. 23 (£15 19s.), and f. 24 (£2 'in full payment'), 12 April 1495.

[13] Jones and Underwood, *The King's Mother*, 180–1; Neil Beckett, 'Henry VII and Sheen Charterhouse', in *The Reign of Henry VII*, ed. Benjamin Thompson (Harlaxton Medieval Studies V, Stamford, 1995), 117–32; Tallis, *Uncrowned Queen*, 212–14.

[14] Tallis, *Uncrowned Queen*, 114; Weir, *Elizabeth of York*, 308–9. For the burial, see B.F. Harvey, *Westminster Abbey and its Estates in the Middle Ages* (Oxford, 1977), 383 n. 4. It may be noted that the couple's first daughter, born in 1489, was named after the king's mother who stood as the child's godmother; she later became queen of Scotland: Jones and Underwood, *The King's Mother*, 148.

[15] Jasper Tudor's will, TNA, PROB 11/10/59, is partially published in *Testamenta Vetusta*, ed. N.H. Nicolas (2 vols, 1826), i, 430–1, and in *Somerset Medieval Wills, First Series, 1383–1500*, ed. F.W.

A surviving inquisition post mortem, which was completed much later on 20 October 1498, recorded that the duke had died on 21 December 1495, but a later addition to the 'Great Chronicle of London', possibly made by William Cary, a London citizen, gives the date as 18 December.[16] It is not known precisely when the funeral took place in Keynsham abbey, but the contemporary Bristol chronicler recorded the event and the subsequent visit by Henry VII and Queen Elizabeth to Bristol as if the two events were related:

> This yere the King and Qwene came to Bristowe with dyuers Lordes spirituall and temporall. And this yere the Duc of Bedford the kings uncle decessid at Thornbury on whois sowle god have mercy, and was buryed at Keynesham. And the saide Maire and his brethren met with the saide Duc in Kyngeswode with ii ml. men on horsbake, all in blake gownes, and so brought his body to Keynesham, for the which the saide Maire and his brethren had grete thankes of the King.[17]

Recording the two events a century and more later, William Adams's chronicle of Bristol tightens the link between them:

> The Duke of Bedford unckill to King Henry died at Thornbury and buried at Keinsham. The maire of Bristowe and his brethren with 2000 men on horseback all in blacke met the said duke in Kingswood, and so brougte his body to Keinsham and, for which the King and queene coming short afteirwards to Bristow, gave the mair and councell of heartie thankes.[18]

Among the 'dyuers Lordes ... temporall' who accompanied the king and queen is likely to have been Giles, Lord Daubeney, who had succeeded Sir William Stanley as the king's chamberlain and as early as September 1485 had been gifted for life the royal chase of Kingswood where the large Bristol contingent met the duke's body on its way to burial at Keynsham abbey. Daubeney was also an executor of Jasper Tudor's will.[19] Henry and his queen began their progress across southern England in June; they could hardly have set off sooner while Elizabeth was in the latter stages of

---

Weaver (Somerset Record Soc., xvi, 1901), 327–9. For discussions based on the published versions, see R.S. Thomas, 'The Political Career, Estates and "Connection" of Jasper Tudor, Earl of Pembroke and Duke of Bedford (d.1495)' (PhD thesis, Wales, Swansea University, 1971), 353–7, and (with some inaccuracies) S.E. Roberts, *Jasper, the Tudor Kingmaker* (Stroud, 2015), 114–15.

[16] *CIPM Henry VII*, iii. 396 (from TNA, C142/23/162); *The Great Chronicle of London*, ed. A.H. Thomas and I.D. Thornley (1938), 275 and (for Cary) 422. The surviving inquisition covers only Herefordshire and part of the Welsh march and seems not well informed. It was not uncommon for inquisitions to be taken one or two years after death, perhaps especially so in this case: see Claire Noble, 'Writs and the Inquisitions Post Mortem', in *The Fifteenth Century Inquisitions Post Mortem: A Companion*, ed. M.A. Hicks (Woodbridge, 2012), 188–9.

[17] Robert Ricart, *The Maire of Bristowe is Kalendar*, ed. L.T. Smith (Camden Soc., new series, v, 1872), 48. The duke's entrails were buried in the Slimbridge chantry in Thornbury church: *CPR, 1494–1509*, p. 114 (2 May 1497).

[18] Bristol RO, Bristol MS 13748/4, Chronicle of Bristol by William Adams, 1625, under '1495', a reference I owe to Margaret Condon and Evan Jones. A shorter version of his chronicle merely states – but with a suggestion of a link between the duke's funeral and the king's visit – that 'The Duke of Bedford died at Thornbury and was buried at Kainsham; and the King and Queene came to Bristow to St Austine's': *Adams's Chronicle of Bristol, 1623* (Bristol, 1910), 77.

[19] *Materials for a History of the Reign of Henry VII*, ed. William Campbell (2 vols, RS, 1873), i. 83.

pregnancy before the birth of Princess Mary on 18 March. They are known to have reached Bath and Bristol on 11–18 August, towards the end of their progress, and in view of the gathering of temporal and spiritual lords, and especially of the large company of Bristol men, the funeral may have been delayed for some months after the duke's death until the king himself could attend. He made offerings while he was at Keynsham abbey and to St Anne's chapel 'in the wood' nearby.[20]

Henry and Elizabeth were almost certainly accompanied by Lady Margaret Beaufort on the progress. While Margaret was visiting her Dorset estates en route, both she and her son made an offering at Wimborne Minster where her parents (and therefore the king's grand-parents) were buried. Later, and while the party was at Bristol, Henry VII recalled his and Jasper Tudor's exile at Vannes in southern Brittany by making an offering at the chapel and hermitage dedicated to St Vincent Ferrer (d. 1419) above the Avon gorge. The saint had died at Vannes where his cult was popular by the time Henry, his uncle and their exiled company were staying there: the offering may have seemed an appropriate gesture following Jasper's funeral. Indeed, Henry VII maintained his contact with Vannes cathedral and later commemorated St Vincent Ferrer in his new lady chapel at Westminster abbey and in the design of his own tomb.[21] Such progresses might have several purposes that embraced family and friends, and their estates and interests, as well as more political – even security – objectives. Marking the burial of Jasper Tudor gave the progress of 1496 added significance for Henry VII, while the king's gratitude to Bristol may have resonated in his new charter to the city in 1499 which extended the powers of Bristol's merchant elite.[22]

The duke of Bedford was well into his sixties when he died, on or very shortly before the day that parliament ended. The only adult duke in the realm, he had been among those summoned on 15 September 1495 to attend parliament at Westminster a month later. It met on 14 October in the shadow of continuing plotting at home and abroad by Perkin Warbeck, whose threats became particularly serious with an attempted invasion in the summer of 1495, and Warbeck's arrival in Scotland to plan a further incursion. Both the record of the proceedings of this parliament and the terms of Jasper's will in some respects signal the close relationship between the king and his uncle. They suggest that Henry VII, who was named as the will's supervisor, was aware of the testamentary intentions before the will was written, and that certain acts of the parliament anticipated that Jasper would die in the very near future. Paul Cavill judged this parliamentary session to be 'the most productive session of the reign', in which the king showed himself ready 'to deal with the problems of the realm'.[23] One of its main purposes was to confirm the truce with France

---

[20] See the king's itinerary reconstructed in Gladys Temperley, *Henry VII* (1917), 415, supplemented by TNA, E101/414/6, ff. 42v, 43 (references I owe to the kindness of Margaret Condon).

[21] TNA, E101/414/6, f. 41. The 1496 progress is noted by Susan Powell, 'Lady Margaret Beaufort: A Progress through Essex and East Anglia, 1498', in *The Elite Household in England, 1100–1500: Proceedings of the 2016 Harlaxton Symposium*, ed. C.M. Woolgar (Harlaxton Medieval Studies XXVIII, Donnington, 2018), 295–316, quoting TNA, E101/414/6, ff. 39–41. For Henry, Vannes and St Vincent Ferrer, see R.A. Griffiths and R.S. Thomas, *The Making of the Tudor Dynasty* (3rd edn, Stroud, 2021), 88, 90, 94, 112, 117–19, 124, 196–7.

[22] See James Lee, 'Urban Policy and Urban Political Culture: Henry VII and His Towns', *HR*, lxxxii (2009), 493–510 (esp. 501–7), for Bristol's warm relations with Henry VII and his government in the 1490s.

[23] P.R. Cavill, *English Parliaments of Henry VII, 1485–1504* (Oxford, 2009), 16, 74–7. For the parlia-

which had been agreed by Henry VII and Charles VIII at Etaples in November 1492 and which Henry hoped would neutralise French support for the pretender Warbeck. Jasper was present at the formal ratification ceremony on 27 October. Some weeks later, before the parliament ended, he left Westminster and made his way to Gloucestershire.[24] Probably towards the end of the session, several king's bills were passed which affected Jasper, the king and his family, and which were intended to take effect immediately after the duke's death. That Jasper was aware of their nature is suggested by several clauses of his will and by his nomination of the king as the will's supervisor, presumably with Henry's consent, 'for myne to his grace olde service doon'.[25]

A significant act of this parliament was the generous settlement of the Stafford properties, during the minority of Edward, duke of Buckingham, on Jasper's wife, Katherine Wydeville, Duke Edward's mother (and the queen's aunt), thereby securing her life interest in the entire Stafford estates. This explains why Jasper's will includes only one mention of Katherine and no significant additional provision for her. A second important act provided for the reversion of Jasper's own estates, whether granted to him by Henry VI or Henry VII, to his nephew the king and his heirs, properties which the parliament resolved should then be vested in the king's second son, Henry, the young duke of York, aged four, and his male heirs 'immediately after the death of [King Henry's] dear uncle'. They were envisaged as a patrimony for the king's second son, but – 'which God forbid'– if Prince Henry were to become the heir apparent then the estate should revert to the king as part of the crown estate. The only exception from this grant to the duke of York was the marcher lordship of Builth; the parliament resolved that after Jasper's death this should pass directly to the king, apart from an annuity of £113 6s. 8d. which had already been granted to Prince Henry's elder brother, Arthur, prince of Wales.[26] There can be no doubt about the importance of these acts for the future of the crown estate, or that Jasper Tudor was aware of them shortly before his death.

At the beginning of his will, Jasper Tudor proudly recorded his own ancestry which was also the ancestry of the king. He left money to Keynsham abbey to support four priests to sing perpetually for the souls of his father, Owen Tudor; 'the lady of noble memorie Kateryne, some tyme Quene of Englond, my mother' and Henry V's consort; Edmund 'late Erle of Richemonde, my brother', Henry VII's father; and 'all other my predecessours'. In default of these arrangements being carried out, he bequeathed as an alternative the substantial sum of £100 for the same purpose. Although Owen Tudor was not mentioned by name in the will, Jasper additionally bequeathed the sum of £20 to the Grey Friars church at Hereford 'where my Father is entered', one of the largest sums left for religious purposes in the will.[27] These commemorations in the will would not have come as a surprise to Henry VII who himself

---

mentary record, see *Rot. Parl.* vi. 458–508, and TNA, C65/128 and C49/42/2 in *PROME*, xvi. with commentary by R.E. Horrox, 236–7.

[24] For Jasper's presence at the ratification of the treaty of Etaples, see *Foedera*, xii. 710–13. Among the triers of petitions in the parliament were Lord Daubeney, Viscount Welles, the king's step-uncle, and the earl of Derby, Henry's step-father.

[25] *PROME*, xvi. 235–7.

[26] *Ibid.*, 164–7.

[27] It is perhaps going too far to suggest that Jasper (and the king in other contexts) purposely concealed the identity of Owen Tudor because of his family's allegedly 'low birth': C.S.L. Davies, 'Tudor: What is in a Name?', *History*, xcvii (pt 1) (2012), 24–42 (at 24–7). Rather is it more likely that Jasper did not

showed an interest in his ancestry after 1485. Ten years later the specific mention of Jasper's brother seems to have coincided with thoughts about an enhanced memorial for Edmund, earl of Richmond, at Carmarthen, as well as one for the queen's uncle and Henry's predecessor, Richard III, at Leicester. And soon afterwards Henry VII was also contemplating his own burial in Westminster abbey where his grandmother, Queen Katherine, was interred. The death of the king's daughter Elizabeth and the failing health of his uncle, Jasper Tudor, may have prompted Henry VII and his family to ponder the implications of mortality. The several acts of memorialisation in the years that followed suggest a narrative of commemoration to underpin and sustain the legitimacy and security of the new dynasty.

In the latter part of 1495, plans were being laid to raise a tomb appropriate for the former king at the Grey Friars church in Leicester where Richard III had been hastily buried with muted ceremony. Why the decision was made to erect a tomb for King Richard ten years after his death as an act of memorialisation has been unclear. The initiative may have come from Henry VII himself, or from Queen Elizabeth, Richard's niece, or from both. It may have been considered appropriate to accord a crowned king a memorial other than the bare burial at Leicester for someone who was acknowledged to be king 'in deed and not in right'. Most immediately, if the construction of a new tomb were to become widely known at a time of continuing danger from the pretender's foreign allies, it might be taken as a signal – including from Queen Elizabeth herself – that the events of 1483 should be consigned firmly to the past. And it might undermine further the claims of the pseudo-duke of York by offering reconciliation to some at least of his potential supporters, complementing in this respect the creation of Prince Henry as duke of York.[28]

Shifting attitudes in Yorkist circles may even have penetrated the household of the matriarch of the Yorkist house, Cecily Neville, duchess of York, at Berkhamsted castle. Some members of her entourage had been implicated in treason alongside Sir William Stanley in the winter of 1494–5, and when the duchess made her will on 1 April 1495 – and set her seal to it on 31 May on her deathbed – she was uncertain whether Henry VII would respect her wish to be buried beside her husband, Richard, duke of York (d. 1460), at Fotheringhay: 'if myn executours by the sufferaunce of the King finde goode sufficient therto. And elles at the kings pleasure.' Describing herself as 'wif unto the right noble prince Richard late Duke of Yorke Fader unto the most christen prince my Lord and son king Edward the iiiith', she studiously avoided all reference to her other kingly son, Richard III, and her will included no provision for personal prayers, other than for the souls of her husband and herself. She had ample possessions with which to meet her funeral expenses and required no financial help from the king.[29]

---

wish to draw attention to Owen's family's kinship with Owain Glyn Dŵr and their role as prominent Welsh landowners during his rebellion – which Owen Tudor would have been too young to join.

[28] S.B. Chrimes, *English Constitutional Ideas of the Fifteenth Century* (Cambridge, 1935), 55–6. It may be significant that the act of attainder (the so-called 'De Facto Act') that raised the issue of kings *de facto* and *de iure*, was introduced in the parliament which met in October 1495: Cavill, *The English Parliaments of Henry VII*, 43.

[29] *Wills from Doctors' Commons*, ed. J.G. Nichols and John Bruce (Camden Soc., lxxxiii, 1863), 1–8; A.J. Speding, '"At the King's Pleasure": The Testament of Cecily Neville', *Midland History*, xxxv (pt. 2) (2010), 256–72, for the will (at 265–71) and commentary. The will was proved with little delay at Lambeth palace on 27 August 1495. For the plotting in her household, see Arthurson, *The Perkin*

In the event, as the grandmother of King Henry's queen, she need not have worried about her last resting place at Fotheringhay. Cecily bequeathed gifts to the king and queen and to the king's mother and 'my lord prince' [Arthur], and then, significantly by both name and title, 'to my lord Henry, Duke of Yorke'. Moreover, prominent among her executors were three of King Henry's councillors who were his foremost advisers: Bishop Oliver King, his secretary, and Sir Reynold Bray and Sir Thomas Lovell. She would have known Oliver King well since he had served as Edward IV's secretary and was dismissed and imprisoned by Richard III, but to name all three specifically in the will as 'councellours to the kings grace' suggests that they were not entirely the duchess's own choice. It is noteworthy that one of Cecily's executors, Master Richard Lessy, the dean of her chapel, had earlier been arrested and fined for misprision of treason and yet he was commissioned to administer the will when it was proven on 27 August 1495. Moreover, Cecily asked King Henry himself to appoint a supervisor of the will. Thus, in the weeks before Cecily's death, steps were evidently being taken to encourage reconciliation with persistent Yorkist loyalists.[30]

The decision to erect 'a fair tomb' for Richard III was purposeful and bold. Queen Elizabeth was, of course, a niece of the dead king and is likely to have been consulted by King Henry and his advisers. There was no suggestion of translating the body to Westminster abbey where Richard's wife, Anne Neville, had been interred in March 1485, or to Fotheringhay. In a petition addressed to the chancellor, and which elicited a reply on 1 July 1496, it was claimed that about a year previously none other than Sir Reynold Bray and Sir Thomas Lovell, the king's closest councillors, had concluded a contract with a Nottingham alabaster-man to provide such a monument at a cost of £50. Later in the year, a further contract was evidently needed with a gentleman from Rockingham in Northamptonshire who was paid £10 1s. by the king on 11 September 1495 for work on 'King Richard tomb'. When it was completed and in what form is not certainly known, though the existence of the petition suggests that it was unfinished in the summer of 1496. Whatever form the monument took, it lasted no more than a generation. Following the dissolution of the Grey Friars monastery in 1538, two property developers acquired the site and proceeded to demolish the buildings (and presumably their furniture) and cleared the site.[31]

In about 1497 or soon afterwards, Henry VII was contemplating a second memorialisation of a long-dead kinsman, that of his father, Edmund Tudor, earl of Richmond

---

Warbeck Conspiracy, 87–8, although J.L. Laynesmith, *Cecily Duchess of York* (2017), 170–1, downplays its significance.

[30] Although King is identified as bishop of Bath in Cecily Neville's will, the papal bull of translation from Exeter to Bath and Wells was not issued until 6 November 1495: A.B. Emden, *A Biographical Register of the University of Cambridge to 1500* (Cambridge, 1963), 343–4. The remaining executors were clerical members of the duchess's household; for Lessy, see J.L. Laynesmith, 'Richard Lessy, Dean of Cecily Duchess of York's Chapel', in *Yorkist People: Essays in Memory of Anne F. Sutton*, ed. C.M. Barron and Christian Steer (*The Ricardian*, xxxiii, 2023), 225–36; Laynesmith, *Cecily Duchess of York*, 166–7, 178, regards the choice of royal councillors as Cecily's own.

[31] For a recent account, see Nigel Ramsay, 'The Tomb of Richard III', *The Ricardian*, xxix (2019), 85–99, quoting George Buck, *The History of King Richard the Third* (1619), ed. A.N. Kincaid (Gloucester, 1979), 217. The sums assigned on the king's orders suggest that it was a table tomb, perhaps with an incised picture of the king. For the costs of stone or alabaster monuments of the 'higher aristocracy', between £40 and £200 and settling at about £100, see Saul, *English Church Monuments*, 109–10.

(d. 1456). Lady Margaret Beaufort had earlier considered commemorating Edmund, her first husband. Following the death of Henry, Lord Stafford, her second husband, in December 1471, she composed a will (1472) that provided for her own eventual burial at Bourne abbey in south Lincolnshire; at the same time, she set aside some money so that Earl Edmund's remains could be transferred from distant Carmarthen, where Edmund was buried in the Grey Friars church, to a new tomb at Bourne. Sir Reynold Bray's important role in Lady Margaret's service is indicated by the payment he made on her behalf in 1473–4 for 'the making of my lord Tomb', but this may not have been for Earl Edmund whose body remained at Carmarthen, but rather a tomb for Lord Stafford at Pleshey in Essex.[32]

However, in about 1497 Henry VII himself took steps to erect a tomb for his father in the Grey Friars in Carmarthen, doubtless with his mother's encouragement. If they needed any prompting, the will of Jasper Tudor with its prayers for Earl Edmund and its benefactions to Carmarthen's Grey Friars church was a recent reminder. Henry VII now authorised Sir Rhys ap Thomas, his stalwart supporter in Wales since Bosworth and a member of his household, to oversee the building of a new tomb for the body of Edmund Tudor. Forty years after the earl's death, the king assigned £43 10s. from the clerical subsidy of 1496–7 due to be collected in the archdeaconries of St David's and Cardigan, for 'the making of a newe tombe for our most dere fadre', and from part of an annual gift of alms which presumably was already being given to the church. Sir Rhys, who died in 1525, is likely to have commissioned the fine tomb-chest in Purbeck marble which has stood in St David's cathedral since its removal from Carmarthen at the dissolution of the monasteries.[33] In 1531, heralds visiting Carmarthen's friary noted that 'in the myddest of the quere, lyeth buryed in a tombe of marbill the body of Edmund Tudor'.[34]

The king's memorialisation of his father had several echoes. Not only did Henry arrange with the abbot of Westminster for an annual stipend of £8 to be paid for a chantry priest to sing for the soul of his father at Carmarthen, but when, in 1498, the king began the construction of a new building after a disastrous fire destroyed much of the royal manor house at Sheen, he named the new palace Richmond.[35] Queen Elizabeth and Lady Margaret Beaufort were no less attentive to the soul of Edmund

---

[32] For speculation otherwise, see Ramsay, 'The Tomb of Richard III', 90–1, and for the will of 1472, Jones and Underwood, *The King's Mother*, 137–8, quoting St John's College, Cambridge, MS D56.195.

[33] TNA, E404/84 unsorted, Warrants for Issues 17–19 Henry VII, 18 Henry VII (16 May 1503); Westminster Abbey Muniments, 28018 (25 September 1517); R.A. Griffiths, *Sir Rhys ap Thomas and his Family: A Study in the Wars of the Roses and Early Tudor Politics* (2nd edn, Cardiff, 2014), 23–4, 49, 51–2.

[34] *Visitations by the Heralds in Wales*, ed. M.P. Siddons (Harleian Soc., 5th series, xiv, 1996), 70. The present nineteenth-century brass on the tomb-chest replaces one put there in Sir Rhys ap Thomas's day but removed from the cathedral by parliamentarians in the seventeenth century: E. Allen, 'The Tomb of the Earl of Richmond in St. David's Cathedral', *Archaeologia Cambrensis*, 5th series, xiii (1896), 315–20.

[35] Westminster Abbey Muniments 6634, the indenture between king and abbot, 7 July 1502; H.M. Colvin and John Summerson, 'The King's Houses, 1485–1660', in *The History of the King's Works, Volume IV, 1485–1660 (Part II)*, ed. H.M. Colvin (1982), 222–34. The king's chantry in the Grey Friars, Carmarthen, is noted in the foundation charters of 1504 between Henry and the abbot and convent of Westminster: Margaret Condon, 'God Save the King! Piety, Propaganda and the Perpetual Memorial', in *Westminster Abbey: The Lady Chapel of Henry VII*, ed. T.W. Tatton-Brown and Richard Mortimer (Woodbridge, 2003), 88.

Tudor. In 1502, Elizabeth assigned money (5*s.*) from her chamber to Westminster abbey 'at the obyt of the Kinges Fader holden at Westminster'. For her part, when in 1505 Lady Margaret founded Christ College, Cambridge, she ordered prayers to be said for Edmund's soul at the college and that his arms should be placed on her own tomb in due time. Soon afterwards, in March 1506, she went further and arranged for two priests to offer prayers at Westminster abbey for the souls of Edmund as the king's father and her own parents, and then for the souls of her more recent husbands and Queen Elizabeth and her dead children: the order of souls is significant.[36]

Unlike Richard III's tomb at Leicester – and indeed that of Jasper Tudor at Keynsham – Edmund's tomb survived the Dissolution and was transferred to a more prominent site, St David's cathedral. In 1538 the future of the tomb of King Henry VIII's grandfather needed to be considered, not least because Bishop William Barlow was eager to transfer the centre of his see from St David's to the Grey Friars church in Carmarthen as being more accessible to all parts of the sprawling diocese. On 30 August 1538, the friary's contents were ordered to be delivered to Bishop Barlow and the vicar of Carmarthen, Thomas Pritchard, with the mayor of Carmarthen taking charge of the pall which lay on Earl Edmund's tomb.[37] A year later, the mayor and aldermen of Carmarthen petitioned Henry VIII that the site and buildings of the former friary, which were being neglected, might be adapted for use as a grammar school at the cost and charges of Master Thomas Lloyd, precentor of St David's, whose own plans for a grammar school in his home town of Carmarthen had received the king's endorsement as early as January 1536. As for the earl's body and its tomb-chest, with its incised brass depicting the dead earl, Henry VIII himself may have ordered their removal to St David's. More than likely, the tomb's installation before the high altar at St David's was assigned to the cathedral's precentor, Lloyd, to arrange, for in 1542 he identified the former Grey Friars buildings as the most suitable site for the new school which he and the canons of St David's had been planning. On 30 January 1543 Henry VIII at last granted the site and the friary's property in Carmarthen to him for what the king designated as 'the King's Scole of Karmerden of Thomas Lloyds fundacion'.[38]

A third memorialisation was even more ambitious and dynastically significant: that of King Henry VI, Henry VII's uncle. The king's mind turned to plans for his own burial in the early 1490s, at a time when he was also showing growing interest in the veneration of the last Lancastrian king, a veneration which he shared with his mother, Lady Margaret Beaufort, who was the dead king's kinswoman and had known him personally. The focus was on St George's chapel, Windsor, whence Henry VI's body had been transferred on the orders of Richard III from Chertsey abbey, not far away, and buried opposite the tomb of Edward IV. Moreover, on 8

---

[36] TNA, E36/210, f. 58, Queen Elizabeth's book of payments; *Privy Purse Expenses of Elizabeth of York*; *Wardrobe Accounts of Edward the Fourth*, ed. N.H. Nicolas (1830), 55 (3 Nov. 1502); *CCR, 1500–9*, pp. 290–1; Harvey, *Westminster Abbey and its Estates*, 399; Tallis, *Uncrowned Queen*, 45, 224–5, 265, 279.

[37] *Letters and Papers*, xiii (pt 1) 235 (pt 2), 86 (31 Mar. 1538).

[38] *Ibid.* (pt 1), 123. Lloyd was precentor of St David's from at least 1529 until his death in 1547: Bridget Jones, *John le Neve: Fasti Ecclesiae Anglicanae, 1300–1541, XI: The Welsh Dioceses* (1965), 57. See Glanmor Williams, '"Thomas Lloyd his skole": Carmarthen's First Tudor Grammar School', *The Carmarthenshire Antiquary*, x (1974), 49–75, and 'Carmarthen and the Reformation, 1536–58', in *Carmarthenshire Studies: Essays Presented to Major Francis Jones*, ed. Tudor Barnes and Nigel Yates (Carmarthen, 1974), 147.

June 1492 Edward's widow, Queen Elizabeth Wydeville, died at Bermondsey abbey, near London, where she had spent the last four years in relative seclusion. In her will two months earlier, she had requested burial beside her husband at Windsor, as he had wished. There can be little doubt that her eldest daughter, now Henry VII's queen, who was conspicuously commended in the will and appointed one of its supervisors, would have ensured that her mother's wishes were respected – including the simplicity of the funeral, 'without pompes entering or costlie expensis done thereabought'. The younger Elizabeth did not attend her mother's funeral perhaps because she was in the latter stages of pregnancy, aside from the demands of protocol; nor did her next sister, Cecily, Viscountess Welles, perhaps for a similar reason, though Cecily's husband, John Welles, took a prominent role at the interment.[39]

Although the burial of Elizabeth Wydeville at Windsor was accompanied by only modest funeral ceremonial, it may have prompted serious thought about burials and commemorations associated with the new dynasty. Whatever private thoughts Henry VII may have had on the subject, they are likely to have been discussed with his queen and with his mother, Lady Margaret, whose experience and knowledge of royal lineages went back decades, and also with his most intimate advisors such as Jasper Tudor and loyal servants like Sir Reynold Bray and Sir Thomas Lovell. Henry and especially his mother had encountered Henry VI at close quarters before his death in 1471, and by the 1490s they had come to embrace the growing belief in the dead king's sanctity. Significantly, when Henry and his mother visited Wimborne Minster during the progress of 1496, not only did they make offerings at the tomb of Henry's grandparents, but they also acknowledged the cult of Henry VI which Lady Margaret had probably introduced there a few years earlier.[40]

At that stage, there was no reason why Henry VII should not have contemplated his own burial in St George's chapel, and indeed he continued to fund building works there during the 1490s. However, by March 1498 – possibly as early as December 1497 – the plans had changed in favour of Westminster abbey which, as the abbot of Westminster insisted, had been Henry VI's own preference for his last resting place. Westminster abbey also housed the tomb of Henry V's queen, Katherine of Valois, Henry VII's grandmother. The traditional mausoleum of English kings may, therefore, have come to appeal to Henry VII on several grounds as he sought to emphasise his own claim to the blood royal and to express his reverence for Henry VI whose canonisation he had been urging on the pope since 1492.[41] Henry VII's

---

[39] PROB 11/9/207: *Testamenta Vetusta*, ed. Nicolas, ii. 24–6, has a detailed calendar of the will, which was published in *A Collection of all the Wills ... of the Kings and Queens of England*, ed. John Nichols (1780), 370–1. For the funeral and burial in accordance with the will, including a herald's later account from BL, Arundel MS 26, ff. 29v–30, see A.F. Sutton and Livia Visser-Fuchs, with R.A. Griffiths, *The Royal Funerals of the House of York at Windsor* (2005), 66–74. For the two daughters of John and Cecily Welles, who died young, see *CP*, xii (2), 449 n.g.

[40] Jones and Underwood, *The King's Mother*, 218, for Margaret's known devotion to Henry VI; C. Cornish-Dale, 'Cuthburga and Saintly King Henry: Two Royal Cults at Wimborne Minster, Dorset, 1403–1538', *Sixteenth-Century Journal*, xlix (pt 4) (2018), 963–86 (at 963–4, 971–3), for evidence of the cult at Wimborne by 1494–5.

[41] H.M. Colvin, D.R. Ransome and John Summerson, *The History of the King's Works*, vol. III (1485–1660), part 1 (1975), 305–9; C. Wilson, 'The Functional Design of Henry VII's Chapel: A Reconstruction', in *Westminster Abbey: The Lady Chapel of Henry VII*, ed. Tatton-Brown and Mortimer, 141–88 (esp. 153–60 for the king's interest in Henry VI and Westminster). See R.A. Griffiths, 'The Crown and the Royal Family in Later Medieval England', in *Kings and Nobles in the Later Middle Ages: A Tribute to Charles Ross*, ed. R.A. Griffiths and James Sherborne (Gloucester and

plans involved the removal of Henry VI's body to a new lady chapel at Westminster with the intention of harnessing his uncle's saintly reputation, while the pivotal place of Queen Katherine in his and his father's lineage had been underscored in Jasper Tudor's will. The new lady chapel would house a shrine and altars for Henry VI who, it was hoped, would soon be canonised.[42] The foundation stone for the new chapel was laid on 24 January 1504, a year following the death of Henry VII's queen who was buried at Westminster. Both she and the king's mother, who died on 29 June 1509 and was also buried in the lady chapel, are certain to have concurred in the king's grandiose dynastic interment plans. These were amended early in his son's reign: Henry VI was never canonised and his tomb remained at Windsor.[43]

The king's plans for Westminster abbey were known to his uncle, Viscount Welles, by the time he died on 9 February 1499. John Welles, Lady Margaret Beaufort's half-brother, died at 'Palmer's Place' in the city of London, apparently from an attack of pleurisy.[44] In 1483 he had joined the exiles who gathered around Jasper Tudor and his nephew Henry in Brittany and he returned in 1485 to fight at Bosworth, where the new king knighted him. Thereafter, he remained particularly close to his half-sister and became a trusted member of the royal circle. He was created a viscount and elected to the Order of the Garter, and by December 1487 he had married the queen's sister, Cecily of York, thereby becoming not only the king's uncle but also his brother-in-law! Welles proved a reliable if unspectacular supporter of the new regime, not least in the east midlands where his estates mainly lay. However, in 1490 he was also granted the former Mortimer lordships of Caerleon and Usk in the southern march of Wales adjoining the lordships of the duke of Bedford and the duchy of Lancaster; and about the same time – during 1489–90 – Lady Margaret granted him the lands in Yorkshire (especially Holderness) and Lincolnshire which she held as custodian of the young Edward Stafford, duke of Buckingham.[45]

Prior to joining the royal expedition to France in the autumn of 1492, Welles composed his will and sought burial in St George's chapel, Windsor, where Henry VII himself at that time was planning to be interred.[46] But by the time that Welles died in 1499, he was aware that the king had changed his mind as to his own burial place: in the lady chapel of Westminster abbey instead of in St George's. Welles may even have been party to discussions within the royal family about the preference for Westminster. On the day before his death, he made his last will as 'uncle to the Kynge, oure soveraigne lorde, and brodre to the right noble prynces, Margaret, countes of Richemond, natural and dere modre to oure said soveregne lord'. Welles left the choice of burial site (though not responsibility for the burial costs) to the king, the queen and Lady Margaret, who were named as overseers of the will, as well

---

New York, 1986), 15–26 (at 22–3), for emphasis on the royal blood; and 'Succession and the Royal Dead in Later Medieval England', 108–9, for the importance attached to Westminster by heralds who recorded royal funerals in the late fifteenth and sixteenth centuries.

[42] R.A. Griffiths, 'The Burials of King Henry VI at Chertsey and Windsor', in *St George's Chapel, Windsor: History and Heritage: Dedicated to Eileen Scarff*, ed. Nigel Saul and T.W. Tatton-Brown (Wimborne Minster, 2010), 100–7 (at 106–7).

[43] Condon, 'God Save the King!', 59–98 (esp. 59–61 for the king's vision).

[44] M.A. Hicks, 'Welles, John, Viscount (d.1499)', *Oxford DNB*. For the cause of death, which seems to have been quite sudden, see M.A.E. Green, *Lives of the Princesses of England from the Norman Conquest* (1849), 419–28 (at 426).

[45] TNA, E40/14584; Jones and Underwood, *The King's Mother*, 108–9, 125, 133–5.

[46] Jones and Underwood, *The King's Mother*, 133–5.

as to his wife Cecily: 'in suche place as the kynge, the queen, my lady, his moder, and my lady, my wife, shalbe thought most convenient'. The making of his tomb – and its costs – was also left to the discretion of the same royal quartet. He concluded by beseeching the king 'to shewe his mooste gracious favour for the welthe of my sowle in the premysses as he did to me in my life'.[47] The administration of the will was committed to his wife and the ubiquitous Sir Reynold Bray, one of the most senior and long-serving councillors of the king and his mother; indeed, the practical accounting for the will's execution was made Bray's responsibility. These were unusual arrangements.

There can be no doubt of the special place that Welles occupied in Henry VII's family circle. The king respected Welles's last wishes and at the same time took the opportunity to signal his own intentions for future royal burials. Aside from the duke of Bedford who had arranged for his own burial, John Welles was the first adult member of the royal family to die during the king's reign, and the arrangements made for his funeral and burial at Westminster abbey were of uncommon interest to the heralds who organised the ceremonies. A detailed record was made, probably by John Writhe (d. 1504), Garter king of arms since the beginning of the reign, and thereafter the record remained in the collections of Writhe's successors for future reference. Among the earliest surviving accounts is that among the archives of Writhe's son (and successor as Garter king of arms), Sir Thomas Wriothesley (d. 1534).[48] Immediately after her husband's death, Lady Cecily informed the king at Greenwich

> to know the pleasir wher his grace wold have his corps buried and how then his grace ordeyned and commanded dyvers of his conceil to have a communicacion upon the same and over that his plaisir was expressed to have his bodye buried at Westmynster in our Ladye Chappelle wher his grace entendith to be.[49]

The discussion revolved around a series of questions as to the appropriate ceremonies to be adopted at Welles's funeral. Following the king's decision, it was decided that the body should be borne from London to Westminster overland accompanied by 'the best of the courte' and interred in the abbey's lady chapel.[50] Henceforward,

---

[47] TNA, PROB 11/11/657. The will was proved relatively quickly, on 22 June 1499. It is published, with some omissions, in *Testamenta Vetusta*, ed. Nicolas, ii. 437–8, and *North Country Wills, being Abstracts of Wills relating to the Counties of York, Nottingham, Northumberland, Cumberland and Westmorland at Somerset House and Lambeth Palace, vol. 1, 1383–1558*, ed. J.W. Clay (Surtees Soc., cxvi, 1908), 68–9.

[48] BL, Add. MS 45131, ff. 14, 60v–61. See Adrian Ailes, 'Writhe, John', and Robert Yorke, 'Wriothesley, Sir Thomas', both in *Oxford DNB*. A further, independent copy is among the heraldic records of Sir William Dethick (d. 1612), who succeeded his father as Garter king of Arms in 1586: BL, Arundel MS 26, f. 35v; A.R.J.S. Adolph, 'Dethick, Sir William', *Oxford DNB*.

[49] BL, Arundel MS 26, ff. 35v–36.

[50] BL, Additional MS 45131, f. 14, for the questions discussed. An elaborate and well-preserved lead coffin excavated in 2015 may be that of John Welles: see Matthew Payne and John Goodall, 'Elizabeth Woodville and the Chapel of St Erasmus at Westminster Abbey', *Journal of the British Archaeological Association*, clxxv (pt 1) (2022), 235–65 (at n. 78), brought to my attention by Matthew Payne. The coffin was well illustrated in BBC, Channel 5, 'Westminster Abbey: Behind Closed Doors', 22 October 2022.

the official account of John Welles's funeral and burial had a significant place in the portfolio of heraldic funeral records during the two centuries that followed.[51]

The execution and burial of Queen Elizabeth's cousin, Edward, earl of Warwick, the son and heir of George, duke of Clarence (d. 1478), effectively brought the main Yorkist threat to the new dynasty to an end. His execution in November 1499 was ordered by Henry VII, doubtless with the acquiescence of the queen, and the costs of his burial were met by the king himself. It may be noted, too, that Warwick, along with Elizabeth of York, had been placed temporarily in the charge of Lady Margaret Beaufort immediately after the battle of Bosworth and Lady Margaret's opinion in 1499 may have been sought.[52] Although the earl had been soon transferred to the Tower of London, he continued to be a focus of impersonations and plots, and most recently he was alleged to have helped Perkin Warbeck to escape from the Tower; both were recaptured and executed on 24 November. In Warwick's case, the burial at the king's expense took place at Bisham abbey, the mausoleum of earlier earls of Warwick on his mother's side, not far from Windsor castle, rather than more distantly at Tewkesbury abbey in Gloucestershire where his parents were interred. There is a likely comparison to be drawn with the burial of Sir William Stanley, not least in that decisions in both cases were taken within the royal family and in the interests of state security – possibly sweetened by the knowledge that two considerable landed inheritances would now fall into the king's hands.[53]

The Spanish ambassador, De Puebla, who had recently been negotiating the marriage between Prince Arthur and Catherine of Aragon, was able to report enthusiastically (if with some exaggeration) to the Spanish monarchs early in the new year that 'England has never been so tranquil and obedient as at present. There have always been pretenders to the crown of England; but now that Perkin and the son of the Duke of Clarence have been executed, there does not remain "a drop of doubtful Royal blood", the only Royal blood being the true blood of the King, the Queen, and, above all, of the Prince of Wales.'[54] The management of royal burials and planned memorialisations in recent years had played its part in the search for dynastic and political stability.

At the heart of the king's court in the 1490s stood the interconnected personal relationships and households of the king, the queen and the king's mother, with links to the households of other senior members of the royal family like the duke of Bedford and Viscount Welles, and perhaps also – though in more strained circumstances – Cecily, duchess of York. Burials and reburials within this circle involved the king personally and would likely have been discussed with his closest relatives. Those who executed his decisions were among their most influential servants, with loyalties forged during 1483–5, and often as exiles in France.

Among the most prominent were Sir Reynold Bray, Sir Thomas Lovell and Sir

---

[51] See, for example, College of Arms, WB, a vol. of Sir William le Neve (d. 1661), Clarenceux king of arms, digested by Sir Edward Walker, Garter king of arms, 1664, ff. 37–8; and College of Arms I/3, ff. 2, 32 et seq. (16th century), summarised in Green, *Lives of the Princesses*, 426–8.

[52] Tallis, *Uncrowned Queen*, 173–4.

[53] 'The Chamber Books of Henry VII and Henry VIII': TNA, E101/415/3, f. 6, and BL, Add MS 7099, f. 64, for four bills for the burial of Warwick amounting to £121 8s. 2d.

[54] *Calendar of State Papers, Spanish*, i. 213 (11 Jan. 1500). Christine Carpenter, *Locality and Polity: A Study of Warwickshire Landed Society, 1401–1499* (Cambridge, 1992), 437–8, 595, stresses Henry VII's relief from insecurity by 1499.

Giles Daubeney (who was swiftly raised to the peerage). They had deserted Richard III in 1483 and after 1485 moved easily between the three royal households and were often in the entourages of Bedford and Welles. Bray and Lovell were the king's principal financial officials and therefore intimately involved in the funding of burials and memorialisations ordered by the king.[55] Both were also closely associated with Queen Elizabeth. For example, they are represented alongside the king, the queen and their son Arthur in the Magnificat stained-glass window in the nave of Great Malvern church, Worcestershire, which may have been donated in about 1501 by Bray and Lovell as well as by the young Prince Arthur.[56] Bray had long served the king's mother since her marriage to Henry, Lord Stafford, and continued to serve her after she married Thomas, Lord Stanley. Bray's wife, Katherine Hussey, also joined the Stanley household and after 1485 she moved into the royal household as one of the queen's gentlewomen.[57]

In implementing the decision to commemorate Edmund Tudor at Carmarthen, the king relied on his lieutenant in south Wales, Sir Rhys ap Thomas, who, though not joining the exiles in Brittany, had a decisive role to play in the Bosworth campaign.[58] As for Daubeney and Welles, they were near neighbours of Jasper Tudor in the West Country and the southern march of Wales, and Daubeney was named as executor of Bedford's will. He had a commanding role at the court of Henry VII from the outset and was one of very few to be ennobled by the king and then made a knight of the Garter; after the execution of Sir William Stanley in February 1495 he became the king's chamberlain. Like Welles, he was buried in Westminster abbey 'where my said soveraigne lorde entendeth his [Henry VII's] bodye to be entired'.[59] Another executor of Bedford's will, the lawyer Morgan Kidwelly, came from the same exiled stable and was enlisted to serve the king as well as his uncle, while having honed his abilities and reputation in Yorkist service. This was a pattern that included several others on whom the king and queen and both Bedford and his sister-in-law, Lady Margaret Beaufort, relied.[60] The letters which Queen Elizabeth wrote in 1493 to Bedford, her 'Ryght trusty [and] entyerly belovyd uncle', may reasonably suggest an affection for the elderly duke as she sought his 'good lordship' for one of

---

[55] M.M. Condon, 'Bray, Sir Reynold (c. 1440–1503)'; S.J. Gunn, 'Lovell, Sir Thomas (c. 1449–1524)', both in *Oxford DNB*. For Bray and his acquisition of office, property and wealth during Henry VII's reign, see Margaret Condon, 'From Caitiff and Villain to Pater Patriae: Reynold Bray and the Profits of Office', in *Profit, Piety and the Professions in Later Medieval England*, ed. Michael Hicks (Gloucester, 1990), 137–68.

[56] Katherine Wells, *Tour of Great Malvern Priory* (2nd edn, Malvern, 2013). For Lovell's service to Queen Elizabeth as her first treasurer and for Bray's association with Lady Margaret Beaufort and the queen, see Weir, *Elizabeth of York*, 163, 216, 448–9.

[57] Powell, 'Lady Margaret Beaufort: A Progress', 295–316 (at 305, 311–12).

[58] Griffiths, *Sir Rhys ap Thomas*, 40–5.

[59] TNA, PROB 11/16/16 (1508). For Daubeney and his closeness to the king as courtier and councillor, see S.J. Gunn, 'The Courtiers of Henry VII', *EHR*, cviii (1993), 23–49 (at 29–30), and *idem*, 'Daubeney, Giles, first Baron Daubeney (1451/2–1508)', *Oxford DNB*. For a less charitable view of Daubeney's own motives, see Dominic Luckett, 'Crown Patronage and Political Morality in Early Tudor England: the Case of Giles, Lord Daubeney', *EHR*, cx (1995), 578–95.

[60] For example, Richard Hill, dean of the chapel royal after 1485 and bishop of London from 1489, was another of Bedford's executors: R.C.E. Hayes, 'Hill, Richard (d.1496)', *Oxford DNB*, which notes his connection also with Lady Margaret and Sir Reynold Bray.

her servants; they were written from Collyweston, Lady Margaret's manor house in Northamptonshire.[61]

If Henry VII and his family shared the Spanish ambassador's optimism at the beginning of 1500, their confidence was shaken somewhat in the opening years of the new century. For all the awareness of the fragility of young lives shown in 1495 at the disposition of Jasper Tudor's estate, the deaths within a short period of time of two of the three sons born to Henry and his queen were a blow to the family and posed a threat to the stability of the realm. Elizabeth had given birth to the third of her surviving sons in February 1499. The baby was named Edmund after the king's father and his godmother was Lady Margaret Beaufort. On 15 June 1500 he died, possibly of plague.[62] Like his sister Elizabeth in 1495, he was buried in Westminster abbey, in Edward the Confessor's chapel, and for all that it was the interment of a baby, the burial costs amounted to the not inconsiderable sum of £242 11s. 8d. paid by the king to the abbot and convent of Westminster.[63]

Less than two years later, the elder of the king's surviving sons, Prince Arthur, fell ill and died at Ludlow castle on 2 April 1502. The death was as swift as that of the king's uncle, Viscount Welles, in 1499 and may have been as a result of a similarly rapid onset of deadly respiratory disease. Be that as it may, neither the king nor the queen attended the elaborate and costly funeral which was held at Worcester cathedral, not far away, rather than in Westminster abbey on which the king's mind was now firmly set as the appropriate mausoleum for his dynasty.[64]

Shortly afterwards, Henry VII did not begrudge paying for the burial of Owen 'Tidder' (or Tudor), who must surely have been related to the king, though the relationship is unclear. He may have been the youngest son of Owen Tudor and Queen Katherine who became a monk at Westminster, or perhaps more likely Owen Tudor's son by a later liaison who thereafter took his father's surname. If the latter, then he also had an illegitimate brother, David (ap) Owen: both brothers entered King Henry's service from the beginning of the reign. Owen Tudor died just weeks after Prince Arthur's death. The king had occasionally supported him with a modest gift; then, in June 1502, when he was managing the enormous cost (£666 16s.) of Arthur's funeral at Worcester, Henry authorised his lawyer-servant, Morgan Kidwelly, who had been one of Bedford's executors, to spend 61s. 2d. on Owen's burial at Westminster. One further link with the past was broken at a time when the king and his family were adjusting to present calamity.[65]

---

[61] W.R.B. Robinson, 'Two Letters of 1493 from Queen Elizabeth to Jasper Tudor, Duke of Bedford, concerning the Will of her Servant, Thomas Kemeys of Newport', *The Monmouthshire Antiquary*, xxii (2006), 105–9. The letters were dated 9 October 1493 during a visit with the king to Collyweston.

[62] Jones and Underwood, *The King's Mother*, 148–9: Lady Margaret lavished gifts on the baby at his only Christmas. For the outbreak of plague in London in 1499–1500, see L.H. Voigts, 'Plague Saints, Henry VII, and Saint Armel', in *Saints and Cults in Medieval England*, ed. Susan Powell (Harlaxton Medieval Studies XXVII, Donnington, 2017), 105–6.

[63] 'The Chamber Books of Henry VII and Henry VIII': BL, Add. MS 7099, f. 67; TNA, E101/415/3, f. 20v. For the Westminster burials, see Harvey, *Westminster Abbey and its Estates*, 383 and n. 4.

[64] See Sean Cunningham, *Prince Arthur: The Tudor King Who Never Was* (Stroud, 2016), for possible causes of Arthur's death (175–8) and the funeral ceremonies at Worcester (178–91).

[65] 'The Chamber Books of Henry VII and Henry VIII': TNA, E101/414/16, f. 36 and BL, Add. MS 7099, f. 49 (a payment of 40s. to 'Owen Tidder' in 1498); TNA, E101/415/3, f. 98v and BL, Add. MS 7099, f. 75. See R.A. Griffiths, 'Tudor, Owen [Owain ap Maredudd ap Tudur] (c. 1400–1461)', *Oxford DNB*. For Sir David Owen, created a knight of the body in 1485, see J.C. Wedgwood, *History of Parliament: Biographies of the Members of the Commons House, 1439–1509* (1936), 654–5. An alternative, if

Less than a year later, on 11 February 1503, Queen Elizabeth herself died following childbirth. It would have been seen as beyond question that she should be buried at Westminster. Although the precise location in the abbey is not known, the body was later moved to the new lady chapel where the king and his mother would also be buried. These recent deaths 'heightened the prospect of renewed vulnerability' for the dynasty after it had seemed reasonably secured by 1499.[66] Henry VII was understandably prudent in harbouring and managing his financial resources; yet his expenditure on the burials of the 1490s do not suggest a king who was overly avaricious or miserly at that stage of his reign, but rather one who was resourceful yet prudent, and motivated by sentiment and obligation which had an intensely political dimension to ensure the durability of his kingship.[67] In this, he was advised and supported by his closest family and assisted by dependable companions of his exile.

---

speculative, suggestion of the identity of Owen Tudor is in Matthew Payne, 'The Lost Tudor', *History Today*, lxxiii, no. 3 (2003), 62–7.

[66] Harvey, *Westminster Abbey and its Estates*, 384; Cavill, *Parliaments of Henry VII*, 200–1 (for the quotation).

[67] See Cavill, 'The Enforcement of the Penal Statutes in the 1490s: Some New Evidence', *HR*, lxxxii (2009), 482–92, which examines the king's motives in 1495; and M.R. Horowitz, 'Henry Tudor's Treasure', *ibid.*, 560–79, which notes (at 560) contemporary observations of his avarice after 1499.

JUSTICE, GOOD LADYSHIP AND THE QUEEN'S COUNCIL IN LATE MEDIEVAL ENGLAND, 1450–1550[1]

Laura Flannigan

'A presumed fundamental aridity may render administrative history unattractive to many as an area of research. The process of institutions expanding and fragmenting into smaller and yet more bureaucratic units seems a guarantee of dullness, not to say tedium. Such a view is too narrow and surely ill-judged.'[2] It was with this defence of institutional histories that Dr Archer prefaced her initial endeavours to articulate 'something of what it was like to be a woman of property' in late medieval England. Thirty years on, to prioritise procedure over people might still be branded a particularly dry and thankless approach to any given subject – and especially to the otherwise vibrant field of gender and authority. Clearly, understanding how things worked is an essential precursor to addressing questions about where power lay, the principles upon which it was enacted, and to what end. Yet so often the material required for such a study, particularly when it comes to institutions headed by women, is still so 'scattered and ... fragmentary' that identifying any such 'bureaucratic units' is not so much dull as simply difficult to do.[3] As recently as 2020 it was recognised that a lingering aversion to administrative history had left certain activities of even the most substantial female landowners of this period – the queens consort – 'understudied'.[4] This includes, most obviously, the work of their councils.

In the much older tradition of constitutional histories of *king*ship, the fifteenth and sixteenth centuries are associated with crucial developments in central government, and especially in the royal council. Yet the scholarship that has carefully plotted the stages of these advancements has much less – usually nothing at all – to say about the councils of the successive queens consort in those same years.[5] Likewise, these

---

[1] Unless otherwise specified, all manuscript sources cited in this essay are held by The National Archives, Kew.
[2] Rowena E. Archer, '"How ladies ... who live on their manors ought to manage their households and estates": Women as Landholders and Administrators in the Later Middle Ages', in *Woman is a Worthy Wight: Women in English Society, c.1200–1500*, ed. P.J.P. Goldberg (Stroud, 1992), 149.
[3] Ibid.
[4] Michele Seah and Katia Wright, 'The Medieval English Queen as Landholder: Some Reflections on Sources and Methodology', in *Women and Economic Power in Premodern Royal Courts*, ed. Cathleen Sarti (Leeds, 2020), 9–10.
[5] E.g. J.F. Baldwin, *The King's Council in England during the Middle Ages* (Oxford, 1913); *Chapters in the Administrative History of Mediaeval England*, ed. T.F. Tout (6 vols, Manchester, 1920–33); John

conciliar bodies have not featured much in the published research on their other closest comparator, the noble or baronial council (including the admittedly limited work on Margaret Beaufort's administration in the midlands).[6] Elsewhere, the study of queenship in western Europe has been shaped more by the currents of social and cultural histories into which it was born in the later twentieth century than by the high-political, institutional approaches already by then seen as outdated. What has emerged is a vibrant body of scholarship which continues to chart new inroads into the material culture, ritual, and theory of monarchies through a range of biographical and survey studies of queens and their office.[7] However, one ramification of the focus on the socio-cultural over the structural, at least in the English scholarship, has been that the queen's council tends to be subsumed within analysis of the wider court and household.[8] It remains on the periphery of governmental and monarchical histories of this period.

This council was perceived to be a discrete part of the queen's administration, with its own space and duties, by at least the fourteenth century. In 1404 a new chamber at Westminster was set aside specifically 'for the management of [the queen's] council and businesses', and by the middle of that century petitions might be directly addressed to '*Dame la Royne & a son essage counseile*' for grace and intercession.[9] Plaintiffs of the early Tudor period addressed their English bills to 'the Queen's most honourable and discrete council', or even to 'the Quenes graces right honorable counsel in her graces counsell chamber at Westminster'.[10] These references properly account for a *series* of councils active under successive queens consort rather than one abiding institution. Like any other institution orbiting a magnate or monarch, they could be interrupted by the disinterest, unavailability (due to age or illness), or the absence of any presiding authority – particularly where more mundane, judicial work was concerned. Nonetheless, comparison between respective queens' councils across this period illustrates gradual formalisation of these capacities.

Watts, 'Counsel and the King's Council in England, c.1430–c.1540', in *The Politics of Counsel in England and Scotland, 1286–1707*, ed. Jacqueline Rose (Oxford, 2016), 63–87. Robert Somerville's work on the duchy of Lancaster and its administration does briefly consider the queen's council: *History of the Duchy of Lancaster* (2 vols, 1953), i. 209–10.

[6] Of which the key studies remain Carole Rawcliffe, 'Baronial Councils in the Later Middle Ages', in *Patronage, Pedigree and Power in Later Medieval England*, ed. Charles Ross (Gloucester, 1979); eadem, 'The Great Lord as Peacekeeper: Arbitration by English Noblemen and their Councils in the Later Middle Ages', in *Law and Social Change in British History: Papers Presented to the Bristol Legal History Conference*, ed. J.A. Guy and H.G. Beale (1984); A.E. Levett, 'Baronial Councils and their Relation to Manorial Courts', in *Studies in Manorial History*, ed. H.M. Cam, M. Coate and L.S. Sutherland (Oxford, 1938).

[7] J.L. Laynesmith, *The Last Medieval Queens: English Queenship 1445–1503* (Oxford, 2004); Theresa Earenfight, *Queenship in Medieval Europe* (Basingstoke, 2013); *Tudor and Stuart Consorts: Power, Influence and Dynasty*, ed. Aidan Norrie et al. (Basingstoke, 2022); *Later Plantagenet and the Wars of the Roses Consorts: Power, Influence and Dynasty*, ed. Aidan Norrie et al. (Basingstoke, 2023).

[8] E.g. Hilda Johnstone, 'The Queen's Household', in *Chapters in the Administrative History of Mediaeval England*, ed. Tout, v. 231–89; Laynesmith, *The Last Medieval Queens*, ch. 5; Lisa Benz St John, *Three Medieval Queens: Queenship and the Crown in Fourteenth-Century England* (Basingstoke, 2012), 65–81.

[9] *CPR*, 1401–5, p. 473. By the middle of the fifteenth century, this room was known as 'the council-house of queen Margaret' [of Anjou], even after Edward IV had displaced Henry VI and his queen: *CPR*, 1452–61, pp. 113–14; 1461–7, p. 273; SC8/42/2075, 59/2946, 75/3718, 87/4344, 103/5129, 162/8051, 8082, 181/9034, 339/15976.

[10] E 163/11/48/9.

Conciliar development in the queen's side of government was driven by the same motivation as it was in the king's administration or a nobleman's household: the demands of managing a substantial landed estate. At the time of their marriages the late-medieval English queens received a considerable jointure, granted to them for life. The lands included in this portion, drawn partly from the duchy of Lancaster, could cover as many as twenty-five counties in southern and eastern England, as well as more estates in the Welsh marches.[11] At its height these holdings, with their rents, fee farms and dues, brought the English queens an annual income in the region of £4,500, rivalling that of the realm's principal noblemen and helping to fund their own households.[12] Any major landowner required a council staffed with clerks, auditors, surveyors, receivers and legal professionals to travel their lands and to treat with their tenants over rents, services, and disputes. *Unlike* other private, seigneurial councils, the queen also had more convenient recourse to the advice of the king and the services of his councillors and clerks. Her council also eventually came to dispense justice on the procedural model of the crown's courts of 'equity'.

Where the 'good ladyship' of the queen's extensive estate has received assessment it has usually been only in reference to a one-way stream of revenue.[13] Biographical studies of queenship have often set out to compare consorts as either especially voracious (Margaret of Anjou) or timid (Elizabeth of York) in gathering their dues.[14] A similar emphasis dominates studies of the manors and tenants in the queens' remit; in Marjorie McIntosh's survey of the royal liberty of Havering-atte-Bower the councils of the queens holding that manor appear only when extracting money from a disgruntled tenantry.[15] More reciprocal dimensions of estate management – and how the queen's tenants benefitted from her lordship – remains just out of frame. Certainly, many late-medieval English people would have 'seen at first hand the queen as a local landholder and lord of the manor'.[16] But it was her council's other duties, namely in the dispensation of justice, which increased this visibility and fostered a two-way dialogue about life on her estates.

Exceptions to the general lacuna of scholarship on this council's judicial side come in the form of several article-length studies, by N.R.R. Fisher in 1991, Dakota

---

[11] For summaries, see Seah and Wright's map of Margaret of Anjou's holdings: 'The Medieval English Queen as Landholder', 27; Derek Neal's appendices on the lands of Elizabeth Wydeville and Elizabeth of York: 'The Queen's Grace: English Queenship, 1464–1503' (MA thesis, McMaster University, Ontario, 1996), 161–7; and Somerville, *History of the Duchy of Lancaster*, i. 207–10, 238–40, 339–40.

[12] Laynesmith, *The Last Medieval Queens*, 234–6.

[13] E.g. Hilda Johnstone, 'The Queen's Exchequer under the Three Edwards', in *Historical Essays in Honour of James Tait*, ed. J.G. Edwards, V.H. Galbraith and E.F. Jacob (Manchester, 1933), 149; eadem, 'The Queen's Household', 251–2, 255; Laynesmith, *The Last Medieval Queens*, 232–4, 236–7; Louise Tingle, 'Aurum Reginae: Queen's Gold in Late Fourteenth-Century England', *Royal Studies Journal*, vii (pt 1) (2020).

[14] E.g. Alec Myers' studies of the household accounts of Margaret of Anjou and Elizabeth Wydeville, reproduced in *Crown, Household and Parliament in Fifteenth Century England*, ed. C.H. Clough (1985); also, more recently, Michele Seah, '"My Lady Queen, the Lord of the Manor": The Economic Roles of Late Medieval Queens', *Parergon*, xxxvii (pt 2) (2020). Recent exceptions are Michelle Beer's 'A Queenly Affinity? Catherine of Aragon's Estates and Henry VIII's Great Matter', *HR*, xci (2018), 426–55 (at 253); Neal, 'The Queen's Grace', ch. 4.

[15] M.K. McIntosh, *Autonomy and Community: The Royal Manor of Havering, 1200–1500* (Cambridge, 1986); eadem, *A Community Transformed: The Manor and Liberty of Havering, 1500–1620* (Cambridge, 1991).

[16] Beer, 'A Queenly Affinity?', 444.

Hamilton in 1998, and Anne Crawford in 2001. As a historian of seventeenth-century England, Fisher sought precedent for the courts overseen by the early Stuart queens consort, chasing up claims made in the 1640s by Sir John Lamb, chancellor to Queen Henrietta Maria, that 'the Queenes of England have antiently had their Courts for the Government of the Tennants of their joynture lands and decision of controversies betwixt them'.[17] It was within paperwork produced during Katherine Parr's queenship that Fisher, like Lamb, identified the most convincing evidence for an earlier conciliar court engaged in such judicial work.[18] Crawford's study looked further back in time, identifying the queenships of Eleanor of Provence and Eleanor of Castile in the thirteenth century as heralding a more 'sophisticated' conciliar system with 'judicial, administrative, and advisory' capacities. Examining some newly reclassified documents for its judicial business under Margaret of Anjou and Elizabeth of York, she observed the 'overwhelming importance of its legal work' by the late fifteenth century.[19] Hamilton's work assessed the early Tudor period, arguing that these years saw the queen's council properly distance itself from the household and undergo sustained 'professionalization'. On the evidence of the few petitions and pleadings to this council still surviving, Hamilton specified that while it 'did not constitute a formal legal court' it could 'summon individuals connected with her properties ... and hear and arbitrate disputes concerning her tenants and officers', though she said little more about the nature of these disputes other than them being 'irksome' to resolve.[20] These three short studies broadly concur about a general trajectory in the development of the queen's council as a judicial forum for royal tenants between c. 1450 and c. 1550.

A more joined-up survey of what the council's justice looked like, how it worked, and who it served might still be valuable, however. Such a project is admittedly hampered by the patchy survival of pleadings, registers and memoranda that would illustrate the queen's conciliar justice. We might suppose that the lack of institutional continuity between consorts precluded any consistent record-keeping, though anecdotal references to a once-extant central archive of sorts give us cause to think otherwise. Several of Lamb's letters from the mid-seventeenth-century remark that entire trunks full of 'bills aunswers replicacions orders decrees &c of matters formerlie in the Queenes Court', some from 'the time of H. 7 & of H. 8', had been moved from the Treasury to the 'Long Howse at Westm[inster]' before apparently disappearing.[21] Today a few pockets of this paperwork remain, scattered across the exchequer miscellanea at The National Archives. This includes a series of fifty-four documents in E298 (papers of the 'Queens' Councils'), divided into 'Proceedings in Equity' and 'Administrative Documents and Memoranda', which formed the evidentiary basis of Crawford's study.[22] Material of similar substance and volume for the early Tudor consorts can be found in E111 ('Miscellaneous Equity Proceedings') and E135 ('Miscellaneous Ecclesiastical Documents'); likenesses in the outer labels of

---

[17] SP16/483, f. 126.
[18] N.R.R. Fisher, 'The Queenes Courte in her Councell Chamber at Westminster', *EHR*, cviii (1993), 315, 318.
[19] Anne Crawford, 'The Queen's Council in the Middle Ages', *EHR*, cxvi (2001), 1203, 1209.
[20] D.L. Hamilton, 'The Learned Councils of the Tudor Queens Consort', in *State, Sovereigns and Society in Early Modern England: Essays in Honour of A.J. Slavin*, ed. Charles Carlton (Stroud, 1998), 91, 97.
[21] SP16/483, f. 205; 484 f. 24.
[22] Crawford, 'The Queen's Council'.

Justice, Good Ladyship and the Queen's Council

these documents and the presence of paperwork for one case in both classes indicate that they might represent parts of a larger whole. More miscellaneous paperwork, including those letters and orders of Katherine Parr which have been interpreted as evidence for her more formalised council, is among the State Papers.[23]

Together, these materials comprise a roughly consistent set of pleadings, writs and even determinations made out to and in the name of councils belonging to Margaret of Anjou, Elizabeth Wydeville, Elizabeth of York, Catherine of Aragon, Anne Boleyn, Jane Seymour, Anne of Cleves, Catherine Howard, and Katherine Parr. Alongside the miscellaneous memoranda from across this period they also provide evidence for around sixty-five separate civil cases. Rather than re-examining the measurable force of these queens' personalities on the activities of their councils, this essay seeks to use this latter type of evidence to establish the place of the queen's council within the legal and administrative structures of late-medieval England. Focusing as much on the perspective of petitioners as the work of the councillors, it also looks to tie the giving of justice into the better-known processes of revenue collection that bound the queen and the localities together.

* * *

The facility for petitioning the queen and receiving some justice represented an extension of the medieval consort's role as intercessor between subjects and sovereign. This duty manifested itself most dramatically in those chronicled performances wherein public displays of queenly mercy offset the harshness of the king's law: from Philippa of Hainault's deliverance of the Calais citizens from execution in 1347 to Catherine of Aragon's pleading on behalf of the Evil May Day rebels of 1517.[24] Those with the connections and know-how had long been able to invoke the queen's intervention in more personal matters, through a flurry of private letters, warrants and behind-the-scenes discussions. The handful of bills among the 'Ancient Petitions' that are addressed to the queens consort further demonstrate the utility of direct, personalised appeal for those with existing ties to the royal households. In c. 1320 one Hugh de Snitterby from Kirton in Lindsey (Lincolnshire) petitioned Isabella of France to complain that his efforts to convict another man of trespass in his capacity as constable had caused him to be violently attacked. He requested that she in turn petition the king to establish an oyer and terminer commission to confirm his initial trespass suit.[25] Later, in c. 1384, a petition from a Florentine merchant to Anne of Bohemia leaned on prior connections to that queen's family to request aid in securing letters of safe conduct to trade in England. An endorsement scrawled along the top

---

[23] Fisher, 'The Queenes Courte', 318; SP1/191, ff. 201–2.
[24] A.J. Musson, 'Queenship, Lordship and Petitioning in Late Medieval England', in *Medieval Petitions: Grace and Grievance*, ed. W.M. Ormrod, Gwilym Dodd and Anthony Musson (York, 2009), 158–60; Garrett Mattingley, *Catherine of Aragon* (1950), 136. For the wider scholarship, see L.L. Huneycutt, 'Intercession and the High-Medieval Queen', in *Power of the Weak: Studies on Medieval Women*, ed. Jennifer Carpenter and Sally-Beth MacLean (Chicago, IL, 1995), 126–46; John Carmi Parsons, 'The Queen's Intercession in Thirteenth-Century England', in *ibid.*, 147–77; M.L. Beer, 'Between Kings and Emperors: Catherine of Aragon as Counsellor and Mediator', in *Queenship and Counsel in Early Modern Europe*, ed. Helen Matheson-Pollock, Joanne Paul and Catherine Fletcher (Basingstoke, 2018), 35–58; Benz St. John, *Three Medieval Queens*, ch. 3.
[25] SC8/87/4327. This commission was granted in Oct. 1320: *CPR, 1317–21*, p. 541. The oyer and terminer procedure is discussed in Benz St John, *Three Medieval Queens*, 89–90.

of the bill confirms that this was duly granted by Richard II '*a le requeste la reyne*'.[26] Obtaining the queen's justice, even as her servant or tenant, depended on proximity and access. It has thus been supposed that even in this context petitioners ultimately 'hedged their bets', approaching the queen as intercessor with her husband rather than as an arbiter in her own right.[27] Yet, as Joanna Laynesmith reminds us, we must be cautious not to overplay intercession as some apotheosis of queenly power.[28] Nor should we see the queen's power as residing only in occasional, informal extensions of mercy and patronage.

A survey of the disparate records for the judicial business of the queen's council in the period 1450 to 1550 confirms that, like any other seigneurial administration, it was routinely engaged in peace-keeping within the jointure estates at the behest of inhabitants. The majority of recorded suits involved plaintiffs who claimed to be tenants of their queen, whether according to a copyhold from the local manor or honour court, as 'farmers' or lessees of the queen's farms, or, most commonly, as her 'dayly bedemen'.[29] A smaller number of informants were the queen's officers, including those receivers, stewards, bailiffs, reeves, beadles, parkers, keepers, woodwards, haywards and clerks working to further her interests on the ground by collecting rents and dues, maintaining woodlands and hedgerows, and keeping accounts.[30] These resident royal representatives were just as likely to be the *targets* for petitions to their mistress, however. A similar proportion of named defendants – around a quarter of the total known – were competing, neighbouring landlords of some description. They included abbots, abbesses and priors of religious foundations within or adjoining the queen's estates, accused of asserting their own franchises, as well as several secular authority figures such as mayors and neighbouring lords, who came under fire for encroaching into common land and trying to enforce their own taxes and customs. Local gentry who hunted in the queen's parks and forests were a continual concern for her council, too.[31]

Unsurprisingly, then, many of these cases illustrate the depth of knowledge about the queen's landlordship among her tenantry. Petitioners and witnesses often rehearsed an understanding that parcels of land in their neighbourhood were 'howldyth of the Quene', or that they had 'herd meny owld men say' so.[32] Others expressed a more technical understanding of how particular properties were held, even relating to their historical ownership. One long set of articles contesting the intercommoning arrangements in land held of 'the castell of Berkhampsted wiche is

---

[26] SC8/222/11079. This was granted on 14 September 1384: *CPR, 1381–5*, p. 458.
[27] Musson, 'Queenship, Lordship and Petitioning', 165.
[28] Laynesmith, *The Last Medieval Queens*, 263. This dichotomy between intercession and governmental power was present in Huneycutt, 'Intercession and the Queen', 131; Parsons, 'The Queen's Intercession', 149.
[29] For the copyhold cases, see E111/7, 9; E298/20; for more typical examples, see E163/11/47/2.
[30] The figures in full are as follows: of the fifty-one cases with identified plaintiffs, thirty-one involved self-proclaimed tenants of the queen, eleven involved officers, one came from a neighbouring landlord, and three made no assertion of any formal relation to the queen (though they each concerned land within her jointure estates). A further six were pursued in the queen's name, through writs and warrants.
[31] E.g. E111/49, 60; E135/22/15; E163/10/11, 11/47; E298/1/1, 2, 19, 22, 23, 27, 28, 39. The breakdown of the fifty-one identifiable defendants is sixteen tenants, thirteen officials, thirteen neighbouring lords or tenants, and nine without explicit connection with the queen.
[32] E.g. E111/68.

nowe in the qwenes handes' lamented that 'the qwenes tenauntes were never interrupted nor overleyn of ther comen till ... the deth of my lady of Yorke' – referring to Cecily, duchess of York, whose death in 1495 had brought substantial estates to her grand-daughter, Elizabeth of York, and to the jointure parcels of the queens consort thereafter.[33] Local memory of the duchess's lordship ran deep in Wendover, Buckinghamshire, too, though there appears to have been some confusion about who governed the lordship after her death. When the town's under-bailiff, Thomas Wilcox, happened to pass a widow of one of the late duchess's servants on the road there, he asked her '[w]hose shepe be they in yonder close[?]'. He went on to chide her that 'she showlld medyll no more with yt for yt was the kynges'. The widow's neighbours clearly disagreed, since the information that eventually came before the queen's council insisted that this Wilcox 'toke ye *quenes* tymber', that the current user of the lands had done so with the agreement of the '*quenys* cowncell', and that this dispute harmed 'the *quenes* tru tenawntes'.[34] A similarly sophisticated knowledge of property ownership was displayed by supplicants who relayed that 'their auncetours & predicessours' had held lands and tenements 'of the Erledom of Marche', whose estates in Suffolk had passed through Edward IV to Elizabeth of York, 'the whiche ys now in the possession of your noble grace'; and also in those cases where petitioners described themselves as both living 'withyn the dochy of Lancaster' and as 'tenauntes of the quens moost excellent highness'.[35] These tenants conceptualised their rights within 'the quenes place'.[36]

So, even where disputes unfolding in these lands were interpersonal, between warring neighbours, they also touched upon the administration of the queen's estates and revenues. A frequent concern presented to her council through petition was the proper allocation of land for horses, cows, hogs and sheep – in what numbers, during which seasons, and at what price. One such complaint saw the prior of Walsingham accused of having grazed his 'xii hundred' strong flock for so much of the year that 'he dothe ete up the commons'.[37] It was well within the interests of both the queen *and* her tenants to clarify these privileges and the customs which determined them. Several surviving memoranda record the efforts of surveyors to investigate the principles of 'yoksylver' and 'chynnage', determining the prices for grazing livestock at Margaret of Anjou's Havering-atte-Bower, and to establish hog-rearing privileges at pannage and masting times in the woodlands of Catherine of Aragon's Berkhamsted.[38] The overlap between the council's economic and judicial imperatives is even more apparent in cases which tested the very extent of the queen's 'place'. Several of those gentlemen and farmers accused of venturing into royal forests to hunt and fish were also presented for digging up 'old marke stakes & dowles' and casting 'new boundes' on the edge of estates, slicing off lands and,

---

[33] E111/49. Other cases concerning lands once in the possession of the duchess of York include E298/38 (Bisley, Gloucestershire).
[34] E298/4 (my emphasis). This confusion about the ownership of Wendover could reflect the fact that at the parliament of 1495 it had been resumed into the crown's estates and then granted to the queen specifically 'for t[er]me of her life ymmediatly after the deth of oure seid Sov[er]eign Lord': *Rot. Parl.* vi. 459–60 (11 Hen. VII c. 32).
[35] E163/11/47/2, 48/10.
[36] E298/13.
[37] E298/39.
[38] E163/28/2; E298/8; E111/49.

by extension, profits.[39] It was on this basis that one John Lovelace of Kingsdown on the Kent coast was accused of having felled trees and wasted woodlands 'to the grett detrement of the quenes grace', with the specific figures supplied in a list of articles by Catherine of Aragon's farmer. So much confusion emerged here that her councillors at one point visited Kingsdown to re-measure the bounds of the land in question. In this case as in others, those living on and around the queen's estates might opportunistically take advantage of ambiguities arising from the complexities of managing such disparate holdings; some, like Lovelace himself, could even claim that contested lands were 'never in no quenys possession'.[40]

Internal conflicts of authority also demanded swift clarification from the queen's council. The tenantry did not always respond well to the seigneurial exactions pursued by resident administrators. Hence an undated bill brought by John Cavell, an official at the hundred of Milverton and Bridgwater Castle, Somerset, complained that one of his bailiffs had been indicted and attached for felonies after collecting amercements owed by one of the tenants 'unto the Quenes grace'. Citing 'the welth of the seid ffraunchise', Cavell asked that this tenant be punished. How, exactly, he did not say; presumably he hoped that the council would relieve the bailiff of this charge and send a signal about the queen's rights in the franchise.[41] A hostile writ sent by Catherine of Aragon herself to the mayor and burgesses of Bridgwater in a different dispute, warning them against imposing their own tolls and appointing their own officers, certainly suggests that intervention might be enacted directly.[42] Where tenants presented grievances against officers they put an even greater strain on the queen's authority, expecting her to act in their favour. John Raymond of Great Leighs, Essex, claimed to have been 'tenaunt unto the seid quene & other her predecessors the space of xl yere[s]', and protested against the recent imposition of a higher rent by the new farmer of the manor, Thomas Sorrell, asking that he instead be allowed 'from hensfforth [to] contynue tenaunt to the seid quene as he have byne in tyme past', at the usual rate.[43] In c. 1527 the queen had demised to Sorell that manor, which she held from the duchy of Lancaster, for thirty-one years, and so Raymond presumably hoped that she might use her position as lessor to apply pressure.[44] Similarly, two tenants of Tolleshunt in Essex complained to 'our late Quenes councell' (possibly meaning that of Jane Seymour) that their bailiff had seized a parcel of land in nearby Bradwell 'to the quenes use' according to the notion that one of them had been 'a bondman to her grace', a fact already denied by the homage there.[45] Presuming their opponents to be acting in bad faith or on false information, petitioners on either side of these clashes asked that the queen's council restore the status quo, 'according to righte equitie and good consciens'.[46]

More complicated was the fall-out from encroachments into the queen's lands and liberties by the landlords of adjoining estates. A case in point is that which arose from Alderholt, Dorset, where Catherine of Aragon's tenants contested the right of

---

[39] E.g. E298/9; E111/49.
[40] E298/8–10. Further examples of bills and memoranda concerning money lost by the queen through poaching, fishing and encroachment are E298/15, 24, 35, 45, 51; SP1/244, f. 260.
[41] E163/11/19.
[42] E298/19.
[43] E163/11/48/10.
[44] E210/10309.
[45] E.g. E111/36; E163/10/32, 11/47/2; E298/37.
[46] E298/37.

the lords of nearby Midgham – Richard North and his son, John – to graze hundreds of sheep on their commons. In a commission conducted in May 1527 by Sir Robert Poyntz, the queen's chancellor, Alderholt's eldest tenants attested that 'the lordes of Migeham neither ther ffermers had eny shepe peasably in theth of Alderholt but [were] distrained & empounded', although servants of the Norths claimed that they had been allowed to bring sheep there in the daytime without them being 'folded'. John North himself reverted to the common claim that 'he hath not knowen any of his auncestors to be admytted [to the pasture] by eny of the kynges or quenes counsel herbifor'.[47] Conversely, the queen's council might be called upon to investigate misbehaviours committed by her own tenants against adjoining estates. A petition brought to Anne of Cleves's council by Walter Chalcott, a sergeant-at-arms and tenant of Sir John Baker in Wokefield, Berkshire, alleged that on 10 December 1540 several tenants of the queen's manor there had entered Chalcott's lands and impounded his cattle. They acted, he said, on the false pretence that his groves and crofts were actually 'the premisses of the Quenes grace'; he demanded that the council recompense him for his harmed livestock.[48] In short, the people residing on the edges of the queen's estates might suffer the interventions of her council, but they could also take advantage of its inherent interest in the adjudication of these jurisdictional grey areas.

For the same reasons the council also battled against infringements committed by heads of ecclesiastical foundations whose authority and remit perceptibly overlapped with the queen's estates. A brief glimpse into one such clash is afforded by a short memorandum informing the queen's council that the abbess of Elstow in Hertfordshire 'claymythe a lete' court in Hitchin – brought to the crown through the duchess of York and granted as Catherine of Aragon's jointure along with its view of frankpledge – according to a charter made to the abbey by Henry I which granted it the town's church and tithes.[49] In other such quarrels competing ecclesiastics eschewed paperwork in favour of physical action. On one spring day in 1513, so the queen's tenants at Berkhamsted reported, the prior of Kings Langley and his friars and 'souldyors' set upon a group of men discovered fishing in the ponds within the priory's franchise. Calling them 'knaves and drevyls [devils]', two of the friars 'lept into the water and pulled the seid tenauntes by the[ir] hedes ... and toke awey their wepons and their nettes'.[50] This was one phase in a long-term dispute about the boundaries between the respective estates of this priory and the late medieval queens. At some point in Henry VIII's reign, the prior and convent petitioned the 'Quenes honorable Councell' to complain that they had been seeking confirmation of their title to parks, woods, and closes adjoining their priory for some time without resolution. In the early 1530s, perhaps in response to these grumblings, the council took greater pains to resolve a feud between the priory and the queen's steward, John Verney, concerning various rights of way within the same locality.[51] This matter proved so troublesome that Thomas Cromwell was forced to intervene, and the council's eventual concession of all the rights and access demanded – including a key for

---

[47] E163/10/11.
[48] E163/10/32.
[49] E298/23.
[50] E298/27.
[51] E135/22/31; E298/28.

the gate to the queen's park – indicates the need for compromise with wealthy and well-favoured lords, over whom the queen had little authority.[52]

Not all cases concerned such high-profile conflicts of interest; occasionally the council's role was to restore order and punish bad behaviour rather than to call in its debts. An unusual variation on the tenants-versus-officials theme is the grievance submitted by the people of Highworth in Wiltshire against their vicar, Nicholas Inglesham (or Ynglesem), for his refusal to administer the sacraments, leaving some of his parishioners to die 'withoute shriffte or housell' and denying others 'holy water and holy brede' so often that they had been driven to attend another church. We might speculate that this complaint deliberately played into conservative religious sympathies on the eve of the Reformation, though it cannot be firmly dated. When resumed from the duchess of York's estates and regranted to Elizabeth of York, Highworth *did* come with 'advousons of chirches, as of other benefices what so ever they be', so it was likely on these technical grounds that its parishioners turned to the queen for direction 'as may be acceptable to god & [the] salvacion of our soules'.[53] Elsewhere, information emerging out of Bisley, Gloucestershire, reported that a servant of the troublesome lord of nearby Lypiatt Park had been 'arrested to the peace by one of the quenes tenauntes' because he had 'bette and yll intretyd the said tenaunt and his wyff'. Yet this man had 'desyrid that he might goo to his owne house ... and when he was there [he] escaypyd oute of the bakesyde' and into the safe house of his master, leaving the queen's tenants without remedy.[54] Cases like these stand out as being less directly about the queen's financial interests, and more explicitly about the absence of justice across various social and geographical boundaries.

Indeed, this overview of disputes and their litigation not only confirms that matters in the queen's manors were 'irksome' but also that her councillors '[saw] themselves as responsible for the quality of justice' in the communities within their remit.[55] As one bill had it, the primary duty of 'the quene is most discrete councellors in all her maters consernyng her grace lordeshippis & her tenauntes and by twene her tenaunt & tenaunt [is] to reforme ... the enormities of her cortes aftur the lawys of good concience'.[56] Invocations of 'right', 'conscience', and even 'equity', were part of the established rhetoric for appealing to seigneurial and royal authorities alike, all of which might offer arbitration over lower judicial systems.[57] But this statement also reflects the more functional view that the queen's council served as a 'review jurisdiction' at the top of a defined hierarchy of officials and tribunals.[58] These firmer geographical and institutional parameters puts the queen's council closer in jurisdictional terms to the administrations surrounding the realm's noblemen and women

---

[52] E289/29; SP1/82, f. 8, 100, f. 100. See also *Letters and Papers*, vii. no. 11; ix. no. 1154. Another judgment in this case appears in E211/306.
[53] *Rot. Parl.* vi. 460; E135/23/45.
[54] E298/38.
[55] Hamilton, 'Learned Councils of the Tudor Queens Consort', 91; M.K. McIntosh, 'Central Court Supervision of the Ancient Demesne Manor Court of Havering, 1200–1625', in *Law, Litigants and the Legal Profession*, ed. E.W. Ives and A.H. Manchester (1983), 87.
[56] E298/2.
[57] For such terminology in the context of noble councils, see *Paston Letters and Papers of the Fifteenth Century*, ed. Norman Davis (2 vols, Oxford, 1971, 1976), ii. no. 849; and Robert Catesby's petition to the duke of Buckingham from the 1440s: E163/29/11, m. 2.
[58] McIntosh, 'Central Court Supervision', 87–93; *eadem, Autonomy and Community*, 332–40.

than to the king's council and its more general purview over all English subjects, whether or not they resided within the ancient demesne.

In the case of the queen's council this jurisdiction extended as far as maintaining the very infrastructure of justice-giving within her estates. It was not only in Hitchin that the right to administer a court was thrown into question; in early sixteenth-century Bury St Edmunds, the abbot would allegedly 'not suffre [the queen's] cortes to be kepte & holden ... [as] in tymes past'.[59] Anne Boleyn's tenants in Edlogan (in the lordship of Usk in south Wales) even held their queen responsible for regulating and funding their courthouse. In a petition to Anne's council they objected, firstly, to their court being held not in nearby Llanfrechfa, as had been agreed during a visit by Anne's commissioners just after she had been made marchioness of Pembroke, but in the liberty and lordship of Caerleon. This, they claimed, had meant that they could not obtain justice without being 'manassed & threatened ... onlesse then they will geve veredict according to the pleasures & myndes of some of the burgeses of the said towne'. Secondly, they lamented that they had recently been forced to gather for sessions 'in open street and wynde & rayne', and demanded that the queen help fit out their own 'fayre new cort howse or yeld hall'. After all, they remarked rather slyly, the queen had seen fit to pay 'xij d every cort for a letill shop' to house the judges in Caerleon.[60]

The queen's council also played a supervisory role in the daily business of these courts. In 1531 one William Odynham reported to Catherine of Aragon's council that he had 'prayed to be admytted tenaunte' in her manor of Leyham, Suffolk, and that the 'hoole homage' had been called to make confirmation, but that one of the tenants, the widow Elizabeth Bendish, 'beyng ffermor to the quenys grace', refused his admittance. Apparently an outsider to the manor, he emphasised his correct use of legal procedure – that he had entered 'in to the seid court by his suffycyent attorney and ther in due forme made his peticion' – and asked that the council authorise 'some wurshipfull jentilmen of this partyes' to investigate.[61] Similar respect to the ultimate authority of the council was observed in Hitchin in 1529, when upon the death of one of the queen's tenants her under-steward had made a 'precept' to certain claimants to the now-vacant lands 'yt they scholde nott take nor occupy none of the londes holden of the quenes grace by coppy unto suche tyme that they had bene affore ye quenes councell to know ther pleasure'.[62] In these instances the council was expected to affirm a court's actions, but things were not always so simple. Where the stewards, under-stewards and particularly the lessees of manors under the queen visibly corrupted these processes, the tenantry there might justifiably argue that they could not 'have any indifferent tryall'.[63] And, as one bill of articles presented against the bailiff of Hampstead Marshall, Berkshire, insisted, the stakes for the queen in such instances were dire: where 'tenauntes hath ben so grievously intreted' they might 'at the cortes there holden ... not present of the menyfold iniuries which they know yor grace suffrith onles it be before suche persones as will save them harmeles'.[64]

[59] E163/11/47/2, 28/2.
[60] E298/33.
[61] E298/20.
[62] E111/7.
[63] E.g. E298/7, where a tenant of Hundon, Staffordshire, complained that the queen's feodary and officer, Hugh Danyell, would not grant a copy of the court roll.
[64] E298/13.

In turn, it was this pragmatic connection between the microcosm of the manor and the order of the wider realm – and *not* the notions of queenly mercy and clemency that we might expect to see in documents pertaining to this period's consorts – that informed how plaintiffs framed themselves before the queen as judicial authority.[65] Her supplicants typically stressed the importance of 'savyng ... the Quenes enheritance & hir pore tenauntes', or of preventing the 'utter undoyng & impoverysshyng of the qwenes tenauntes', and they claimed to be without remedy altogether 'onles your grace be unto tham mercifully shewed' – phrases common to petitions to the king by this time, too.[66] Yet the tenurial contract between most of these complainants and the receiving councillors granted additional lines of justification for choosing this route for remedy, emphasising the seigneurial as much as the monarchical contract in the balance. Hence those suits in which title to land was at odds could be framed as ensuring that 'the seyd most gracious quene might lawfully be intytelyd' as well, appealing to the council's desire to maximise profits from the queen's estates.[67] The mayor and commonality of Sudbury even boldly reminded Catherine of Aragon that 'your grace ys soveraign lady & owner of the seid towne duryng your lyff the reversion therof after your decesse to your sovereign lord the kyng & hys heyrs', meaning that their losses 'may retorne to hys losse in tyme commyng'.[68] The perfunctory tone of much of this petitioning reminds us, again, that justice-giving in the context of estate management was a reflection of the queen's 'good ladyship rather than any uniquely queenly quasi-Marian role'.[69]

A further implication of this capacity to appeal to the queen on 'several different levels' – as the source of intercession, as a font of charity, as landlady – is that the judicial element of her council functioned as yet another forum to which well-placed, savvy litigants might apply for remedy.[70] Yet its place within the sprawling legal network of medieval England is difficult to discern when we take its work in a vacuum. Examining the wider context of one case, that presented by Alice Warner of Bury St Edmunds, is more revealing. Warner petitioned Catherine of Aragon alleging that her husband had been attacked and 'wounded ... grievously bothe in the hede & in other partes of his body' by a servant of the sacristan of the abbey of Bury St Edmunds, such that after a week or so he had died from his injuries. This seems an unusually straightforward matter to present to the queen, for it was presumably triable at common law. Warner's tactic becomes more obvious towards the end of her petition, where she asked only that the queen 'be gracious meane for your sayd pore bedewoman unto the kinges good grace', encouraging him to see her receive recompense, and made casual reference to troubles between the officers and the townsfolk going back 'x or xij yere' which were 'nowe dependynge in the lawe'.[71] Here she referred to a wider set of suits already winding their way through numerous central conciliar courts contemporaneously. The town of Sudbury also joined the

---

[65] Parsons, 'The Queen's Intercession', 149.
[66] E.g. E111/49; E298/12, 21.
[67] E163/11/48/11.
[68] E163/11/47/1. Similar phrasing appears in the plea of the tenants of Walsingham against the prior's encroachment on their commons: E298/39.
[69] Laynesmith, *The Last Medieval Queens*, 243.
[70] M.L. Beer, 'Practices and Performances of Queenship: Catherine of Aragon and Margaret Tudor, 1503–1533' (PhD thesis, University of Illinois, Chicago, 2014), 40–2.
[71] E135/22/15.

fray, with its mayor reporting in a separate petition to the queen's council that the abbot believed the town to belong to his own franchise and imposed 'forren officers' to collect fines for his own coffers.[72] Around the same time, several other tenants of Bury St Edmunds lodged a similar complaint, echoing the allegations that the abbot had drawn rents and profits from their tenements to the abbey's use.

While these petitioners recognised that the queen was their landlord, they also admitted having turned first to the 'kinges moost honorable councell' and to the chancellor for redress. Possibly they had done so in the absence of a queen consort, as Elizabeth of York had died in 1502. But they had just as likely exploited the ambiguity in their rights, as inhabitants of a town partly farmed out by the queen to the abbot but otherwise within the abbot's own liberty of St Edmund, to shop for justice.[73] After all, much like Alice Warner, the Bury tenants' primary request was that Catherine of Aragon merely induce the abbot to 'surcease in [his] seyd sute' at the common law rather than to examine the matter herself.[74] Likewise, the Sudbury delegation was at pains to insist that they did *not* wish to have the abbot 'callyd in … to answer' but hoped only 'that your grace & your noble councell may be instructed & informed of the grett wronges injuries & extorcions commytted be the officers of the seid abbott': in fact, they ultimately sought 'direccion & order … be comen lawe'.[75] In the later 1510s the case came before Star Chamber, and an answer submitted by the abbot not only recounted deliberations 'bifor the Quenes honorable counceile' but also another round of hearings before the king's council, at Barnard's Castle and at Westminster, followed by various efforts by Archbishop Thomas Wolsey to arbitrate a resolution in 1517.[76] In other words, the tenants of Bury and Sudbury continued to seek the king's justice before, during and after their pleas to the queen. We might draw two conclusions from this episode: first, that the impression of any straightforward review provision offered by the queen's council might be qualified by evidence that it served as just one in a constellation of potential routes for trying existing disputes, and was used opportunistically; and second that even the queen's tenants saw her jurisdiction and her authority as having defined limits.

A factor determining litigants' decisions to sue to the queen's council was, presumably, what this court could do for them and against their opponents. Evidence for its procedures and rulings is, unfortunately, now quite scarce. Surviving letters from earlier medieval queens show that where problems had arisen within their dower lands – gentry trespassing into parks, or the king's officers behaving 'underhandedly and maliciously' – they had traditionally written to the chancellor, asking that he initiate investigations or legal action.[77] By the middle of the fifteenth century, Margaret of Anjou herself sent letters to those vexing her tenants and officers, warning that they should 'put th'examination of your said suit to us and to our counseil, where we shall by good deliberation and advis see that ye shull have al that that rightfully

---

[72] E163/11/47/1.
[73] *Letters and Papers*, i. no. 94 (35).
[74] E163/11/47/2.
[75] E163/11/47/1.
[76] STAC2/7, ff. 159–63. A recognisance binding numerous tradesmen of the town to stop their suits against the abbot, dated 17 September 1517, appears in STAC2/7, f. 165 and SP1/232, f. 56.
[77] *Letters of the Queen of England*, ed. Anne Crawford (Stroud, 1994), 79, 98–9. One petition addressed to Katherine de Valois in the late 1420s asked similarly that the chancellor intervene to have an obligation restored: SC8/306/15298.

belongeth unto you in that bihalf'.[78] This bears the hallmarks of the direct, extemporaneous treatment of disputes by all major landlords; for example, as countess of Richmond and Derby, Lady Margaret Beaufort (the only other woman in this period granted status of *femme sole* during her husband's lifetime) similarly had her officials convey parties from her estates in the Midlands to appear before her council at Collyweston.[79] From the later fifteenth century onwards, however, the evidence suggests that the queen's council initiated judicial proceedings through the more formal and regular mechanism of the queen's seals, in a manner not dissimilar from the crown's equity courts. Accordingly, the mayor of Sudbury indicated that the abbot of Bury could be 'callyd in by prive seale ... to answer' before the queen, while the warrant sent by Catherine of Aragon to the mayor of Bridgwater demanding that he show 'what auctorite ye have to justifie yor doynges' in the town was issued from Lambeth Palace under her signet seal.[80] This not only made the personal more procedural, but also followed the general pattern set by the king's council of using the privy seal to summon and the personal seal to warrant or command.

That said, as late as the 1540s petitioners might ask Katherine Parr's council to award 'the *kynges* graces writ of privey seal', even though the dispute in question concerned offences committed within the queen's estates.[81] One of the few surviving original writs was, indeed, issued under the king's privy seal, requiring that the recipient 'be and personally appere beffore the counseyll off our most dere and ryght enterely welbeloved wiffe the quene in her counsell chamber at Westm[inster]', again despite the matter pertaining to 'our saide wiffis libertys'.[82] The date and intended recipient of this writ are unknown, but the aforementioned petition to Katherine Parr levelled accusations about the spoilage of woodlands against two men from Yardley, Worcestershire, a manor then in the crown's possession.[83] It is therefore not implausible that in these instances the queen had no authority to compel the named defendants to appear, necessitating recourse to the king's side of the administration. In other words, procedures moving the queen's justice became more formalised in the sixteenth century, but the geographical limit of her authority meant that there might be circumstances in which her writs did not run.[84]

Where issues arose within the queen's estates, and thus firmly within her jurisdiction, it has been noted how much her council 'relied on its local officers to settle these disputes'.[85] Certainly, many of the surviving suits saw the 'quenes gracys commyssyon' empowered to take depositions on the basis of pre-prepared interrogatories, to collect defendants' answers, and sometimes to help the parties come to some resolution – to 'handle the said matier by yor discrecions the mooste pollitiquely

---

[78] *The Letters of Margaret of Anjou*, ed. Helen Maurer and B.M. Cron (Woodbridge, 2019), 83–4, 88, 111.
[79] *The Household Accounts of Lady Margaret Beaufort (1443–1509): From the Archives of St John's College, Cambridge*, ed. Susan Powell (Oxford, 2022), 275, 288.
[80] E163/11/47/1; E298/19.
[81] E163/11/48/5 (my emphasis).
[82] E298/42.
[83] E163/11/48/5. Yardley had been granted to Catherine of Aragon as part of her divorce settlement in 1533, then returned to the crown on her death: *VCH Worcestershire*, iii. 239.
[84] For more on the queen's various possible approaches to disputes brought before her, see *The Letters of Margaret of Anjou*, ed. Maurer and Cron, ch. 5.
[85] Hamilton, 'Learned Councils of the Tudor Queens Consort', 92.

ye can'.[86] The men appointed to this work included a range of secular and ecclesiastical figureheads resident in the relevant area, and not just those in the queen's employ. We find among those recorded in the extant paperwork an abbot and three esquires nominated in Southfrith, Kent, 'acordyng to a letter missife ... derected by our grasius Quene' in 1519; and, in 1527, a 'comyssion by [Catherine of Aragon's] Counsell' was made out to two knights and a gentleman of Alderholt.[87] Petitioners were aware of this option and sometimes asked for it in the first instance. For example, in his numerous pleadings to Catherine of Aragon's council the mayor of Sudbury requested that she send 'your gracious lettres unto the right honorable Erle of Oxford' and the high steward of the town, asking them to see that the townsfolk could live free from the abbot's oppression.[88] It is worth noting that this degree of delegation was a consistent feature of justice at all levels, including the royal courts (indeed, as Carole Rawcliffe suggested, the king's conciliar courts perhaps borrowed this on-the-ground style of mediation from the nobility).[89] We should not, therefore, interpret its use by the queen's council in terms of an over-reliance on local authorities or a dilution of its own influence. After all, sometimes the issues in dispute were simply to be scrutinised locally and certified back to that council, so that they could 'take suche order therin as may stande with equyte and justyce'.[90]

To make any order the council heard and hashed out the details of given disputes in-house. By at least the late fifteenth century, this meant soliciting more evidence through the flexible, vernacular English bill procedure that was already common to the royal courts of Chancery, Star Chamber and Requests. Defendants submitted answers setting out their arguments, raising objections to their opponents' claims, and insisting that they could present proof before the court.[91] A warrant sent by Anne Boleyn's council to two commissioners, ordering that they take an answer to an especially elderly defendant in person 'so that she [may] make first a corporall othe for the truethe of hir saide aunswer', both indicates the lengths taken to secure this response from accused parties and the significance of the oath in trying the conscience of the respondent and opening him or her up either to self-incrimination or to perjury.[92] The adversarial nature of party-to-party litigation extended in some instances to the full range of replications and rejoinders, too.[93]

Little evidence for the results of this council's deliberations now survives – at least, nothing equivalent to the registers left by various of the king's conciliar courts from the late fifteenth and early sixteenth centuries.[94] The sole exception is a single, fragmentary page said to contain 'Acts of the Queen's Council' during Catherine of Aragon's queenship (dating to c. 1526, according to another document with which it is filed). Visible on either side of this leaf are entries of a few lines each,

---

[86] E111/7, 9, 49; E163/10/11; SP1/231, f. 326.
[87] E111/68; E163/10/11.
[88] E163/11/47/1.
[89] Rawcliffe, 'The Great Lord as Peacekeeper', 52–3.
[90] SP1/245, f. 80.
[91] E111/25
[92] E298/32.
[93] Examples survive in E111/35 and 49.
[94] That is, akin to those surviving in DL5 and REQ1; the transcripts from the now-lost main council registers in Huntington Library, San Marino, CA, Ellesmere MSS 2654, 2655; and the record of hearings kept for Star Chamber, calendared in *Star Chamber Reports: BL Harley MS 2143*, ed. K.J. Kesselring (List and Index Society, special series, lvii, 2018).

some in Latin and some in English, recording interlocutory decisions in judicial disputes pending before this body. For example, one reads: 'M[emoran]d[um] it is agred before the quenes Counsaill that Thomas Motyng of Estdereham and Richard Ivony of the same towne hathe aperid before the said Counsaill by vertue ~~uppo~~ of a privey seale to theym directed in that behalf &c Wheruppon bothe the said parties be licenced to departe for that mater ~~in~~ towchyng the said privey seale and John Hynde the lerned man ys admitted theire attorney to make answer for them …'. The names of the manors in question and the parties in variance appear in the left-hand margins. Between some of the entries are headings with dates – the clearest being 'Saterday the xx[th] day of May' – and some also include a list of the councillors in attendance at certain meetings. Listed as present on that Saturday are 'Mr Chauncellor Mr Attorney Mr Griffith Mr Scott [and] Mr Solicitor'.[95]

All told, this page confirms some existing impressions of how this part of the council's work functioned day to day. It was overseen by a mixture of leading officials like the chancellor, estate administrators such as the receiver-general and surveyor, and retained lawyers including the attorney-general and solicitor. Household officers like the treasurer, chamberlain or steward were noticeably absent from the lists on this page and from all other surviving documents. The estate-focused side of the council sat specifically for the furthering of judicial business it seems. Aside from admitting parties' attorneys, the aforementioned page of entries records decisions to summon the prior and canons of Royston, Hertfordshire, to defend their distraint of cattle; to certify a decision of the homage of Wendover, Buckinghamshire; and to accept obligations concerning the queen's park in Stondon, Hertfordshire. We can safely assume that this business was conducted from the 'quenes graces counsaill chembre' at Westminster Palace, from whence Anne Boleyn's council issued its warrants.[96] Although the council's use of particular authorising seals could vary, as we have seen, its hearings were more routinised; signs of pre-planning emerge from one order recorded in the register page for a party's appearance on the following Saturday and by writs filed elsewhere which asked defendants to attend by similarly specific days (for example, 'on Thursdaye next commyng'). It is not implausible that consistent record-keeping was another part of this picture of greater institutionalisation, and that this fragmentary page once belonged to an entire register that is now lost. After all, an entry in Elizabeth of York's household accounts of 1502 notes a payment of 10s. made to William Trende 'for the making of a Cheste and Almorys in the quenes counsaill Chambre for to put in the Bokes', and in 1544 Katherine Parr's new auditor was in receipt of 'all such bokes … towching ye Quene her graces possessions'.[97]

Certainly, given the range of cases received by the queen's council, its members 'would have had to work very hard to sort out disputes to everyone's satisfaction', though their options were inflected by who or what was actually at stake.[98] A brief endorsement in Latin noted on the reverse of one bill of articles records its receipt

---

[95] E163/26/6. 'Griffith' likely refers to Griffith Richards, Catherine of Aragon's chancellor, and 'Mr Scott' perhaps means John Scott, an apprentice at law retained in 1529: *Letters and Papers*, iv. no. 6121 (51).

[96] E298/32, 34; E163/11/49/9 (which is also addressed 'To the Quenes graces right honorable counsel in her graces counsel chamber at Westm[inster]').

[97] E36/210, f. 89; SP1/195, f. 192 (*Letters and Papers*, xix (pt. 2), no. 722).

[98] Hamilton, 'Learned Councils of the Tudor Queens Consort', 92.

by Edmund Chaderton, Elizabeth of York's chancellor, her attorney Richard Eliot, and others of her council, and summarises their own determination ('*adjudicatum & decretum est ...*') that a common-law judgment made between parties in the queen's own court at Cookham, Berkshire, should be annulled because of errors described in the bill.[99] A more extensive record of the same stage of procedures is a series of responses 'ordered and decreed' by Catherine of Aragon's council in the case between the prior of King's Langley and her steward there. The surviving version appears to be a rough draft, with interlineations and an additional hand (perhaps that of the chancellor, Robert Dymmock, to whom the document was addressed) adding the caveat '*salvo jure cuiuscumque*' to orders regarding the use of certain gardens and roads in that area – which, as we have seen already, were determined in the priory's favour.[100] To make decisions in such matters the council not only gathered witness testimonies and perused local court rolls but also, in some cases, sought 'thadvice of all the kynges juges and seriauntes and of dyvers oþer lerned in the lawe'.[101] Another, similarly detailed decree is that awarded by Katherine Howard's council to the college of Fotheringhay, concerning its clerks' rights to wages and to 'mary & tary', made while the queen and her entourage were staying at nearby Fotheringhay castle in late June 1541.[102] This order was written directly into the final leaf of one of the college's own books, where it was signed off by Katherine's chancellor, attorney, surveyor and clerk. It recorded that these councillors had 'delyberatly and advysedly seen and examyned the said ffundacion corporacion and Statutes of this saide Colledge' (many of which were copied into this same book) and had decided that the clerks ought to obey their master, 'mynding thencreasse of unytie and obedyens ... and eschewing of the contrary'.[103] In this and the other scattered examples just described we can discern this council's capacity for clarifying rights through documented procedures as well as offering arbitration-style intervention in complex, interpersonal disputes – its ethos being to secure both profit and peace.

Who benefitted from the queen's justice, then? We have observed that her authority had some practical limitations: when facing a prestigious neighbouring landlord, the only recourse was to bring their councils together or seek a third party to mediate. It was such complexities, presumably, which had caused Elizabeth Wydeville to seek examination 'by the councell lerned of kyng Edward the iiijth' before entering into jurisdictional wrangling with the prior of King's Langley; and which, in a later phase of that dispute, had resulted in one of that prior's successors complaining that he had pursued the matter for years without receiving any 'ordre or fynall direccion therin'.[104] As an ultimately advisory body with a geographically bounded jurisdiction, the queen's council could not formally impose any order on people outside its remit. Otherwise, where more straightforward, internal disputes – between tenants in a specific manor – were resolved, the council's orders were written up and disseminated around the queen's dispersed estates. Resident officials acted as conduits: the trou-

---

[99] E298/2.
[100] E298/28.
[101] E298/44.
[102] E317/417, ff. 26v–27; *VCH Northamptonshire*, ii. 175. The councillors who signed this decree were the chancellor Thomas Denys, Robert Chydley, attorney, Geoffrey Danyell, surveyor, and Thomas Smythe, clerk of the council.
[103] E315/147, ff. 26v–27.
[104] E298/28.

blesome vicar of Highworth received a letter from the council 'in the quens courte of Seven Hampton', where it was read out to him by her under-steward; and one of Catherine of Aragon's officers in Worcestershire wrote to her attorney, Charles Bulkeley, in reference to 'the [a]warde ... which I browght downe ffrom you'.[105]

In turn, the council's determinations were legitimised and executed by those same local courts over which it retained oversight. In Hitchin, 'at the petycion' of certain tenants and 'by the advice of her Counceile', Catherine of Aragon once urged her steward to utilise a court session to grant lands and tenements according to her judgment, and to record this new arrangement in the court rolls.[106] Likewise, at Cookham, the plaintiff aggrieved by errors in judicial processes prayed that 'the record & jugement ayenst her be ... adjugid by yor seid lordeshippes voyd & of no force' but also that this annulment be 'sent downe in to the seid cort of Cokeham with a comaundement in the next cort ... to the stuard of the same corte' to make note of this 'voyd record'.[107] Here, in the communication between institutions, do we glimpse the clearest synergy between queen and her localities.

* * *

This essay has joined a growing body of administrative histories which, combined with the scholarship on the culture of queenship and the biographies of individual consorts, continue to map out the spheres in which queenly power operated.[108] Analysis here has been inclined more towards the structural than personal, meaning, most obviously, that it cannot definitively say much about how far the quality or scope of justice-giving reflected the disposition of any individual queen, or what degree of independence the queen's side of the administration held from the king's. There is far more surviving material for Catherine of Aragon's council compared to Elizabeth Wydeville's, but we must resist equating patchiness of evidence with absence of activity. The concentration of warrants and writs during Katherine Parr's queenship seems to relate more to her regency in 1544 than to any independent development in her own council. Moreover, whether or not the surviving records prove any of these queens to have been 'equal to a male landowner', or to their husbands, with regard to their personal hand in government is a moot point.[109] After all, it was rare for the king himself to be personally engaged each day in the kind of civil rulings of justice between tenants undertaken by his side of the administration.

To return to the institutional questions that opened this essay: was there a clear judicial element – even 'a Court of Equitie (as well as of Revenue)' – within the queen's council by the turn of the sixteenth century, as described in the 1640s and by historians since then?[110] Attempting to pinpoint anything like 'equity' must come with certain caveats, seventeenth-century definitions of that term being shaped by the many doctrinal developments and jurisdictional conflicts that had unfolded by that time. We have observed the use of the vocabulary of 'right and equity' in relation to this council's judicial ethos, but this was neither exclusive to royal courts nor even

---

[105] E135/23/45; SP1/239, f. 197.
[106] E298/16.
[107] E298/2.
[108] E.g. Beer, 'A Queenly Affinity?'; Seah, "My Lady Queen, the Lord of the Manor".
[109] Seah and Wright, 'The Medieval English Queen as Landholder', 24.
[110] SP16/483, f. 126v; Fisher, 'The Queenes Courte', 315; Crawford, 'The Queen's Council', 1193.

to judicial contexts in this period, when it represented a generalised ideal of fairness rather than a juridical doctrine. Nevertheless, in so far as 'equity' before the mid-sixteenth century might refer to a lack of deference to common law, a general ethos of morality and even-handedness, and a specific form of flexible bill procedure that litigants found preferable, the queen's council might certainly be classified an 'equity' tribunal of sorts. These qualifications help us to further illuminate the relationship between the queen's administration and the developments of central government in this period, where the ethos of seigneurial governance met with the procedures of crown bureaucracy in emerging judicial forums.

They also direct our attention, importantly, to consumers of justice and their experience of its procedures, not just the officials who dispensed it each day or the queen in whose name it ran. Reconstructing the full process of justice-giving better informs 'our understanding of the queen's importance in the localities', beyond the household and court, where her authority was felt most directly by her wide-ranging tenantry and cadre of officers.[111] The remaining evidence illustrates the various contributions made by the queen and her council in the administration of money, land and sheep; their hand in the production of royal writs and orders flying all over the country; their attention to the administration of justice in a network of local courts; and their care for maintaining peace within the complex network of officials, farmers and tenants in crown lands. In turn, tenants taking up the mantle of litigation invited the queen into their disputes on the basis that she would, in the process of determining where justice lay, establish her own rights. This two-way dialogue was key to how these royal women managed their estates.

---

[111] A line of inquiry that Laynesmith has suggested: *The Last Medieval Queens*, 264–5.

THE 'LAST YORKIST' REVEALED? RICHARD DE LA POLE, CHARLES, DUC DE BOURBON, AND A CONTENTIOUS PANEL PORTRAIT OF THE 1520s[1]

Anthony Gross

A great part of history is fantasy. We read and research. But it is human to visualise. Each of us hosts a pictorial construct of the past, founded on shared principles but also thoroughly individual. Here, the art of the personal portrait has a very particular place. The desire to know what people looked like, to put a face to the name, is stronger now than ever, sustained by the swelling tide of digitally recreated living images of those long dead.[2] The costume drama will soon give way to reanimation, the immediacy lending an additional veneer of certainty to dramatisation that must, at the very least, be partial and distorted. It was against this background that, in 2013 when I spoke at the conference organised by Dr Rowena Archer at Christ Church, Oxford, I argued that the sitter seen in the panel portrait discussed in this essay is not Charles, duc de Bourbon, the traitorous cousin of François I, as previously thought, but Richard de la Pole, putative duke of Suffolk and one of the last serious Yorkist claimants to Henry VIII's crown.[3] My case rested on the sitter's cap badge which clearly shows the white hart at rest, the emblem of King Richard II. The subject was advertising his family relationship to Richard II and was therefore, most plausibly, Richard de la Pole.[4]

---

[1] It is fitting that for a *festschrift* in honour of Rowena Archer the principal subject of this essay, Richard de la Pole, should have been a grandson of Alice Chaucer, duchess of Suffolk. I wish to thank my research assistant Dr David Harrap for his help in the preparation of this essay, both by checking my original research and by making judicious comments as I have reassessed my argument.

[2] Perhaps the most famous visualisation of recent times is the craniofacial reconstruction of Richard III, commissioned by the Richard III Society and carried out by Professor Caroline Wilkinson of Liverpool John Moore's University, which has raised the public profile of both these tools and also the historical and ethical quandaries associated with their use. Only a sample of the recent literature can be given here: Roberta Gilchrist, 'Voices from the Cemetery', *Medieval Archaeology*, lxvi (pt 1) (2022), 120–50, at 139–41; Susan Hayes, 'Faces in the Museum: Revising the Methods of Facial Reconstructions', *Museum Management and Curatorship*, xxxi (pt 3) (2016), 218–45, at 219; Richard Toon and Lauri Stone, 'Game of Thrones: Richard III and the Creation of Cultural Heritage', in *Studies in Forensic Biohistory: Anthropological Perspectives*, ed. Christopher Stojanowski and William Duncan (Cambridge, 2016), 43–66, esp. 55–6.

[3] See Figure 1. All the images of Richard de la Pole/Charles III, duc de Bourbon, that are referred to in this article are listed in the Appendix. The best account of de la Pole's life is that given in W.E. Hampton, 'The White Rose Under the First Tudors, Part 3. Richard de la Pole, "The King's Dreaded Enemy"', *The Ricardian*, vii (1987), 525–40.

[4] Through his mother (the sister of Edward IV and Richard III), de la Pole was descended from Lionel, duke of Clarence, Richard II's eldest uncle.

Figure 1 Anon., *Richard de la Pole*, ante 1525, private collection.

I remain of that view. As Dr Alexandra Zvereva, presently the principal authority on French Renaissance portraiture, put it to me in personal discussion there are two separate portrait traditions for Bourbon.[5] They cannot both be correct. When the panel, which had long been in the possession of the Tempest family at Tong Hall in Yorkshire, came up for sale at Christies in December 2010, Dr Timothy Hunter was entirely correct in asking the auction house to announce, just as the bidding was about to start, that the picture was part of a long sequence of related images identified as the constable de Bourbon.[6] What Dr Hunter couldn't know is that that identification is in fact completely apocryphal and that this panel, arguably the progenitor of that series of portraits, would lead to the unravelling of several centuries worth of entrenched assumption and edge us towards a tentative identification of the actual sitter, the near contemporary who for so long took on the identity of Charles de Bourbon in the historical imagination.[7] De la Pole is and will remain the most plausible candidate. But since I have never claimed conclusiveness for my identification, it is interesting that in the years since the conference at Christ Church and the brief notice in *The Times* which happened concurrently, the painting has become a staple of internet websites and blogs aimed at those interested in the Wars of the Roses.[8] The television dramas based on the writings of Philippa Gregory, as highly detailed as they are romanticised, have increased the popular awareness of the remnants of the Yorkist dynasty ready to press a claim to the Tudor throne. Anyone who googles Richard de la Pole, will see it immediately and in several locations including YouTube.[9] To the best of

---

[5] For these traditions, see Louis Dimier, *La Peinture de Portrait en France au XVIe Siecle* (3 vols, Paris, 1924–6), iii. 160, nos 41, 42.

[6] 'Old Master & 19th Century Paintings, Drawings & Watercolours (Day Sale): Lot 176', Christies, 8 December 2010: https://tinyurl.com/ykvwyher (accessed June 2023).

[7] At this point, it should be acknowledged that another portrait tradition exists, which putatively depicts Charles de Bourbon. This is based on an image that is now held by the Museu Bellas Artes in Valencia, see Figure 2 and Appendix, no. 7. This painting, at one point attributed to Titian, belonged to the collections of Thomas Howard, 14th earl of Arundel, as witnessed by Titian's great nephew at the beginning of the seventeenth century: Tizianello, *Vita dell'insigne pittore Tiziano Vecellio, 1622* (Venice, 1809), p. xiii. The attribution to Titian recurs in the print of the same image, which was made by Lucas Vosterman during the 1620s, see Figure 3. The authorship was challenged by Johannes Wilde, who preferred Giampietro Silvio, Titian's collaborator, as the work's author, based on a comparison with a portrait now in the collections of the Kunsthistorischen Museum in Vienna: Wilde, 'Zwei Tizian Zuschreiben des 17. Jahrhunderts', *Jahrbuch der Kunsthistorischen Sammlungen in Wien*, viii (1934), 161–72, at 164. This attribution also appears in Harold Wethey's catalogue of Titian's work, *The Paintings of Titian* (3 vols, 1971), ii. 156, no. X–14. The *milieu* of the portrait's provenance is fairly certain; the posture and colouration of the image is typical of Venetian portraiture of the mid-sixteenth century. Yet there is no reason to think that it was originally meant to be an image of Charles de Bourbon, let alone that it was taken from life.

[8] Anon., 'Rebel found with the Hunchback's Badge', *The Times*, 10 September 2013: https://tinyurl.com/2s4xydxc. This notice led to a refutation by Frederick Hepburn: 'NOT Richard de la Pole', *Ricardian Bulletin* (March 2014), 42–3. Yet while Hepburn has an unquestionable expertise in the field, his argument rests on the long tradition which identified this image as Charles de Bourbon – a tradition which the present essay contends is apocryphal and based on an early misidentification. Similarly, Hepburn's assertion that the absence of any jewel on the coif tells us that the panel portrait is a copy made *after* the first engravings of the image is belied by the early date provided by the dendrochronology.

[9] For example, Matthew Lewis, 'The Fate of the House of York', Matt's History Blog, 24 October 2014: https://tinyurl.com/39edxnkf; David Crowther, 'The Family De la Pole', The History of England, 17 October 2016: https://tinyurl.com/4en3upv5; Matt Lewis, 'On This Day: 24 February 1525, Death of Richard de la Pole', YouTube, 24 February 2020: https://tinyurl.com/26spttr8; in 2021 a photo of the

Figure 2   Anon., *Charles de Bourbon*, Colección del Museo de Bellas Artes de València.

my knowledge, none of these sites discusses the reasons for the identification of the sitter. That is simply taken as a given. And, while that might be considered flattering, it goes too far. It falls into exactly the same error made centuries ago when, by dint of repetition, the image was unquestioningly accepted as Bourbon. Nowadays, of course, we don't need copyists or the printing press to reinforce the reputation of an image by replication. It can be done in a moment by capturing it online and embedding. So, it is not surprising that while some bloggers claim the face on the panel for de la Pole, other internet resources still use it along with its successors to illustrate the life of Charles de Bourbon. The Royal Collection's descriptions of its two versions of Thomas Leu's engraving follows the printmaker's assertion that he based his design on a true likeness of Bourbon.[10] Bourbon's Wikipedia page presently displays the portrait which bears his title from the gallery of notables at the Chateau de Beauregard.[11] But, as is shown below, both of these are among the many late derivatives related to the early panel under discussion here, which is not a portrait of Bourbon at all. Even the panel itself, so often now certified as a portrait of de la Pole, still appears on the Wikimedia entry for Charles, duc de Bourbon, with a reference to Christies and a dating of 1630, which would place it after the creation of the print by Thomas de Leu to which it is closely related, but, as dendrochronology has shown, anterior by some seven decades.[12] It is almost impossible to dislodge from the pic-

---

    panel was added to A.S. Stevens, 'Richard de la Pole', Find a Grave, 2 May 2013: https://tinyurl.com/bdfcdkvy – all accessed June 2023.

[10] See Figure 4: Leu, Thomas de (*fl*.1576–1614): *Charles de Bourbon c.1575–1612*, Royal Collection Trust: https://tinyurl.com/yrhjf5sx and Leu, Thomas de: *Charles duc de Bourbon, c.1756–80*, Royal Collection Trust: https://tinyurl.com/4mrvxvwj (accessed June 2023).

[11] 'Charles III, Duke of Bourbon', *Wikipedia*, updated 23 May 2023: https://tinyurl.com/2ezr4uc4 (accessed June 2023).

[12] '*Charles de Bourbon, connétable de France. Ecole française, vers 1630*', *Wikimedia Commons*, 17

Figure 3 Lucas Vosterman, *Charles III de Bourbon*, 1622–8, British Museum, London © The Trustees of the British Museum.

Figure 4 Thomas de Leu, *Charles, duc de Bourbon*, c. 1600, Royal Collection Trust, London © His Majesty King Charles III.

torial record an image which exists in so many related versions with its title passing through multiple recensions. Even though it is based on a misapprehension, the traditional image of the constable de Bourbon has taken on a historical reality of its own.

At the commencement here, it is worth giving some consideration to the importance attached to the naming of subjects of portraits and the reasons why, now as in the past, incorrect identifications can easily become entrenched. The creation of the accurate personal likeness, an aspect of the Greco-Roman culture of antiquity, returned with increasing force from the mid-fourteenth century onwards. But the use of iconographic formalisation, predominant in the depiction of individuals from the fall of Rome until at least the Black Death, did not entirely disappear. Instead, it formed part of a shifting balance between the literal and the symbolic. Pictorial catalogues of ancient kings, popes and bishops that were avowedly putative were produced alongside portraits derived from life or, in some cases, the immediate aftermath of death. For the medieval period for which visual materials are sparse, those that we have attain an iconic quality increased by recycling through media that now expand exponentially. What we cannot see, we invent or permit to be invented for us. Our visual construct of the past does not readily admit gaps.

Accurate likenesses were also conduits for the expression of hierarchy and authority. At a time when even the most eminent might sit for no more than three or four pictures, it was especially important for artists and patrons to convey as much as possible of what they perceived as meaning. Art and artifice are never far apart. Portraits use the eye and brain to trick the mind. Dabs and strokes of colour, purely abstract on close inspection, take on recognisable association as we retreat from them because of the assumptions and associations that we make. Since the assimilation of an image is an act of belief, it is a powerful vehicle for the expression and consolidation of shared values and knowledge. The artists of the early modern period were aware of the epistemology of their craft. When Giuseppe Arcimboldo, himself a highly accomplished portraitist in the literal style, painted Emperor Rudolf II as a *trompe l'oeil* fruit sculpture, he acknowledged that the function of the artist was to deceive as much as to inform and that there was, in fact, little difference between the two.[13]

When we gaze into a portrait of an historical character, we tend to imagine that we are transported closer to the past. We reinforce the constructive illusion by asserting that we can decipher and indeed move beyond the coded messages included by the artist as if we could inhabit our own perception and theirs simultaneously. But our vision is prismatic. What we see is refracted both through our own learned experience and numerous interpolations of other generations in the form of commentary, alteration or reproduction. This is not to deny the intellectual facility with which we manage our disordered imaging of the past, making distinctions and imposing definitions. But that intellectual process takes place, however fractionally, after the experience of seeing.

The two schools of Fontainebleau offer ample scope for this sort of construction and deconstruction.[14] France has twice seen deliberate efforts to destroy and disman-

---

August 2021: https://tinyurl.com/28t5afdk (accessed June 2023).

[13] Thomas DaCosta Kaufmann, *Arcimboldo: Visual Jokes, Natural History and Still Life Painting* (Chicago, IL, 2009), 91–109.

[14] The idea of Fontainebleau 'schools' and their lineaments were, after all, a nineteenth-century circumscription of the artistic products of the courts of François I and Henri II, albeit with antecedents in the comments of such early critics such Karel van Mander and Florent le Comte. For the prehistory

tle large parts of its physical cultural record and then, faithfully from the contemporary point of view, to restore and reinstate what had been disrupted or destroyed.[15] The revolution recommenced and escalated what had already been begun in the Wars of Religion, but it was unprecedented in its systematic annihilation of heritage. It was easy enough to provide an accurate replacement for the broken bronze statue of Henri IV on the Pont Neuf;[16] other losses were more difficult to replicate. Under Louis Philippe and Napoleon III, the urge to restore or reinstate what had been damaged or destroyed was complicated by an attachment to a picturesque imaginative construct evident in the works of Viollet le Duc and Felix Duban.[17] While their director, Prosper Mérimée, was keenly aware of the line which separates recreation from invention, the process he oversaw made it harder to produce a forensic evaluation of the ways in which perceptions had developed through the preceding centuries.

In the field of portraiture loss and displacement increased an inherent confusion about the identity of sitters. In part this was created by the fashion, particularly favoured in Renaissance France, for depicting sitters in disguise. The 1518 portrait of François I, attributed to Jean Clouet and arguably the finest picture of him, shows the king attired as John the Baptist attended by the lamb of God and a parrot.[18] All European schools of art had long incorporated living people into religious scenes, either as donors or as actors in events. In France as the century progressed sacred identifications were overtaken by heroic ones. The ambiguities which followed are well exemplified by the cult of Diana. By the close of the sixteenth century, it is unclear whether portrayals of the goddess reference Diane de Poitiers, Gabrielle d'Estrées, the mistress of Henri IV, or neither.[19] With the sitters for portraits, let alone those included in religious or mythic scenes often left unnamed, all too often identification rests on comparative physiognomy.

For the French kings of the late fifteenth century there are no more than two or three archetypal portraits from which we can trace lines of near contemporary and

---

of the school(s) of Fontainebleau, see Sylvie Béguin, 'L'École de Fontainebleau: Fortune Critique', in *L'École de Fontainebleau*, ed. Sylvie Béguin *et al.* (Paris, 1972), pp. xxix–xxxiv; for the role of nationalism in its early evaluation (as the importation of what were characterised as decadent, Italianate styles), see pp. xxxiv–xxxv.

[15] For iconoclasm during the Wars of Religion, see Denis Crouzet, *Les guerriers de Dieu* (2 vols, Seyssel, 1990), i. 527–63; Louis Réan, *Histoire du Vandalisme: Les Monuments Destruits de l'Art Français* (2 vols, Paris, 1959), i. 65–105; ii. 298–9 for a list of sites ransacked.

[16] For the overturning of the statues of kings, in particular, see Richard Clay, *Iconoclasm in Revolutionary Paris: The Transformation of Signs* (Oxford, 2012), 170–95. See also Réan, *Histoire du Vandalisme*, i, 187–378; ii. 303–5.

[17] The animating spirit of le Duc's work is perhaps best summarised by his famous definition of restoration: 'To restore an edifice is not to maintain it, repair it or remake it, it is to re-establish it in a complete state that may never have existed at a given moment', Eugene-Emmanuel Viollet le Duc, *The Foundations of Architecture: Selections from the Dictionnaire Raisonné*, ed. Berry Bergdoll (New York, 1990), 195. For Viollet le Duc's restorations, see Martin Bressani, *Architecture and the Historical Imagination: Eugène-Emmanuel Viollet-le-Duc 1814–1879* (Aldershot, 2014). For Felix Duban's efforts to conceive a likely decorative scheme for the ceilings of the chateau of Blois, see Sylvanie Allais, 'Les Plafonds peints de Félix Duban', *Les Amis Du Château et des Musées de Blois*, xxxiii (2002), 7–14. For a brief discussion of the nineteenth-century restorations of Fontainebleau itself and the attending controversy, see Boris Lossky, 'La Restauration de la Galerie de François Ier au XIXe Siecle', in *L'Art de Fontainebleau*, ed. André Chastel (Paris, 1975), 29–30.

[18] Jean Clouet, *Portrait de François Ier en saint Jean Baptiste*, 1518, oil on wood panel, Musée de Louvre, Paris.

[19] Françoise Bardon, *Diane de Poitiers et le Mythe de Diane* (Paris, 1963).

later copies. For François I the numbers are greater but still in single figures.[20] But when it comes to François's overmighty subject, Charles, duc de Bourbon, the material is slender indeed. In 1834, the year after the appointment of Mérimée as Director of Historic Monuments, Louis Philippe commissioned a portrait of the constable for the historical museum at Versailles. The resulting work by Bernard Gaillot configured Bourbon for the romantic age, full length in armour looking upward as if searching for his destiny.[21] But when it came to his subject's physical features, Gaillot aspired to what he understood as historical veracity; his design for Bourbon's face was closely based on the archetypal portrait created by Thomas de Leu in an engraving which appeared in about 1600 and which had always been accepted as a true likeness.[22] Leu followed the convention of accompanying his portrait with an instructive verse encapsulating the subject's character;[23] Bourbon had been a French hero, the terror of the earth and if his fortune had not been cut short by death, he would have been master of the world. The portrait had to do justice to this profile. Bourbon is shown in armour, brooding and severe; he is the anti-hero *par excellence*, magnificent but doomed by his own ambition. This image became the template for a long series of later portrayals in the heroic mode, of which the painting by Gaillot may be considered the consummate expression. But Leu's engraving was not directly based on a recorded lifetime image of Bourbon, and that creates uncertainty. The span of three quarters of a century between Bourbon's death and the production of the engraving was long enough for corruption to creep into the iconography. In fact, there are reasons to believe that Leu's image was derived not from a portrait of Bourbon but from the anonymous panel, which is likely to represent his contemporary Richard de la Pole, nominally duke of Suffolk and presumptive Yorkist heir to the throne of England, painted during the last years of his continental exile shortly before his death at the battle of Pavia, the engagement which also marked the apogee for the rebel constable. We will see later how Leu may have been influenced by portraits that were already circulating in the mid-sixteenth century and most particularly by a picture presented by the Guises to the cardinal and author Paolo Giovio to be displayed in his *museo* on Lake Como.[24] While that picture, the original of which is now lost, purported to represent Bourbon, there are grounds for associating it with de la Pole and placing it at the start of a long repeating pattern of mistaken identity. But in attempting to identify de la Pole as the subject of first instance in this sequence of portraits, it is an essential preparatory step to demonstrate that despite longstanding tradition Charles III, duc de Bourbon, cannot have been the original sitter.

At Chenonceau, during her long political pre-eminence, Catherine de Medici accumulated a large portfolio of crayon portrait studies.[25] Her collection included notables of both sexes from every corner of France and stretched back into the early years of the reign of her father-in-law. It was almost exclusively the work of

---

[20] For portraits of François, see Cécile Scailliérez, *François Ier par Clouet* (Paris, 1996).
[21] Appendix, no. 13.
[22] Appendix, no. 16.
[23] '*Homme soubs qui trembloit iadis la terre e l'onde, De cet Héros françois fut la proye e l'honneur: Et sans la dure Mort qui borna son bonheur Le Monde estoit a luy, ayant la chef du monde.*'
[24] For the contents of Giovio's *Museo*, see L.S. Klinger, 'The Portrait Collection of Paolo Giovio' (2 vols, PhD thesis, Princeton University, 1991).
[25] Alexandra Zvereva's monumental *Portraits dessinés de la Cour des Valois: Les Clouet de Catherine de Medici* (Paris, 2011) traces at 117–94 the history of this collection, from its origins to its dispersal after Catherine's death.

the pre-eminent court painters Jean Clouet and his son François.[26] These artists, originally from the Netherlands, brought accurate personal portraiture to France just as Holbein did to England. The quality of these sketches is remarkable. And Catherine, the widow of a king who was almost as ardent in the patronage of the arts as his father had been, fits quite comfortably into the tradition of great royal collectors of the *haute époque*. Yet, as Alexandra Zvereva's authoritative study has shown, the principle behind this collection was not a simple admiration for the skills of 'Les Clouet'; Catherine wanted to be able to recognise the principal subjects of the kingdom, both those of the present and those of the recent generation,[27] and she wanted her sons to acquire that knowledge as they prepared for their political roles as adults. In part, her collation of earlier works by the elder Clouet may have been prompted by the disjuncture and interruption to the production of court portraits caused by King François's captivity in Madrid after Pavia. While the purpose was instructional, this picture cabinet was no mirror for princes. The emphasis was on identification rather than judgment; it was portraiture made *politique*. Bourbon's treason should not in itself have excluded him from the queen's inventory.

In 1889 the duc d'Aumale purchased Catherine's collection from the earl of Carlisle and installed it at Chantilly. Henri Bouchot, conservator at the *Bibliothèque*, who had seen the collection at Castle Howard and advised Aumale to buy it, compiled a manuscript catalogue. Cautious and scrupulous, Bouchot was nevertheless caught up in a circular logic framed by the wish to find the images of all the most prominent nobility and the fact that an idea of Bourbon's appearance had been entrenched in the popular imagination. He identified an uninscribed crayon drawing of about 1520, number seventeen in his own list, as Bourbon. By 1910 other cataloguers already deemed this tendentious, and most recently Zvereva has confirmed that it is not a portrait of Bourbon.[28] But Bouchot's influence prevails. His portrait seventeen still appears on Wikimedia Commons as a reliable image of the constable.[29]

Fortunately, there is one known titled lifetime portrait of the constable; this is in the Montmor manuscript preserved at Aix en Provence in the Bibliothèque Mejanes.[30] It is not a recent discovery; it was used as long ago as 1911 as the frontispiece to Christopher Hare's biography.[31] Styled 'Monsieur de Bourbon' the drawing is part of an album datable to 1525–6 copied from an original executed by Clouet about ten years earlier. The drawing also bears an enigmatic comment *plus grys*

---

[26] Studies of the Clouets and their work are very numerous. Zvereva's publications on their sketches, however, remain unsurpassed: *Portraits dessinés de la Cour des Valois* and her earlier catalogue *Les Clouet de Catherine de Médicis: chefs-d'oeuvre graphiques du Musée Condé* (Paris, 2002). For a broader consideration of their sketches alongside their painted work and influence, see Etienne Jollet, *Jean et François Clouet* (Paris, 1997).

[27] Zvereva, *Portraits dessinés de la Cour des Valois*, 164.

[28] Ibid., 184–7, 224.

[29] '*Clouet supposé connétable bourbon*', Wikimedia Commons, 20 July 2018: https://tinyurl.com/de9h-kt3d (accessed June 2023).

[30] Figure 5; Appendix, no. 20. According to Vasari, in his life of Baldassarre Peruzzi, there was also a portrait made immediately after Charles de Bourbon's death: during the sack of Rome, the constable's Spanish soldiers, so enamoured of their deceased leader, coerced the hapless artist into creating a portrait based on de Bourbon's corpse. According to a note in the 1879 edition of Vasari's *Vite*, there is a record of a debt incurred to pay his ransom that offers some corroboration of the story. Sadly, the image, if it did exist, has been lost: Giorgio Vasari, *Le vite de'più eccellenti pittori, scultori ed architettori scritte*, ed. Gaetano Milanesi (9 vols, Florence, 1878–85), iv. 601.

[31] Christopher Hare, *Charles de Bourbon, High Constable of France* (1911), frontispiece.

Figure 5   Aix en Provence, Bibliothèque Méjanes
MS 442 (Rés. Ms 20), f. 17.

que vieux one of a series of epigrams which credible sources from the seventeenth century tell us were inscribed by or at the instruction of King François. Assuming that this story is true, what did he mean? When the copy was made, during the king's captivity after Pavia, Bourbon was still alive. But the epigrams were added sometime after François's return to France, probably after the sack of Rome. So, the reference to his age may well refer to his early death. Just conceivably, *grys* might be a play on the use of a grisaille technique in the picture. But it is most probable that the king was saying that premature grey hair, just like premature death, was one of Bourbon's distinguishing characteristics. This tradition probably reached Leu whose print suggests that both his hair and beard were streaked with grey.

Leu may never have seen the Montmor manuscript. For, grey hair aside, he based his image on an entirely different tradition. By the end of the sixteenth century oil paintings and sketches believed to be of Bourbon and showing him older and in

Figure 6   Anon., *Portrait d'homme tourné de profil à gauche, portant un chaperon à résille*, BNF.

profile existed in several versions. They showed a man, purported to be the constable, not in armour but in a costume of high fashion which might date from the late 1520s or early 1530s.[32] An example of this image later passed into the collection of François Roger Gaignières. Best known in England for his studies of medieval monuments, the great Louis XIV antiquary also had an important collection of paintings. The appropriation of Gaignières' property by the crown and the secretive and illicit

---

[32] Appendix, nos 2–5, 21–5.

Figure 7   École Française, *Monsieur de Bourbon*, c. 1590, Musée Condé, Chantilly.

dispersal which followed his death makes the task of reconstruction very difficult.[33] We are dependent on a scattering of pictures with recorded provenance and copies which he had made from the originals in his cabinet. One such copy was a portrait purporting to represent the constable, executed in a style imitative of and perhaps preparatory to an engraving, titled in error Charles II and with the printer's note '*Original dans le cabinet de M. de Gaignières*'.[34]

We have no way of identifying the original model used by Gaignières, but there are related antecedents traceable back into the sixteenth century. The printed image taken from the portrait owned by Paolo Giovio first appeared in Petrus Perna's 1575 edition of the *Elogia*.[35] While the original painting owned by Giovio is lost, one of the small-scale portraits of Bourbon made for the Emperor Ferdinand II's collection

---

[33] For Gaignieres's biography, see Roman d'Amat, 'Gaignieres (François-Roger de)', *Dictionnaire de Biographie Française*, ed. Marcel Prevost *et al.* (22 vols, Paris, 1929–2020), v. 62–3.
[34] Appendix, no. 9.
[35] Paolo Giovio, *Elogia virorum bellica virtute illustrium veris imaginibus supposita quae apud Musaeum spectantur* (Basel, 1575), 281. The *Elogia* had first been printed in Florence in 1551, but without images.

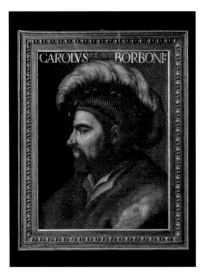

Figure 8 Anon., *Ritratto di Carlo di Borbone*, ante 1568, Uffizi Gallery, Florence.

at Schloss Ambras may be a copy.[36] It suggests that the portrait acquired by Giovio in 1549 was already a rather debased version of the original panel, though retaining some of the softness in the facial features of the sitter. Numerous versions of this portrait exist painted in oils. The best known, in the *Galerie des Illustres* at the Chateau de Beauregard, a group of 327 historical and political portraits commissioned by Paul Ardier between 1617 and 1638, may relate quite closely to the tradition derived from Giovio's original.[37] Other versions of this image in crayon, found in major collections, principally but not exclusively in France, introduce a variant physiognomy, sharpening the facial features which purported to represent those of the constable.[38] An early and interesting example was incorporated into the collection of the nineteenth-century architect and bibliophile Hyppolyte Destailleur.[39] This picture is titled twice in the same hand: 'Monsieur de Bourbon' and 'Charles de Bourbon Connetable de France'. It has been dated to the 1560s, but the palaeography suggests the possibility of a later date, perhaps as late as 1580.

What is now clear is that the oil on panel under consideration in this essay is the earliest of this closely related series extant and that it may in fact be the archetype for the entire group. Notably, it stands apart from all the drawings and other oils in that it shows the sitter's hands, so that all of the rest are probably truncated head and shoulders copies from an earlier work. Only the Gaignières print shows the complete figure as it appears in the painting from Tong Hall.[40] There are also differences which discount the possibility that the print was made from this very painting. Gaignières's painting, the whereabouts of which are unknown, must have come from a separate stem of the same family of pictures. Dr Daniel Miles of the Oxford

[36] Appendix, nos 3, 4. A further probable copy, albeit a much later one is Appendix, no. 2.
[37] Appendix, no. 8.
[38] Appendix, nos 21–5.
[39] Figure 7; Appendix, no. 21.
[40] Figure 1; Appendix, no. 1.

Dendrochronological Laboratory has analysed the Tong Hall panel and, taking a last ring date of 1508 and allowing for the presence of some sapwood, found a felling date for the timber not earlier than 1516.[41] The limitations of a *terminus a quo* are manifest. But it is fair to say that this painting could quite plausibly have been executed between 1523, the year of the planned invasion of England in de la Pole's interest, and 1527 when Bourbon perished at Rome.

The picture was preserved at Tong Hall in Yorkshire in the hands of the Tempest family from which it passed by marriage to the Viscounts Mountgarret to whom it belonged until that collection was dispersed on the art market a few years ago. The Tempests and the Mountgarrets were benefactors of the Cartwright Gallery in Bradford and this painting was loaned to the gallery for an exhibition of historical paintings in 1943.[42] Family tradition identified it as Philip the Fair, king of Castile. It was through the sharp eyes and excellent memory of Dr Hunter that, while the picture was at Christies, the association between this painting and the Bourbon portraits was made apparent. The Tempests are an ancient family, well recorded from the fourteenth century, but there is no certain evidence as to when this painting came into their hands.

By comparison, the seventeenth century painting at Beauregard is a clumsy copy. Even so, its context adds to our insight. The purpose of Ardier's gallery was designed to provide a visual *polychronicon* and a basis for moral instruction. Its spiritual antecedent was as much Hartmann Schedel's *Weltchronik* as it was Catherine de Medici's collection of Clouets. On stylistic grounds the great part of Ardier's gallery may be attributed to one or two unnamed artists working from copies held in similar historical collections, formed by Henri IV, Sully's brother Philippe de Bethune and a little later by Cardinal Richelieu.[43] These galleries set out their stalls to be comprehensive and encyclopaedic. There was no great figure that could not be portrayed, no portrait that could not be named. The epic tragedy of Bourbon's treason and dramatic death at Rome meant that no collection of historic figures could be complete without him – that is why we find copies of this image, not just at Beauregard and Schloss Ambras but at the Chateau d'Eu and at the castle of the nobleman and author Roger de Bussy Rabutin.

This was an environment in which there was a temptation to mistaken identification, and it was in this milieu that Thomas de Leu made his engraving at the end of the sixteenth century, creating what would become the definitive image of Bourbon. Francis Haskell showed years ago how the artists of this time were prepared to stretch the materials available to them to create the historical impression they wanted.[44] Print makers, in particular, freely transposed the heads of famous people to unrelated bodies in order to create the effect they desired. From the corpus of work available to him Leu distilled the image of Bourbon that served his purpose, turning the subject to the left, dressing him for battle, changing the letter for a sword.

---

[41] Oxford Dendrochronology Laboratory Report 2013/15.
[42] Bradford Art Galleries and Museums, *Exhibition of Historical Portraits from Tong Hall* (Bradford, 1943), no. 62.
[43] For Richelieu's gallery, see Friederich Polleross, 'La Galerie de portraits entre architecture et littérature: essai de typologie', in *Les Grands Galeries Européennes XVIIe–XIXe Siècles*, ed. Claire Constans and Mathieu de Vinha (Paris, 2010), 67–90, at 76.
[44] Francis Haskell, *History and its Images* (New Haven, CT, 1993), 26–68; see also Polleross, 'La Galerie de portraits', 67–90.

Figure 9   BL, Add. MS 17385, ff. 25v–26.

Taken as a whole, what we see here are the staging posts in the creation of a myth. The complexity is such and the evidence for provenance and authorship so thin that it is impossible to define the relationship between the copies of this portrait fully and accurately. For every version that we know of, there must be several that have been lost or which have yet to be recorded. There is a hierarchy in this iconography, a family tree that we can discern but not clearly define, one within which variant forms we see hint at separate lineages. The discovery of a version of this image so much earlier than the others, very possibly a prototype created in the sitter's lifetime, simplifies the task but also raises radical questions. A detailed comparison between the oil painting from Tong Hall and the copied Clouet from the Bibliothèque Mejanes largely discounts the possibility that the portrait tradition still conventionally identified with the Constable de Bourbon actually derived from his likeness at all.

The established view, that these are separate images of the same man, does not stand up to close analysis. Bourbon, as depicted by Clouet, has a pronounced chin and eyes set well back with rather swollen bags over the sockets. Assuming that the Clouet copyist was accurate, Bourbon's nose was small with no obvious bridge, almost *le nez retroussé*. By contrast the painting depicts a man whose nose is quite long and protruding with quite a distinct bridge. Approximately one year after Bourbon's death at Rome, Nicolas de Martin and Laurent Pillard presented a eulogis-

Figure 10 Anon., medal depicting Renée de Bourbon and Antoine de Lorraine, 1520–9, British Museum, London © The Trustees of the British Museum.

tic memoir to his sister Renée, duchess of Lorraine.[45] Denis Crouzet, who included a lengthy discussion of this text in his biography of Bourbon, describes a work in which realism coexists with romance and a sense of the sacred, setting it squarely in the context of the early Renaissance.[46] The same is true of the drawings created for it (Figure 9). They cannot be construed as realistic portraits, but they are not the schematic representations typical of medieval art either. As with the hammered coins produced at about this time, we can discern an emerging attempt to produce a personal likeness. That is significant because the manuscript was produced for the personal contemplation of Duchess Renée. She certainly had a very clear memory of her brother's appearance. The images of Bourbon seen here bear no relation to the panel portrait or its descendants.[47] In fact, the titled drawing of the constable's reception on the Fortunate Isle, shows a face very comparable to that seen on the portrait medal of Renée cast at about this time (figure 10); something like *le nez retroussé* is visible in both. Equally, the drawing depicts Bourbon with hair down the length of the nape of his neck, whereas the sitter in the panel has his hair cut short. Even more telling than the length of the hair seen in the oil painting is its colour. A striking feature is the sitter's fine head of reddish-brown hair visible outside the headdress. There is not a shred of grey in it. If the inscription '*plus grys que vieux*' on the copy taken from Clouet does refer to the fact that Bourbon was prematurely grey, the author of the painting did not reflect that. The most plausible reason for the discrepancy is that the works record different sitters.

This is confirmed when the comparison is extended to the crayon drawing from the collection of Hippolyte Destailleur. The artist in this case seems to have been

---

[45] BL, Add. MS 17385.
[46] Laurent Pillard (Pilladius) (1503–71), canon of St Dié, was the author and Nicolas Martin, another of the canons, wrote the dedicatory epistle, see Denis Crouzet, *Charles de Bourbon, connétable de France* (Paris, 2003), 26–7.
[47] The portraits occupy double pages, see BL, Add. MS 17385, ff. 25v–26, 49v–50.

aware of the tradition that Bourbon was grey.[48] The picture demonstrates great care and skill in portraying the hair and beard as heavily peppered. There are other discrepancies too. The chin and beard in the Destailleur drawing protrude rather more than in the painting. There are also two birthmarks evidently displayed on the sitter's cheek. These are not visible in the painting. But similar marks are detectable, in slightly different positions on the Montmor manuscript. These features are replicated in the other drawings related to Destailleur. On the other hand, Gaignières's eighteenth-century print, which as we have seen came from a different stem of the same family of pictures, repeated and further accentuated the protrusion of the chin and beard, adding severity to the sitter's expression, but did not reflect any greying of the hair or show the birthmarks. I think there is enough evidence to suggest that there was a process of modification by which a portrait incorrectly believed to be Bourbon was intentionally but innocently changed to eliminate inconsistencies and to take account of knowledge derived from other records.

While the portrait which provided the source for this iconography of the constable did not represent him, it is more difficult to identify the real sitter with confidence. There is one powerful factor which points towards de la Pole: both the portrait from Tong Hall and the copy of the painting owned by Gaignières both show a hat badge decorated with the white hart which most closely resembles the white hart at rest, the emblem of Richard II.[49] Just as in the case of the resting hart commissioned by Richard, duke of York, for the misericords at Ludlow there is no suggestion of a collar. Perhaps the collar was taken to represent the crown, its absence indicating that the crown had been lost. In France in the early 1520s the only man with an incentive for wearing the badge of Richard II in a portrait was Richard de la Pole, the Yorkist heir presumptive.

In a personal communication sent to me shortly after the Christies sale, Dr Hunter maintained that the sitter was indeed Bourbon and went on to say that there was no reason for Bourbon to advertise his support for a defeated and dwindling Yorkist cause when he spent most of his life fighting in northern Italy, first for the Valois then for the Hapsburgs. In his view, the stag on the hat badge has nothing to do with Richard II and is much more likely to be associated with the cults of St Hubert or St Eustace.[50] This suggestion seems all the more plausible when we remember that this conversion story was incorporated into the golden legend and that a chivalric order of St Hubert, the patron saint of hunters, was founded in 1444.[51] But the conversion story is quite specific in describing a stag not at rest but in flight from the hunt, when it turns and stands, so that the saint can see that there is a crucifix between its antlers. The presence of the cross is absolutely fundamental. That is not what is depicted on

---

[48] For Destailleur's collection, which was bought by the duke of Aumale in 1896 and to which the sketch belongs, see Dimier, *La Peinture*, 43, 45.

[49] M.V. Clarke, 'The Wilton Diptych', *The Burlington Magazine for Connoisseurs*, lviii (1931), 283–94, at 284–7; J.M. Bowers, *The Politics of Pearl: Court Poetry in the Age of Richard II* (Cambridge, 2001), 97.

[50] The lives of both St Eustace and St Hubert record conversion narratives in which a cross appears between the antlers of a stag, although Hubert was not associated with the stag vision until the fifteenth century: Judith Golden, 'Images of Instruction, Marie de Bretagne, and the Life of St Eustace as illustrated in BL. Ms. Egerton 745', in *Insights and Interpretations: Studies in Celebration of the Eighty-fifth Anniversary of the Index of Christian Art*, ed. Colum Hourihane (Princeton, NJ, 2002), 60–84. For Hubert, see 83, n. 29.

[51] Jacobus de Voragine, *Legenda Aurea*, ed. Giovanni Paolo Maggioni (2 vols, Florence, 1998), ii. 1090.

the hat badge. On the other hand, the context of the St Eustace legend certainly helps to explain the occurrence of the motif within the decorative and emblematic schemes of royalty and aristocracy.

At about the same time as Richard II adopted the insignia of the white hart Charles VI of France adopted the beast as his own principal device. Froissart gives the account of the king's dream in which a winged stag appears, allowing him to rescue a favourite falcon which had escaped during the hunt.[52] This also honoured his favourite uncle, Louis de Bourbon, whose family already employed the device. The addition of the royal connection further entrenched it in their family iconography. At the time of his rebellion or just before, Charles de Bourbon carried a closely related badge, partly to advertise his right to the estates of his late wife and his close connection to the crown. In 1515 in his role as constable, he arranged an aquatic display to celebrate the entry into Lyon of his new king, François I. A miniature of the event shows a large model of a hart, elaborately winged, moving through the water, presumably carried on the shoulders of men wading beneath, while another man stands on the back of the figure, holding a flaming sword.[53] But while this hart was sometimes portrayed at rest, submitting itself to the service of Charles VI in the forest, its defining character is that of the '*cerf vollant*'. Resting or in flight, it is always the *cerf ailé*; it is always winged. In 1559, when the young Pierre de Bourdeille was invited into the chapel at Gaeta where Bourbon was buried, he saw a banner of yellow taffeta prominently hung above the sepulchre, embroidered with flaming swords, the legend *Esperance* and several *cerfs vollants*.[54] These harts were decidedly winged. Bourdeille's guide, the castellan once a servant of the constable, explained that Bourbon frequently used this crest when outside France and that he carried a deer's hoof as a protective charm.[55] The resting hart in the Tong Hall painting, which is quite carefully drawn, does not appear to have wings. The decorative background of the escutcheon could just about be interpreted as a flawed attempt to represent them, but it is more likely to be a reference to the shell of Santiago.[56]

All of this suggests an explanation for the complex development in the portrayal of this sitter. If we find it difficult to be absolutely sure about the intention of the badge in the painting, then artists working in the sixteenth century and their connoisseur clients may have faced a similar difficulty. There are points of association which

---

[52] Jean Froissart, *The Chronicles of Froissart*, trans. John Bourchier, Lord Berners, ed. George Campbell Macaulay (1924), 282–3. See also Émile Picot, 'Note sur une tapisserie a figures symboliques conservée au musée des antiquités de Rouen', *Bulletin de la Société de l'histoire de Normandie*, xi (1910–12), 111–20. A somewhat earlier story, reported by a monk of St Denis, states that when Charles VI was hunting in the forest of Senlis in 1380, his servants captured a white hart with a collar bearing the inscription *Caesar hoc michi donavit*. From this, it was assumed that the stag had been resident in the forest since the time of the emperors, and Charles had the superannuated beast released. The encounter prompted the king to adopt the device of a winged hart (*cervum volantem*): Anon., *Chronique du religieux de Saint-Denys: contenant le règne de Charles VI, de 1380 à 1422*, ed. Louis Bellaguet (6 vols, Paris, 1839–52), i. 70–1.

[53] Wolfenbüttel, Herzog August Bibliothek, Codex Guelf. 84 extravagantes, f. 7v.

[54] Pierre de Bourdeille, Seigneur de Brantome, *Recueil des Hommes*, in *Oeuvres complètes de Pierre de Bourdeilles*, ed. Prosper Mérimée and Louis Lacour (13 vols, Paris, 1858), i. 75–382, at 329.

[55] Ibid., 330.

[56] Duke Antoine, incidentally, had a *Galerie des Cerfs* at his palace in Nancy. Painted between 1524 and 1529 by Hughes de la Faye, the series of panels compared the life of Christ with the life of a stag, terminating with the crucifixion/stag hunt; see Adolph Cavallo, *Medieval Tapestries in the Metropolitan Museum of Art* (New York, 1993), 355.

intertwine the lives of these two men, loose but real and significant, which add depth to this speculation. De la Pole spent much of his exile at Metz, where, despite the town's independent status, he depended on the protection of Charles de Bourbon's sister Renée de Bourbon Montpensier and her husband Antoine, duc de Lorraine.[57] In 1521, King François plotted a Yorkist coup on behalf of de la Pole, reviving a plan first laid by Louis XII seven years before and intended to deprive the emperor of his English alliance,[58] and Bourbon participated personally in a Netherlands campaign designed to pave the way for an invasion of England in the interests of both the Scottish regent James Stuart, duke of Albany, and de la Pole.[59] In February 1521, as these manoeuvres gathered momentum, Cardinal Wolsey's spies reported that de la Pole had left Metz and had been seen 'with his usual train', accompanied by Duke Antoine's treasurer.[60] This would not be enough to encourage Bourbon to wear the badge of Richard II; for him, de la Pole's claim to the English throne was a familiar but peripheral feature of the diplomatic landscape. But it would have made the clearest sense for de la Pole himself to wear the emblem which both spoke of his own royal ancestry and suggested a flattering association with the powerful military ally whose family bore a closely related device. The interconnection between the two lives reached its conclusion in de la Pole's death at the hands of troops commanded by his former ally at Pavia.[61] The pathos may not have been lost on the constable. It is said that he arranged for de la Pole's interment in a splendid tomb in the Basilica

---

[57] De la Pole was a burgess of Metz by February 1515: *Letters and Papers*, ii. no. 105. And although his relationship with the king of France gave his neighbours cause for nervousness, he was apparently something of a socialite, entertaining the principal persons of the town with daily banquets: *ibid.*, ii. no. 2081. Metz was the focus of espionage efforts against de la Pole; the musician and scribe, Peter Alamire and the musician Hans Nagel, were dispatched there to insinuate themselves into his household, and it was in the vicinity of Metz that individuals, whose names were given as Captain Thibianville and Captain John Russell, proposed, in exchange for substantial emolument, to murder the pretender while he coursed hares. The plan was, apparently, never approved, although in February 1516 a report circulated that an Englishman captured in Champagne had been sent to assassinate de la Pole: *ibid.*, ii. nos 1163, 1581. For Duke Antoine and the history of his duchies, see William Monter, *A Bewitched Duchy: Lorraine and its Dukes 1477–1736* (Geneva, 2007), 38–49.

[58] Reports of de la Pole's possible departure reached England in July 1521: *Letters and Papers*, iii. no. 1403. The plan took on a more menacing aspect on 23 June 1522, when François I sent a proposal to the duke of Holstein that de la Pole be sent to England via the ports of that dukedom; he even offered a marriage between de la Pole and the duke's daughter. A similar plan was still, apparently, underway in August of that year, when the Hanse merchant, Perpoynte de Vauntter, confided that de la Pole was preparing for an invasion of England with the help of the king of Denmark: *ibid.*, iii. no. 2340. Louis XII's original plan had germinated in June 1512, when Venetian ambassadors reported that he had recognised de la Pole's claims (*ibid.*, i. no. 1223), and rumours of the alleged material support afforded by Louis or François for these claims, or of the pretender's imminent departure to either Scotland or England in support of the duke of Albany recurred almost right up until de la Pole's death – the panic peaked twice in 1515 and in the early 1520s. As late as 5 September 1524, Sir William Sandys, treasurer of Calais, corresponded with Cardinal Wolsey to report a rumour that François I would give de la Pole 40,000 men for the invasion of England 'within a few days' (*ibid.*, iv. no. 631), but by this point Wolsey was justifiably sceptical of such reports: in a letter to Thomas Howard, 3rd duke of Surrey, undated but probably sent in late 1523, he opined that François had quite enough trouble to occupy him in Italy, and that reports of substantial commitments to de la Pole's cause were almost certainly fanciful: *ibid.*, iii. no. 3447.

[59] *Ibid.*, iii. nos. 1456, 1557, 1581, 1631, 1651, 1662, 1727, 1748, 1817.

[60] *Ibid.*, no. 2035.

[61] Initial reports on the defeat at Pavia were garbled, with at least one stating that de la Pole had been captured rather than killed, but the reality swiftly became apparent: *ibid.*, iv. nos. 1131, 1175.

del Ciel d'Oro, burial place of St Augustine.[62] If that is true, then it is surely possible that he also kept some form of portrait as a keepsake of his fallen adversary. No other Frenchman had a better reason for doing so. A memento of this sort could explain how later generations soon transposed the image of one man for the other.

At the same time, we cannot discount the possibility that there were personal portraits among the items of de la Pole's property which remained in Metz following his death in Italy. Judging by the printed and painted versions derived from it, the lost painting displayed in Paolo Giovio's gallery as a likeness of Bourbon was more distantly related to the early panel than the example owned by Gaignières.[63] But it is distinguished by its early date and by the likelihood that it originated from Metz. In July 1548, Giovio reported to Girolamo Dandini with some excitement that he had acquired portraits of the duc de Guise and Charles III, duc de Bourbon. These had been received from 'the Cardinal de Guise'.[64] This was Jean de Lorraine, who was also bishop of Metz.

What we know of de la Pole's tastes and conduct suggests that he may well have commissioned fine portraits of himself. On a widening in the river which circumscribed Metz he constructed a fortified residence in the early Renaissance style. Funded by his aunt, Margaret, duchess of Burgundy, the palace of Haut Pierre was designed to express the regal pretensions of its occupant. It was built on the site of the abbey of St Symphorien which had been demolished when the French besieged Metz in 1444, so that de la Pole was able to secure a lease from the cathedral chapter. He had spent some time at the court of Ladislaus II of Bohemia, heir to the courtly magnificence of Matthias Corvinus and once he had settled at St Symphorien he made his house a magnet for poets, goldsmiths, racehorse fanciers and landsknechts aspiring to a lucrative mission.[65] He was an adventurer and a *condottiere*. De la Pole's principal usefulness to his patrons was his ability to recruit Swiss mercenaries and it was this capacity that fuelled his hope that he might one day seize an opportunity to reclaim his English status. He was the kind of man who would have expressed his ambition in his dress. His most famous guest was Peter Alamire, a spy for Henry VIII who turned his coat to serve de la Pole. Alamire was also a highly accomplished illuminator of musical manuscripts who adorned his pages with vivid and realistic images which often included portraits of his patrons.[66] Metz itself, though better known for its glass painters than its portraitists, most especially for the atelier of Valentin Bousch, was just the kind of entrepot that would have produced paintings which blended influences from north and south of the Alps, east and west of the Rhine.

The association between this series of portraits and the duchy of Lorraine is strengthened by the medal referred to above (figure 10), which depicts Renée to one

---

[62] According to Joseph Addison, *Remarks on Several Parts of Italy* (1761), 24–5, who also transcribed the epitaph erected in 1582 by de la Pole's nearest surviving blood relative Charles Parker, titular bishop of Man. Addison also asseverated that Bourbon 'though an enemy, assisted at his funeral in mourning'.

[63] Appendix, no. 9.

[64] Paolo Giovio, *Lettere*, in *Pauli Iovii Opera* (8 vols, Rome, 1956–72), i. 126.

[65] Hampton, 'The White Rose', 525, 532.

[66] Alamire was recruited in October 1515 and was due to depart for Metz by December. However, by April 1516, Thomas Spinelly was reporting his mistrust of Alamire to Henry VIII, and in a report from Cuthbert Tunstal, dated September 1517, Thomas Stanley, illegitimate son of William Stanley (Henry VII's steward), was said to have referred to Alamire as de la Pole's spy: *Letters and Papers*, ii. nos 981, 1339, 1822.

side and her husband Duke Antoine to the other, for the obverse depicts the latter using a strikingly similar design to that of the Tong Hall portrait. The medal was cast at Nancy at about the same time as the panel sold at Christies was painted, most likely a few years earlier. It is sophisticated, Italianate in style and execution. While Duchess Renée is portrayed with striking realism, the design of the obverse, which displays her husband, bears an unmistakable relation to the series of portraits which came to be identified as Duke Antoine's brother-in-law Charles de Bourbon. He is shown in profile, bust length, his hat and clothing configured in a manner closely related to those found in the panel portrait sold at Christies and its derivatives. The cap badge is given particular emphasis, clearly stamped with a capital A for Antoine. This stylish medal has been attributed to Florentin Olriet, the master of the mint at Nancy.[67] The portraiture seen on the coinage produced for Duke Antoine is by contrast with this medal typically late medieval. But Olriet, of whom little else is known, certainly had Italian origins and probably maintained contacts there. In Italy it was quite common for masters of the mint to be accomplished medallists. As the daughter of Clara Gonzaga, Renée de Bourbon maintained contact with the court of Mantua and helped to bring its influence to Nancy.[68] This medal survives in considerable numbers, so it must have circulated quite widely.[69] It helps to place the panel portrait in Lorraine by showing that the model used was current there at the time it was painted. But the fact that this medal carried a portrait of Duke Antoine so similar to the panel portrait on one side and Renée the constable's sister on the other, also points towards a social and artistic context in which confusion over identity appears as a credible possibility.

So, in 1549 when Giovio, who trawled far and wide for what he regarded as reliable portraits of notable men, set out to find a portrait of Bourbon, the cardinal bishop of Metz seemed like a sensible person to ask. But most of those who had known Bourbon personally were dead – Duke Antoine had died in 1544, and the constable's sister had predeceased him by some five years. While de la Pole was not entirely forgotten (Montaigne would refer to the fate of his family in his essays), the symbolism of his association with the badge of Richard II can no longer have been obvious.[70] By contrast, the *cerf ailé* had become so inextricably associated with the historical reputation of the constable that the French crown, which had used it quite

---

[67] The medal has been variously attributed: in addition to Olriet, Jacques Gauvain (a Lyonnaise engraver) and Regnault Danet (a Parisian goldsmith and jeweller) have been proposed as possible creators. For a summary of these, see J.G. Pollard, *Renaissance Medals* (Oxford, 2007), 611. For the attribution to Olriet, based on his work as a moneyer for the dukes of Lorraine, see Henri Lepage, 'Notes et Documents sur les Graveurs de Monnaies et Médailles', *Mémoires de la Société d'archéologie Lorraine*, iii (1875), 7–110, at 30–1, 44. The attributions to Gauvain are based on a comparison with self-portrait medals: Jean-Baptiste Giard, *The Currency of Fame*, ed. Stephen Scher (1994), 313; Natalis Rondot, *Jacques Gauvain, orfèvre, graveur et mèdailleur à Lyon* (Lyon, 1887), 29–30 and plate; Fernand Mazerolle, *Les Médailleurs Français* (2 vols, France, 1902–4), i, pp. xvii–xxi. The attribution to Danet is likewise based on a comparison with his known work: Mark Jones, *A Catalogue of French Portrait Medals in the British Museum* (2 vols, 1982–4), i. 51–2.

[68] Julia Cartwright, *Christina of Denmark, Duchess of Milan and Lorraine, 1522–1590* (New York, 1913), 259–60.

[69] For a list of the surviving examples of this medal, Jones, *Catalogue of the French Medals*, i. 53, no. 29. A lead matrix for this medal also survives at the National Museum of Art in Washington, DC, see Pollard, *Renaissance Medals*, ii. no. 611.

[70] Michel de Montaigne, *The Essayes of Michael Lord of Montaigne*, trans. John Florio (2 vols, 1928), i. 41.

regularly before 1525 completely abandoned it since it was emblematic of Bourbon's treason.[71] It is therefore entirely possible that by 1549 those around the cardinal de Lorraine in Nancy and Metz had access to an early version of the panel portrait considered here and, incorrectly, took the presence of the white hart as certain evidence that Bourbon was the sitter, discounting the possibility that the beast advertised the Plantagenet ancestry. There is one indication of an uncomfortable sense that the hart depicted in the sitter's cap badge was not shown in the form usually associated with Bourbon: later editions of Giovio's work incorporated an image of a crest depicting a hart at rest which is uncannily like that seen in the devices of Richard II but for the addition of prominent wings.[72] These may have been an afterthought, intended to iron out a perceived discrepancy. By the mid-1560s, when the first of the crayon versions of the portrait titled with Bourbon's name was probably made, the last of the generation that had known Bourbon personally and would instantly have recognised his likeness was dying out: Diane de Poitiers, whose father had connived in Bourbon's rebellion, died in 1566 and Anne, duke de Montmorency, who had fought at Pavia, died a year later.

So, having prefaced this subject by expressing a personal view about the evanescent and personal nature of historical perception, I must now turn turtle by imbuing this image with a subjective imaginative construct. If the white hart is the symbolic key to the identity and political significance of the man portrayed here, it can be argued that there are other features of this unusual composition which increase the likelihood that the original sitter was indeed de la Pole. The first point to be made is that this painting does not slot neatly into the traditions of the French school. It is not by Jean Perreal.[73] Although the hands may be compared with those in Jean Clouet's portrait of François I's librarian Guillaume Bude, it is certainly not by him or even a close follower.[74] The positioning of the sitter in full profile, reminiscent of a medal portrait, led Alexandra Zvereva to suggest a transalpine origin.[75] It is very unlikely that a Baltic oak panel would have been used in Italy, leaving us with the possibility that it is a very early northern copy from an Italian original or that it was executed by an Italian working north of the Alps. The sitter's elaborate costume is unusual. With ribbon ties and with the hat badge supported on a cushioned extension of a day cap embellished with gold thread and seed pearls, it is at the cutting edge of fashion in a way which is quite flamboyant by standards of the French court portraiture

---

[71] Luc Duerloo and Stephen Thiry, *Heraldic Hierarchies: Identity, Status and State Intervention in Early Modern Heraldry* (Leuven, 2021), 195–204.

[72] This first appears in Paulo Giovio, *Diologo dell'Imprese militari et amorose* (Lyon, 1559), 11, illustrating Giovio's remark that he had seen the constable's insignia at the battle of Agnadello in 1509. Giovio does not describe the emblem, except to say that it depicted a winged hart (*cervo con l'ali*) and to discuss its symbolism. The engraving did not appear in the first edition (Rome, 1555), 10. The same image is reproduced in Louis Bourdery and Émile Lachenaud, *Léonard Limosin, peintre de portraits* (Paris, 1897), 16, where it is used to illustrate a discussion of an enamel depiction of de Bourbon/de la Pole in the Tong Hall panel tradition. For the enamel, see Appendix, no. 31.

[73] For Jean Perreal, see Jules Renouvier, *Iehan de Paris, varlet de chambre et peintre ordinaire des rois Charles VIII et Louis XII* (Paris, 1861); Luisa Nieddu, 'L'art du portrait dans l'oeuvre de Jean Perréal et ses liens avec le Nord', in *Arts et Artistes du Nord à la cour de François Ier*, ed. Laure Fragnart and Isabelle Lecoq (Paris, 2017), 163–76.

[74] Jean Clouet, *Guillaume Budé, c. 1536*, oil on panel, 39.7 x 34.3 cm., Metropolitan Museum of Art, New York.

[75] Alexandra Zvereva, in discussion with the author, July 2013. See John Pope-Hennessy's discussion of profile portraits in Italian painting of the period, in *The Portrait in the Renaissance* (1963), 35–48.

at this period.[76] In some respects the style is more German, finding echoes in the more ornate costume recorded in contemporary works by Lucas Cranach and Hans Baldung Grien.[77] In terms of execution the flesh tones are very thinly laid while the background blue is more thickly applied. This is a technique associated with Holbein and, by the mid-1530s, with works attributed to Corneille de la Haye.[78] As we have already seen, these eclectic aspects of the painting fit in well with the life story and tastes of de la Pole.

More specifically, the sitter wears a collar of leopard skin. While fur collars are a feature frequently seen in portraits of this date, leopard is distinctive. It was a sign of high status associated with the cult of St John the Baptist.[79] Jean Clouet had used it in his portrait of King François as St John. Here it is shown against a blue background. The arms of a de la Pole were three leopard heads against an azure ground.[80] He holds a letter in his gloved left hand. The letter is closed so that its contents cannot be read. The indication is that it is about to be dispatched. His right hand is free, resting on the second glove, and, while his gaze is directly to the left, his index finger points outwards towards the viewer as if they are the intended recipient of the letter. Taken together with the possible reference to the arms of de la Pole and most of all with the hat badge of the resting white hart there is more than a hint of a clandestine message here.

Because the early provenance of this painting is obscure, we can only speculate about the reasons for which it was painted or the intended recipients, but it is a strange coincidence that it came into the hands of the Tempests. While Richard was still duke of Gloucester, before he became Richard III, Nicholas Tempest of Bracewell had married the daughter of his chamberlain, John Pilkington,[81] and members of the family fought for him as king at Bosworth.[82] By the 1520s, the Tempests were not

[76] The sketches by Jean and François Clouet, collected by Zvereva, may be taken as broadly indicative of contemporary courtly fashions. While the combination of decorated hat brim and badge became ubiquitous after 1530, there are fewer instances among the sketches dated earlier: Zvereva, *Portraits*, nos 28, 49, 50, 58, 59, 60, 61, 64, 68, 69. Of these, the only individual sporting a similar combination of decorated hat and coif was the veteran courtier and François's *capitaine de la porte*, Louis, Seigneur de Chandio – nos 58, 59. Ribbon ties are not in evidence in the collections assembled and published by Zvereva.

[77] See Max Friedlander and Jakob Rosenberg, *The Paintings of Lucas Cranach* (Ithaca, NY, 1978), Cat. nos 58, 323 for similar collars. The headgear recalls that of Grien's self-portrait in his St Sebastian triptych of 1507: Das Martyrium des Heiligen Sebastian, 1507, oil on panel, 121.2 x 78.6 cm (central panel), Germanisches Nationalmuseum, Nuremberg.

[78] Norbert Wolf, *Hans Holbein the Younger 1497/8–1543, the German Raphael* (Cologne, 2004), 82; A.D. de Groër, *Corneille de la Haye dit Corneille de Lyon (1500/1510–1575)* (Paris, 1996), 52, 81.

[79] The association of leopard skin with John the Baptist, present in several artistic depictions by Leonardo da Vinci, Andrea del Sarto and others, rests on an identification of the New Testament prophet with Bacchus. That identification is itself grounded in the symbolism of the vine: John 15, verses 1 and 5: 'I am the true vine, and my father is the gardener, I am the vine; you are the branches.' For this association, see S.J. Freedberg, 'A Recovered Work of Andrea del Sarto with Some Notes on a Leonardesque Connection', *The Burlington Magazine*, cxxiv:cml (1982), 281–8, at 285, 287–8, where the garment is referred to as a 'panther's skin'.

[80] Bernard Burke, *The General Armory of England, Scotland, Ireland, and Wales: Comprising a Registry of Armorial Bearings from the Earliest to the Present Time* (1884), 810.

[81] Alan Davidson, 'Tempest, Sir Richard (c.1480–1537), of Bracewell and Bowling, Yorks.', in *The History of Parliament. The House of Commons 1509–1558*, ed. S.T. Bindoff (3 vols, 1982), iii. 430–1; Eleanor Tempest, 'Tempest Pedigrees', ed. John Scheurman, *Medieval Genealogy*, [undated], i. 144: https://tinyurl.com/y9uvzhn2 (accessed June 2023).

[82] Sir Richard Tempest is reported to have joined Richard III's army with his cousin William Tempest,

really likely Yorkist recidivists, but as important figures in the political and military management of northern England, they were precisely the kind of family whose old Yorkist loyalties would have to be revived if de la Pole's adventure was to succeed.

In the winter of 1522, as the kingdom prepared for a campaign in France and a possible counter invasion from Scotland, rumours circulated of a dangerous fifth column building in the de la Pole interest. At East Dereham in Norfolk two local men had approached the watch and promised them money if they bound themselves to Richard de la Pole 'who had been kept from his rights for many years'.[83] One hundred men, they were told, had already pledged their support to the cause. If men were to be expected to fight for a new king, they would have to recognise him. It was the familiar problem of facial recognition which would later inspire Catherine de Medici's collection of Clouets, and de la Pole and his supporters had every incentive for resolving it. Unlike the impostors they had no need to fear the comparison of his image with that of a man he was impersonating.

We should not underestimate the intensity of the polemical struggle between the agents of the Tudor king and the advocates of the pretender supported by the French. John Skelton's damnation of the 'starke cowarde' the duke of Albany, commissioned in about 1524, does not dignify de la Pole with a mention by name.[84] But the import is clear. Albany's professed intent was 'to undertake our royall kinge his owne realme to forsake'. The open profession of the de la Pole claim, which as Greg Walker has noted, undermined Henry VIII through dishonour, had to be demolished in images as well as in words. After his death panoramic paintings of the battlefield of Pavia circulated in England. These were based on a Flemish cartoon and detailed de la Pole's corpse among the dead. One of the surviving examples formed part of the Ashmolean Museum's founding collection.[85]

The pretender's image can have counted for no less in life than it did in death. If, as suggested, de la Pole was seen wearing the badge of Richard II, the insult to Henry VIII was acute. His ally Albany was well known for his patronage of French artists and craftsmen some of whom he took with him to Scotland.[86] He was acquainted with Lorenzo de Medici and Leonardo da Vinci. It is not impossible that Albany took images of the prospective king with him when he campaigned in England. In fact, it stands to reason that he would have done so. It can be argued that the painting owned by the Tempests is too fine a work to be a copy used for distribution in a political campaign. At the same time, the number of later copies of this image suggests that there may have been more than one created at the time of first production. Printed polemical broadsheets were more suitable for large-scale distribution than oil paint-

---

according to the account of Thomas Stanley, earl of Derby, in BL, Harley MS 542, ff. 31–33v. The account is transcribed in William Hutton, *The Battle of Bosworth Field* (1813), 204–19.

[83] *Letters and Papers*, iii. no. 2737.

[84] Greg Walker, *John Skelton and the Politics of the 1520s* (Cambridge, 1988), 207, 210–11. Skelton's poem, *The Doughty Duke* was not his first treatment of Richard de la Pole: in 1513 or 1514, his interlude *Hick Scorner*, probably composed for performance in the household of Charles Brandon (who had taken over the de la Pole dukedom of Suffolk), depicts Richard (the titular Hick) as a pimp and coward, travelling about fruitlessly with a shipload of vices: Greg Walker, *Plays of Persuasion: Drama and Politics at the Court of Henry VIII* (Cambridge, 1991), 43–6.

[85] Anon. [Flemish], *The Siege and Battle of Pavia, 1525–30*, oil on panel, 117 x 202 cm, Ashmolean Museum, Oxford.

[86] Bryony Coombs, 'The Artistic Patronage of John Stuart, Duke of Albany, 1520–30', *Proceedings of the Society of Antiquaries of Scotland*, cxlvii (2018), 175–217.

ings. But at this date only a master such as Durer working with copper plates at the most detailed level attainable could produce a facial likeness to rival a moderately accomplished oil or drawing. But exactly how this painting came to the Tempests is likely to remain lost in the disjuncture between the written record and what remains to us in images.

In words, there is a recorded scene from Henry VIII's French campaigns that gives us one last tantalising glimpse of the face of de la Pole. In May 1524 an English emissary visited the French camp near Calais to deliver letters to Charles de Bourbon's cousin, the duc de Vendôme. As barbed remarks were thrown back and forth between the two parties, Richard de la Pole entered the tent. Vendôme presented him to the ambassador with the words 'Here is your King'.[87] We cannot be certain that the face seen by the English emissary in 1524 was the same as the one in the painting from Tong Hall. The historic accretion of myth and dubious identification presents a barrier that is difficult to overcome, but it does not exclude the real possibility that the painting represents de la Pole rather than Bourbon. Whatever the truth of his physical appearance, by 1524 the presentation of de la Pole as king was idle bombast. His fortunes were waning. His ally Albany had attempted a raid on the castle of Wark which had ended in a humiliating flight back to Scotland.[88] Bourbon, alienated by the king's determination to claim to the estates of his widow, had already defected to the emperor and acknowledged the right of Henry VIII to the French crown. Once funds arrived, he would cross the Alps to lay siege to Marseilles, pursuing an adversary weakened by defeats in Italy and the loss of its champion Bayard. The pressure on the French in the Mediterranean theatre was now so severe that the prospect of King François seeking relief by opening up a front in the north aimed at supplanting Henry VIII, appeared more remote than ever. De la Pole would shortly follow Bourbon into the Italian vortex that would prove mortal to both of them. And the defeat and captivity of François I would also create a dark moment in the development of French aristocratic portraiture which meant that no definitive visual image of either was passed to posterity.

---

[87] *Letters and Papers*, iv. 335.
[88] D.M. Head, 'Henry VIII's Scottish Policy: A Reassessment', *Scottish Historical Review*, lxi (1982), 1–24, at 8; Raymond Paterson, *My Wound is Deep: History of the Anglo Scots Wars, 1380–1560* (Edinburgh, 1997), 159. For a somewhat different take on Albany's fortunes, see Neil Murphy, *Henry VIII, the Duke of Albany and the Anglo-Scottish War of 1522–1524* (Woodbridge, 2022), 46–52.

APPENDIX: LIST OF IMAGES OF DE LA POLE/BOURBON

Paintings

1. Anon., *Richard de la Pole*, ante 1525, oil on panel, 21 x 27 cm, private collection.
2. Anon. [Italian], *Ritratto de Carlo di Borbone* [ante 1568], oil on panel 60 x 45 cm, Uffizi Gallery, Florence.
3. Anon. [French], *Bourbon Charles Herzog v., Konnetabel 1519, gestorben 1527*: GG 4872 [undated] oil on wood, 13.2 x 10.2 cm, Kunsthistorisches Museum, Vienna.[89]
4. Anon., *Bourbon Charles Herzog v., Konnetabel 1519, gestorben 1527: GG 4873* [undated] oil on wood, 13.2 x 10.3 cm, Kunsthistorisches Museum, Vienna.
5. Anon. [Italian], *Karl von Bourbon (1490–1527), Connetable von Frankreich: GG 8240* [undated], oil on canvas, 204 x 97 cm, Kunsthistorisches Museum, Vienna.
6. Anon., *Charles III duc de Bourbon* [undated] oil on wood, 178 x 91.5 cm, Chateau d'Eu.
7. Anon., *Charles de Bourbon* [undated], oil on canvas, 100 x 76 cm, Colección del Museo de Bellas Artes de València.
8. Anon., *Charles de Bourbon*, c. 1617–1638, oil on panel, Chateau de Beauregard, Cellettes.
9. Anon., *Portrait d'homme tourné de profil à gauche, portant un chaperon à résille* [undated], gouache on parchment, 28.8 x 18.5 cm, BNF.
10. Anon., *Charles III, duc de Bourbon, connétable de France*, seventeenth century, oil on panel, 59.5 x 49 cm, Chateau de Bussy Rabutin, Bussy-le-Grand.
11. Anon. [Italian?], *Charles III Duke of Bourbon (1490–1527)*, seventeenth century, oil on canvas, 64.6 x 50.5 cm [private collection; present location not known].[90]
12. Anon., *Portrait de Charles III de Bourbon, dit le connétable de France (1490–1527)*, c. 1750–1800, oil on canvas, 30 x 23 cm, Musée d'Art et Histoire, Geneva.
13. Bernard Gaillot, *Charles III, Duc de Bourbon, Dit le Conetable de Bourbon, Connetable de France*, 1835, oil on canvas, 215 x 140 cm, Chateau de Versailles.

Printed media

14. Guillaume Rouillé, *Promptuarium Iconum Insigniorum* (2 vols, Lyon, Guillaume Rouillé, 1553), ii. 228.
15. Paolo Giovio, *Elogia Virorum Bellica Virtute* (Basel, 1575), 218.
16. Thomas de Leu, *Charles duc de Bourbon*, c. 1600, ink on paper, 15.8 x 10.6 cm, Royal Collection Trust, London.
17. Léonard Gaultier, *Charles de Bourbon, Conestable de France*, [1601], ink on paper, 4.4 x 2.7 cm, Chateau de Versailles.
18. Lucas Vosterman, [*Portrait of Charles III de Bourbon*], [1622–8], ink on paper, 30.3 x 22.5 mm, British Museum, London.
19. André Thevet, *Les vrais pourtraits et vies des hommes illustres grecz, latins et payens* (Paris, 1584), 351.

---

[89] Items 3 and 4 originally came from the collections of Schloss Ambras.
[90] For its sale, see 'Old Masters Day Auction: Lot 139', Sotheby's, 7 July 2023: https://tinyurl.com/4b2up888 (accessed June 2023).

Sketches[91]

20. Aix en Provence, Bibliothèque Mejanes MS 442 (Rés. Ms 20), f. 17.[92].
21. École Française, *Monsieur de Bourbon – Recueil Béthune. Provient de Philippe de Béthune (1561–1649)*, c. 1590, pencil on paper, 28.6 x 19 cm, Musée Condé, Chantilly.
22. Anon., *Charles de Bourbon, IIIe du nom, duc de Bourbon, Connétable de France*, [undated], pastel on paper, 26 x 19 cm, Cabinet des Dessins de la Louvre, Paris.
23. Adhémar and Moulin, 'Les Portraits dessinés du XVIe siecle au Cabinet des Estampes', 185, no. 513.
24. Ibid., 189, no. 553.
25. Ibid., 331, no. 597.

Medals

26. Anon., *Medal* (no reverse), sixteenth century, cast lead, 4.1 x 2.9 cm, British Museum, London.
27. Anon., *Medal* (no reverse), sixteenth century, cast lead, 5.6 x 5.6 cm, British Museum, London.

Manuscripts

28. Wolfenbüttel, Herzog August Bibliothek, Codex Guelf. 84 extravagantes, f. 7v.
29. BL, Add. MS 17385, ff. 25v–26, 49v–50.
30. Vienna, Kunsthistorisches Museum MS GG 9691, p. 271.[93]

Enamel

31. Anon., *Portrait of Charles, comte de Montpensier, connetable de Bourbon*, [undated], enamel on copper, 21 x 16.5 cm, Legion of Honour Museum, San Francisco.

---

[91] Numerous sketches in the same tradition as the Tong Hall panel are to be found in several collections. The following list is intended to be illustrative rather than exhaustive. For a brief notice of the item in the collections of the Hermitage, in St Petersburg, see Louis Dimier, *La Peinture de Portrait en France au XVIe Siecle* (3 vols, Paris, 1924–6), iii. 65. Owing to the fact that the BNF possesses three rather similar items, the reference below is to their respective places in Adhémar and Moulin's catalogue rather than to their physical characteristics, to better distinguish them from one another.

[92] A selection of the manuscript's contents has been printed as Etienne Rouard, *François Ier chez Madame de Boisy; Notice d'un recueil de crayons ou portraits au crayon de couleur, enrici par le roi François Ier de vers et de devises inédites* (Paris, 1863). For the notice of Bourbon's portrait, see p. 26, no. 15.

[93] This is the portrait book of Leopold Beck. For more on its contents and context, see Wolfgang Neuber, 'Visual Exegesis and Social History: Hieronymus Beck von Leopoldsdorf (1525–1596) and his Strategies of Self-Aggrandisement', in *Imago Exegetica: Visual Images as Exegetical Instruments, 1400–1700*, ed. Walter Melion *et al.* (Leiden, 2014), 667–82.

IMPERIAL ECHOES: ENGLISH GASCONY AND BRITISH INDIA. A PRELIMINARY SURVEY[1]

Malcolm Vale

Is it medieval Aquitaine or modern India whose government he is studying? ... [witness] the multifarious nature of the administration; the multitude of English families engaged in the process; the interchange of products; the action and reaction of the two countries upon one another in peace and war; and the extremely delicate nature of their mutual relations.[2]

The honorand of this volume has worked and published primarily on the English nobility and gentry – female as well as male – in the later Middle Ages. But her teaching has extended widely over continental European topics, including the Hundred Years' War and Anglo-French relations in the fourteenth and fifteenth centuries. No student of that prolonged episode, or episodes, can embark on their study without taking account of the central role and position of Gascony (or, more correctly, the duchy of Aquitaine or Guyenne) in that conflict. The post-1066 continental possessions and holdings of the medieval English crown, of which Gascony was to be, with the sole exception of Calais, the longest-lasting part, have certainly attracted a very large and distinguished body of scholarship. But few who have ventured into those stormy waters, possibly for fear of total shipwreck, have sought to draw comparisons with other periods in England's – and subsequently Britain's – so-called 'imperial' past. The British intervention in, and ultimate control of, the Indian sub-continent is a case in point. Distinguished works have certainly appeared on the Norman, Angevin and Plantagenet 'empires', but few have sought to allude in any depth to later manifestations of England's (or Great Britain's) overseas interests and commitments, apparently considering that these were fundamentally and incomparably different from their medieval forbears. So this study will, inevitably, be as much an historiographical as a comparative one.

The academic study of the history of modern Empires – and in particular, the British Empire – emerged in Great Britain in the 1880s with the Cambridge professor J.R. Seeley's groundbreaking and best-selling book *The Expansion of England*.[3] It prompted the first Chichele Professor of History at Oxford, Montagu Burrows (1819–

---

[1] I am most grateful to Hannah Skoda for her constructive comments on this contribution and also to Ross McKibbin and Peter Hacker for their helpful observations.
[2] Montagu Burrows, *The History of the Family of Brocas of Beaurepaire and Roche Court* (1886), 18.
[3] (1883, 2nd revised edn, 1919).

1905), to make a broad comparison in 1886 between the 'empire' of the Angevins and Plantagenets and that of the house of Saxe-Coburg-Gotha (later Windsor).[4] Burrows did not share Seeley's belief that the creation of what he called a 'larger Britain' began only with the English colonisation of North America (Virginia) in 1606, followed by a vast expansion of British-held territories, in whole or in part, during the eighteenth and early to mid-nineteenth centuries.[5] He claimed, quite unlike Seeley, that the 'expansion of England' under the Hanoverian monarchy was largely, in effect, the 'restoration of an old position'.[6] It is the purpose of this short contribution to pursue Burrows's comparison further, while always remaining mindful of what is, and what is not, strictly comparable.

To define 'empire' is always fraught with difficulties as the term is to a large extent time-bound, carrying rather different meanings and characteristics in different historical and geographical contexts. John Le Patourel, in his work on the Norman Empire, cited a definition by John Gilissen, where the 'notion of empire' encompasses entities forming 'at least a great power within a regional context that, in this setting, possesses the other necessary qualities: sovereign state, power-concentration, complex composition, hegemonic tendency, at least regionally, larger territorial area than other states, and relatively long duration'.[7] The Angevin-Plantagenet complex certainly shared many, if not most, of these characteristics. 'Feudalisation' or the creation of 'feudal empires' could thus, Le Patourel argued, be a source of strength, not weakness, to a ruler, creating and sustaining a stronger bond between rulers and ruled.

In order to avoid misunderstandings, a brief digression is perhaps required to explain the title of this contribution. It is derived from that of a celebrated military march, 'Imperial Echoes', composed by Arnold Safroni (1873–1950) in 1913, originally as a solo piano piece, subsequently arranged for military bands in 1928 by James Ord-Hume (1864–1932). It became the signature tune of the BBC's Radio Newsreel (1940–70), recorded by the Central Band of the Royal Air Force, and that of the BBC World Service until 1988, when it was no longer deemed appropriate.[8] In 1913, the 'echoes' of empire may not yet have been a nostalgic celebration of a regime that was already passing away. The huge territorial extent of that empire was still largely unchanged and undiminished. But the beginning of the end of British hegemony in the Indian sub-continent could be said to have been furthered very soon after by the action of Brigadier-General Reginald Dyer at Amritsar in 1919, as well as by the cumulative effects of the seemingly inexorable rise of Indian nationalism represented largely by the Congress Party.[9] Dyer's brutal suppression of a demonstration in favour of the Congress party at a time of breakdown of public order in

---

[4] Burrows, *Family of Brocas*, 18–19. Burrows followed up his work on the Brocas family with an article on the significance of the Gascon rolls as a source in his 'The Publication of the Gascon Rolls by the British and French Governments, Considered as a New Element in English History', *TRHS*, vi (1892), 109–24. He argued that more attention should be paid to the history of the 'sea-separated' and 'sea-divided' areas and subjects of the medieval (and later) English crown: 114.

[5] Seeley, *The Expansion of England*, 11.

[6] Burrows, *Family of Brocas*, 115.

[7] John Le Patourel, *The Norman Empire* (Oxford, 1976), 323. My translation.

[8] See https://en.wikipedia.org/wiki/Imperial_Echoes.

[9] For a recent study, see K.A. Wagner, *Amritsar 1919. An Empire of Fear and the Making of a Massacre* (New Haven, CT and London, 2019). A further and perhaps even more significant factor in the rise of Indian disaffection from the British Raj was the experience of well over 100,000 Indian troops on the

Amritsar, using Indian (Sikh, Balochi, Rajput) and Gurkha troops, with the loss of at least 379 Indian lives and 1,500 wounded, led to outrage in both India and Britain. He was dismissed from the service, although he was not without his defenders in both Britain and India. But it could be argued that the Amritsar (or Jallianwala Bagh) massacre/punitive action fuelled a growing movement of disaffection from which the British regime in India never fully recovered.[10]

A comparison between two apparently vastly dissimilar contexts – in both time and place – might be greeted with some scepticism, but comparative history and, in particular, the comparative history of ritual, which will be a major concern of this contribution, can be as valuable for what it tells us about differences as about similarities.[11] The English regime in Gascony (1152–1453), as it had evolved by the later thirteenth century, might (perhaps surprisingly) offer scope for the exercise of cautious but potentially fruitful comparison with the British Raj in India, as it evolved after 1858, especially over the period culminating in the great Delhi durbar of 1911.[12] Montagu Burrows may not have been entirely wrong or misguided to point to similarities and analogies between them, but all generalisations about such perceived similarities must be subject to substantial qualification and strict limitation. This contribution will focus upon just two main areas of potential comparison: on the one hand, relations and interactions between the English administration and the Gascon nobility and, on the other, those between the British imperial power and the Indian princes and nobility. Apart from fundamental differences in religious allegiance – Catholic Christianity universally in Gascony, starkly contrasted with Hindu, Muslim, Sikh and other ethnic and sectarian groupings in India – there were of course also major contrasts in territorial extent and demographic size and structure.[13]

Western front in the First World War. The myth of white superiority was broken by that experience. I owe this point to Dr Peter Hacker.

[10] The aftermath and legacy of the event are discussed in Wagner, 251–66.

[11] That said, could it be argued that all 'imperial' regimes tended, sometimes in very different manners, to resort to highly ritualised forms of rule, e.g. from ancient Egypt to nineteenth-century Europe? I was prompted to pose this important question by Dr Ross McKibbin. For an excellent comparative example, see Stuart Tyson Smith, 'Colonial Gatherings: The Presentation of Inu in New Kingdom Egypt and the British Imperial Durbar: A Comparison', in *Gatherings Past and Present. Proceedings from the 2013 Archaeology of Gatherings International Conference* (Oxford, 2017), 102–12. For recent discussions of comparative history, in the context of empires and imperialism, and of the history of ritual, see S.J. Tambiah, 'A Performative Approach to Ritual', *Proceedings of the British Academy*, lxv (1979), 115–69, and Maya Jasanoff, 'How Can we Write the History of Empire?', in *What is History Now? How the Past and Present Speak to Each Other*, ed. Suzannah Lipscombe and Helen Carr (2021), 84–100; also, from a very extensive literature, John Darwin, *After Tamerlane: The Rise and Fall of Global Empires, 1400–2000* (2007), and E.J. Hobsbawm, *The Age of Empire, 1875–1914* (New York, 1987).

[12] Burrows's points were to some (albeit limited) extent taken up, but not developed at any great length, in M.W. Labarge, *Gascony. England's First Colony, 1204–1453* (1980), xi–xii: 'Although it is no longer [1980] historically fashionable to make comparisons across the centuries, Montagu Burrows ... was fascinated by the likenesses between the English administration in Aquitaine and nineteenth-century India ... [when] England experimented for the first time with the government of an overseas possession where it was essential to keep the loyalty and support of its inhabitants', and p. 235: 'The duchy [of Aquitaine] was a training-ground for administrators as well as diplomats. Separated from the centre of authority by some 500 miles and slow communications, the men in charge in the duchy had to show initiative and ability to deal with the very different conditions, customs, temperament and manners characteristic of Gascony.'

[13] Although there were fundamentally vast differences in variety and scale, the geophysical and climatic

The territorial area of the British Indian empire in 1911 was immense. It comprised 1,802,912 square miles (4,667,660 square kilometres), greater than the whole of Europe excluding Russia.[14] By comparison, English Gascony was tiny, comprising about 70,000 square miles (181,300 square kilometres) – the size of today's Syria or Cambodia – at its fullest extent.[15] In terms of population, British India in 1911 held 315,132,537 people.[16] English Gascony had an estimated population in 1316 of at least 625,000, forming one-seventh of that of the English kingdom.[17] Both India and Gascony witnessed the presence of significantly important nobilities within their boundaries. The Indian princes and nobles held no fewer than 563 'states', some no larger than an aristocratic landed estate, described as 'feudatory states', of vastly differing territorial extents. They ranged from Hyderabad (98,000 square miles/253,818 square kilometres), that is 28,000 square miles (72,519 square kilometres) larger than English Gascony in its entirety, to Pataudi (50 square miles/129.5 square kilometres).[18] The major states were Hyderabad, Baroda, Mysore, Kashmir, Jaipur, Jodhpur, Gwalior and thirty-five others in the next rank down in the hierarchy.[19] In Gascony there were just four greater lordships held by counts and fifteen by viscounts, of whom the most significant within the duchy were those of the Albret, plus a very large number of lesser fiefs, some held by those styled 'baron'.[20] But the majority were very small in area and were sometimes held on a basis of shared lordship, often with members of the same or related families (co-seigneurie). In 1323, the English crown could call for military aid against the Scots from 202 Gascon nobles, all to be paid under contract for their services.[21] The major lordships, including those held by nobles styled 'baron', were Buch (the Captaux), Caumont, Castelnau, Castillon, Curton, Durfort, Escoussan, Fossat, Lamothe, Lescun, Lesparre, Madaillan, Montaut, Montferrand, Pommiers and Sescas. All owed personal homage and oaths of fealty, sworn in person to the king's lieutenant or the seneschal of Aquitaine.

In 1911, no fewer than 335 Indian princes and nobles paid homage in person to George V as king-emperor of India; but in 1363–4 a total of 1,747 persons (of whom 652 were secular lords) had paid homage and/or fealty in Gascony to the Black Prince as representative of the sovereign power and as immediate lord of the

---

variations – between low-lying coastal areas, hilly and mountainous regions, fertile river valleys and relatively unproductive plains – found within both Gascony and India were not entirely dissimilar.

[14] See www.nationalarchives.gov.uk/first-world-war/a-global-view/Asia/India. citing the census of 1911.

[15] Estimated from the territorial area marked on the map published in *Roles Gascons, III 1290–1307*, ed. Charles Bémont (Paris, 1906).

[16] See www.nationalarchives.gov.uk/first-world-war/a-global-view/Asia/India.

[17] See Yves Renouard, 'Conjectures sur la population du duche d'Aquitaine en 1316', in his *Etudes d'Histoire Medievale* (2 vols, Paris, 1968), i. 169–70. Renouard reckoned this figure of 625,000 to represent about one twenty-seventh of the population of the French kingdom and one seventh of that of the kingdom of England.

[18] See the detailed statistics contained in J.T. Wheeler, *The History of the Imperial Assemblage at Delhi. Held on the 1st January 1877, to Celebrate the Assumption of the Title Empress of India by H.M. the Queen*, including *Historical Sketches of India and Her Princes, Past and Present* (1878), 186 (Hyderabad) and 208 (Pataudi).

[19] The figures in 1877 were as follows: Hyderabad=9 million (*ibid.*, 186); Baroda=2 million (187); Mysore=5,055,412 (188); Kashmir=1,537,000 (204); Jaipur=1,995,000 (196); Jodhpur=2 million (197); Gwalior=2,500,000 (189).

[20] Malcolm Vale, *The Origins of the Hundred Years War. The Angevin Legacy, 1250–1340* (Oxford, 1996), 84.

[21] *Ibid.*, 110.

region.[22] Of them, twenty-one were women; at Delhi in 1911 there was a single woman – Shah Jehan Begum, lady member of the (British) Order of the Star of India – performing homage in person for her state (Bhopal).[23] The three Delhi durbars all took place at one fixed location. The homage and fealty rituals in Gascony, however, were performed and received in many different places as the Black Prince travelled through his newly-created principality. In 1363–4 they took place at Bordeaux (in the cathedral of St-Andre and the archbishop's palace), Bergerac (in the castle chapel), Agen (the church of the Dominicans), Perigueux (the church of St-Front and the castle chapel), Poitiers (the cathedral of St-Pierre, the prince's palace and the church of the Franciscans), St-Maixent (the prince's hotel and the abbey), Angouleme (the castle), Saintes (the cathedral of St-Pierre), St-Jean d'Angely (the church of St-Jean-Baptiste), La Rochelle (the church of the Franciscans), Benon (the castle) and Cognac (the castle). The prince's tour of the principality began on 9 July 1363 and ended on 6 April 1364, the longest and most far-reaching ever undertaken by a king-duke or his representative since the reign of Edward I.[24]

Our knowledge of homage-taking rituals in Aquitaine is substantially increased by the unique surviving record of a tour of the duchy by Sir Ralph Basset, seneschal of Aquitaine, between 25 September and 28 October 1323.[25] Apart from the record of homages pledged to the Black Prince, this is the most detailed account of oath-taking and receiving procedures in the duchy that we possess. Basset had been appointed seneschal of Aquitaine on 11 June 1323 and was acting there from 18 September, embarking on his tour of the duchy a week later.[26] His eight months' tenure of the office was to see the onset of the most serious crisis to break out over the duchy for many years. A local incident ignited a conflagration which was to lead to the Anglo-French War of Saint-Sardos. On the night of 15–16 October a band of armed men, retained by Raymond-Bernard de Montpezat, one of the less law-abiding nobles of the Agenais, wrecked the site of a newly founded bastide at Saint-Sardos, burning down some of the buildings of the priory there and killing the French royal serjeant who was to proclaim the creation of the new settlement. They proceeded to lynch him from the stake bearing the French royal fleurs-de-lis which had been erected there, signalling and symbolising royal protection.[27] It was a profound insult to the crown of France. But Basset did not interrupt his oath-taking tour of the duchy, leaving the sub-seneschal of the Agenais to investigate it. Another noble from the Agenais, Amanieu du Fossat, had told Edward II in January 1319

---

[22] See *The Historical Record of the Imperial Visit to India, 1911* (1914), 168; and for the homages to the Black Prince, *Le Livre des Hommages d'Aquitaine*, ed. J.-P. Trabut-Cussac (Bordeaux, 1959), 70–117; also P. Capra, '*L'Apogee Politique au Temps du Prince Noir (1355–72)*', in *Bordeaux Sous les Rois d'Angleterre, III*, ed. Yves Renouard (Bordeaux, 1965), 394–6, and carte 9 (p. 381).
[23] Wheeler, *History of the Imperial Assemblage*, 190.
[24] *Le Livre des Hommages d'Aquitaine*, 70–110.
[25] TNA, C47/26/17. See Vale, *Origins of the Hundred Years War*, 234–6; Guilhem Pépin, 'The Oath-taking Circuits of the Seneschals of Gascony and their Origins: the Case Study of Ralph Basset of Drayton's Circuit (1323)', in *Anglo-Gascon Aquitaine: Problems and Perspectives*, ed. Guilhem Pépin (Woodbridge, 2017), 27–47, and map 2.2 (on p. 37). The roll, written by Eliot Gaucelme, clerk of Aubert Mege, registrar of the court of Gascony, is of seven membranes; m.1 is damaged and stained but the remainder in good condition. I intend to devote a further study to this important document.
[26] TNA, C61/35, m. 10 (11 and 20 June 1323).
[27] *The War of Saint-Sardos (1323–5). Gascon Correspondence and Diplomatic Documents*, ed. Pierre Chaplais (Camden Soc., 3rd ser., lxxxvii, 1954), introduction and pp. 2–3.

that although such progresses were essential, the frequent replacement of seneschals meant that each new appointee 'can hardly undertake the tours of his seneschalcy in one year' (something of an exaggeration) 'which he must do ... because of the oath which he must perform to the people and the people to him'. Furthermore, he continued, 'just when he has gained knowledge of the duchy and of the people, and so ought to remain there, in order to benefit both you and them and, after taking the oaths, journey through the land, punishing wrongdoers, reforming the country, and putting it in order, he is removed'.[28] This was a not infrequent complaint. Basset had refused to interrupt his oath-taking and receiving tour as he believed that 'it was imperative for him to go to Saint-Sever, Dax' [and other places, missing in the damaged record] '... to receive the oaths accustomed to be performed to, and by, a newly-appointed seneschal, because he had already assigned certain days for this purpose ... to the nobility and others of the aforesaid regions, which consumed many days, so much so that there was hardly an hour to spare'.[29]

The form and text of the seneschal's oath on taking office was recorded on the Gascon rolls as it was sworn by Basset's successor, Richard de Grey, in April 1324:

> You swear that you will, well and loyally, with all your mind and all your strength, hold the office of the seneschalcy of the duchy of Aquitaine, and do justice to all in those matters which concern you; and keep the towns, castles, forts, lands and tenements of our lord the king in that duchy, to his and his heirs' profit, and deliver them only to him or his heirs, or to whomsoever brings you his letters patent; and guard and maintain his honour, estate, rights and lordship with all your strength; and if any of his rights, of whatever kind, should be withdrawn or concealed, you should resist this and restore such rights to their due form, as your loyal duty; and if you cannot do this, you should make it known to the king.[30]

The varying forms of the oaths sworn and taken (in the vernacular, that is in *lingua romana*) during Basset's itineration of the duchy are set out in the record as follows. At Bordeaux, the seneschal swore 'That he will be a good and faithful lord, and will protect their fors [privileges] and customs, and defend them from wrong and force from whomsoever, as long as he shall be seneschal of the duchy of Aquitaine, with his loyal power, saving his loyalty to our lord the king and duke.'[31] In return, the nobles, mayors and jurats (town councillors) of the Bordelais swore: 'That they will be good and loyal subjects, faithful and obedient, as long as he shall be the

---

[28] TNA, C47/25/2/30.
[29] *War of Saint-Sardos*, ed. Chaplais, 8.
[30] TNA, C61/35, m. 4d. My translation. The French (Anglo-Norman) text reads: *Vous jurrez qe bien et leaument, a tut vostre sen et a tut vostre poair, garderez loffice de la seneschalcie de la duchee de Guyenne, et droit fere a touz en ce que vous appent, et les villes, chasteux, fortalesces, et terres et ten' nostre seignour le Roi en cele duchee garderez, al oeps de lui et ses heirs, et ne les livrez a nul forsque a lui ou a ses heirs, ou a celui qi vous portera ses lettres patentes, et soen honour, son estat, ses droitures et sa seignourie garderez et meintendrez a tut vostre poair, et si rien de ses droits en queue chose qe ceo sait, soit soutztrete et concele, vostre loial peine mettrez de ceo repeller et remectre en estat doeu, et si vous ne le pourrez faire, vous le facez savoir au Roi.*
[31] TNA, C47/26/17, m. 1 (26 Sept. 1323). My translation. The Gascon text reads: *Que en lors sera bon senhor e leyau, e los gardera lurs fors e lurs costumas, eus gardera de tort e de force de ed medis e dautruy, tant cum sera senescaut deu dugat de Guiayna, a son leyau poder, sauba la fieutat de nostre senhor lo Rey e duc.*

seneschal of the duchy of Aquitaine, and will protect his life and limbs with all their loyal power.'[32] The oaths continued to be taken, in very similar forms but with local variations, throughout the seneschal's journey across the duchy. They were sworn on the Gospels and the crucifix. In some places, a wider group was encompassed, when members of the populus also swore the oath, 'raising their hands towards the ... Holy Gospels and cross'.[33] But there was no bodily contact between the seneschal and those performing the oaths. In that respect these rituals had more in common with the Indian homage ceremonies rather than with the homages taken by the Black Prince in 1363–4 where a kiss of peace was also exchanged.

Any comparative study must always take account of (often profound) structural differences between polities and societies in many respects, including the differing social and political configurations of a state and its functions. In the Anglo-Gascon-Indian case, grounds for comparison seem rather more compelling, largely because of the vital role played by their respective elites in the very existence and survival of the regimes under which they were governed. Other grounds for comparison can certainly be found, such as the part played by bureaucracy in both India's and Gascony's day-to-day, as well as longer-term, government; the extent to which, as in British India, Gascony provided a training ground for English diplomats and administrators, many (in the Gascon case) on their way to promotion to higher office in Church and State; the degrees of independence accorded by the 'imperial' or colonial power to regional and local elites; or the role played by a perceived common enemy in holding these often fragile structures together. They will be considered in another, quite separate study. Burrows identified a further point of apparent similarity when he wrote that 'No colonial dependency of England has ever offered a similar parallel [as did England and Gascony] nor, it may safely be said, ever will. In Aquitaine and India alike the Englishman was, and is, a foreigner, with a home elsewhere; [whereas] in our colonies men, with their families, settle, and only now and then return.'[34] India was indeed different from other British overseas territories in that it was ranked as a 'dominion', not a colony, aspiring to a status comparable with that of the so-called 'white' possessions (Canada, Australia, New Zealand).[35] It was always considered as being to some degree superior to other, non-white, largely African, areas of the British Empire. In his exhaustive narrative study of the visit of George V and Queen Mary to India in 1911, Sir John Fortescue could make the comparative point that India had 'a nobility prouder and with longer and more sublime traditions of chivalry and heroism than any ... between the Atlantic and the Ural Mountains'. He claimed that the German Guelph emperors of the European Middle Ages seemed to 'pale' before the Rajputs.[36] The 'medievalism' of the British vision of India, and its transla-

---

[32] There were some significant variations in the oaths sworn by the representatives of towns, especially at Bonnegarde (m. 4), Bayonne, Arcangues, Hastingues and Dax (m. 5). The Gascon text (my translation) of the oath of the Bordelais 'barons, nobles, mayors and jurats' sworn on 26 September reads: [*Que*] *en seran bons sotzmes et loyals, fieus et obediens, tant quant sera senescaut deu dugat de Guiayna, engarderan vita et membres a* [*lur leyau*] *poder* (m. 1).

[33] TNA, C47/26/17, m. 4.

[34] Burrows, *Family of Brocas*, 18.

[35] For a discussion of dominion status and a comparison of later medieval commissions and contractual forms with royal commissions to American colonial governors, see Julius Goebel, 'The Matrix of Empire', in J.H. Smith, *Appeals to the Privy Council from American Plantations* (New York, 1950), pp. xiii–lxi, esp. lvii–lix.

[36] John Fortescue, *Narrative of the Visit to India of their Majesties King George V and Queen Mary and*

tion into practice at the durbars – and how both that vision and practice changed over time – is worthy of a study in itself. Further parallels spring to mind when one reads the succinct summary of English rule in Gascony by Charles Bémont, early editor (and a very fine one) of the Gascon Rolls, where he observed 'The English regime was not oppressive, less [oppressive] perhaps than it was in England; the clergy and nobility retained a full degree of independence compatible with the allegiance owed to their sovereign ... the urban bourgeoisie obtained privileges from which their administrative, economic and social life developed ... [English officers] normally respected the laws and usages of the province, while reserving to the central power the rights of decision and control.'[37] Bémont identified an important aspect of the Anglo-Gascon polity when he alluded to the fact that the indigenous nobility (and clergy) 'retained a full degree of independence compatible with the allegiance owed to their sovereign'. Their support was critical to the survival of the regime. Their allegiance and loyalty were secured not only by the mutual oath-taking and oath-receiving which was conducted between them and the king-duke's representative in the duchy (the king's lieutenant or seneschal) but also by the purposeful distribution of rewards and grants of privileges. In British India, the princes and nobility were similarly crucial to the regime's continued survival. Their allegiance was bolstered and furthered by the granting of titles, lands and lordships, emblems, pensions, annuities, gifts of confiscated lands, banners, coats of arms, elephants and kettle-drums, and by induction into the membership of newly created orders of chivalry such as the Star of India (1861).[38] What was in effect a form of service nobility was in the process of creation, sharing some, but by no means all, of the characteristics of its Mughal predecessors. The traditional Mughal durbar was for example retained, but was shorn of one of its most fundamental elements – the giving of gold coins (nazar) by the liegeman as tribute to the emperor, and the reciprocal gift (khilat) of clothes and robes by the Mughal, signifying incorporation into the emperor's body.[39] Under

---

of the Coronation Durbar held in Delhi. 12th December 1912 (1912), 5; and also his account of the forms of homage performed at the durbar: 152–5.

[37] Charles Bémont, *La Guyenne pendant la Domination Anglaise, 1152–1453* (1920), 10: *Le regime anglais n'avait pas ete oppressif, moins peut-etre qu'il ne l'avait ete en Angleterre ... la bourgeoisie urbaine obtint des privileges a l'abri desquels se developpa sa vie administrative, economique et sociale ...* [English officers] *respectaient d'ordinaire les lois et usages de la province, tout en reservant au pouvoir central les droits de decision et de controle.*

[38] Among a very extensive literature, especially important for relations between the British Raj and Indian princes are P.L. Chudgar, *The Indian Princes under British Protection* (1929), esp. 135–54; A. Ikegame, 'Space of Kinship, Space of Empire: Marriage Strategies amongst the Mysore Royal Caste in the 19th and 20th Centuries', *Indian Economic and Social Review*, xlvi (2009), 343–72, esp. 347–9, 368; C.J. Keen, 'The Power behind the Throne: Relations between the British and the Indian States, 1870–1909 (PhD thesis, University of London, 2003), esp. 18–35, 240–65 (hierarchy and ritual), 295–6; C.W. Nuckolls, 'The Durbar Incident', *Modern Asian Studies*, xxiv (1950), 529–59, esp. 530–5; Dick Kooiman, 'The Invention of Tradition in Travancore: a Maharajah's Quest for Political Security', *Journal of the Royal Asiatic Society*, 3rd ser., xv (2005), 151–64; P. O'Donoghue, 'Heralds at Delhi Durbars', *The Coat of Arms. The Journal of the Heraldry Society*, 3rd ser., ii. no. 212 (2006), 107–24.

[39] Fundamental to any study of the durbars and of British authority in India (though not without its biases and partis pris) is the lavishly illustrated volume *Power and Resistance. The Delhi Coronation Durbars*, ed. J.F. Codell (The Alkazi Collection of Photography, Mumbai, 2012). For an authoritative and unrivalled study of the durbars and their context, B.S. Cohn, 'Representing Authority in Victorian India', in *The Invention of Tradition*, ed. E.J. Hobsbawn and Terence Ranger (Cambridge, 1983), 165–209, and Cohn, 'The Command of Language and the Language of Command', in his

the British, incorporation was replaced by the performance of homage and fealty, literally at arm's length or at an even further distance from the sovereign than under the Mughals. No bodily contact was acceptable. Nonetheless, however, the British regime underwent a striking change of approach to such rituals between the durbars of 1877, 1903 and 1911, progressively adopting (and adapting) Hindu, Islamic and Mughal forms to a much greater degree. Moreover, at the highest level, the new Queen-Empress Victoria's proclamation of 1858, creating the new British imperial regime, undertook to respect the 'rights, dignity and honour' of the princes and nobility 'as our own', cognisant of their 'ancient rights, usages and customs'.[40] This kind of obligation would not have been out of place in an Anglo-Gascon context where a fundamental bedrock of the English regime was the observance of closely guarded local rights and privileges. Lord Lytton, as viceroy, summed up the prevailing situation in India well when he wrote in 1876 of the Indian 'feudality' as 'a great feudal aristocracy which we cannot get rid of [!]; which we are avowedly anxious to conciliate and command, but which we have as yet done next to nothing to rally round the British crown as its feudal head'.[41] Attempts were then made over the following thirty-five years to address this perceived omission. They were to a certain extent responsible for stemming the tidal wave of nationalism and self-determination, at least for a time, until that wave broke, in the mid- and later 1940s, through the diminished storm defences of the British Raj.

Yet that regime could certainly be censured as 'oppressive' when responding, as did other colonial powers, to perceived threats to its security, above all at times of crisis. This certainly was the case in the aftermath of the Indian Mutiny/First War of Independence of 1857 or the Amritsar massacre/punitive action of 1919.[42] But the norm tended to be a less directly intrusive style of government, above all in the princely states, where a third-party, adjudicatory role in local disputes was often adopted by the British. Within those states, considerable latitude was normally allowed to the princes whereby their state could be administered without undue interference from the 'paramount power'. Attempts were certainly made by the representatives of the Raj to reform what was considered the misuse or abuse of princely power. But non- or limited direct intervention (except in cases of what was viewed as flagrantly un co-operative, contumacious or corrupt behaviour) was normally the policy, especially in the administration of justice, collection of revenue, estate

---

Colonialism and its Forms of Knowledge (Princeton, NJ, 1996), 276–329; P.K. Nayar, 'Nineteenth-century Imperial Pageantry and the Politics of Display', *Journal of Creative Communication*, v (2010), 75–87; B. Shivran, 'Mughal Court Rituals: the Symbolism of Imperial Authority during Akbar's Reign', *Proceedings of the Indian Historical Congress*, lxvii (2006–7), 331–49, and 'Court Dress and Robing Ceremony in Mughal India', *ibid.*, lxvi (2005–6), 404–22; M.P. Kalim, 'A Right Royal Tamasha: Imagining Queen Victoria as Kaiser-i-Hind', *Vides*, iv (2016), 210–18; G.A.M. van Meersbergen, 'Ceremonies of Submission: Diplomacy in a Multiple Register', in *Ethnography and Encounter. Dutch and English approaches to Cross-cultural Contact in Seventeenth-century South Asia* (Leiden, 2021), 143–72; S. Saha, 'The Darbar, the British and the Runaway Maharaja: Religion and Politics in Nineteenth-century Western India', *South Asian Research*, xxvii (pt 3) (2007), 271–91.

[40] Sarvepalli Gopal, *British Policy in India, 1858–1905* (Cambridge, 1965), 299–304.
[41] Keen, 'Power behind the Throne', 260–1.
[42] The extent of the oppressiveness of the British Raj is set out, not without some biases, in Wagner, *Amritsar 1919*, chs 6, 9–10, and above all in 'Conclusion. An Empire of Fear', 251–9. For a recent polemic directed against some current – and some more long-standing – interpretations, which are seen by the writer to play down 'imperial violence', see D. Hicks, 'Glorious Memory', in *What is History Now?*, ed. Lipscombe and Carr, 101–15.

management and dealings with the local nobility. Where local customs and usages seemed compatible with the effective exercise of justice and administration, they tended to be observed.

Something of a sea-change, however, was coming over British attitudes from the 1880s onwards. That decade saw, in effect, the birth of 'imperial' history and the beginnings of a closer scrutiny and, perhaps paradoxically, a questioning of British imperial policies, aims and ambitions. Historiography, it could be argued, was here beginning to have a certain effect upon contemporary politics and even policies. This seminal period was also to see the further professionalisation of academic history in Great Britain and the development of a new, more rigorous 'record history', relying as much on documentary as on narrative sources.[43] Seeley already (in 1883) saw the potential beginnings of the end of empire, concluding pessimistically that the greatest danger to the British Raj was the rise of Indian nationalism, and predicting that there was to be no long-term imperial future there.[44] But the study of the 'imperial' past, again perhaps paradoxically, now assumed a much more central and fundamental place in British historical scholarship. Burrows, in an article published in 1892, as the edition of the Gascon rolls got under way, noted the 'silence' on English rule in Gascony, 'which the most cursory reader must have observed in the histories of both countries [Britain and France]', claiming, with some justification, that many British medieval historians and their reading public saw 'the royal provinces in South-West France as personal and very troublesome appendages to the Crown of England' which were 'to be deplored and despised' because they gave rise to Anglo-French conflicts.[45] The British professoriat, led by Stubbs and Freeman, largely shared and propagated this view, to be opposed only by the Mancunian voice of T.F. Tout and his subsequent disciples.[46] But Burrows could make a convincing case for at least some of his argument by broadening the field of vision to embrace the history of a foreign policy which advocated that 'the coasts extending opposite to the South-Eastern shores of England should be, if not in the hands of the English sovereign, at least in the hands of friends ... For three centuries an almost independent Aquitaine and a scarcely less independent Britanny, grievously blocked the way of the French monarchy'.[47] The overall aim was to keep England free from invasion and to hold on to at least some of the cross-Channel territories brought to the English kingdom by the Normans, Angevins and Plantagenets. And that aim, until 1453 (the loss of Gascony) and 1557 (the loss of Calais) was largely achieved.

A detailed study of ritual and ceremony, as well as other topics, in the twin contexts of Gascony and India may occasion some surprise. But it can be claimed that there are sufficient grounds for potentially fruitful comparison. The homage-taking and receiving ceremonies in both contexts provide only starting points for wider ranging approaches. The transition from Mughal and subsidiary princely rule to British imperial rule in India brought with it many changes. In Gascony, there were certainly changes over the period of English administration. But the consistency

---

[43] For a brief survey, see M.D. Knowles, 'Some Trends in Scholarship, 1868–1968 in the Field of Medieval History', *TRHS*, xix (1969), 139–50.
[44] Seeley, *The Expansion of England*, 271.
[45] Burrows, 'The Publication of the Gascon Rolls', *TRHS*, vi (1892), 112.
[46] Tout's views are best found in his *France and England. Their Relations in the Middle Ages and Now* (Manchester, 1922), esp. 1–17, 158–62.
[47] Montagu Burrows, *A History of the Foreign Policy of Great Britain* (New York, 1895), 4.

with which the mutual performance of homage and fealty and the acceptance of its obligations took place is striking. The periods stretching from the *Recogniciones Feodorum* of Edward I (1273–4) to the *Livre des Hommages* of 1363–4 and from the Durbar ceremonies of 1877 to those of 1911 saw the establishment and consolidation (at least at first sight) of two seemingly totally dissimilar colonial or quasi-colonial regimes. But the ritualised and other bases upon which those regimes were in many ways built, merit a comparative study which has not so far been attempted. The sources for a detailed study of the subject are rich and varied, including (for the durbars) material on a Pathe News film.[48] The virtues, as well as the pitfalls, of comparative history have often been preached – or decried – especially in recent years. In this case it needs to be put to the test.

[48] A fourteen-minute newsreel of the 1911 Durbar: https://player.bfi.org.uk/free/film/watch-delhi-durbar-1911-online.

CONTRIBUTORS

Margaret Condon's main research interests lie in the reign of Henry VII and in English administrative history. A founder member of the University of Bristol's Cabot Project (started in 2009), she was a researcher on the Tudor Chamber Books Project in 2015–18; she is currently working on a co-authored monograph on the English discovery voyages of the late fifteenth century.

Sean Cunningham is Head of Collections (Medieval, Early Modern and Legal) at The National Archives.

Diana Dunn is Emeritus Research Fellow in the department of History and Archaeology at the University of Chester.

Laura Flannigan, Junior Research Fellow at St John's College, Oxford, has written about litigation, society and politics in late medieval and Tudor England; her book *Royal Justice and the Making of the Tudor Commonwealth, 1485–1547*, was published in 2023.

Ralph A. Griffiths OBE, Emeritus Professor of Medieval History at Swansea University, has among his publications *The Principality of Wales in the Later Middle Ages: South Wales, 1277–1536* (2nd edn, 2018), *The Reign of King Henry VI* (3rd edn, 2020), (with R.S. Thomas) *The Making of the Tudor Dynasty* (4th edn, 2020), *Sir Rhys ap Thomas and his Family: A Study in the Wars of the Roses and Early Tudor Politics* (2nd edn, 2014), and *Free and Public: Andrew Carnegie and the Libraries of Wales* (2021). His continuing interest in the politics and society of later medieval England and Wales has been sustained by the collegiate companionship of such fifteenth-century scholars as Rowena Archer.

Anthony Gross, an Associate Fellow of the Institute of Historical Research in the University of London, is the author of *The Dissolution of the Lancastrian Kingship* (1996), a study of political culture during the Wars of the Roses. He is presently working on a book examining the relationship between central government and local society during the reigns of Edward II and Edward III.

Samuel Lane, a Postdoctoral Associate Member of the University of Oxford's History Faculty, completed a D.Phil. on the political activities of English bishops in the reign of Edward III and is currently undertaking professional training to become a barrister.

Contributors

Simon Payling has worked at the History of Parliament Trust since 1993. He has known Rowena since the early 1980s when they were both graduate students, supervised by Gerald Harriss, and habitues of Duke Humphrey's Library.

Edward Powell was a Fellow and Director of Studies in History at Downing College, Cambridge, between 1982 and 1989, after studying alongside Rowena as a research student of Gerald Harriss in Oxford in the 1970s. He now writes biographies of more recent figures such as *King Edward VIII* (2018).

Carole Rawcliffe, Professor Emeritus of Medieval History at the University of East Anglia, has published widely on medicine, health, institutional care and urban life in late medieval England.

James Ross is Reader in Late Medieval History at the University of Winchester. His D.Phil. on the de Vere earls of Oxford 1400–1513 was supervised by Rowena and his publications on various aspects of the late medieval nobility and political society include *John de Vere, Thirteenth Earl of Oxford, 1442–1513* (2011), *Henry VI* (2016), and *Robert de Vere, Earl of Oxford and Duke of Ireland, 1362–1392* (2024).

Hannah Skoda, Fellow and tutor in medieval history at St John's College, Oxford, works on the social and cultural history of the later Middle Ages. In 2023 she published *A Companion to Crime and Deviance in the Middle Ages*.

Malcolm Vale, an Emeritus Fellow of St John's College, Oxford, has written on Anglo-French history and the cultural history of northern Europe in the later Middle Ages and early Renaissance, publishing most recently *The Renaissance in Northern Europe* (2020).

DR ROWENA E. ARCHER

Rowena has been an inspiration to generations of Oxford undergraduates and postgraduates, to students and audiences far beyond its dreaming spires, and through her publications and support for academic endeavours to the wider scholarly community.

Rowena herself would recognise the importance of her undergraduate years at the University of Bristol in the shaping of her career (she received her BA from the university in 1977, having written her undergraduate dissertation on 'The Court Party during the Ascendancy of the Duke of Suffolk, 1444–50') from the teaching of Charles Ross, James Sherborne and Malcolm Lambert, to the long-lasting, professional relationships and friendships with former Bristol students, a number of whom have contributed to this *festschrift* and some of whom are sadly no longer with us. Nor should the importance of her doctoral research at Oxford on 'The Mowbrays, Earls of Nottingham and Dukes of Norfolk, to 1432', completed in 1984, under the supervision of Gerald Harriss, be underestimated. With Simon Walker, Rowena co-edited a volume dedicated to their supervisor in 1995.[1]

Rowena strongly believes in the value of education for all, old and young, and this was the most prominent theme at the event held in her honour to mark her retirement at Christ Church in June 2023, with former undergraduate and postgraduate students testifying to her boundless care, support and incisive feedback on their work. What should also be emphasised, as they are not covered by the appreciations below, are Rowena's talks to schools, local branches of the Historical Association and Adult Education groups, such as those attending Special Interest weekends at Rewley House, Oxford, and the Cambridge International Medieval Studies summer schools which she helped to organise as well as devoting two weeks of her time every August to teach mature students, many of whom returned year after year.

The first part of what follows focuses on Rowena's formative undergraduate years. Following that are four appreciations based on tributes offered to Rowena at the event at Christ Church. From the many tributes delivered that day, by former students, colleagues and friends, it is hoped that the following selection can stand for all, and, in their focus on Rowena's undergraduate teaching, doctoral supervision, collegiality and scholarship within the broader study of the late Middle Ages, show the full range of her contributions to the late medieval academic community of which she is so much a part, and to Oxford University.

Diana Dunn and James Ross

---

[1] R.E. Archer and Simon Walker, *Rulers and Ruled in Late Medieval England. Essays Presented to Gerald Harriss* (1995).

Dr Rowena E. Archer

The Bristol Experience, 1974–7

The years 1974 to 1977 were good ones to be a history undergraduate at the University of Bristol, which was especially strong in the teaching and research of medieval history. It was hardly surprising that the most popular first-year optional course 'Richard III, William Shakespeare and the Wars of the Roses', taught by Charles Ross, was heavily oversubscribed, necessitating the head of department to put names into a hat to allocate places! Rowena was among the lucky ones and thus began a lifetime's study of, and enthusiasm for, fifteenth-century history. Ross, a brilliant teacher, quickly engaged the minds of his rather timid but highly receptive, mainly female group of students, in the examination of the personality of a king who had attracted considerable criticism from the Tudors onwards. At a time when there were few published scholarly works about Richard III, Ross encouraged his students to read widely and to keep an open mind, and was prepared to include books such as Josephine Tey's *The Daughter of Time* (1954) in his bibliography. He particularly recommended Paul Murray Kendall's *Richard the Third* (1955), which he admired for the author's ability to portray the king as a real person and the product of his violent age. Shakespeare's *Richard III* came alive through the medium of film, notably the unsurpassed Laurence Olivier version.

As a result of this stimulating first-year experience, many students in the group became hooked on medieval history and, with careful selection of options, it proved possible to follow a history course with a strong medieval strand culminating in a final year special subject on 'English Politics and Society during the Wars of the Roses'. By this time Ross had published his major study of *Edward IV* (1974) and his highly readable *The Wars of the Roses* (1976), and was working on his study of *Richard III*, published in 1981. His students benefitted from their close engagement with his latest ideas as he challenged much of what had previously been written on the period.[2] In addition to stimulating lectures and productive seminars, history was brought alive by field trips, particularly memorable among them a visit to Skenrith, Goodrich and White Castle in Monmouthshire in the company of Maureen Merrison, who taught a popular second-year option on 'The Reign of King John'.

It was hardly surprising that, among the fifty-two history students who graduated in July 1977, there were five with First Class Honours, including Rowena. The Bristol student experience provided a model for anyone wanting to pursue a career in history teaching and research: a friendly and supportive environment, a rigorous approach to the use of source material and respect for the views of others. This method has informed Rowena's style of teaching and general approach to the subject throughout her long working life.

Diana Dunn

---

[2] A full appreciation of Charles Ross as teacher and researcher is provided by Keith Dockray in *Medieval History*, ii (1) (1992), 140–52.

Teacher

Dr Rowena E. Archer has been an inspirational figure to generations of history students in Oxford. This was apparent at the event held to mark her retirement at Christ Church on 30 June 2023. While there were many common themes in the tributes given in her honour – such as her dedication to her students, her kindness and her memorable use of props, from helmets to swords – it was also striking how each speaker emphasised something different about her. For some, it was her 'old school' style of teaching which struck them, with recollections of how she instructed her students to read out their essays at the beginning of tutorials, and continued to lecture at Exam Schools in her gown, even when the majority of her colleagues had abandoned that practice. For others, it was the extent and importance of the pastoral care she offered which stayed with them, prompting memories of how she walked with them around Christ Church Meadow during the COVID-19 pandemic, and how she was prepared to support and guide them through a whole plethora of problems. While I have tried to reflect the observations of others, what follows is very much a personal tribute to Rowena, with an emphasis on her teaching of undergraduates.

I had the great privilege to be taught by Rowena for seven of my eleven undergraduate papers; thereafter, she supervised my MSt in Medieval History, and served as my college advisor (and *de facto* second supervisor) while I engaged in research for a D.Phil. As the tutor who gave me my very first tutorial, in the halcyon days of 2012, and as one of the people I immediately rang up after finishing my doctoral *viva*, she was a constant source of encouragement, help and advice throughout my time in Oxford. A remarkable tutor of undergraduates, her tutorials, which some have described as 'legendary', were always demanding but never unrewarding. With the benefit of hindsight, four aspects of her teaching particularly stand out, as she helped to turn students like me from naïve and nervous freshers to fledgling historians ready to tackle Finals. First, she forced us to read, by giving us extensive reading lists and expecting us to get through them; there was no place to hide for those who had prepared insufficiently. But she also stressed the value of reading critically, of 'gutting' books for the passages of most value and relevance, and of engaging with older scholarship – such as J.H. Wylie and W.T. Waugh's *The Reign of Henry the Fifth*, Eileen Power's *Medieval Women* and the original *Oxford History of England* series – rather than just the most recent tomes. Secondly, she demanded that we should think for ourselves, rather than simply parroting the opinions of others. Thus, in the first essay I wrote as an undergraduate, one of her many marginal comments read: 'too much the views of historians; too little your views'. Through innumerable similar remarks, she encouraged us not to hide behind the statements of earlier scholars, but to stand on our own two feet, to work out what we thought and to express it in our own words.[3] Thirdly, Rowena frequently reiterated the importance of argument; she had little patience for undergraduates – or, indeed, for politicians on the *Today* programme – who ducked the question that they had been asked, and instead delivered a response to a different one. On the contrary, she insisted that we read the precise question she had set, and taught us to deconstruct it, stick to it and answer it.

---

[3] Indeed, later – when I was a graduate student – Rowena would remind me of the advice which Gerald Harriss had once given her in her early days in Oxford, namely to stop hiding behind secondary sources.

She also trained us to respond to questions in a clear and coherent way, pushing us to take a position and drawing attention to the logical flaws or gaps in our reasoning. Finally, Rowena helped us to write: when marking essays, she would often highlight typographical errors, put a line through clauses which added little of value, suggest changes to inelegant prose and point out when sentences were too long. By meticulously correcting our style, over time she helped us to write more clearly, engagingly and fluently. Consequently, when she taught us she not only imparted her encyclopaedic knowledge of the Middle Ages, but also instructed us to read, think, argue and write like historians.

Of course, Rowena did not merely make her students better scholars, she also inspired us to enjoy medieval history. When I came up to Oxford as a fresher, I was determined to focus on the Tudors. Yet that determination had essentially dissipated by the end of my first term, during which I studied 'British History II, 1042–1330' with Rowena. Eschewing more modish subjects, she principally gave tutorials on traditional topics – such as the Anglo-Saxon kingdom, the Norman Conquest, Thomas Becket and the reigns of Stephen, John and Edward I – and taught them in an utterly compelling manner. But if 'British History II' turned my head towards the Middle Ages, it was the 'English Chivalry and the French War, 1330–1400' optional subject which set my course for the next decade. Tutorials with Rowena brought the fourteenth century alive, as we discussed the chaos of the battlefield, the colour of heraldry and the mechanics of siege warfare. Furthermore, she helped the contemporary sources of the period to speak to us. While Froissart's *Chronicles* were a great read in their own right – and all the more so when Rowena urged us to think about the author's style, patronage and sources – other set texts, such as the Black Prince's register, that seemed a little dry at first glance, became when taught by her fascinating windows into the political and military culture of fourteenth-century England. And so, like many of Rowena's students before and after me, I became so gripped that I took more and more late medieval papers, and ultimately stayed on for graduate research. Had I never studied with Rowena, that simply would not have happened.

Perhaps the most impressive aspect of Rowena's teaching was the effort and attention she gave to all her students. This was underlined at the event in June, when some of those attending highlighted how she always went 'above and beyond', while others spoke of her going 'the extra mile'. When I was taught by Rowena as an undergraduate, she did not just teach me in tutorials and mark my essays, but also made time to meet me on other occasions. For instance, at the start of my first term at Christ Church, I struggled with the transition from writing A-Level essays to undergraduate ones, and Rowena set aside time to see me, answer my questions and break down how to write a good essay, which meant that things suddenly clicked into place. Likewise, when she was my supervisor for my MSt, she did not just read my thesis – in characteristically forensic detail – but also read through my other essays, and whipped them into shape. Finally, as my college advisor during my doctoral studies, she did not restrict herself to seeing me once a year (which was her only obligation), but read through hundreds of pages of my thesis, rooting out typos, making stylistic suggestions, and pointing out places where my argument might be sharpened. Moreover, Rowena has done so much beyond even all that, including posting me books during the COVID-19 lockdown, reading through drafts of numerous articles and writing countless references.

Both Rowena's exceptional teaching and her going 'above and beyond' were founded on the fact that she cares: she cares deeply about Oxford, about medieval history, about her students and about how they develop, both as scholars and as people. That is something for which I – alongside a great many others – are profoundly grateful. In her *Oxford DNB* entry about her own supervisor, Gerald Harriss, Rowena described how he was 'deeply humane', 'devoted to his students' and a 'superlative and dedicated teacher', who 'sought to inculcate in his charges that same clarity, rigour, and directness that was the hallmark of his own work'.[4] Much to the benefit of her own colleagues and charges, these qualities and ambitions were all ones which Rowena shared.

Samuel Lane

Supervisor

Rowena's office, in the days when she was my D.Phil. supervisor, was in a tower, approached by a spiral staircase. Walking up these stairs always felt like a thoroughly appropriate way to initiate a supervisory meeting. Despite a very heavy teaching load, Rowena always made time for me, whether meetings were planned or not, and her comments on draft chapters were always so full that it seemed a wonder that she found time to do them. Frequently, the backs of my one-sided printed drafts were covered in pencil comments; on some pages she had written more on the back than I had on the front. Supervisory sessions were calm and constructive, and Rowena's phenomenal memory for detail and eye for argument were fully deployed.

One apt description of Rowena as a supervisor would be 'meticulous'. Eagle-eyed in spotting poor use of English or inconsistent citation in footnotes, she would correct such errors and make clear that they should be learnt from and not repeated. She was meticulous too in other areas: no name dropped into the thesis without context ever escaped notice. Rowena was demanding in terms of secondary reading, both new and old: notes such as 'You need to gut Holmes' would appear regularly (a reference to G.A. Holmes, *Estates of the Higher Nobility*, rather than a command to eviscerate Sherlock) and would be followed up on. Equally, she was content to allow me freer rein when she was confident I could cope. Rowena was challenging as a supervisor too. Her own knowledge about the late medieval nobility (and indeed so many other subjects) was deployed to challenge, compare and contrast with my nascent doctoral study on the de Vere earls of Oxford, and she quickly disposed of ill-supported assertions. My least favourite comment from her, seen on more than one draft chapter, was 'James, you need to go away and think about this'; yet she was always right, and the matter did need further reflection.

None of this meant that Rowena was anything other than supportive – perhaps the hallmark of her professional career – as a doctoral supervisor, going far beyond the basic confines of the role, and indeed she remained supportive far beyond the years when I was her student, as draft articles have been read, requested references written and advice dispensed ever since. Whatever strengths I have as a historian, I owe in large measure to Rowena's early guidance and ongoing wisdom.

James Ross

---

[4] Rowena E. Archer, 'Harriss, Gerald Leslie', *Oxford DNB*.

Dr Rowena E. Archer

Colleague

It has been a great honour to work with Rowena Archer, ever since my career at St John's Oxford began in 2010. We taught together on the special subject focused on Joan of Arc, and I remember the very first class when one of the students was asked why Joan had claimed to see Saints Margaret, Michael and Catherine: why these particular saints? The student looked at Rowena as if she were mad, and said 'because those were the ones who appeared to her!' Rowena's response was, of course, respectful, challenging and rigorous, as was her approach to all her teaching and research.

When I began teaching at Oxford, I found the experience stimulating yet daunting. Rowena was the most staunch and wonderful supporter; she generously allayed my nerves, and offered both practical and moral support. The Joan of Arc paper, established by Malcolm Vale, engages with an enormously wide range of themes: the dramatic events of Joan's life and career; a decisive moment in the Hundred Years' War; a critical period when the meaning of 'Frenchness' or 'Englishness' mattered; a fascinating time of cultural change despite all the upheaval. It is a paper based on a wide range of diverse sources – from letters, to chronicles, to trial records and exquisite images. Rowena has always guided her students through the morass of factional shenanigans in fifteenth-century France with no-nonsense aplomb, challenging assumptions and stimulating curiosity in equal measure.

When choosing between options, students tend to speak to those in the year above: the popularity of Rowena's teaching meant that her papers were often over-subscribed and her astonishing work ethic pushed to its limits. And I can see why her teaching has always appealed so much: she leads discussions with great clarity, and brings to life the period's political geography, showing how much it matters to know where the principal rivers are, to get a grip on the challenges of travel, to understand the topography of the land. She has an encyclopedic knowledge of who was who, and how people were related; suddenly in her hands complex relationships make sense, and the overlaying of the personal, factional and political becomes so much clearer. Her pedagogy relies on startlingly sharp questions: how many swords did Joan of Arc have? When did a particular battle take place and why does this matter? And she is a master of the counterfactual – a favourite question is 'what would have happened had this been John of Arc?' – it is an ingenious way of crystallising so many of the contentious issues around Joan. Chocolates and biscuits were supplied to sustain students through the trauma of watching Robert Bresson's *Trial of Joan of Arc* from 1962 and Karl Theodor Dreyer's *Passion of Joan of Arc* from 1928 – both extraordinary cinematic masterpieces, the latter rediscovered locked away in a mental institution near Oslo in 1981 and restored. Students were treated to wonderful excursions, notably a trip to the Beauchamp chapel in Warwick, an annual treat guided by Rowena's encyclopedic knowledge.

I count it a real privilege to have worked with Rowena. She has a very different historiographical perspective from my own, and this is enormously salutary, pushing me in different scholarly directions in a way that is highly productive, and for which I am very grateful. Where I might be focused on Joan's subjectivity and gender, Rowena will ask 'Where was she? When? Who supported her?' – in other words, rooting flimsy constructions back into the evidence. Where I might wax lyrical about Joan's visions and theories of what she might have seen (perhaps related to the statues in the church at Domrémy and ways of seeing in this period which were as much miraculous as representational), Rowena will remind me to trace precisely who Joan saw, at what date, and when she said this. Where I might get caught up in the tangled web of methodological considerations around Joan's trial, Rowena will root the analysis back in the surviving evidence about procedure. Her very grounded approach is a model of academic rigour and insight; here we all have so much to learn.

So, Rowena is a wonderful tutor and an inspiring scholar, and her career has been a model of how these two qualities can be intertwined.

Hannah Skoda

Scholar

It is for me both an honour and a pleasure to have been invited to offer this brief tribute to Rowena and her work. Many of us in the History Faculty have memories and appreciations of her contributions to teaching, research and university life here in Oxford. Contributions, that is, to the Faculty and as College Lecturer and Fellow to no fewer than six colleges of which she has been a member. During those years, significant changes have taken place in the now well-ploughed and abundantly sown field of later medieval studies, defined (broadly) from the later thirteenth to the early sixteenth centuries. Above all, those studies have been marked by the continued rise of prosopography; by studies of aristocracies influenced by socio-anthropological concepts of class, caste and status; of material culture, influenced in part by central and east European scholarship, Marxist, post-Marxist, and otherwise; a revived and more broadly based political narrative; of a wide-ranging exploration of women's and gender history in many forms, as well as the history of minorities; and last but not least, more widely comparative studies of the visual arts. All these developments tend to unite rather than divide us. Or at least they should do.

It would be difficult to discuss developments in the study of English later medieval history without mentioning the name of K.B. McFarlane, who died suddenly in 1966. McFarlane, great historian that he was, had also been a kind of ringmaster for a circus in which so many successful candidates for academic posts in medieval history had been his pupils or research supervisees, and those of us who had lain outside that charmed circle had been very much influenced by the master's work, or rather by what relatively little of it had actually been published at that time – in my case, the early 1960s. We went to his lectures and strove to transcribe almost every single word (I still have the notes) knowing that they would be most unlikely to appear in print during our undergraduate years or even perhaps our lifetimes. And the words were certainly worth transcribing, such as the rhetorical fanfare which opened his Henry V lecture: 'If there were a great medieval English king, then Harry of Monmouth was he.' And this is where both Rowena and myself fit into the picture: neither of us were McFarlane's pupils nor research supervisees but received that influence, as it were, at second hand, Rowena through Charles Ross and James Sherborne (both McFarlane supervisees) at Bristol, and then Gerald Harriss, McFarlane's immediate successor, as her D.Phil. supervisor at Oxford. Her thesis was on 'The Mowbrays, Earls of Nottingham and Dukes of Norfolk, to 1432'. And I myself was taught by two Magdalen products and McFarlane pupils – the formidable and sometimes utterly and totally terrifying John (J.P.) Cooper but also by Peter (P.S.) Lewis, always extremely stimulating but never ever terrifying, described by my old tutor Michael Maclagan at the time as 'one of the non-effete' Fellows of All Souls College.

I think it is worth recalling the state of scholarship in later medieval English history at that time. S.B. Chrimes concluded his Foreword to the published papers from the first conference in the UK devoted to later medieval British history, held at Cardiff in 1970, with the following words: 'It is hoped that the publication of this volume ... [by] ... Manchester University Press, will bring – to a wider public – acquaintance with current trends of scholarship, and the advancing bounds of knowledge, of a period which used to be called, but can hardly continue to be called, the "Cinderella" of the centuries of English history.' Cinderellas, of course, also tend to have both ugly sisters and Princes Charming – readers can take their choice. Something similar might even be said about the state, and future, of medieval history in Oxford during the regimes of a particular Regius Professor (1957–80) and a certain Chichele Professor (1970–3), when the subject emerged from a dire period of culling in medieval tutorial fellowships in relatively good health. Thanks to dedicated teachers, including Rowena, taught medieval studies in Oxford have survived and indeed prospered.

But what about research? I recall being told by a senior Fellow of the Queen's College in the mid-1960s that the D.Phil. was a degree 'for tourists and Americans'. Preposterous though it may now sound, the non-researching College Fellow (in many Humanities subjects) was still a notable feature of the Oxford scene at that time. But the death-knell had sounded, and the bell was tolling for the 'sound College man' who eschewed research or, if he (always 'he', you note) did any, never published a word of it. You published – it was claimed – only when you had something important and interesting to say. So it was a very different world indeed from today, and it was, at least in the UK, a rather insular one. Any survey, for example, of the study of later medieval nobilities in this country cannot avoid looking over the English Channel and North Sea for both influences and counter-influences. It was not always thus. The days of total or partial non-comprehension between some British and French or German historians appear to have (mercifully) come to an end. I remember once being told at a conference in France by one of the doyens of the profession that my approach was 'trop Britannique'. I never really discovered what that meant. But this was offset by that excellent later medievalist and Directeur des Archives de France, Jean Favier. He (at another such event) gathered the British and selected French participants together to drink a toast to 'nous quinziemistes' – translated, I suppose as something like 'we fifteenth-century-ists' or 'fifteenth-century-ites'.

Now the drinking of toasts reminds me of another of Rowena's interests. She has been Senior Member of Bacchus, the Oxford University Wine Society, and among her interests listed in her online profile, 'Burgundy' features beside garden restoration, trees and music. Again, if I may reminisce again for a moment, the study of Burgundy here carries something of a double entendre – of the most proper kind, however. The history of Valois Burgundy in the later fourteenth and fifteenth centuries has not featured among her published work but it has certainly been part of her teaching, not least in the Joan of Arc special subject. She and I taught it together for some years. But the 'Burgundy' to which her profile refers is also, I'm assuming, the wine. When I was a second-year undergraduate, I recall a conversation with Michael

Maclagan at Trinity, during a tutorial in which he said 'Excellent essay. You seem to have learnt a good deal about Burgundy in the fifteenth century but, perhaps, not so much about it today. Would you care to join me in a glass?' The tutorial continued with both tutor and pupil on their hands and knees, scrutinising a huge genealogical table, spread out over the floor, tracing the dukes of Burgundy and their affiliations.

Now Rowena and I taught the current Oxford undergraduate special subject on 'Joan of Arc and her Times', with its substantial Burgundian component, from its inception onwards. Joan of Arc or, if you prefer, St Joan, is a historical figure around whom myth, legend and vastly differing views have clustered. But allow me to resort once more to the anecdotal. During the 1968 Parisian student protests, a British student found himself caught up in a street riot near the Sorbonne. In a vain and misguided attempt at self-protection from the advancing forces of the Compagnies Republicaines de Securite (CRS), he tried waving his British passport at a riot policeman, but he was met with a baton blow and the words 'Ca, c'est pour Jeanne d'Arc!' – 'Take that, it's for Joan of Arc!' So you see such feelings can run very deep indeed. They were also exemplified at a memorable conference on Joan of Arc held at Orleans in 1979, to which a number of British later medieval historians were invited. I vividly remember an episode during one of the sessions, which were open to the public, held in a secularised redundant church. A long table had been set up in the former chancel, where the altar had once stood, at which sat a distinguished company of French erudits, looking for all the world rather like the disciples at the Last Supper. A young French Jesuit very bravely gave a paper on Joan's trials, her judges and assessors, concluding that had he been there, with their theological, intellectual and canonical formation and backgrounds, he too would have condemned her, whatever his political partisanship may have been. Something like consternation then broke out in the audience. From the back of the church an elderly lady, clad in widow's black and carrying a furled umbrella, advanced menacingly towards the podium. Brandishing the umbrella at the Jesuit she exclaimed: 'Mon pere, Jeanne etait vraiment sainte, n'est-ce-pas?' – 'Father, Joan was truly a saint, was she not?' A section – but not all – of the audience burst into spontaneous applause and the Society of Jesus was put firmly in its place.

Since that time, something of sea-change has taken place in later medieval studies. Medieval noblemen were of course often accompanied, aided, abetted and sometimes challenged, even driven to distraction, by noblewomen. Horace Walpole, old misogynist that he was (quoted, by the way, by McFarlane), could refer cattily in a letter of July 1745 to 'a dozen antediluvian dowagers whose carcasses have miraculously resisted the wet'. In 1984 Rowena published her early article on 'Rich Old Ladies: the Problem of Late Medieval Dowagers'. This was before the days when women's history had really taken off as a subject in its own right. She followed it up in 1992 with her article on 'How Ladies... Who Live on Their Manors Ought to Manage Their Households and Estates: Women as Landholders and Administrators in the Later Middle Ages'. But the deficiency has now been more than remedied with excellent studies of great and less great ladies, including Isabella de Forz, dowager of Aumale, Lady Margaret Beaufort, Joan, Lady Abergavenny (called by one chronicler that 'second Jezebel'), and – eagerly awaited – Rowena's own forthcoming study of Alice Chaucer, duchess of Suffolk, with a foretaste of that work in her article of

2015 on Alice's East Anglian estates;[5] not to mention the many popular biographies pouring out on later medieval queens and princesses. How anyone could ever have doubted the central and vital role of many aristocratic women of the period remains something of a mystery to some of us. But prejudice and unfounded assumption can often influence, if not command, the field in more than one historiographical area, and the most cursory reading of, for example, the Paston letters, should surely have confounded the deniers and sceptics. But there is of course the objection, voiced by some critics, that this was all very much history from above, rather than from below, where women of much lower social rank and economic status used to be thought not to play any significant part. But again, studies of women as trades-and-craftspeople such as embroiderers, tapestry weavers, vintners, innkeepers and shop-owners, both on their own account and as partners in their husbands' businesses, let alone great and powerful women of religion and authors of devotional literature, have opened up new vistas on the English – and indeed European – social landscape. But that lies beyond the scope of this contribution. What perhaps could be emphasised is that cultivating the study of aristocratic women during this period can yield plentiful fruit largely because of the nature of the surviving sources. And perhaps one should always be reminded to 'spurn not the nobly born with love affected, nor treat with virtuous scorn, the well-connected'.

May I conclude this very cursory survey with an expression of hope, albeit tinged with some anxiety, for the future of the studies which Rowena and others have both pioneered and followed up over many years? There is clearly an undying public appetite for later medieval history in all its manifold (and sometimes perplexing) guises. Rather like Lancastrian finance in the fifteenth century there is, I think, an intriguing disparity today between the public and private spheres in this respect. As the Lancastrian exchequer was progressively emptied of funds, and levels of taxation did not rise to compensate fully for that, great wealth accrued to members of the nobility, gentry and mercantile classes. Today, while governments and misguided university politicians and administrators withdraw funding and support for medieval studies, the public appetite for them among both young and old appears all the greater. When, if ever, will they learn? But let me conclude on a lighter and happier note. For sheer entertaining pleasure may I recommend Rowena's article of 2009 on 'Piety, Charity and Family: the Cartulary and Psalter of Sir Edmund Rede of Boarstall (d. 1489)'? Not the most auspicious of titles, perhaps, but her discussion of tenurial horns, and even of the very status-conscious Sir Edmund's heraldic achievement with its (I quote) 'crescendo of impalings and quarterings', can at least raise a smile. And, in similar vein, her comment in a book review on Henry VI who had by c. 1453 'become a virtual cabbage' echoes McFarlane's celebrated dictum that 'his head was too small for his father's crown'. Let us hope that retirement will enable her to complete the first-rate work that we shall look forward to seeing in print.

Malcolm Vale

---

[5] 'Alice Chaucer, Duchess of Suffolk (d.1475) and her East Anglian Estates', in *Wingfield College and its Patrons: Piety and Prestige in Medieval Suffolk*, ed. Peter Blore and Edward Martin (Woodbridge, 2015), 187–207.

INDEX

Abergavenny, Joan, Lady 17, 216
Acton Burnell, Salop 127
Adams, William, chronicle of 135n
Agincourt, battle of (1415) 35, 49
    campaign 31n, 34
Aiscough, William, bishop of Salisbury 58
Aix en Provence, France 176–7, 194
Alamire, Peter, musician and spy 186n, 187
Alberton, Richard, deputy butler 99, 115
Aldeburgh, William, of London 43
Alderholt, Dorset 156–7, 163
Aldham, Suff. 3, 4n, 19
Aldobrandino of Siena, physician 69, 77, 79
Almshouses 67–91
    air quality 69, 78, 80
    avoidance of stress 69, 82
    barbers 78–9
    celibacy 79
    chimneys 80
    cleanliness 78
    diets 69–70, 75, 77
    expulsions from 79, 82–4
    for clergy 73, 86, 88
    gardens 68
    prayers 83–5, 87
    privacy 80, 83
    privies 80
    regulations 67, 71, 72n, 73
    sleep 69, 82
Alston, John, deputy butler 109, 111n, 115
Amritsar, India, massacre at 196–7, 203
Andalucia, Spain 100
Angers, France 56n, 66
Anjou, France 51, 61
    René, duke of 47, 50, 56n, 60
        Isabelle of Lorraine, wife of 47
Anne of Bohemia, queen to Richard II 153
Aquitaine, duchy of 95n, 195, 197n, 198–201, 204
    homage-taking rituals 198–9, 201, 203
    oath-taking 199–202
    seneschals of 25, 198–202
Arc, Joan of 213, 215–16
Archer, Rowena E. 1, 20n, 62n, 67n, 112, 131, 149, 167, 195, 206, 208–17
Arcimboldo, Giuseppe, artist 173
Ardier, Paul 180–1
Aristotle, *Politics* 25
Arnald of Villanova, *De conservanda juventute et retardanda senectute* 77n, 81

Arras, France 50
Arronamendi, Juan, of Castile, shipmaster 98
Arundel, Suss., almshouse 68n, 73n, 85
Arundel, earls of, *see* Fitzalan, Howard
    Thomas, bishop of Ely 5
Ashby, George, clerk of queen's signet 57
Ashton, Herefs. 119
Atkins, Elizabeth 119, 122
Australia, dominion status of 201
Avicenna (Ibn-Sīnā), *Canon* 74, 77
Aylleswy, William, servant of Maud de Vere 15

Bacon, Roger 69n, 78
Baker, Geoffrey le 33
    Sir John 157
Barberd, John 16
Bardolf, William, lieutenant of Calais 24–5
Barlow, William, bishop of St David's 141
Barnet, battle of (1471) 117
Baroda, India 198
Barraclough, Geoffrey, Chichele professor 215
Barstaple, John, of Bristol 85
Basset, Sir Ralph, seneschal of Aquitaine 199–200
Bath and Wells, bishop of, *see* King
Bath, Som. 24n, 136
Baugh, Albert 20
Bawde, Thomas, executor of Sir John Fortescue 107
Beauchamp, Richard, bishop of Salisbury 90
    Richard, earl of Warwick 49, 59
    Isabel, wife of 59
Beaufleur, Geoffrey, deputy butler 114
Beaufort, Edmund, duke of Somerset 49, 61–3
    Henry, cardinal 50, 74n, 91
    John, duke of Somerset 51
    Margaret, countess of Richmond and Derby 51, 132–4, 136, 140–1, 145–7, 162, 216
    Thomas, earl of Dorset 34–5
Beaumaris castle, Anglesey 125
Beaupyne, Thomas, of Bristol 93n, 114
Beauregard, France 171, 180–1, 193
Beauvais, Vincent of, *De moralis principis instutione* 54
Bedford, duchess of, *see* Jacquetta of Luxembourg
    dukes of, *see* John of Lancaster, Tudor
Bekynton, Thomas, king's secretary 33
Belknap, Robert, chief justice common pleas 42

Index

Bell, Susan 56
Bémont, Charles 202
Bendish, Elizabeth 159
Benet, John, chronicle of 52
Berkhamsted, Herts. 138, 155, 157
    castle 138, 154
Berkshire 50
Berland, Sir William 12n
Bermondsey abbey, Surr. 142
Bernard, G.W. 132
Bethune, Philippe de 181
Beverley, Yorks., St Giles's hospital 67, 85
Bhopal, India 199
Bilk, Thomas, of London 43
Bisham abbey, Berks. 145
Bishop, John, of Aston, Suff. 15
Bisley, Glos. 158
Bitfeld, John, shipmaster 110
Blois, Henry de, bishop of Winchester 91
Blondel, Jacques, avener 63n
Bockingfold, Kent 8–9, 14, 19
body corporate, the 37–45
Bole, Nicholas, of London 43
Boleyn, Anne, queen to Henry VIII 153, 159, 163–4
    Geoffrey, mercer 76n
    Robert 16
Bond, Thomas, of Coventry, draper 78, 81, 86
Bonet, Honoré, *Arbre des batailles* 53
book production and trade 54–5
Bordeaux, Gascony 24n, 95, 97, 100, 103n, 104, 199–200
    archbishop of 33
    council at 26
Boston, Lincs., customs accounts 97, 109
Bosworth, battle of (1485) 119–21, 125, 127, 129–30, 132–4, 140, 143, 145–6, 190
Boteler, Sir Ralph, Lord Sudeley 93–4, 115
Bouchot, Henri, conservator 176
boundaries, disputed 157–8
Bourbon, Charles, duke of 168–94
    Louis de 185
Bourdeille, Pierre de 185
Bourgchier, Sir William 11n
Bourne abbey, Lincs. 140
Bracewell, Yorks. 190
Bradford, Yorks. 181
Bradwell, Essex 156
Brampton Bryan, Herefs. 122
Bray, Sir Reynold 109, 134, 139, 142, 144–6
    Katherine (née Hussey) wife of 146
Braybrooke, Robert, bishop of London 8, 44
Brayham, Nicholas 15
Brentford, Mdx., almshouse 74n, 85
Bresson, Robert, *Trial of Joan of Arc* 213
Bridgwater, Som. 96n, 99n, 104, 156
    mayor and burgesses of 156, 162
Bristol 26, 92–115, 127, 134–6
    Barstaple's almshouse 68, 85

    chapel of St Thomas the Martyr 45
    charter (1499) 136
    prior of St James 105–6
    St Magdalen priory, prioress of 102
    university 208–9, 214
    visit of Henry VII 102n, 135–6
    voyages of discovery 108, 110–11
Britanny, France 129, 136, 143, 146
    expedition to 124
    truce with (1419) 23, 24n
British Empire 195, 201
Brocas, family 196n
Broke, John, receiver-general of de Vere estates 3
Bromhill, Thomas 127
Brooke, Robert, *Abridgement* 43
Brotherton, Margaret of 4
Brounflete, Thomas, chief butler 114
Browne, Nicholas, deputy butler 109, 115
    Richard, bedesman 81
    William, of Stamford, clothier 72, 90
Bruisyard abbey, Suff. 3, 11, 14
Buckingham, duchess of, *see* Neville
    dukes of, *see* Stafford
Buckland, Richard, treasurer of Calais 24n, 25
Bude, Guillaume, librarian 189
Builth, Breconshire, lordship of 119, 137
Bulkeley, Charles, attorney 166
    Robert, valet of queen's chamber 57
Bulkley, Richard 82
Bulwer-Lytton, Robert, earl of Lytton, viceroy of India 203
Burgayne, John de, alien 99
Burghersh family 59
Burgundy 215–16
burials 131–48
Burrows, Montagu, Chichele professor 195–7, 201, 204
Burscough priory, Lancs. 134
Bury St Edmunds, Suff. 160
    abbey, abbot of 15, 159, 161
    sacristan of 160
    hospital of St Saviour 73, 86
Bussy Rabutin, Roger de 181
butlerage 92–115
Butterfield, Ardis 29

Cabot, John 108
Cache, Robert, of Wareham 93n
Caen, Normandy 24n, 32
Caerleon, Wales 143, 159
Calais, Picardy 24n, 50, 95, 153, 192, 195, 204
Cambridge 37n
    Christ College 141
    King's College 60n
    Queens' College 60
    St Catharine's College 38
Canada, dominion status of 201
Canterbury, Kent, St John's hospital 84, 86

Canterbury, archbishops of, *see* Chichele, Courtenay
Cardiff, Wales   100, 215
Cardigan, archdeaconry   140
Carlisle, bishop of, *see* Layburne
Carmarthen, Wales   102, 138, 140–1, 146
   grammar school   141
   Grey Friars church   140–1
   mayor and aldermen   141
Carpenter, John   71
Carta Mercatoria (1303)   95
Carus-Wilson, Eleanor   94–5
Cary, William, of London   135
Casteleyn, Simon, of London, mercer   15
Castle Howard, Yorks.   176
Catesby, Robert   158n
   William, deputy butler   115
Catherine of Aragon, marriage to Prince Arthur   145
   queen to Henry VIII   153, 155–7, 159–66
Cavell, John, of Som.   156
Cavendish, John, chief justice king's bench   41–2
Cavill, Paul   129, 136
Caxton, William   27
Chaderton, Edmund, chancellor to Elizabeth of York   164
Chalcott, Walter, sergeant-at-arms   157
Chalgrave, Beds.   44
Chamberlain, John, of London   43
Chamberlayne, Margaret, dressmaker   55n
Chancery   23, 26, 30, 39–42, 67, 101, 121, 124, 163
Chantilly, France   176, 179, 194
chantries, perpetual   39, 43–5
Chaplais, Pierre   33
Charles VI, king of France   185
Charles VII, king of France   51, 60–1
Charles VIII, king of France   137
Charlton, Kent   10–11, 14n, 18
Chaucer family   59
   Alice, duchess of Suffolk, *see* Pole
   Geoffrey   47
   Thomas, chief butler, Speaker of House of Commons   47, 94, 101, 105, 114–15
Chenonceau, France   175
Chepe, Robert, of Bristol   45
Chepstow, Wales   100, 108n, 109n
Chertsey abbey, Surr.   141
Chesham, Bucks.   8, 13, 14n, 19
Chichele, Henry, archbishop of Canterbury   68n, 71, 75, 78, 80, 84, 87
Chichester, bishop of, *see* Polton
chief butlers   92–4, 96–103, 106, 108–9, 111, 114
Chrimes, S.B.   131–2, 215
Church Stretton, Salop   121
Clarence, dukes of, *see* Lionel of Antwerp, Plantagenet, Thomas of Lancaster
Claron, William, shipmaster   108

Cleves, Anne of, queen to Henry VIII   153, 157
Clifford, Sir Lewis   102
Clouet, Jean, artist   174, 176, 181–3, 189–91
   François, son of   176, 190n, 191
Clyst Gabriel, Devon   73, 86
Coke, Sir Edward   42
Colbrooke, John   10
Coldbrook, Monmouthshire   119
Collyweston, Northants.   147, 162
Colman, John, of Polstead   16
Constance, Council of   29, 35
Cook, Katherine, wife of John   17
Cookham, Berks.   165–6
Cooper, J.P.   215
Corbet, Sir Richard of Moreton Corbet   117–24, 126, 129–30
   Elizabeth (née Devereux), wife of   118, 119n
   Elizabeth (née Hopton), mother of   118, 120, 122
   Robert, of Wigmore   124
Cork, Ireland   94n
Cornwall, duchy of   108
Cornwall, Sir Thomas   117, 119
coronation office of butler   93
corporation law, development of   39
Couper, John le, warden of Kyngeston's almshouse   87
court of common pleas   7–8, 12, 15–16, 40–2, 45
Courtenay, family   17
   Edward, earl of Devon   5
   Richard, bishop of Norwich   34–5
   Thomas   56
      Marie, daughter of Charles, count of Maine, wife of   56
   Thomas, earl of Devon   56
   William, archbishop of Canterbury   10
Courteys, John, rector of Ewelme   54
Coventry and Lichfield, bishop of, *see* Smith
Coventry, Warws.   64
   charterhouse   102
   Thomas Bond's almshouse   78, 80–1, 86
   William Ford's almshouse   72, 74, 78n, 79, 86
Cowley, Bucks.   19
Cranach, Lucas, artist   190
Crawford, Anne   56n, 152
Croft, Herefs.   117, 119, 123
Croft, Sir Edward   117n
   Sir Richard, constable of Beaumaris castle   116–30
   Edward, son of   122n, 123
   steward of England at Henry VII's coronation   120
   steward of Prince Arthur's household   125
   Thomas, bastard son of   122, 123
   treasurer of households of Edward, prince of Wales, Richard III and Henry VII   116, 118, 120, 126, 128–9

Thomas, deputy butler   93n, 100n, 115
Cromwell, Ralph, Lord   90
    Thomas   157
Cron, Bonita   46n, 50
Crouzet, Denis   183
Croydon, Surr., Elias Davy's almshouse   71, 86
Cruswiche, Essex   4n, 6n, 16n, 17n, 19
Cunningham, Sean   132
Curry, Anne   21

D'Estrées, Gabrielle, mistress of Henri IV   174
Dampierre, France   66
Dandini, Girolamo   187
Danvers, William   13
Danyell, Geoffrey, surveyor   165n
    Hugh, queen's feodary   159
Dartford, Kent, priory, prioress of   103
Dartmouth, Devon, butler's accounts   97, 107
Daubeney, Giles, Lord, chamberlain to Henry VII   134–5, 137n, 146
David ap Owen   138n, 147
Davies, C.S.L.   117
Davy, Elias, of London, mercer   71, 82, 86
Dawe, William, of London, whittawer   39–40
De retardatione accidentum senectutis   69n, 78
Deane, Henry, bishop of Salisbury   68
Dele, Roger, deputy butler   109n
Delhi, India   197, 199, 205n
Denbigh, lordship of   119
Denys, Martin, Portuguese merchant of London   100
    Thomas   165n
deputy butlers   93, 99, 101, 111
Derby, countess of, *see* Beaufort
    earl of, *see* Stanley
Derby, Nicholas, deputy butler   114
    Walter, deputy butler   93n, 114
Destailleur, Hyppolyte   180, 183–4
Devereux, Walter, Lord Ferrers of Chartley   118
Devon, earls of, *see* Courtenay
Dinham, Joan, Lady   17n, 102n
Dodd, Gwilym   22, 23n
Doddinghurst, Essex   6n
Dorchester, Oxon.   60
Dorset, earl of, *see* Beaufort
Dreyer, Karl Theodor, *Passion of Joan of Arc*   213
Duban, Felix   174
Dudley, John, Lord, constable of the Tower of London   65–6
Durham, bishop of, *see* Langley
Dyer, Reginald, brigadier-general   196
Dymmock, Robert, chancellor to Catherine of Aragon   165

Earls Colne, Essex   3, 6, 14, 19
    priory   2
East Dereham, Norf.   191

Edgcote, battle of (1469)   119–20
Edlogan, Usk   159
Edward of Norwich, duke of York   102
Edward, the Black Prince, prince of Wales   198–9, 201, 211
Edward I, king of England   199, 205, 211
Edward II, king of England   199
Edward III, king of England   39–40, 44, 58, 102
Edward IV, king of England   38, 45, 65–6, 94, 96, 97n, 103, 116–17, 119, 132, 138, 141, 155, 168n
    'Black Book' of   94
    tomb of   141
Edward V, king of England, deposition   119
    prince of Wales   117, 126
Eleanor of Castile, queen to Edward I   152
Eleanor of Provence, queen to Henry III   69, 152
Eliot, Hugh, deputy butler   109–11, 115
    Richard, attorney to Elizabeth of York   164
Elizabeth (d.1495), daughter of Henry VII   134, 138
Elizabeth of York, queen to Henry VII   58, 65, 66n, 120, 132–6, 138–42, 145–8, 151–3, 155, 158, 161, 164
Elstow abbey, Herts., abbess of   157
Eltham, Kent   59
    palace   134
Ely, bishop of, *see* Arundel
empire, definition of   195–6
estate management   1, 151, 160
Etaples, treaty of (1492)   137
Eton College, Windsor   57, 60
Ewelme, Oxon.   59–60, 65, 68
    God's House   68, 71, 73, 75, 78, 80, 82–3, 86–7
    inventory   54–5, 65
    parish church   59
Exchequer   30, 93, 96–7, 105–6, 108–9, 152, 217
    chamber, court of   42
    reforms of (1323–6)   92
Exeter, Devon
    butler's accounts   97–8, 106–7, 109
    Wynard's almshouse   87
Exeter, bishop of, *see* Stapleton
    Elizabeth, duchess of, sister of Henry IV   9n
    duke of, *see* Holand
expedition to France, 1492   125, 143
Eyton, John, deputy butler   115

Fastolf, Sir John   54–5
Favier, Jean, directeur des archives de France   215
Ferdinand II, emperor   179
Feriby, Agnes   15
    Robert de, steward of Maud de Vere's household   3, 15
Fernandus, Bertillmew, alien   99
Ferrers of Chartley, Lord, *see* Devereux

First English Life of Henry V 20
Fish, John, deputy butler 115
Fisher, J.H. 21
 N.R.R. 151–2
Fitzalan, Richard, earl of Arundel 72
 William, earl of Arundel 122
Fitzwalter, Lord, *see* Radcliffe
 Walter, Lord 8
Fleet, Kent 7–8, 14–15, 18–19
forests, poaching in 154–5
Fortescue, Sir John 27, 38
 In Praise of the Laws of England 27
 Sir John (d.1500), chief butler 100, 106–7, 115
 Sir John (1912) 201
Forthey, John 94n
Forz, Isabella de, dowager of Aumale 216
Fossat, Amanieu du 199
Fotheringhay, Northants. 138–9
 castle 165
 college 165
Fowey, Cornwall 94n, 108
Frampton, Walter, deputy butler 114
France, invasion of (1475) 104, 119
François I, king of France 168, 173n, 174–5, 177, 185–6, 189–90, 192
 portraits of 175n
Frating, Essex 2, 10, 14n, 17n, 19
Frating, Philip de 19n
Freeman, E.A. 204
freightage 94n, 95, 101–2, 104, 107, 109
Fremlyngham, William, skinner 15
Frenssh, Reynold le, deputy butler 114
Froissart, Jean, chronicler 33, 185
 Chronicles 211
Fusoris, Jean, astrologer 32n, 34–5

Gaeta, Italy 185
Gaignières, François Roger, antiquary 178–80, 184, 187
Gaillot, Bernard, artist 175, 193
Galen, of Pergamum 74, 77n
Gancourt, Raoul de 35
Garter, Order of the 143
 knights 146
 robes 59
 statutes 53, 58
Gascoigne, Thomas, theologian 51n, 61
Gascon rolls 196n, 200, 202, 204
Gascony, France 195–205
 bureaucracy 201
 lordships 198
 nobility 200–4
 population 198
Gatley, Herefs., park 123
Gauchi, Henri de, translator 54
Gay, Raoul le, priest 32n, 34–5
George V, king-emperor of India 198, 201

Gibbes, Edward 108n
Gilissen, John 196
Gillespie, James 58
Givio, Paolo, museum of 175, 179, 187, 192
Glanville, Bartholomew 54n
Gloucester, dukes of, *see* Humphrey of Lancaster, Thomas of Woodstock
Glyn Dŵr, Owain 138n
Gonzaga, Clara 188
Goodall, John 60
Gordon, Bernard 75
Gorham family 11n
 Geoffrey de, abbot of St Albans 11
Gorwey, John, shipmaster 110
Gosselyn, Roger of West Firle 15
Gough, Piers 127
Gras, Norman 92
Great Abingdon, Cambs. 18
Great Bentley, Essex 3–4, 6, 19
Great Canfield, Essex 6n
Great Hormead, Herts. 19
Great Leighs, Essex 156
Great Malvern, Worcs., church of 146
Great Yarmouth, Norf., St Mary's hospital 72n, 87
Greenwich, Kent 59, 126, 144
Gregg, John, of Kingston-upon-Hull, merchant 68, 74, 87
 Joan, wife of 87
Gregory, Philippa 170
Grey, Elizabeth, widow of Sir Ralph 52
 Richard de, seneschal of Aquitaine 200
Grien, Hans Baldung, artist 190
Griffiths, Ralph 56–7, 60n
Grimston, Edward, retainer of duke of Suffolk 63n
 Alice, wife of 63n
grotesques 112–13
Gwalior, India 198

Hakeston, John, deputy butler 114
Hale, Matthew 92
Hall, Edward, chronicler 117n
Halle, William, of Ore 10, 19
Hamilton, Dakota 151–2
Hampstead Marshall, Berks. 159
Hampton, John, king's esquire 102
Hare, Christopher, biographer 176
Harfleur, Normandy 24n, 32, 34, 49
Harley, Sir John, of Brampton Bryan 122
Harris, Barbara 18
Harriss, Gerald 37n, 208, 210n, 212, 214
Harroweden, Robert 28
Haskell, Francis 181
Haughmond abbey, Salop 103
Havering-atte-Bower, Essex 151, 155
Hawkes, John, deputy butler 115
Hawksbrook, David 121

Index

Hawley, Thomas, of Lincs. 44
Haye, Corneille de la, artist 190
Hedingham castle, Essex 6n, 7
Hedingham Vaux, Essex 2n, 7–8, 14n, 17n, 19
Helions Bumpstead, Essex 6n
Helwedyn, Thomas, of Kent 16
Hende, John, mayor of London 11, 14, 19
Henri II, king of France 173
Henri IV, king of France 174, 151
Henrietta Maria, queen to Charles I 152
Henry I, king of England 157
Henry III, king of England 2, 21n, 69
Henry IV, king of England 9–10, 13, 15, 32, 42, 116
Henry V, king of England 20–36, 49, 58, 214
   council of 24–5, 31
   founder of Syon abbey 134
   signet letters of 21–4, 28–33, 35–6
Henry VI, king of England 33, 34, 47, 50–4, 56, 58, 61, 64, 71n, 96, 132–3, 137, 141–3, 217
   council of 50
   cult of 142
   readeption 119
Henry VII, king of England 74, 81n, 95, 98, 103–4, 112–13, 116–17, 122n, 129, 131–48
   council of 106, 110, 121–5, 129
   Edmund (d.1500), son of 147
   grotesque of 112
   household plots 126–30, 145
   supervisor of Jasper Tudor's will 136
   ward to earl of Pembroke 118
Henry VIII, king of England 141, 157, 168, 187, 191–2
   council of 161–2
   duke of York 133, 137–9
Hepburn, Frederick 170n
Heraklion, Crete 98
heraldic devices
   badges depicting harts 168, 184–5, 189–90
   de la Pole arms 190
   leopard skin collar 190
Herbert, Sir Richard of Coldbrook 119
   William, son of 119
   William, earl of Pembroke 117–18
Hereford 118, 119n
   Grey Friars church 137
Herefordshire 2, 117, 119, 123–4, 135n
   sheriffs of 118–21
Hethe, Hamo, bishop of Rochester 72, 87
Heytesbury, Wilts., St Katherine's almshouse 71, 73n, 74n, 76n, 79, 81n, 82–3, 87
Hicks, Michael 83
Higden, Ranulph, *Polychronicon* 27
High Wycombe, Bucks. 60
Higham Ferrers, Northants., almshouse 68n, 71, 80, 82n, 87

Highworth, Wilts. 158, 165
Hill, Richard, dean of chapel royal, bishop of London 146n
Hitchin, Herts. 157, 159, 166
Hoker, John, deputy butler 114
Holand, John, duke of Exeter 8–9
   John, earl of Huntingdon 23
Holderness, Yorks. 143
Holmes, G.A., *Estates of the Higher Nobility* 212
Holt, John, king's serjeant 42
Holybrand, William, deputy butler 108, 109n
homage and fealty ceremonies 156, 159, 164, 198–9, 201–5
Hoo, Sir Thomas, Lord, chancellor of Normandy and France 54–5
Hood, Robin, pageant 84
Hopton, Salop, castle 118–20, 122
   'Hagley's Mountain' 119, 121n, 122n
Hopton, Thomas 118
   Elizabeth, daughter of 118
   Walter, son of 118
hospitals for the sick poor 70, 73, 75
Howard, Catherine, queen to Henry VIII 153
   Thomas, 14th earl of Arundel 170
   Thomas, duke of Surrey 186
   Thomas, earl of Surrey 130
Howell, Joan, nurse to Henry VII 102
Hull, Margery, wife of Sir Edward 52
Hulle, John 104
Humphrey of Lancaster, duke of Gloucester 24–6, 59
Hundon, Staffs. 159n
Hungerford, Margaret, Lady 71n, 87
   Walter, Lord 87
Hunt, Andrew, of London, girdler 85, 88
Hunter, Timothy 170, 181, 184
Huntingdon, earl of, *see* Holand
Hussey, John 109
Hyderabad, India 198
Hynde, John, attorney 164
Hythe, Kent, Bishop Hethe's almshouse 72, 87

incorporation in English law 37–8, 44–5
India
   British Raj 196n, 197, 202n, 203–4
   bureaucracy 201
   Congress party 196
   dominion status of 201
   durbars 197, 199, 202–3, 205
   nationalism 196, 203–4
   orders of chivalry, Star of India 199, 202
   population 198
   princes and nobility 202–3
   territorial area 198
Indian Mutiny or War of Independence 203
Inglesham, Nicholas, vicar of Highworth 158
Ireland 7, 95, 105
   duke and duchess of, *see* Vere

Isabella of France, queen to Edward II 153
Islip, Oxon. 68
Ivony, Richard, of East Dereham 164

Jacquetta of Luxembourg, duchess of Bedford 57
Jaipur, India 198
James, Margery 92
Jenks, Stuart 97
Jodhpur, India 198
John of Gaunt, duke of Lancaster, chantry of 44
John of Lancaster, duke of Bedford, regent of France 24–5, 31n, 49
Jones, Evan 95, 135n
Jordan, Ralph, of London, whittawer 39–40, 42

Kashmir, India 198
Katherine de Valois, queen to Henry V 56n, 142–3, 147, 161n
Kemp, John, cardinal and chancellor 63
Kendall, Paul Murray, *Richard the Third* 209
Kent 2–3, 6–8, 27, 156
Keynsham abbey, Som. 134–7, 141
Kidwelly, Morgan 146–7
King, Oliver, bishop of Bath and Wells 139
king's bench, court of 7, 41–2, 122, 124
King's Langley, Herts., priory, prior of 157, 165
Kingsdown, Kent 10–11, 14n, 19, 156
Kingsley, John 33
Kingston-upon-Hull, Yorks. 38, 98
    charter 38
    Gregg's almshouse 68, 74
    Kyngeston's almshouse 72, 87
Kingswood, Glos., royal chase 135
Kirton in Lindsey, Lincs. 153
Knolles, William, of London, grocer 105n
Knyvet, John, chancellor 42
Kyngeston, James de, of Hull 72, 87

Ladislaus II, king of Bohemia 187
Lamb, Sir John, chancellor to Henrietta Maria 152
Lambert, Malcolm 208
Lambeth, Surr., palace 138n, 162
Lancaster, duchy of 18, 44, 64, 127, 143, 150n, 151, 155–6
Lancaster, duke of, *see* John of Gaunt
    Henry, earl of 88
Lane, Samuel 212
Langley, John, deputy butler 115
    Thomas, keeper of the privy seal, bishop of Durham, chancellor 13, 23
languages
    Anglo-Norman 21, 23–6, 28, 33–5
    Cornish 29
    English 20–36, 212
    French 20n, 21–36, 53–6, 65, 69
    Gascon 29, 34
    Irish 29
    Latin 20, 22–6, 28–35, 53, 55, 65, 83, 164
    Occitan 29n
    Welsh 28–9
Laughton, Suss. 8–10, 14n, 19
Lavenham, Suff. 3, 15, 19
Lawe, Agnes 40
Layburne, Roger, bishop of Carlisle 109
Laynesmith, Joanna 52n, 55, 62n, 64, 154
Le Crotoy, France 32
Le Livre de la Cité des Dames 55
Le Patourel, John 196
Leconfield, Yorks. 12n
Leget, Joan 13n
Leicester, Grey Friars church 138, 141
    St Mary's hospital in the Newarke 68n, 76, 88
Leicester, John, chantry priest 43
Leighton, Sir Thomas, of Church Stretton 121, 124
Lennard Brown, Sarah 83
Leominster, Herefs. 121, 123, 125
    riots at 116–17, 119, 123–4, 126, 128, 130
leper houses 70, 78n
leprosy 78
Les Grandes Chroniques de France 56
Lessy, Master Richard, dean of chapel of duchess of York 139
Leu, Thomas de, engraver 171–2, 175, 177, 181, 193
Lewis, P.S. 215
Leyham, Suff. 159
Liber Assisarum 39–40, 42
Lichfield, Staffs., St John's hospital 72n, 73n, 76, 80, 82, 88
limited companies 38
Lincoln, bishop of, *see* Longland, Russell
Lionel of Antwerp, duke of Clarence 168n
Lisbon, Portugal 100
livery, distribution of 123
Livius, Titus, *Vita Henrici Quinti* 20
Llanelwedd castle, Powys 118
Llanfrechfa, Monmouthshire 159
Lloyd, Master Thomas, precentor of St David's 141
Lomner, William 62n
London 24, 32, 41, 64, 92n, 94n, 95–6, 98, 100, 103–4, 107–8, 110, 112, 114, 127, 144
    administration
        butler's accounts 97, 99n, 106, 112
        common council 43
        coroner 93
        court of husting 39
        customs accounts 97
        mayor and chamberlain 40
        mortmain returns 42
    churches
        All Hallows London Wall 39–40
        St Anthony 43

Index

St Mary Aldermary   43
St Michael Paternoster   43
companies and guilds   42–3
  Brewers' Company   22
  Cutlers' Company almshouse   84, 88
  Fishmongers' guild   40
  Girdlers' Company almshouse   88
  Goldsmiths' guild   40, 44
  Grocers' Company   27
  Mercers' Company   89
  Merchant Tailors' almshouse   79, 84, 89
  Saddlers' guild   40
  Skinners' fraternity   66n
  Whittawers' guild   39–44
hospitals
  St Augustine Papey   73, 79, 88
  St Katherine by the Tower   76, 88
  St Anthony's   68, 77, 88
Fleet prison   107
Fleet Street brewhouse, 'Signe of the Walshemane'   128
'Palmer's Place'   143
St Paul's cathedral   58
Tower Hill   128
Tower of   65–6, 130, 145
London, bishop of, *see* Braybrooke, Hill
Longland, John, bishop of Lincoln   84
Lords Appellant   5
Lorraine, duchy of   187–8
  Antoine, duc de   183, 186
  Renée de Bourbon Montpensier, duchess of   183
Lorraine, Jean de, bishop of Metz   187
Louis Philippe, king of France   174–5
Louis XI, king of France   66
Louis XII, king of France   186
Louis XIV, king of France   178
Louviers, France   24n
Lovelace, John, of Kingsdown   156
Lovell, Francis, Lord, Viscount, chief butler   115, 122n, 127
Lovell, Sir Thomas   134, 139, 142, 145–6
Lucy, Joan   17
  Sir William   118
Ludlow, Salop   117, 125–6, 127n, 147, 184
Ludlow, Sir Richard, of Stokesay   121
  William, deputy butler   115
Lunde, Joan   67, 70
Luxembourg, James of   103
Lyhert, Walter, chaplain, queen's confessor   57
Lypiatt Park, Glos.   158
Lytton, earl of, see Bulwer-Lytton

Maclagan, Michael   215–16
Madox, Thomas   92
Madrid, Spain   176
Maidenhead, Berks.   60
Maine, Charles, count of   56

Maine, France   60–1, 151
Maitland, F.W.   38–9, 45
Mantes, France   52
Mantua, Italy   188
March, earl of, *see* Edward IV
  earldom of   120n
Margaret, daughter of Henry VII, queen of Scotland   134
Margaret of Anjou, queen to Henry VI   46–66, 155
  books   49, 54, 56
  coronation   58
  garter robes   59
  jewel and household accounts   48, 57
Margaret of York, duchess of Burgundy   187
Marie, queen to Charles VII   50
Market Overton, Rutland   2, 8, 12–13, 14n, 19
Marouse, Afounso, shipmaster   110
Marseilles, France   192
Martin V, pope   33
Martin, Nicolas de   182
Mary of Teck, queen to George V   201
Maurice ap Hugh, yeoman of the crown   127
McFarlane, K.B.   17, 214, 216–17
McIntosh, Marjorie   83, 151
Meale, Carol   54–5
Medici, Catherine de, queen of France   175–6, 181, 191
  Lorenzo de   191
Medina del Campo, treaty of (1489)   98n
Mediterranean, the   98, 100, 192
memorialization   131–48
Merbury, Nicholas, chief butler   115
Mérimée, Prosper, director of historic monuments   174
Merrison, Maureen   209
Metz, bishop of, *see* Lorraine
Metz, France   186–7, 189
  palace of Haut Pierre   187
Middlesex, justices of the peace   122
Midgham, Dorset   157
Miles, Daniel   180
Milford Haven, Pembrokeshire   119
Milverton and Bridgwater castle, Som., hundred of   156
Mitton, John, servant, Elizabeth, his wife   121
Mohun, Joan, Lady, of Dunster   5n, 14
  John de, Lord   14
Montagu, Thomas, earl of Salisbury   50
Montaigne, Michel de, essays   188
Montivilliers, Normandy   34–5
Montmorency, Anne, duke de   189
Montpezat, Raymond-Bernard de   199
Morice, Davy   127
Mortimer, John   120
Mortimer's Cross, battle of (1461)   117
mortmain licences for chantries   39, 44–5
Mosdale, John   23n
Motyng, Thomas, of East Dereham   164

Index

Mowbray, John, Lord 6
Mowbray earls of Nottingham and dukes of
    Norfolk 1, 208, 214
Mowbray estates 14n
Mysore, India 198

Nagel, Hans, musician 186n
Nancy, France 52, 185n, 186n, 188–9
Napoleon III, emperor 174
Nassington, William of 22
Netherlands, the 55, 176, 186
Neville, Anne, duchess of Buckingham 63
    Anne, queen to Richard III 139
    Katherine, duchess of Norfolk 14n
    Richard, earl of Warwick 116, 118
New Zealand, dominion status of 201
Newcastle upon Tyne, Northumb., Thornton's
    hospital 73, 84, 89, 106
Newton, Geoffrey, chief butler 114
Norfolk, duchess of, *see* Neville
    dukes of, *see* Mowbray
Normandy 21, 49–52
Norris, John, keeper of queen's jewels and
    wardrobe 57
North, Richard 157
    John, son of 157
Northampton, battle of (1460) 118
Northumberland, earl of, *see* Percy
Norwich 71n, 73
    St Giles's hospital, God's House 73, 77,
        83n, 89
Norwich, bishop of, *see* Courtenay, Suffield
Notebeem, William 4n
Nottingham, Plumptre's almshouse 72n, 89
Nottingham, earls of, *see* Mowbray

Odynham, William 159
Old Romney, Kent 10–11, 14n, 19
Oliver, William, of London, skinner 15
Olivier, Laurence 209
Olriet, Florentin, master of the mint 188
Ord-Hume, James, composer 196
Ore, Suss. 10
Orleans, France 216
    siege of 50
Orleans, Charles, duke of 52
Orleton, Salop 125
Orsini, Giambattista, cardinal 32n
Osney, Oxon. 60
Owen ap Reynold, *alias* Owen Glendower 122
Owen, Sir David 147n
Oxford 208
    Ashmolean Museum 191
    Christ Church Meadow 210
    Dendrochronological Laboratory 181
    Rewley House 208
    university 208, 210–16
        All Souls College 215

Brasenose College 37n
Christ Church College 168, 210
Exeter college 54
Merton College 45
Queen's College 60n
St John's College 213
wine society 215
Oxford, countesses and earls of, *see* Vere

Paris, France 34–5, 49, 52, 54
    Pont Neuf 174
    student protests (1968) 216
parliament, house of Commons, speaker of 94
parliaments 29, 31n, 96
    1344 28
    1377 (Jan.) 28
    1380 (Jan.) 28
    'Merciless' 1388 5, 9
    1394 43
    1397 (Sept.) 8
    1399 9
    1404 (Jan.) 12
    1406 13
    1420 30
    1449–50 61
    1450 62
    1464–5 97n
    1484 97
    1485 121
    1487 127
    1495 136–7, 138n, 155n
Parr, Katherine, queen to Henry VIII 152–3,
    162, 164, 166
    regency (1544) 166
Paston family 217
Paston, John 62n
    Sir John 65n
Pataudi, India 198
Pavia, battle of (1525) 175–7, 186, 189, 191
Payn, John, chief butler 114
Payne, John, cofferer and treasurer of Henry VII's
    household 129n
Pearsall, Derek 22
Pelham family 10
Pelham, John, clerk 10n
    John de, parson 3
    Sir John 10, 19
    Joan, wife of 10
Pembridge, Isabel, widow of Sir Fulk 73n, 76,
    80, 91
Pembroke, earls of, *see* Herbert, Tudor
Percy family 12, 116
Percy, Henry, earl of Northumberland 12, 28
    Henry, king's serjeant 41
    Sir Henry ('Hotspur') 12
    Thomas, earl of Worcester 11–12
Perna, Petrus 179
perpetual corporations 38–9, 41, 44

Perreal, Jean, artist   189
Phelip, Sir John   59
Philip the Fair, king of Castile   181
Philip VI, king of France   28
Philippa of Hainault, queen to Edward III   153
phlebotomy   79
Picard, Henry, vintner   100n, 101, 114
Pichard, Edward, servant   16
Picquigny, France   66
Piers, John, deputy butler   115
Pilkington, John   190
Pillard, Laurent   182, 183n
Pisford, William, executor   86
Pizan, Christine de   65n
  Le Dit de la Pastoure   55
  Le Livre des fais d'armes et de chevalerie   53
  Livre des trois vertus   64
Place, Gracian de la, of Worcester, vintner   108n
plagues   70, 83, 147
Plantagenet, Edward, earl of Warwick   132, 145
  George, duke of Clarence   145
  Richard, duke of York
    Cecily (née Neville) wife of   49–50, 52, 54, 63, 117, 138, 184
    Elizabeth, daughter of   65
  Richard of Shrewsbury (b.1473), duke of York, son of Edward IV   126, 133
Pleshey, Essex   10, 140
  college   9–10, 13–14, 19
Plumptre, John, merchant of Nottingham   72n, 89
Plymouth, Devon   108
Poitiers, Diane de   174, 189
Poitiers, France   199
Pole, de la, family   49
Pole, de la, Alice (née Chaucer), countess of Salisbury, duchess of Suffolk   46–67, 82, 168n, 216
  books   49, 54–6, 65
  tomb effigy   59
  John, duke of Suffolk   57, 60, 65
    Elizabeth, wife of   65
  Michael (d.1415)   49
  Michael, earl of Suffolk   49
  Richard, putative duke of Suffolk   168–93
  William, earl, marquess and duke of Suffolk   47, 49–51, 54, 56–7, 59–64, 71, 78, 84n, 86, 208
Pole, Roger, servant   121
Pollard, John, parson of Lavenham   3, 15
Polton, Master Thomas, bishop of Chichester   29, 33
Pont-de-l'Arche, France   24n, 32n
Pontoise, France   51
Popham, Robert, deputy butler   110–11, 115
Portsmouth, Hants   31
  God's house   76, 89
Portugal, merchants of   99n, 100

Powell, Helena   37n
Power, Eileen, *Medieval Women*   210
Poyntz, Sir Robert, chancellor of Catherine of Aragon   157
Preston, Suff.   2n, 7–8, 17n, 19
prisage   92–115
Pritchard, Thomas, vicar of Carmarthen   141
Puebla, Rodrigo Gonzalez de la, Spanish ambassador   145
Purslow hundred, Salop   122

queens of England
  as intercessors   153–4
  councils of   149–67
    councillors   153, 156, 158, 160, 164–5
    judicial function   151–2, 154, 158, 160, 162, 164, 166–7
    managing estates   151, 156
    records   154, 166
  jointures   151, 154–5, 157
  seals   162, 164

Radcliffe, John, Lord Fitzwalter, steward of Henry VII's household   129
  Sir John, constable of Bordeaux castle   24n, 25–6
Radcot Bridge, battle of (1387)   5, 13
Radnor castle, Powys   118
Raglan castle, Monmouthshire   118, 120
Ramsey, Essex   6, 10–11, 14n, 19
Ramsay, J.H.   20, 51n
Rawcliffe, Carole   163
Rawlyns, John, of Leominster   123n
Rayleigh castle, Essex   9
Raymond, John, of Great Leighs   156
Reading, Berks.   60, 125
  abbey   121, 123
Reculée castle, France   66
Rede, Sir Edmund of Boarstall   217
regimen sanitates   69, 74–5, 77, 80–1
Reynolds, Catherine   53–4
Rhayader church, Wales   123
Ricart, Philip, deputy butler   115
Richard II, king of England   3, 9–10, 12–14, 154, 168, 184–6, 188–9, 191
Richard III, king of England   97, 117–20, 127, 129, 133, 138–9, 141, 146, 190, 209
  craniofacial reconstruction   168n
  tomb   132, 138–9
Richards, Griffith, chancellor to Catherine of Aragon   164
Richardson, Malcolm   22
Richmond, Surr.   111, 146
Richmond, Colin   83
Richmond, countess of, *see* Beaufort
  earl of, *see* Tudor
Ringwold, Kent   10–11, 14n, 19
River Severn   100, 105, 109

228 *Index*

Rivers, Earl, *see* Wydeville
Robyn, Henry, of Westwick   16
Rochester, bishop of, *see* Hethe
Rockingham, Northants.   139
Rome, Italy   173, 181–2
   sack of   176n, 177
Rome, Giles of, *De regimine principium*   54
Rosche, John   16
Ross, Charles   209, 214
   James   208, 212
Rouen, Normandy   24n, 32, 47, 49, 51–5, 57, 61
Roueyte, Robert   17
Rowley, Thomas, of Bristol, merchant   98
Royal Air Force, central band of   196
royal household   46, 62, 93–4, 97, 101, 103, 116–30, 146, 153
   ordinances (1478)   94, 103
   steward   94, 128–9, 164
Royston, Herts., priory, prior and canons of   164
Rudd, Roger, of London, whittawer   39–40
Ruddick, Andrea   29
Rudolf II, emperor   173
Rumbold, Nicholas, of London, whittawer   39–42
   Agatha, wife of   39
Russell, John, bishop of Lincoln   88
   John, captain   186n
   Robert, deputy butler   93n, 114
   Thomas, deputy butler   115
Ruther, Philip, gentleman   123

Saffron Walden, Essex, almshouse   74, 76n, 83n, 89
Safroni, Arnold, composer   196
Saint-Sardos, Aquitaine, war of   199
Saints
   Augustine   187
   Catherine   213
   Eustace   184–5
   Hubert   184
   John the Baptist   174, 190
   Louis   53
   Michael   213
   Vincent Ferrer   136
Salisbury, Wilts., Holy Trinity almshouse   78, 90
   St Nicholas's hospital   79–80, 83, 90
Salisbury, bishop of, *see* Aiscough, Beauchamp, Deane
   countess of, *see* Pole
   earl of, *see* Montagu
Sandwich, Kent, St Bartholomew's hospital   76n, 90, 92
Sandys, Sir William, treasurer of Calais   186n
Saul, Nigel   131
Saundres, Thomas, deputy butler   93n, 114
Saxe-Coburg-Gotha, house of, later Windsor   196
Say, Elizabeth, Lady, widow of Lord William   103
Scalant, Anthony, of Castile   100
Scales, Thomas, Lord, seneschal of Normandy   52, 54
   Ismania, wife of   52, 57
Scarborough castle, Yorks.   23n
Schedel, Hartmann, *Weltchronik*   181
Scotland   133, 134n, 136, 191, 192
Seeley, J.R., *The Expansion of England*   195–6, 204
serjeants at law   104
Sesille, William   3
Seymour, Jane, queen to Henry VIII   153, 156
Shah Jeha Begum, ruler of Bhopal   199
Shakespeare, William   51n, 209
   Richard III   209
Sharpe, John, deputy butler   101, 115
Shawbury, Salop   119
Sheen, Surr.   59, 126, 134
   palace of, renamed Richmond   140
sheep, flocks of   155, 157, 167
Shelley, Thomas   8
Sherborne, Dorset, hospital   74, 84, 90
Sherborne, James   208, 214
Shipman, John   99n
Ships
   Carrigon   103n
   Cog John of Bristol   94n
   Magdalen of Errenteria   98
   Mary Belhouse   108n
   Mary Gallant   100
   Matthew   108
   Michael of Bristol   94n
   Nicholas of the Tower   62
   single-masted cogs   95
   triple-masted   95
Shottle park, Derbys.   127
Shrewsbury, Salop   90, 120–1, 127
   battle of (1403)   12
   Water's almshouse   81, 90
Shrewsbury, earl of, *see* Talbot
   Margaret, countess of   52, 58
Shropshire   117–18, 121–4, 127
   parliamentary elections   121, 124
Sigismund, Holy Roman Emperor   35
Silesia, Casimir, duke of   33
Simnel, Lambert   122
Skelton, John, poet   191
Skilling, Michael, king's attorney   40
Skoda, Hannah   214
Slegh, John, chief butler   114
Smith, William, bishop of Coventry and Lichfield   88
Snitterby, Hugh de, of Kirton   153
Somerset, dukes of, *see* Beaufort
Somerset, John, physician   74n, 85
Sorrell, Thomas, of Essex   156
Southampton   33, 98, 100, 106, 112
Southfrith, Kent   16

Index

Southwark, Surr. 124, 129n
Southwell, Robert, chief butler 108–9, 111n, 115
Spinelly, Thomas 187n
Spray, William 15
Spynell, John, yeoman of the crown 127
St Albans, Herts., abbey 11, 14, 19
St David's, bishop of, *see* Barlow
    cathedral and archdeaconry 140–1
St John, Sir John, mayor of Bordeaux 24n, 25–6
Stafford family estates 137
Stafford, Edward, duke of Buckingham 137, 143
    Henry, duke of Buckingham 117
        Katherine (née Wydeville), widow of 134, 137
    Henry, Lord, husband of Margaret Beaufort 140, 146
    John, earl of Wiltshire, chief butler 115
    Ralph, earl of 17
Stamford, Lincs., God's house 72–3, 82, 96
Stanley, Sir William, chamberlain of Henry VII's household 116–18, 120, 122–3, 125–30, 132–5, 138, 145–6
    Elizabeth (née Hopton), wife of 118, 120, 122
    Thomas, Lord, earl of Derby, constable of England 133–4, 146, 191n
Stansted Mountfichet, Suff. 6n
Stapilton, John, deputy butler 93n, 105, 114
Stapleton, Walter, bishop of Exeter 73, 86
Star Chamber 161, 163
statutes
    of Gloucester (1278) 6
    of March (1340) 30
    of Mortmain (1279) 40, 42
    of Pleading (1362) 27
Stodeye, John, vintner 101, 114
Stoke, battle of (1487) 116, 123, 126, 128–9
Stokes, John, deputy butler 114
Stokesay, Salop 121
Stokke, Thomas, of Stamford 90
Stondon, Herts., park 164
Storm, Richard 15
Strete, William, chief butler 114
Stuart, James, duke of Albany, regent of Scotland 186
Stubbs, William 204
Sudbury, Suff., mayor of 160–3
Sudeley, Lord, *see* Boteler
Suffield, Walter, bishop of Norwich 73, 89
Suffolk, duchess, dukes and earls of, *see* Pole
Sumpter, John 16
    John, son of 16
Sumption, Jonathan, justice of the Supreme Court 37n
Surrey, earl and duke of, *see* Howard
Sutton, John 127–9
Syon abbey, Surr. 134

Talbot, Beatrice, Lady 52, 57
    John, earl of Shrewsbury, chief butler 52–3, 101, 115
        'Shrewsbury Book' 52–4, 57–8
    Sir Gilbert, sheriff of Salop 121
    William, Lord 52
Tasburgh, William, parson of Rayleigh 8
Tattershall College, Lincs., almshouse 80, 90
Taylor, Andrew 53
    Craig 53
Tempest family 170, 181, 190–2
Tempest, Nicholas 190
    Sir Richard 192n
    William 190n
Tenby, Pembrokeshire 100
Terry, John, servant 119, 121–2, 124
Tetsworth, Oxon. 60
Tewkesbury, Glos. 110
    abbey 145
    battle of (1471) 65, 117, 119
Tey, Josephine, *The Daughter of Time* 209
Thibianville, Captain 186n
Thomas of Lancaster, duke of Clarence 24n, 25, 26n, 33
Thomas of Woodstock, duke of Gloucester 8–10, 14
Thomas, Sir Rhys ap 140, 146
Thornbury, Glos. 134–5
Thorne, John, prior of Reading abbey 121
Thornton, Roger, of Newcastle, merchant 73, 84, 89
Tiptoft, Sir John, chief butler 35, 114
Titchfield Abbey, Hants 58
Tolleshunt, Essex 156
Tong, Salop, almshouse 73n, 76, 80, 91
Tong Hall, Yorks. 170, 180–2, 184–5, 188, 192, 194n
Touques, Normandy 24n, 31
Tours, France 50–1, 60–1
    church of St Martin 50
    truce of (1444) 50
Tout, T.F. 48n, 94, 204
Towton, battle of (1461) 56
Trende, William, craftsman 164
Trevisa, John 25n, 27
Trevor-Roper, Hugh, Regius Professor 215
Troyes, treaty of (1420) 24n, 30
Tudor, Arthur, prince of Wales 125–6, 130, 132, 137, 139, 145–7
    Edmund, earl of Richmond 132, 137–41, 146–7
    Jasper, earl of Pembroke and duke of Bedford 118, 119n, 120n, 132, 134–8, 140–3, 146–7
    Mary, daughter of Henry VII 136
    Owen, husband of Queen Katherine 56n, 137, 138n, 147
    Owen (d.1502) 147
tunnage and poundage 96–8

Index

Tunstal, Cuthbert   187n
Tutbury, honour of   19n
Tyle, Thomas, chief butler   114
Tyrell, Sir James   119

Ufford, Sir Ralph   2
   Matilda of Lancaster, wife of   2
Usk, Mortimer lordship of   143, 159

Vale, Malcolm   21, 29–30, 32n, 213, 217
Vannes, Brittany   136
Vaux, Katherine   66n
Vegetius, *De Re Militari*   24
Vere, de, family   1, 5, 11, 14, 17–18, 212
Vere, Alice de, countess of Oxford   11n
   Alphonso de   11n
   Aubrey de, earl of Oxford   5, 7–9, 12–14
   John de (d.1350), Elizabeth (née Courtenay), widow of   5
   John de, 7th earl of Oxford   2, 79
   John de (d.1513), 13th earl of Oxford   10, 66, 129
   Richard de, earl of Oxford   12
   Robert de, 9th earl of Oxford, duke of Ireland   10–11
      Phillipa, wife of   4, 13
   Thomas de, earl of Oxford   2
      Maud, wife of   1–19
Verney, John, queen's steward   157
Versailles, France   175, 193
Victoria, queen-empress   203
Viollet le Duc, Eugene-Emmanuel   174
Virginia, America   196
Vosterman, Lucas   170n, 172, 193

Wakefield, Richard   13n
   Thomas, of Leicester   13n
Waldeschef, Walter, of London   43
Wales   95, 105, 109, 116–17, 125, 127–8, 134, 140, 146, 159
   marches of   116, 127, 143, 146
   princes of, *see* Edward, the Black Prince, Edward V
Walker, Greg   191
   Simon   208
Wallingford castle, Oxon.   65
Walpole, Horace   216
Walsingham, Norf.   63, 160n
   priory, prior of   155
Warbeck, Perkin, pretender   125–7, 133, 136–7, 145
Ward, Jennifer   48
Wareham, Dorset   93n
Wark castle, Northumb.   192
Warner, Alice, of Bury St Edmunds   160
Wars of the Roses   37n, 170, 209
Warwick   213
Warwick, earls of, *see* Beauchamp, Neville, Plantagenet

Water, Degory, of Shrewsbury, draper   81, 90
Waters Upton, Salop   122
Watts, John   21
Waugh, W.T., *The Reign of Henry the Fifth*   210
Waynflete, William, bishop of Winchester   63, 91
Welles, Herts.   3, 9, 10n, 14n, 19
Welles, John, Viscount   132, 137n, 142–7
   Cecily (née Wydeville), Viscountess   142–4
Wendover, Bucks.   155, 164
Wenlock, Sir John, Lord, usher of queen's chamber   57, 103, 115
Weobley castle, Herefs.   119n
Wesenham, John, chief butler   92n, 101, 114
West Dean, Suss.   2n, 4n, 9–10, 14n, 19
West Firle, Suss.   15
Westminster   17, 31, 59, 71, 107, 122, 124–6, 128–9, 133, 135, 137, 144, 148, 161
   abbey   58, 63–4, 132–4, 136, 138–9, 141–4, 146–7
   abbot of   122, 140, 142, 147
   almshouse founded by Henry VII   74–5, 77, 80, 81n, 91
   chamber for the queen's council   150, 164
   Edward the Confessor's chapel   134, 147
   Hall   122, 129
   lady chapel   143
   priory of   41
   treaty of (1466–7)   98
Weston, William, of Bristol, merchant   100
Westwick, Herts.   9–11, 14n, 16, 19
Weymouth, Dorset   99n
Whitstable, Kent   8–9, 14n, 19
Whittingdon, Richard   28
Whittington, Richard, of London, mercer   71, 75n, 86
   almshouse   80n, 89
Wickwane, William, archbishop of York   85
Wigmore castle, Herefs.   117, 124
Wigston Magna, Leics.   2, 3n, 7–9, 13, 14n, 19
Wilcox, Thomas, under-bailiff of Wendover   155
Willoughby de Broke, Sir Robert, steward of Henry VII's household   129
Wiltshire, earl of, *see* Stafford
Wimborne Minster, Dorset   136, 142
Winchelsea, Suss.   94n
Winchester, Hants, hospital of St Cross   74n, 80n, 91
Winchester, bishop of, *see* Blois, Waynflete
Windsor, Berks.   59–60, 133, 142–3
   castle and park   60, 66, 145
   St George's chapel   59, 88, 141–3
wines   92–113
   burgundy   215–16
   malmsey   95, 103n
   Rochelle   111
   sweet   100
Wingfield, Suff.   55, 59, 65
Wingfield, Sir William   2, 12, 19n

Index

Witham, Essex, charterhouse   102
Wokefield, Berks.   157
Wolsey, Thomas, archbishop of York, cardinal   161, 186
Wood-Legh, Katherine, *Perpetual Chantries in Britain*   39
Woodstock, Oxon.   60
Woolgar, Christopher   5
Worcester cathedral   147
  common bell   123
Worcester, earl of, *see* Percy
Wotton, Walter de   8
  Alice, daughter of   8
Wrabness, Essex   11, 14n, 19
Wriothesley, Thomas (d.1534), Garter king of arms   144
Writhe, John (d.1504), Garter king of arms   144
Wroughton, Anne, queen's servant   57
Wycliffe, John, writings   26n
Wycombe, John de, deputy butler   114
Wydeville, Anthony, Earl Rivers   115
  Elizabeth, queen to Edward IV   142, 153, 165–6
  Richard   57
Wylie, J.H. *The Reign of Henry the Fifth*   210
Wynard, William, recorder of Exeter   68n, 76n, 87

Yardley, Worcs.   162
Year Books   37–9, 42–3, 45, 122
Yolande, sister of Margaret of Anjou   52
Yolande of Aragon, grandmother to Margaret of Anjou   56n
York   27
  archbishop of, *see* Wickwane, Wolsey
  duchy of   119
  dukes of, *see* Edward of Norwich, Henry VIII, Plantagenet
Yorkshire   122n, 143, 170, 181
  North Riding   117

Zvereva, Alexandra   170, 175n, 176, 189–90

TABULA GRATULATORIA

Lorraine C. Attreed
Caroline M. Barron
Michael Boon
Paul Brand
Paul Cavill
Linda Clark
Margaret Condon
Sean Cunningham
Anne Curry
Elizabeth Danbury
Diana Dunn
Laura Flannigan
Ralph Griffiths
Anthony Gross
David Grummitt
Sam Harper
Kate Heard
Michael Hicks
Michael K. Jones
Maureen Jurkowski

Nicholas Kingwell
Samuel Lane
Elizabeth Matthew
Caroline Palmer
S.J. Payling
Lynda Pidgeon
Edward Powell
Carole Rawcliffe
Euan Roger
James Ross
David Rundle
Harry Southcott
Michael Stansfield
Christian Steer
Laura Tompkins
Malcolm Vale
Livia Visser-Fuchs
John Watts
Jane P. Williams
Bob Wood

CONTENTS OF PREVIOUS VOLUMES

Details of previous volumes can be found at www.boydellandbrewer.com.

X
Parliament, Personalities and Power: Papers Presented to Linda Clark
ed. Hannes Kleineke (2011)

A.J. Pollard	The People and Parliament in Fifteenth-Century England
Simon Payling	'A Beest envenymed thorough … covetize': An Imposter Pilgrim and the Disputed Descent of the Manor of Dodford, 1306–1481
Charles Moreton and Colin Richmond	Henry Inglose: A Hard Man to Please
J.L. Bolton	London Merchants and the Borromei Bank in the 1430s: The Role of Local Credit Networks
James Ross	'Mischieviously Slewen': John, Lord Scrope, the Dukes of Norfolk and Suffolk, and the Murder of Henry Howard in 1446
Carole Rawcliffe	A Fifteenth-Century *Medicus Politicus*: John Somerset, Physician to Henry VI
Elizabeth Danbury	'Domine Salvum Fac Regem': The Origin of 'God Save the King' in the Reign of Henry VI
Matthew Davies	'Monuments of Honour': Clerks, Histories and Heroes in the London Livery Companies
Hannes Kleineke	The East Anglian Parliamentary Elections of 1461
David Grummitt	Changing Perceptions of the Soldier in Late Medieval England
Caroline M. Barron	Thomas More, the London Charterhouse and Richard III

XI
Concerns and Preoccupations
ed. Linda Clark (2012)

Christopher Allmand	The English Translations of Vegetius' *De Re Militari*. What Were their Authors' Intentions?
John Milner	The English Commitment to the 1412 Expedition to France

Rhun Emlyn	Serving Church and State: the Careers of Medieval Welsh Students
Peter D. Clarke	Petitioning the Pope: English Supplicants and Rome in the Fifteenth Century
Frederick Hepburn	The Queen in Exile: Representing Margaret of Anjou in Art and Literature
Anthony Smith	The Presence of the Past: The Bokkyngs of Longham in the Later Middle Ages
Dean Rowland	The End of the Statute Rolls: Manuscript, Print and Language Change in Fifteenth-Century English Statutes
S.P. Harper	Divide and Rule? Henry VII, the Mercers, Merchant Taylors and the Corporation of London

XII
Society in an Age of Plague
ed. Linda Clark and Carole Rawcliffe (2013)

J.L. Bolton	Looking for *Yersinia Pestis*: Scientists, Historians and the Black Death
Karen Smyth	Pestilence and Poetry: John Lydgate's *Danse Macabre*
Sheila Sweetinburgh	Pilgrimage in 'an Age of Plague': Seeking Canterbury's 'hooly blisful martir' in 1420 and 1470
Elizabeth Rutledge	An Urban Environment: Norwich in the Fifteenth Century
Samantha Sagui	Mid-Level Officials in Fifteenth-Century Norwich
Elma Brenner	Leprosy and Public Health in Late Medieval Rouen
Neil Murphy	Plague Ordinances and the Management of Infectious Diseases in Northern French Towns, c.1450–c.1560
Jane Stevens Crawshaw	The Renaissance Invention of Quarantine
John Henderson	Coping with Epidemics in Renaissance Italy: Plague and the Great Pox
Samuel K. Cohn, Jnr.	The Historian and the Laboratory: The Black Death Disease

XIII
Exploring the Evidence: Commemoration, Administration and the Economy
ed. Linda Clark (2014)

S.J. Payling	The 'Grete Laboure and the Long and Troublous Tyme': The Execution of the Will of Ralph, Lord Cromwell, and the Foundation of Tattershall College

Christian Steer	A Royal Grave in a Fifteenth-Century London Parish Church
Matthew Ward	The Livery Collar: Politics and Identity During the Fifteenth Century
David Harry	William Caxton and Commemorative Culture in Fifteenth-Century England
Euan C. Roger	Blakberd's Treasure: A Study in Fifteenth-Century Administration at St. Bartholomew's Hospital, London
Sheila Sweetinburgh	Placing the Hospital: The Production of St. Lawrence's Hospital Registers in Fifteenth-Century Canterbury
Maureen Jurkowski	Were Friars Paid Salaries? Evidence from Clerical Taxation Records
Susanne Jenks	Exceptions in General Pardons, 1399–1450
Martin Allen	The English Crown and the Coinage, 1399–1485
Christopher Dyer	England's Economy in the Fifteenth Century

XIV
Essays Presented to Michael Hicks
ed. Linda Clark (2015)

Caroline Barron	Michael Hicks: An Appreciation
Anne Curry	Disciplinary Ordinances for English Garrisons in Normandy in the Reign of Henry V
Christopher Dyer	Lords in a Landscape: the Berkeley Family and Northfield (Worcestershire)
Mark Page	Hampshire and the Parish Tax of 1428
Gordon Mckelvie	The Livery Act of 1429
A.J. Pollard	An Indenture between Richard Neville, Earl of Salisbury, and Sir Edmund Darell of Sessay, North Riding, 1435
Ralph Griffiths	The Pursuit of Justice and Inheritance from Marcher Lordships to Parliament: the Implications of Margaret Malefaunt's Abduction in Gower in 1438
Peter Fleming	The Battles of Mortimer's Cross and Second St. Albans: The Regional Dimension
S.J. Payling	Widows and the Wars of the Roses: the Turbulent Marital History of Edward IV's Putative Mistress, Margaret, daughter of Sir Lewis John of West Horndon, Essex
Hannes Kleineke	Some Observations on the Household and Circle of Humphrey Stafford, Lord Stafford of Southwick and Earl of Devon: the Last Will of Roger Bekensawe

James Ross	The Treatment of Traitors' Children and Edward IV's Clemency in the 1460s
Anne F. Sutton	Edward IV and Bury St. Edmunds' Search for Self-Government
Matthew Holford	The Exchequer Inquisitions *Post Mortem*
Karen Stöber	Hams for Prayers: Regular Canons and their Lay Patrons in Medieval Catalonia
John Hare	Production, Specialisation and Consumption in Late Medieval Wessex
Winifred A. Harwood	A Butt of Wine and Two Barrels of Herring: Southampton's Trading Links with Religious Institutions in Winchester and South Central England, 1430–1540

XV
Writing, Records and Rhetoric
ed. Linda Clark (2017)

Michael Bennett	*The Libelle of English Policy*: The Matter of Ireland
Julia Boffey	'Stories of Divers Regions and Provinces': Some Digests of History and Geography for Late-Medieval English Readers
J.L. Laynesmith	'To please … Dame Cecely that in latyn hath litell intellect': Books and the Duchess of York
John Milner	A Case Study in Lancastrian Service and Personal Survival: The Career of William, Lord Roos of Helmsley (c.1370–1414)
Ben Pope	Identity, Discourse and Political Strategy: Margrave Albrecht Achilles (1414–86) and the Rhetoric of Antagonism between Town and Nobility in Upper Germany
Tom Johnson	The Redistribution of Forest Law and Administration in Fifteenth-Century England
Sarah Thomas	Well-Connected and Qualified Clerics? The Bishops of Dunkeld and Sodor in the Fifteenth Century
J.M. Grussenmeyer	Preaching Politics: Lancastrian Chancellors in Parliament
Dan E. Seward	Bishop John Alcock and the Roman Invasion of Parliament: Introducing Renaissance Civic Humanism to Tudor Parliamentary Proceedings
Paul Cavill	Preaching on Magna Carta at the End of the Fifteenth Century: John Alcock's Sermon at Paul's Cross

XVI
Examining Identity
ed. Linda Clark (2018)

Claire Macht	Changes in Monastic Historical Writing Throughout the Long Fifteenth Century
David Lepine	'Such Great Merits': The Pastoral Influence of a Learned Resident Vicar, John Hornley of Dartford
Des Atkinson	Getting Connected: The Medieval Ordinand and his Search for *Titulus*
Samuel Lane	The Political Career of William Ayscough, Bishop of Salisbury, 1438–50
Daniel F. Gosling	Edward IV's *Charta de Libertatibus Clericorum*
Simon Egan	A Playground of the Scots? Gaelic Ireland and the Stewart Monarchy in the Late Fourteenth and Fifteenth Centuries
Brian Coleman	An English Gentry Abroad: The Gentry of English Ireland
Zosia Edwards	Identity Theft in Later Medieval London
Charles Giry-Deloison	Dying on Duty: A French Ambassador's Funeral in London in 1512

XVII
Finding Individuality
ed. Linda Clark (2020)

Chris Given-Wilson	Royal Wills, 1376–1475
Samuel Lane	Propaganda, Piety and Politics in the Fifteenth Century: Henry V's Vernacular War Letters to the City of London, 1417–21
Anne F. Sutton	'To Be of Oon Demeanyng and Unite for the Wele of Your Self and of the Contre There': Yorkist Plans for the Lordship of Ireland, the Last Phase
Anthony Gross	A Mirror for a Princess: Antoine de la Sale and the Political Psyche of Margaret of Anjou
Alice Raw	Margaret of Anjou and the Language of Praise and Censure
S.J. Payling	On 'Peyne of their Lyfes … they Should no Verdit gif, but if they Wold Endite the Seid William Tresham of his Owen Deth': the Murder of Lawyers in Fifteenth-Century England
David Grummitt	'Stond Horeson and Yelde thy Knyff': Urban Politics, Language and Litigation in Late Medieval Canterbury

Deborah Youngs	'In to the Sterre Chambre': Female Plaintiffs before the King's Council in the Reign of Henry VII

XVIII
Rulers, Regions and Retinues: Essays Presented to A.J. Pollard
ed. Linda Clark and Peter Fleming (2020)

Gwilym Dodd	Tyranny and Affinity: The Public and Private Authority of Richard II and Richard III
Douglas Biggs	The Commission to ensure Good Governance of 11 May 1402: A Case Study of Lancastrian Counter-Propaganda
Michael Hicks	A Failure in Foresight: the Lancastrian Kings and the Lancastrian Dukes
Andy King	The Strothers: A Tale of Northern Gentle Folk, Social Mobility and Stagnation in Late Medieval Northumberland
Rosemary Horrox	'No Good unto our said King at this Time'
Keith Dockray	Contemporary and Near-Contemporary Chroniclers: The North of England and the Wars of the Roses, c.1450–1471
Hannes Kleineke	England, 1461: Predominantly Provincial Perspectives on the Early Months of the Reign of Edward IV
James Ross	Greater Landowners and the Management of their Estates in Late Medieval England
Ralph A. Griffiths	Lordship and the Social Elite in the Lordship of Gower during the Wars of the Roses
Sean Cunningham	A Yorkist Legacy for the Tudor Prince of Wales on the Welsh Marches: Affinity-Building, Regional Government and National Politics, 1471–1502
Anne Curry	Southern England and Campaigns to France, 1415–1453
Michael Bennett	Last Men Standing: Lancashire Soldiers in the Wars in France
Carole Rawcliffe	Northern Pride goes Before a Fall: The 'Horrorable' History of Adelston Attysle
Anne Curry	Professor Tony Pollard: An Appreciation

XIX
Enmity and Amity
ed. Linda Clark (2022)

Malcolm Vale	England and Europe, c. 1450–1520: Nostalgia or New Opportunities?
S.J. Drake	Mariners and Marauders: A Case Study of Fowey during the Hundred Years' War, c. 1400–c. 1453

Anne Curry *David Cleverly*	Henry V's Army of 1417
Charles Giry-Deloison	'Get out of our land, Englishmen'. French Reactions to the English Invasion of 1512–13
Susan Maddock	Encountering the 'Duche' in Margery Kemp's Lynn
Catherine Emerson	'*C'est le Beaulté de Castille et d'Espaigne, qui le Soleil cler d'Austrice accompaigne*': Jean Molinet makes the Habsburgs Burgundian
Nigel Saul	Magna Carta in the Late Middle Ages, c. 1320–c. 1520
Paul Cavill	The Business of the Southern Convocation in 1462

The Fifteenth Century aims to provide a forum for the most recent research into the political, social, religious and cultural history of the fifteenth century in Britain and Europe.

Contributions are invited for future volumes. Draft submissions or informal inquiries should be sent to the General Editor, Dr Linda Clark: lclark@histparl.ac.uk. Authors should submit an electronic version of their contribution, presented with double spacing throughout and with notes set as footnotes. Contributions should not be longer than 10,000 words. A style guide is available on request.

Authors submitting manuscripts do so on the understanding that the work has not been published previously. Neither the General Editor nor the publisher accepts responsibility for the views of the authors expressed in their contributions. Authors wishing to include illustrations in their articles should contact the General Editor prior to submission. It is the author's responsibility to obtain the necessary permission to use material protected by copyright.